Oh man, it's spring! I always get sleepy in spring... I'm just sleepy... so slee... ...zzz.

—*Masashi Kishimoto, 2004*

岸本斉史

Author/artist Masashi Kishimoto was born in 1974 in rural Okayama Prefecture, Japan. After spending time in art college, he won the Hop Step Award for new manga artists with his manga **Karakuri** (Mechanism). Kishimoto decided to base his next story on traditional Japanese culture. His first version of **Naruto**, drawn in 1997, was a one-shot story about fox spirits; his final version, which debuted in **Weekly Shonen Jump** in 1999, quickly became the most popular ninja manga in Japan.

NARUTO VOL. 22
The SHONEN JUMP Manga Edition

STORY AND ART BY MASASHI KISHIMOTO

Translation & English Adaptation/Mari Morimoto
Touch-up Art & Lettering/James Gaubatz
Design/Yvonne Cai
Editor/Joel Enos

Editor in Chief, Books/Alvin Lu
Editor in Chief, Magazines/Marc Weidenbaum
VP of Publishing Licensing/Rika Inouye
VP of Sales/Gonzalo Ferreyra
Sr. VP of Marketing/Liza Coppola
Publisher/Hyoe Narita

Printed in Canada

Published by VIZ Media, LLC
P.O. Box 77010
San Francisco, CA 94107

SHONEN JUMP Manga Edition
10 9 8 7 6 5 4 3 2 1
First printing, November 2007

THE WORLD'S
MOST POPULAR MANGA

www.shonenjump.com

www.viz.com

PARENTAL ADVISORY
NARUTO is rated T for Teen and is recommended
for ages 13 and up. This volume contains realistic
and fantasy violence.
ratings.viz.com

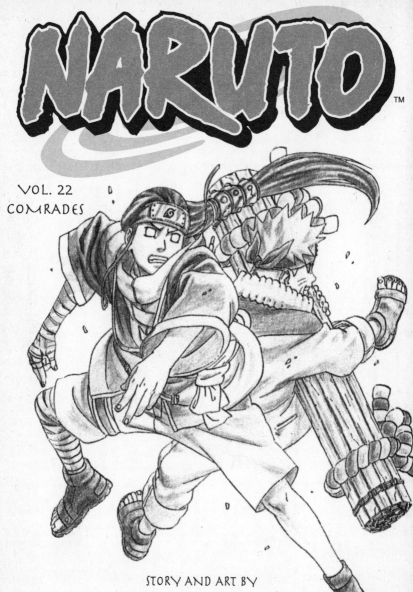

SHONEN JUMP MANGA EDITION

NARUTO™

VOL. 22
COMRADES

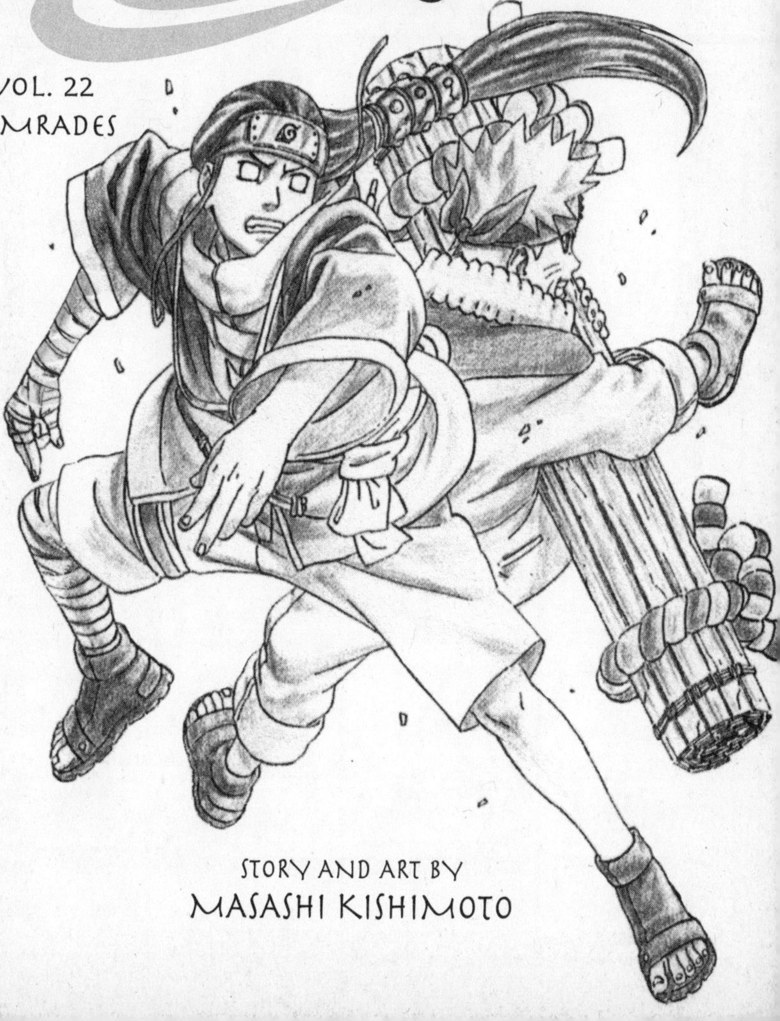

STORY AND ART BY
MASASHI KISHIMOTO

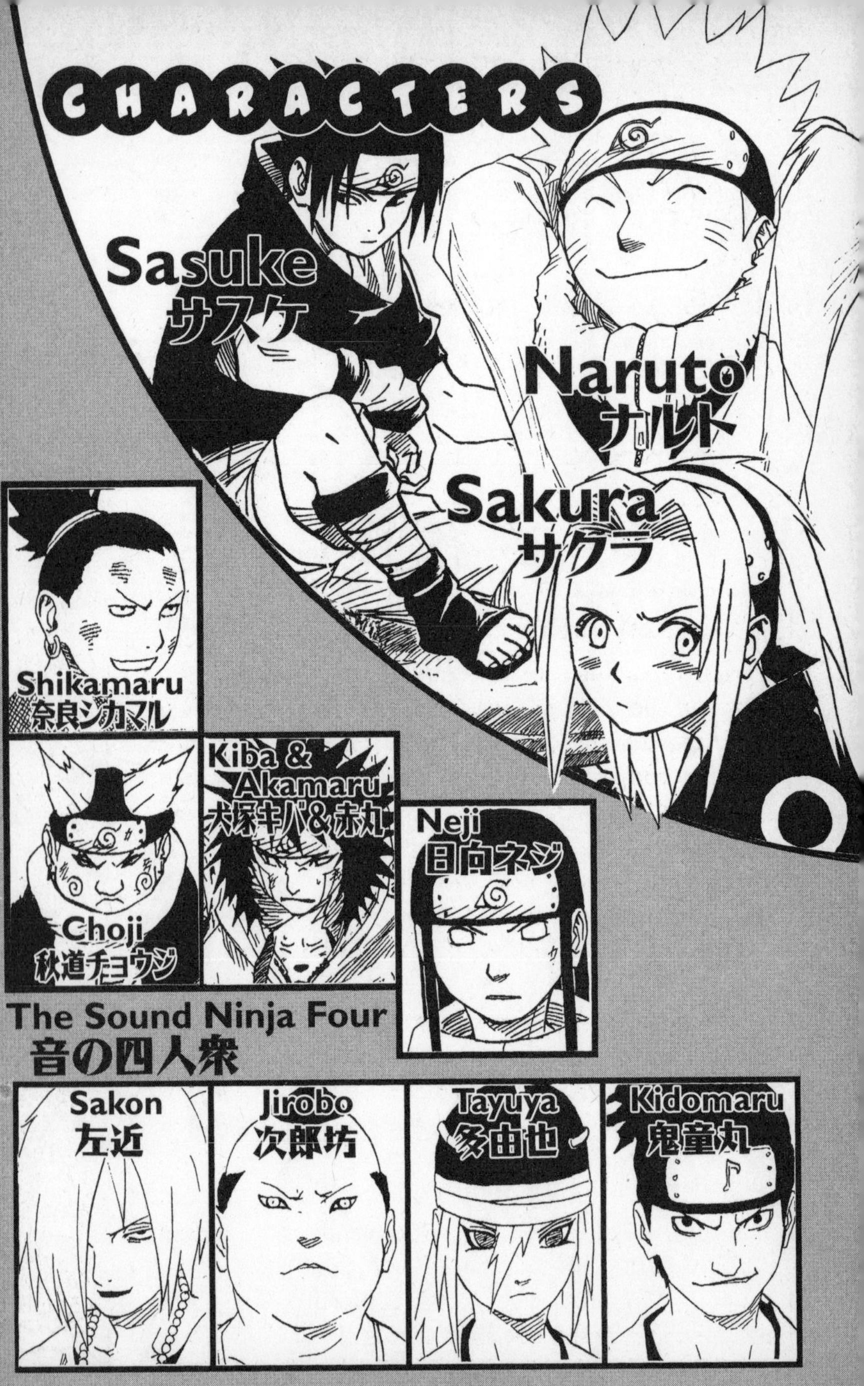
CHARACTERS
Naruto
ナルト
Sasuke
サスケ
Sakura
サクラ
Shikamaru
奈良シカマル
Neji
日向ネジ
Kiba & Akamaru
犬塚キバ&赤丸
Choji
秋道チョウジ
The Sound Ninja Four
音の四人衆
Kidomaru
鬼童丸
Tayuya
多由也
Jirobo
次郎坊
Sakon
左近

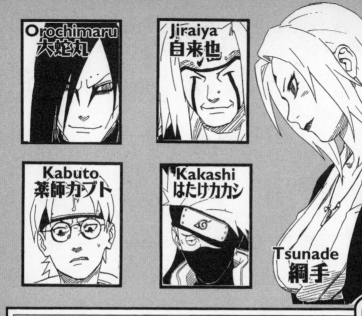

Tsunade
綱手
Jiraiya
自来也
Orochimaru
大蛇丸
Kakashi
はたけカカシ
Kabuto
薬師カブト

The Story So Far...

Twelve years ago, a destructive nine-tailed fox spirit attacked the ninja village of Konohagakure. The Hokage, or village champion, defeated the fox by sealing its soul into the body of a baby boy. Now that boy, Uzumaki Naruto, has grown up to become a ninja-in-training, learning the art of ninjutsu with his teammates Sakura and Sasuke. During the Second Chûnin Exam, Naruto and the others were attacked by Orochimaru, who left a curse mark on Sasuke and vanished…

Naruto and Sasuke proceeded to the Chûnin Exam Finals, but in the middle of the Sasuke vs. Gaara battle, Orochimaru and company launch *Operation Destroy Konoha*, which was stopped when the Third Hokage sacrificed his own life.

Sasuke, healed by Tsunade, who has become the Fifth Hokage, leaves Konoha Village with the Sound Ninja Four… The quintet of Shikamaru, Naruto, Choji, Kiba, and Neji hastily set out after them…!

NARUTO

VOL. 22
COMRADES

CONTENTS

Number 191: Comrades...!!

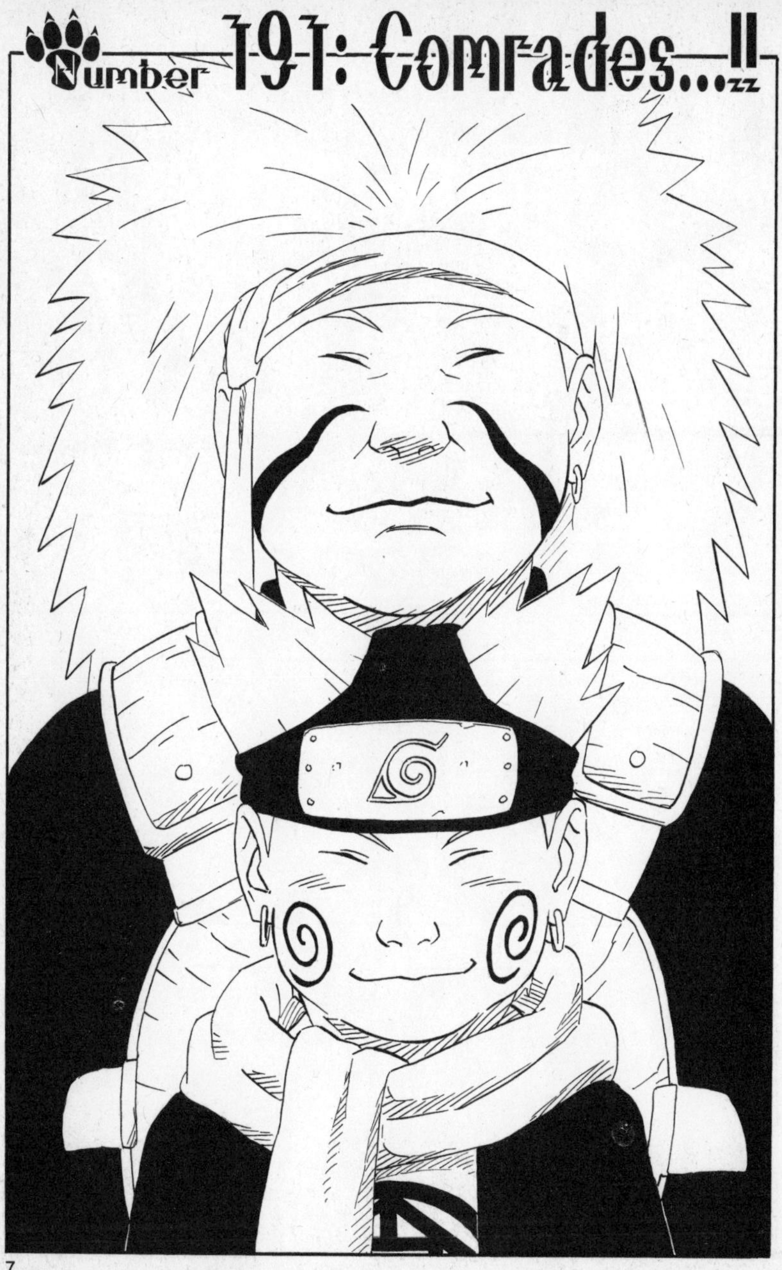

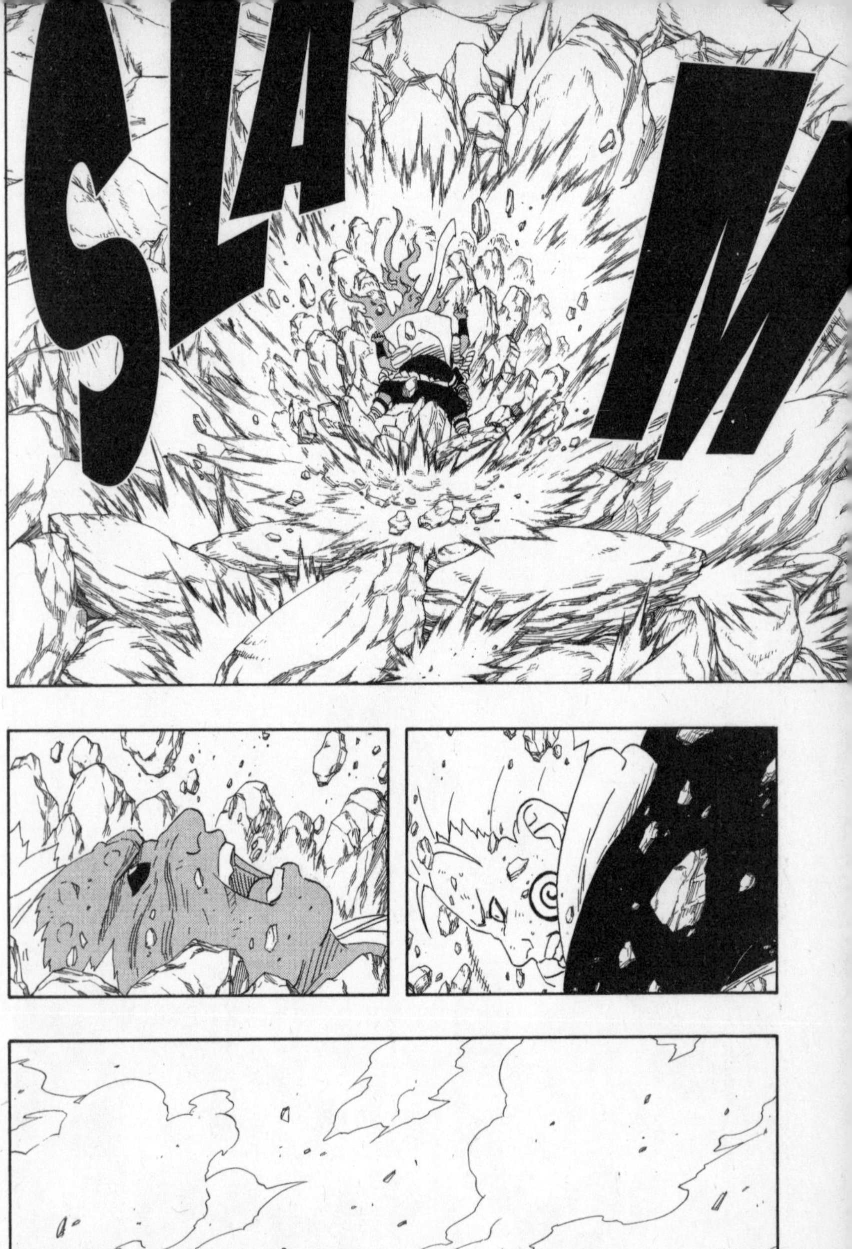
SLAM

READ THIS WAY

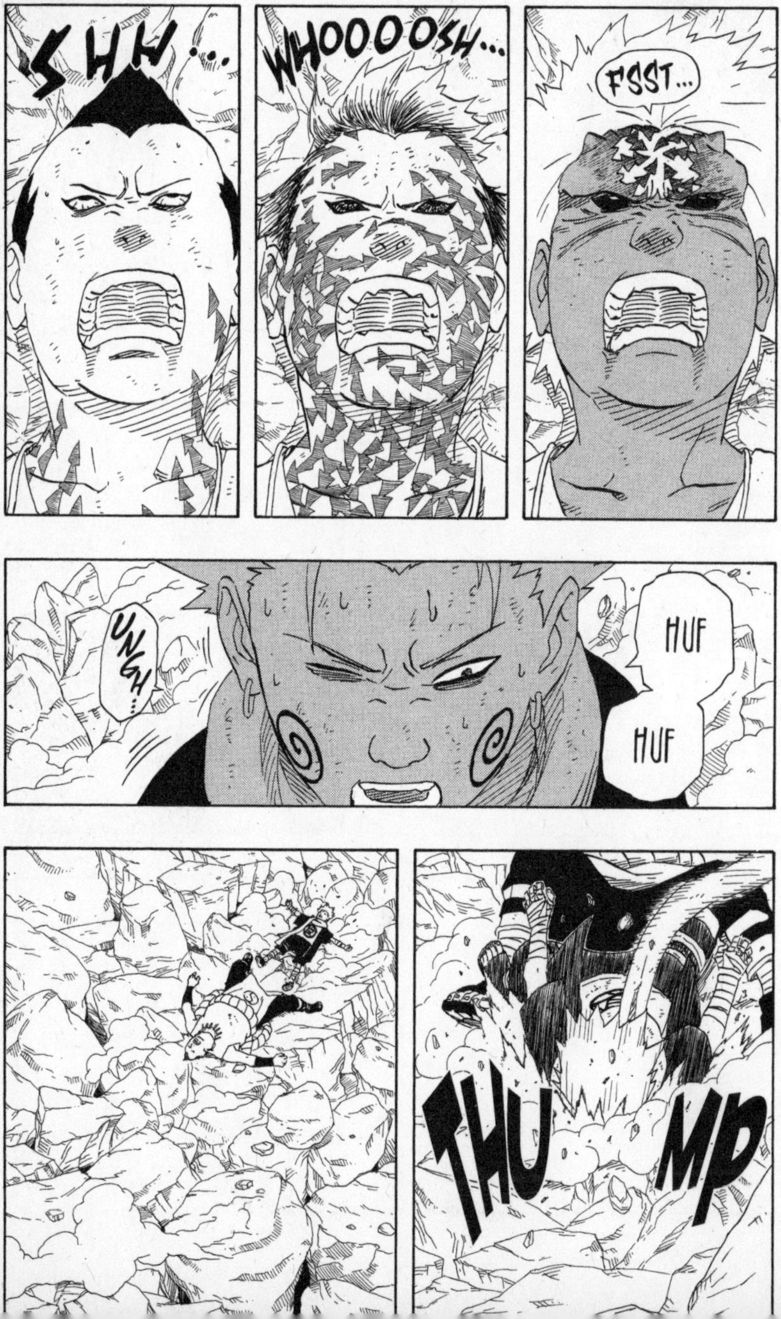
FSST...
WHOOOOSH...
SHH...
HUF
HUF
UNGH...
THUMP

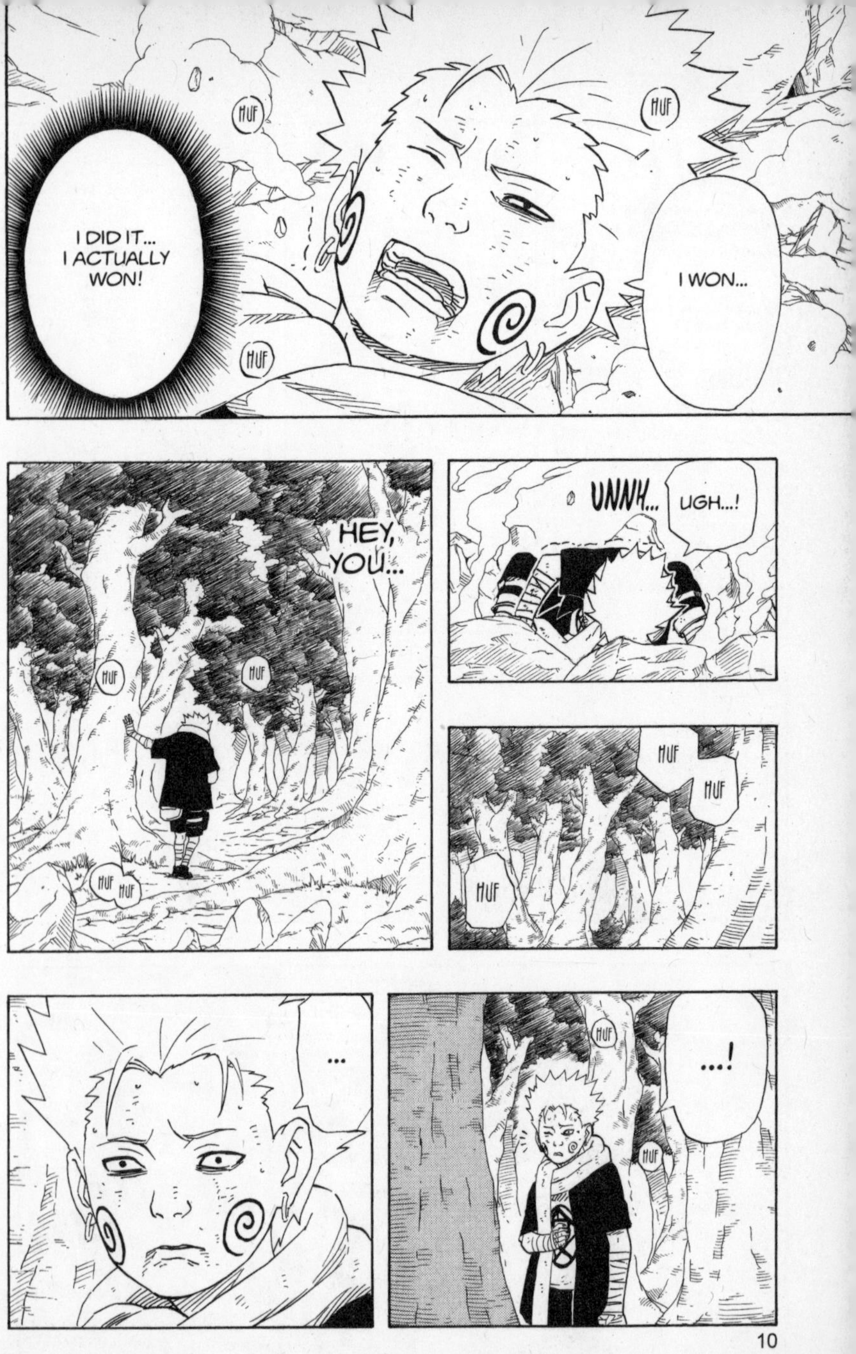
HUF
I WON...
HUF
I DID IT... I ACTUALLY WON!
HUF
UGH...!
UNNH...
HUF
HUF
HUF
HEY, YOU...
HUF
HUF
HUF
HUF
HUF
...!
HUF
...

READ THIS WAY

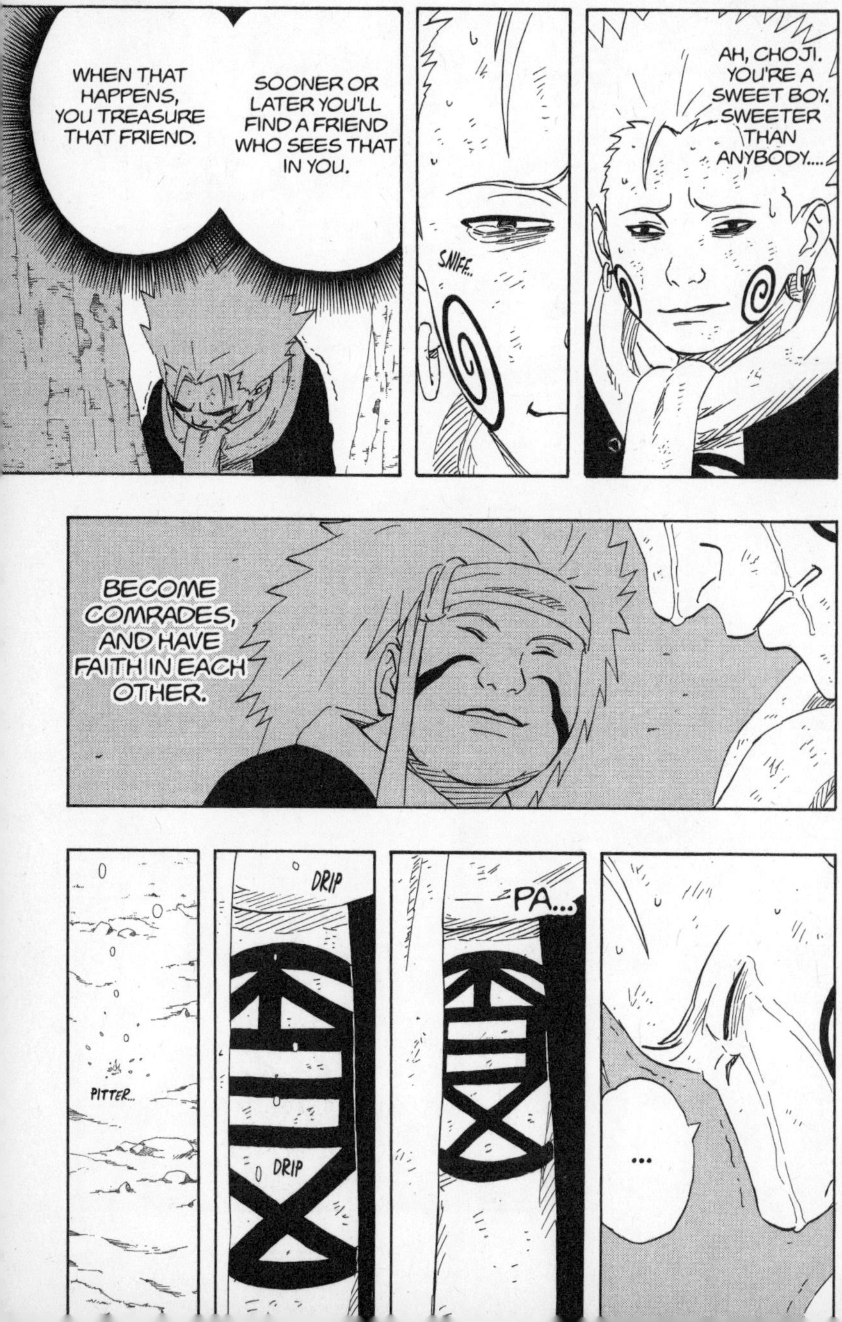

AH, CHOJI. YOU'RE A SWEET BOY. SWEETER THAN ANYBODY....
SNIFF...
SOONER OR LATER YOU'LL FIND A FRIEND WHO SEES THAT IN YOU.
WHEN THAT HAPPENS, YOU TREASURE THAT FRIEND.
BECOME COMRADES, AND HAVE FAITH IN EACH OTHER.
...
PA...
DRIP
DRIP
PITTER...

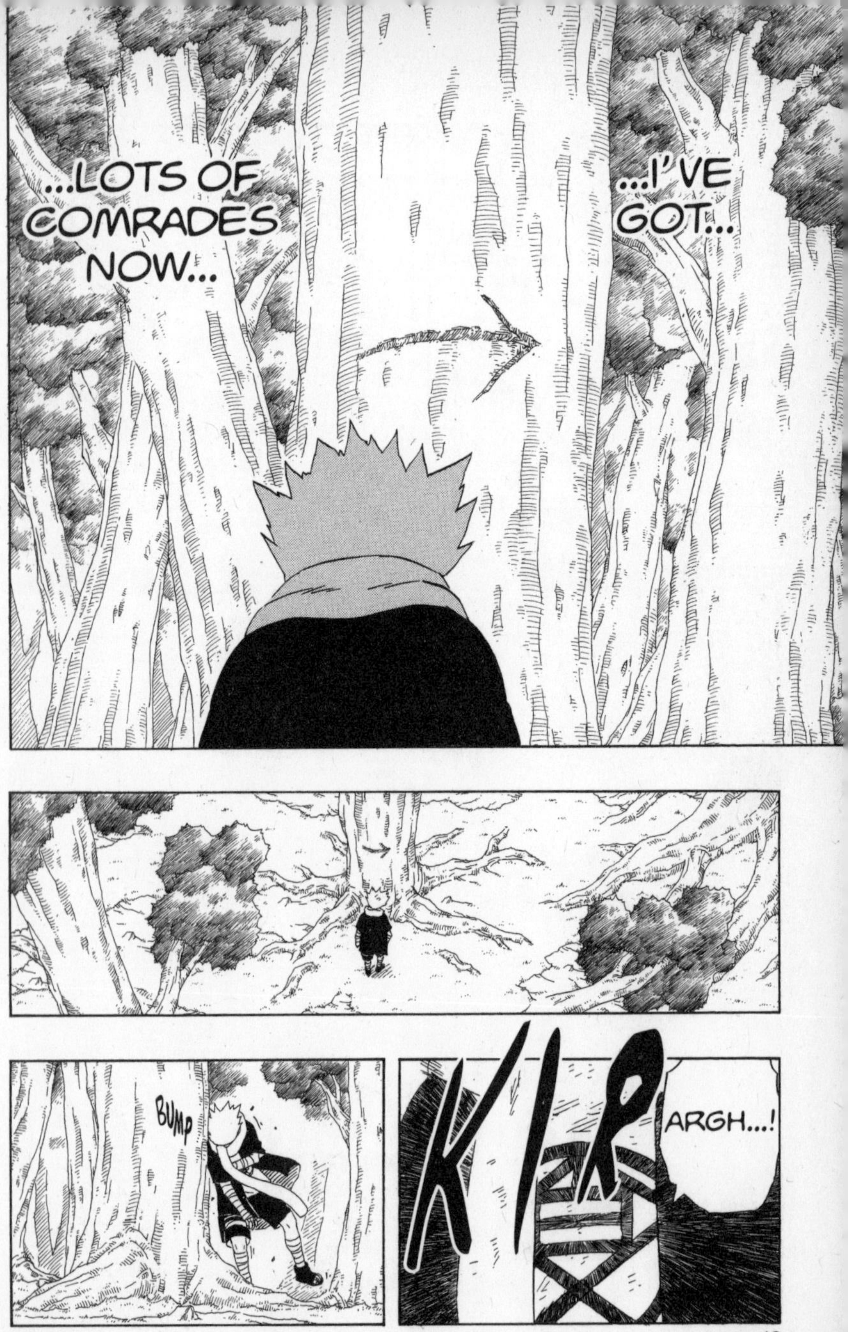
...I'VE GOT...
...LOTS OF COMRADES NOW...
ARGH...!
KIP
BUMP

READ THIS WAY

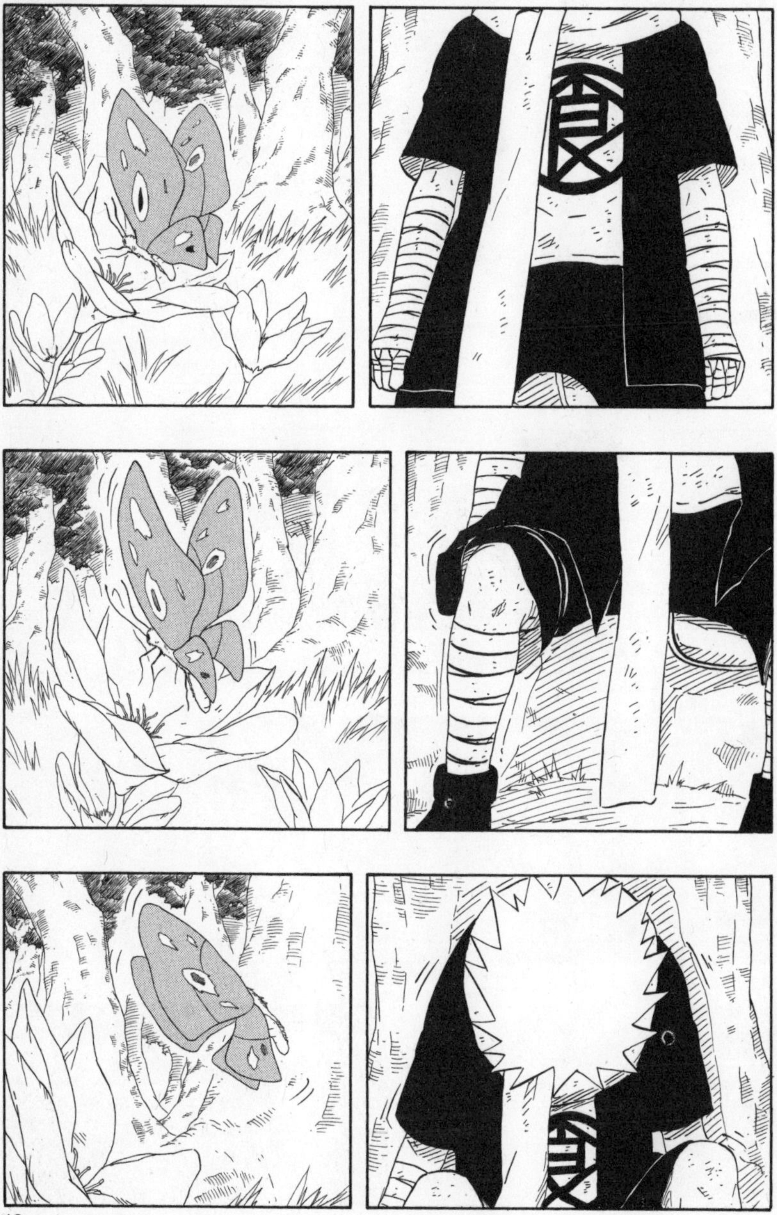

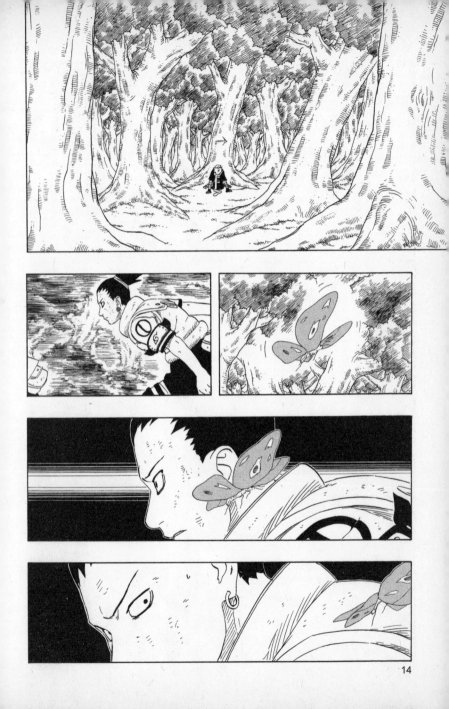

READ THIS WAY

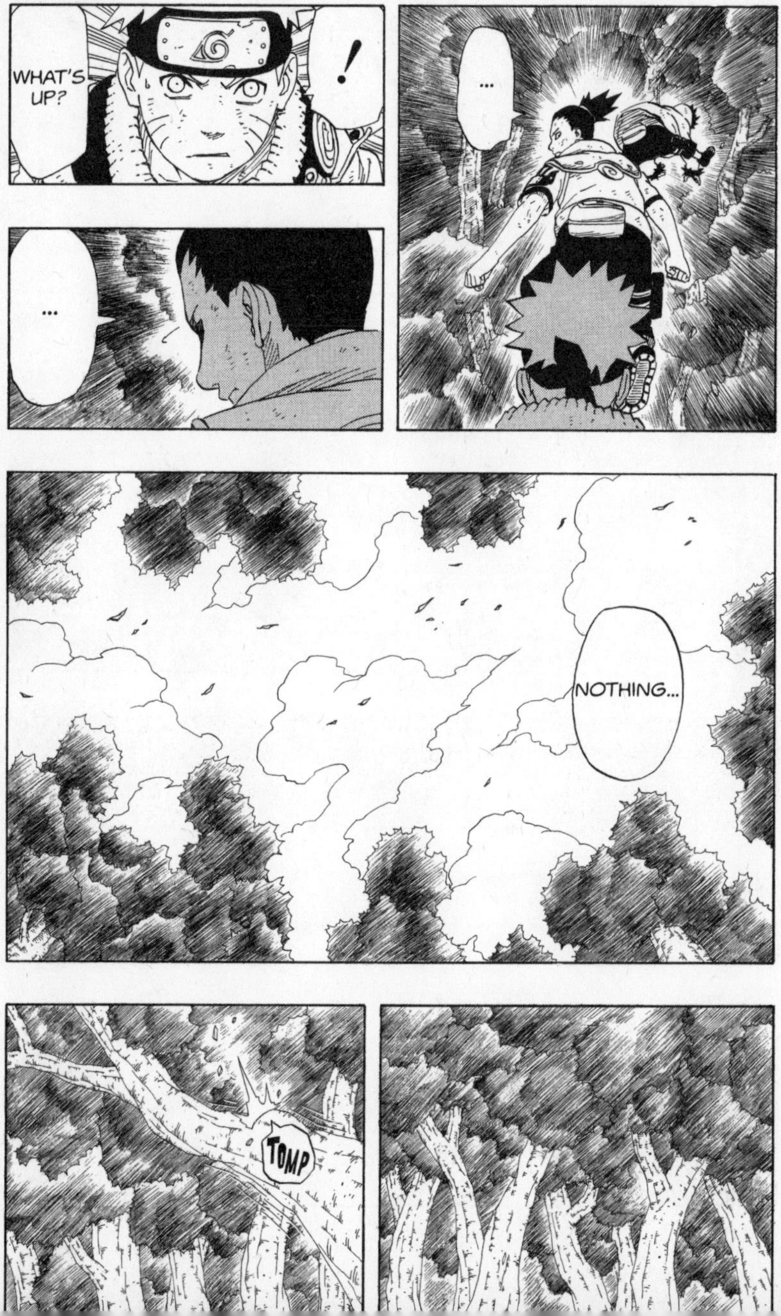
...
!
WHAT'S UP?
...
NOTHING...
TOMP

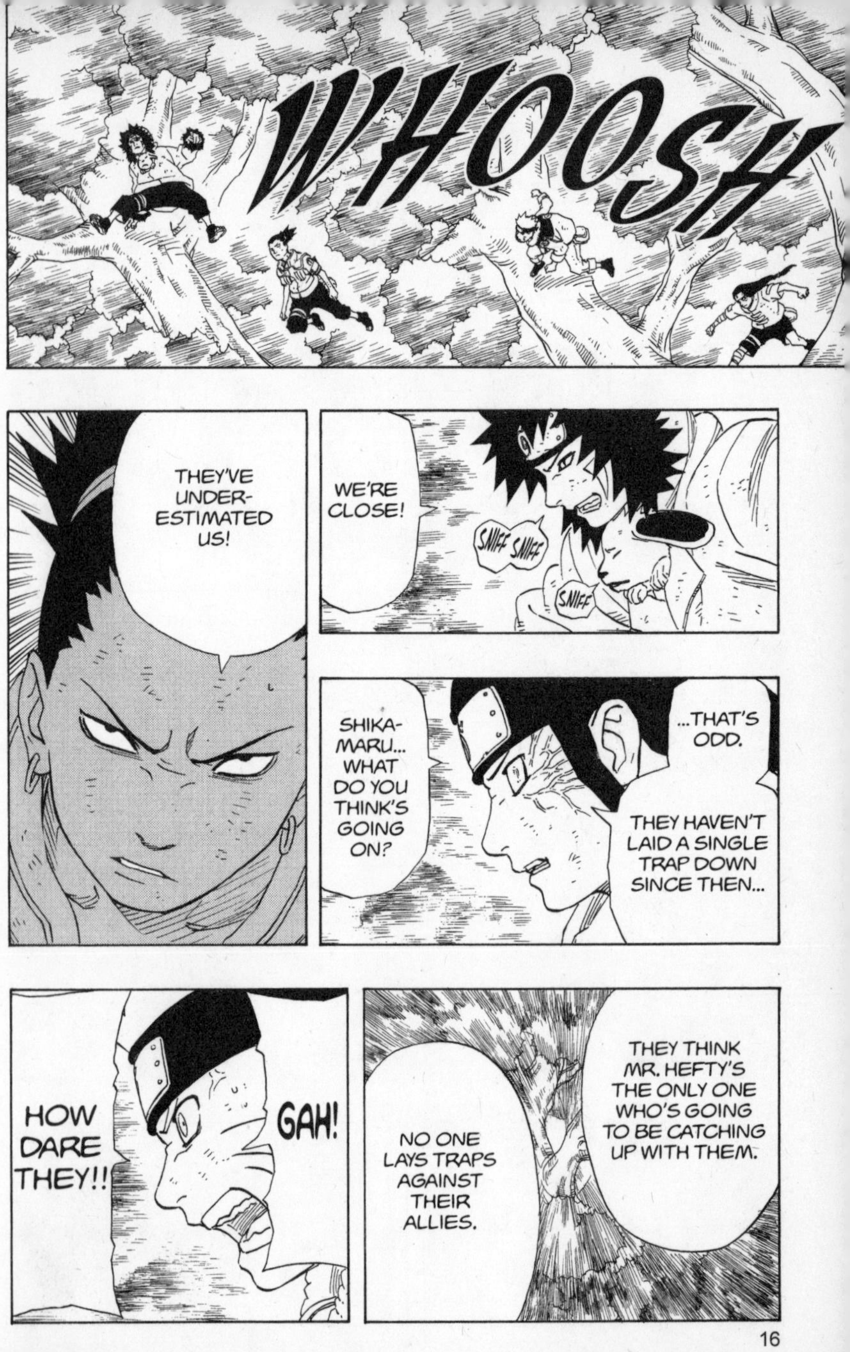
WHOOSH
WE'RE CLOSE!
SNIFF
SNIFF
SNIFF
...THAT'S ODD.
THEY HAVEN'T LAID A SINGLE TRAP DOWN SINCE THEN...
SHIKA-MARU... WHAT DO YOU THINK'S GOING ON?
THEY'VE UNDER-ESTIMATED US!
THEY THINK MR. HEFTY'S THE ONLY ONE WHO'S GOING TO BE CATCHING UP WITH THEM.
NO ONE LAYS TRAPS AGAINST THEIR ALLIES.
GAH!
HOW DARE THEY!!

READ THIS WAY

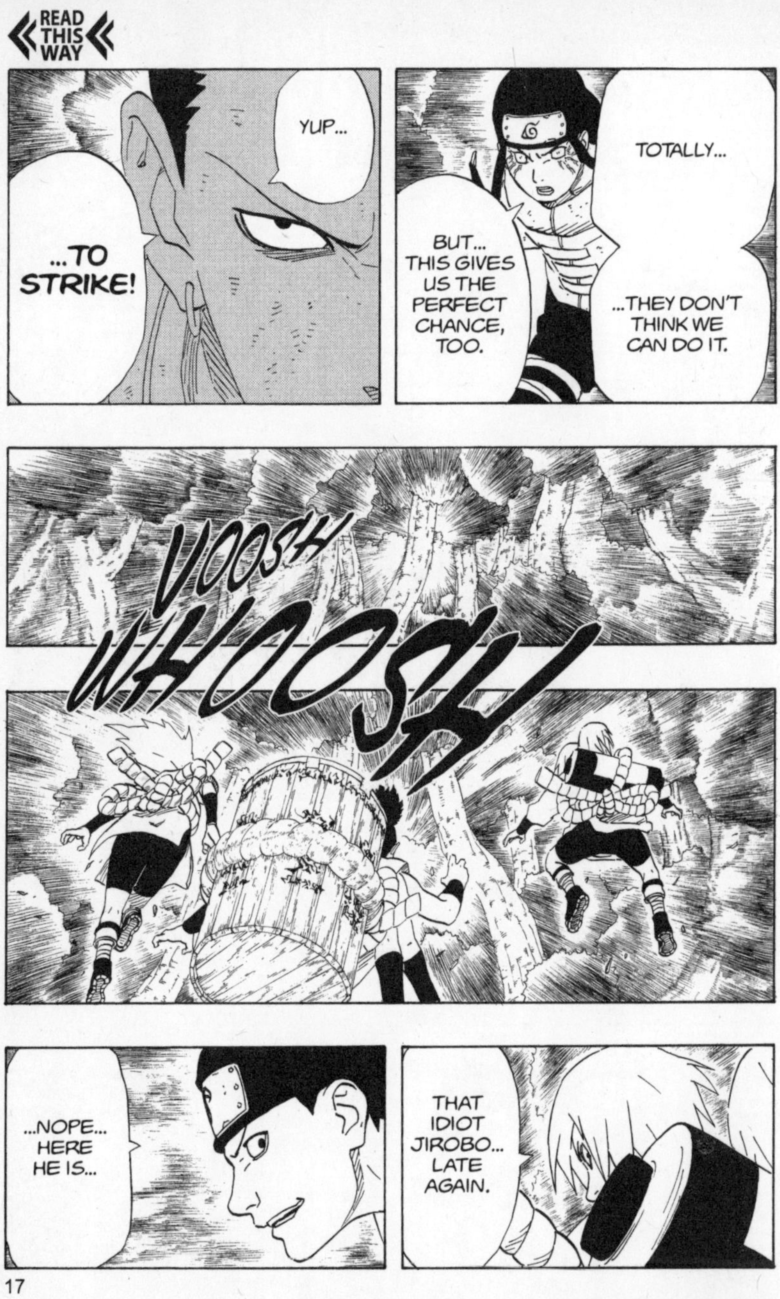
TOTALLY...
...THEY DON'T THINK WE CAN DO IT.
BUT... THIS GIVES US THE PERFECT CHANCE, TOO.
YUP...
...TO STRIKE!
VOOSH
WHOOSH
THAT IDIOT JIROBO... LATE AGAIN.
...NOPE... HERE HE IS...

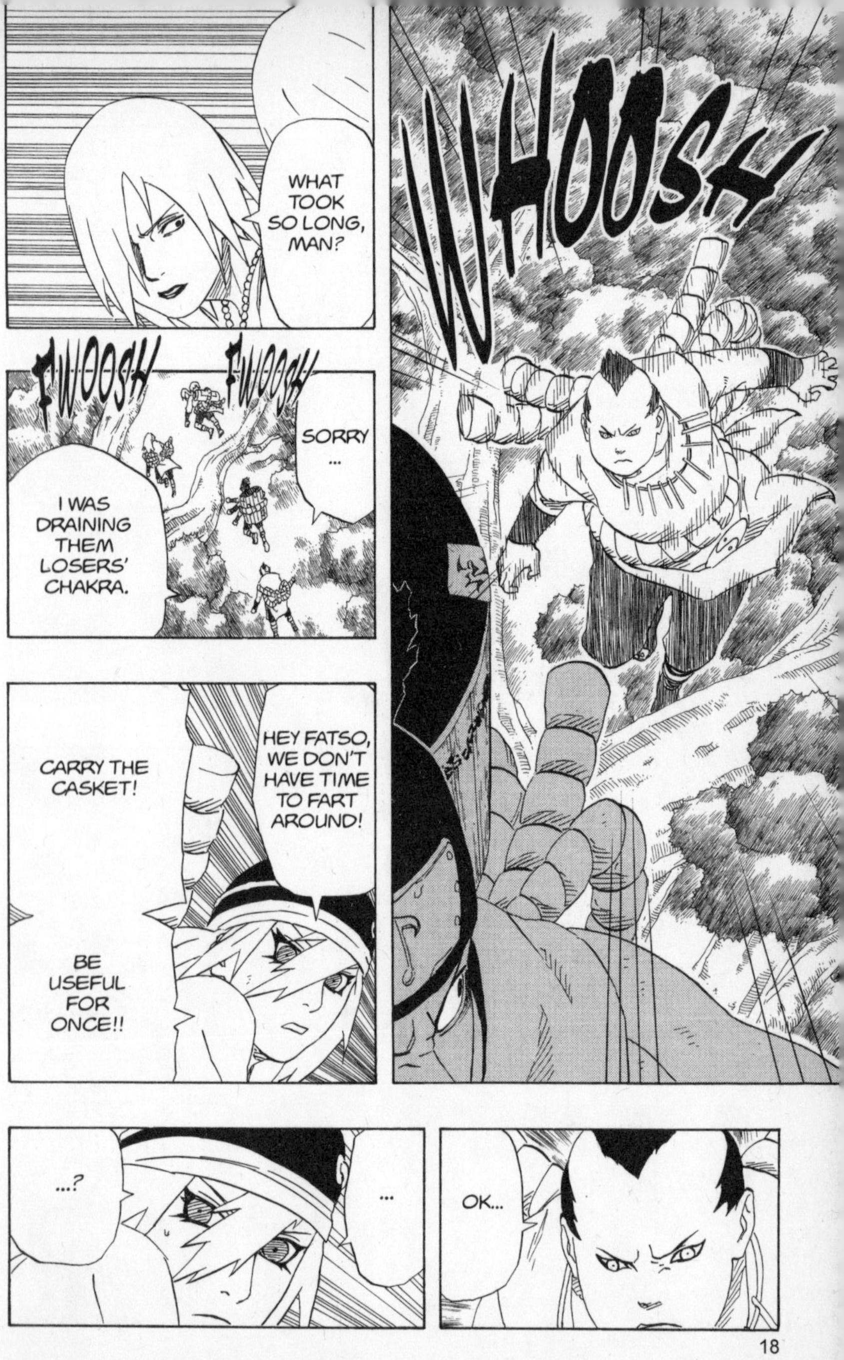
WHOOSH
WHAT TOOK SO LONG, MAN?
FWOOSH
SORRY ...
FWOOSH
I WAS DRAINING THEM LOSERS' CHAKRA.
HEY FATSO, WE DON'T HAVE TIME TO FART AROUND!
CARRY THE CASKET!
BE USEFUL FOR ONCE!!
OK...
...
...?

READ THIS WAY

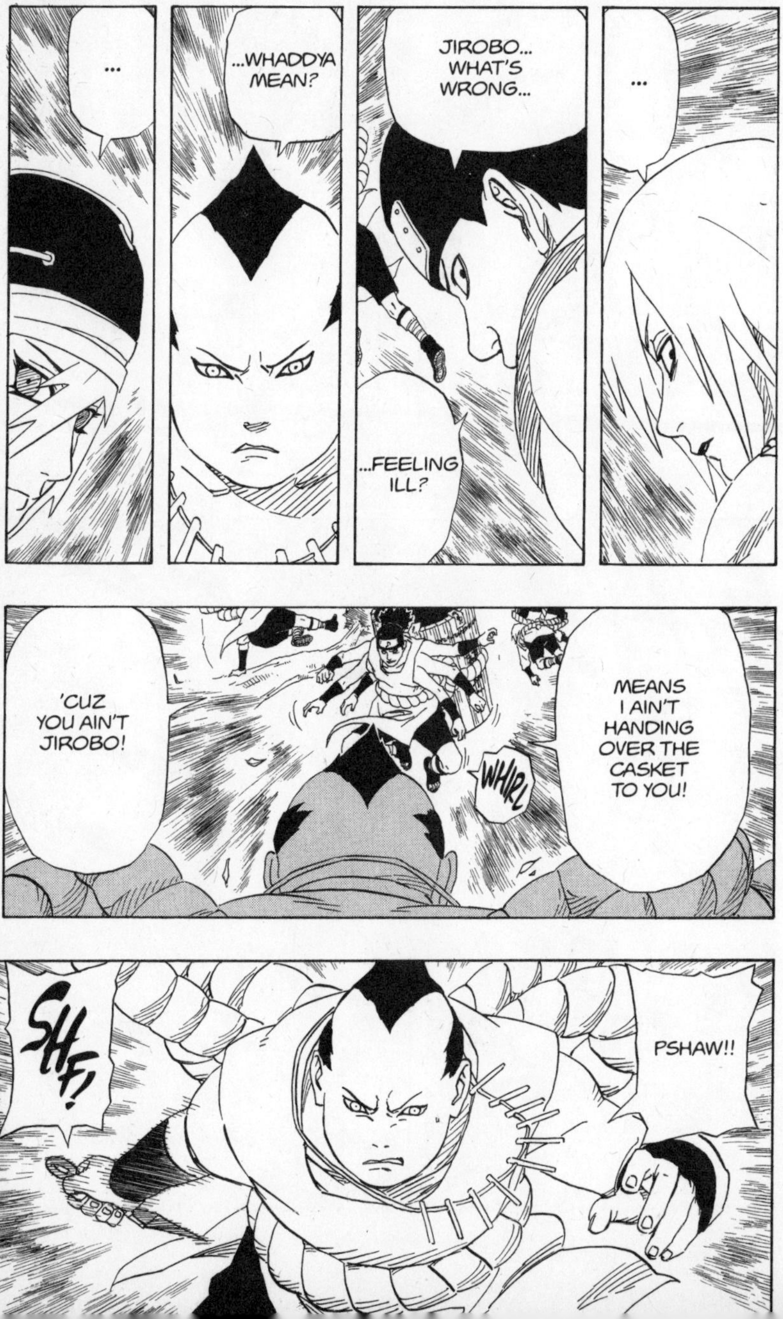

...
JIROBO... WHAT'S WRONG...
...FEELING ILL?
...WHADDYA MEAN?
...
MEANS I AIN'T HANDING OVER THE CASKET TO YOU!
WHIRL
'CUZ YOU AIN'T JIROBO!
PSHAW!!
SHF!

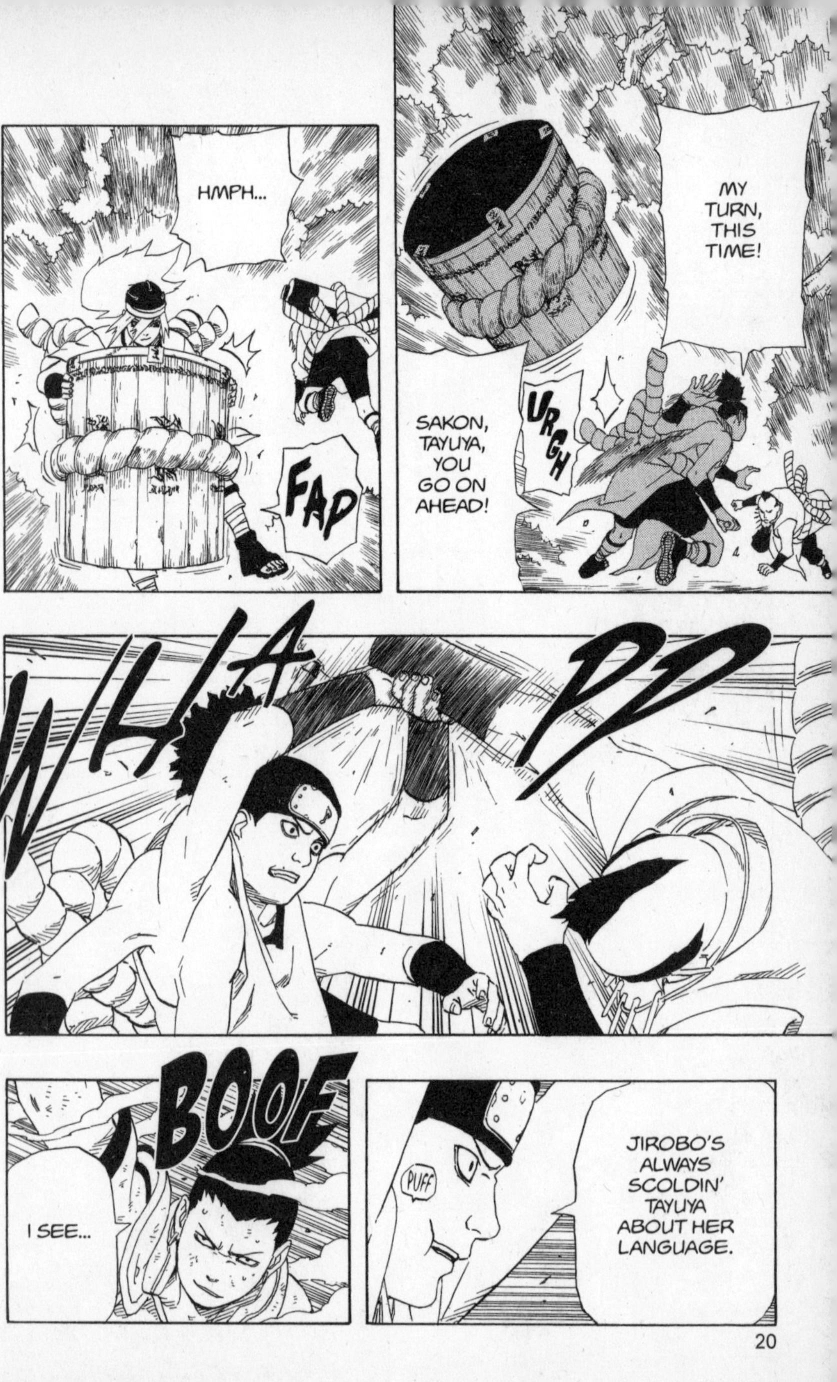
MY TURN, THIS TIME!
URGH
SAKON, TAYUYA, YOU GO ON AHEAD!
HMPH...
FAP
WHAPP
JIROBO'S ALWAYS SCOLDIN' TAYUYA ABOUT HER LANGUAGE.
PUFF
BOOF
I SEE...

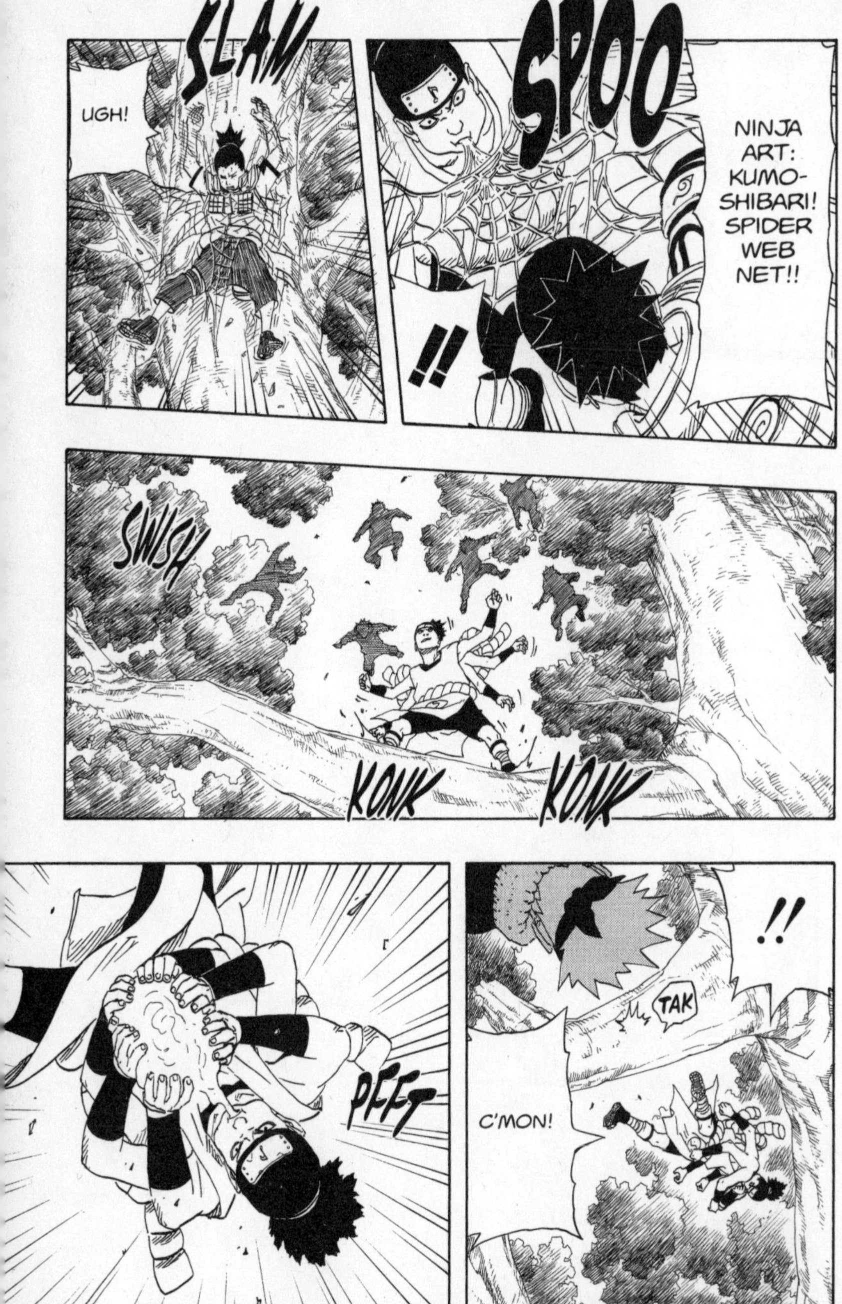
SPOO
NINJA ART: KUMO-SHIBARI! SPIDER WEB NET!!
!!
SLAM
UGH!
SWISH
KONK
KONK
!!
TAK
C'MON!
PFFT

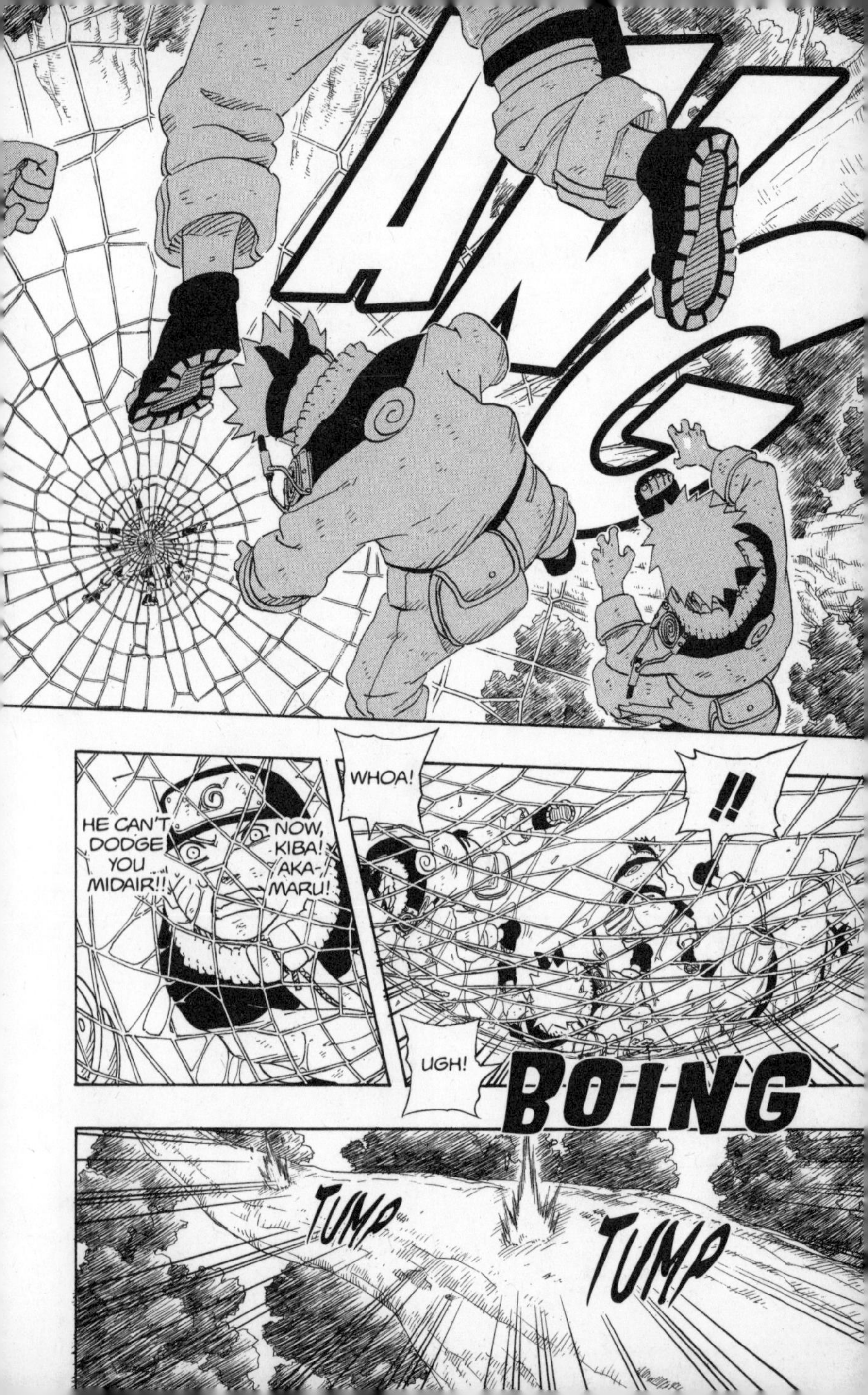
!!
WHOA!
UGH!
BOING
NOW, KIBA! AKAMARU!
HE CAN'T DODGE YOU MIDAIR!!
TUMP
TUMP

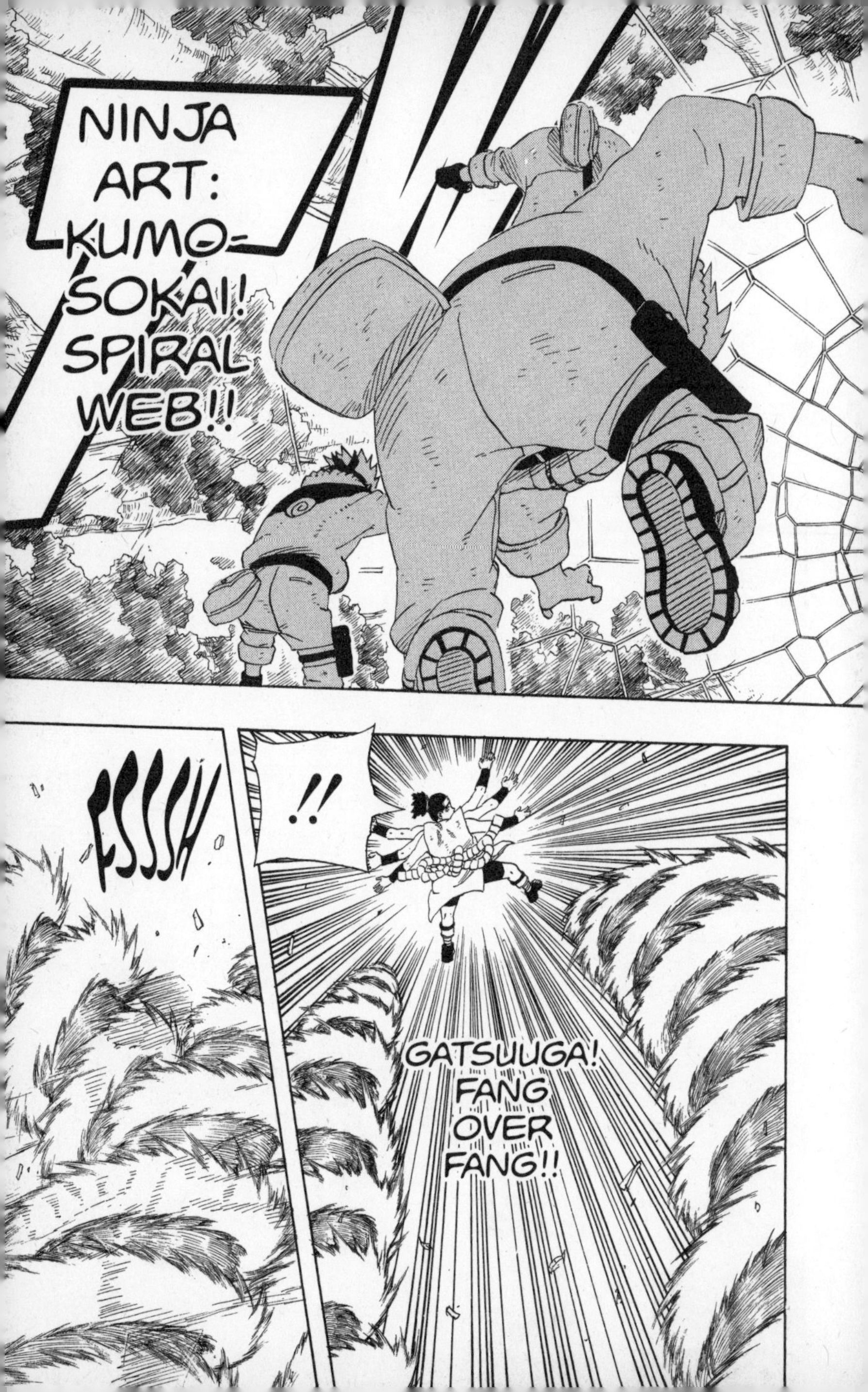
NINJA ART: KUMO-SOKAI! SPIRAL WEB!!
!!
GATSUUGA! FANG OVER FANG!!
FSSSH

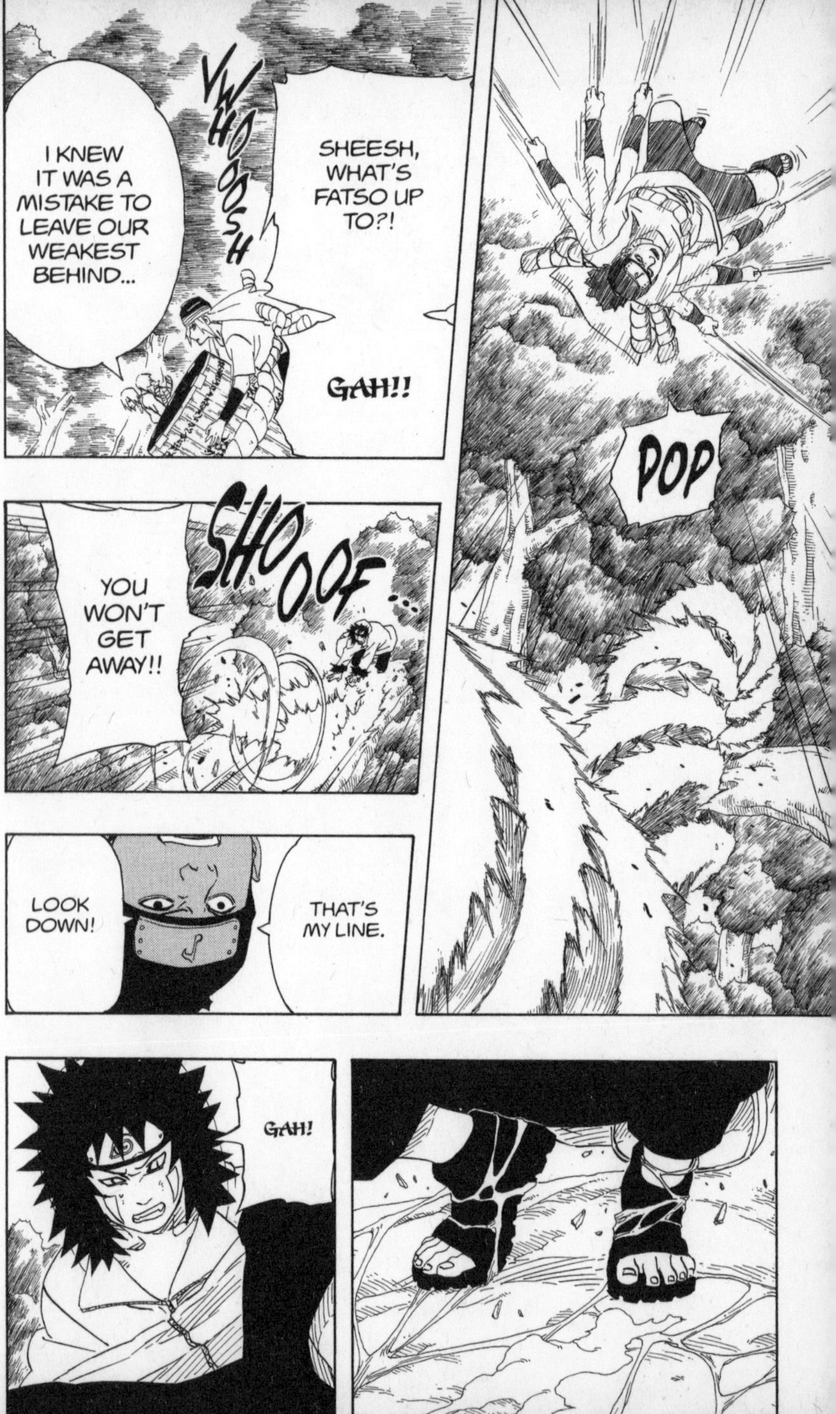
POP
SHEESH, WHAT'S FATSO UP TO?!
VWHOOOOSH
I KNEW IT WAS A MISTAKE TO LEAVE OUR WEAKEST BEHIND...
GAH!!
SHOOOF...
YOU WON'T GET AWAY!!
THAT'S MY LINE.
LOOK DOWN!
GAH!

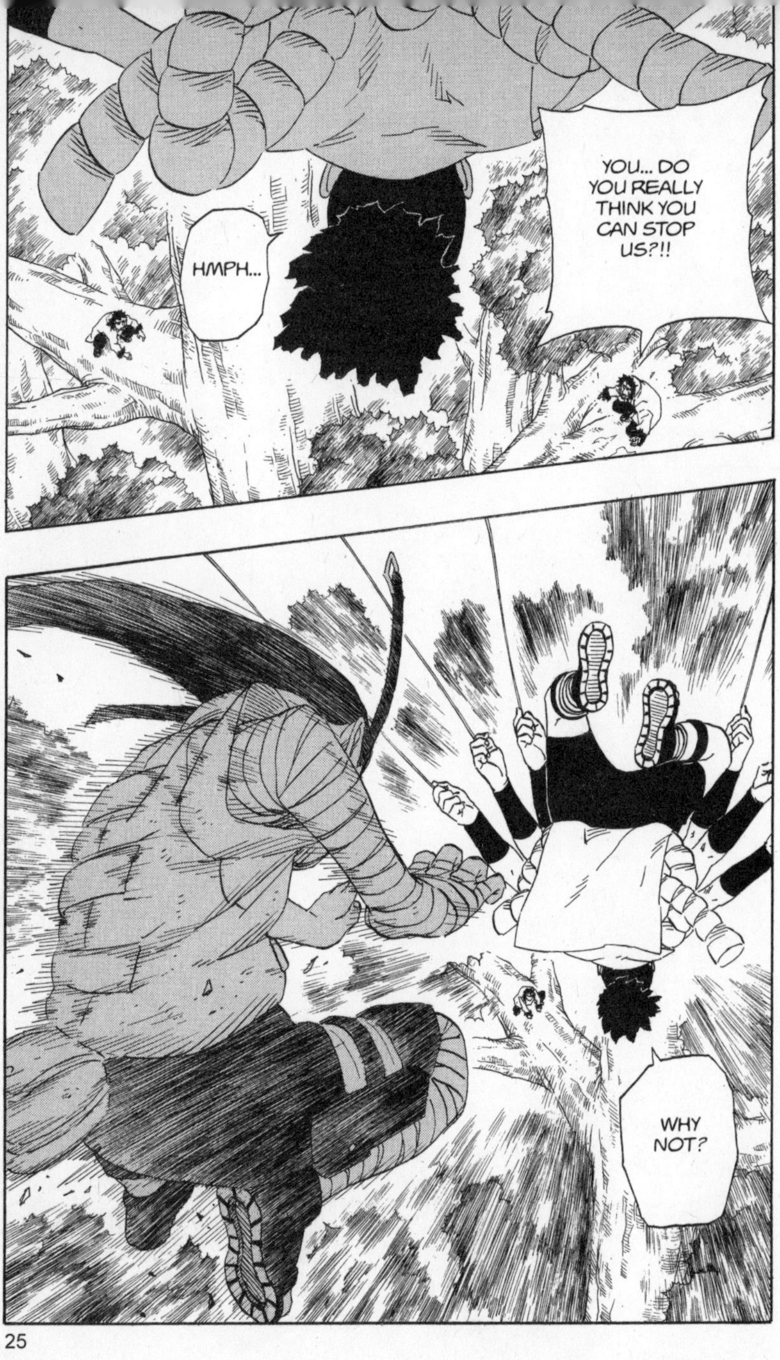
YOU... DO YOU REALLY THINK YOU CAN STOP US?!!
HMPH...
WHY NOT?

NARUTO™

Number 192: The Plan...!!

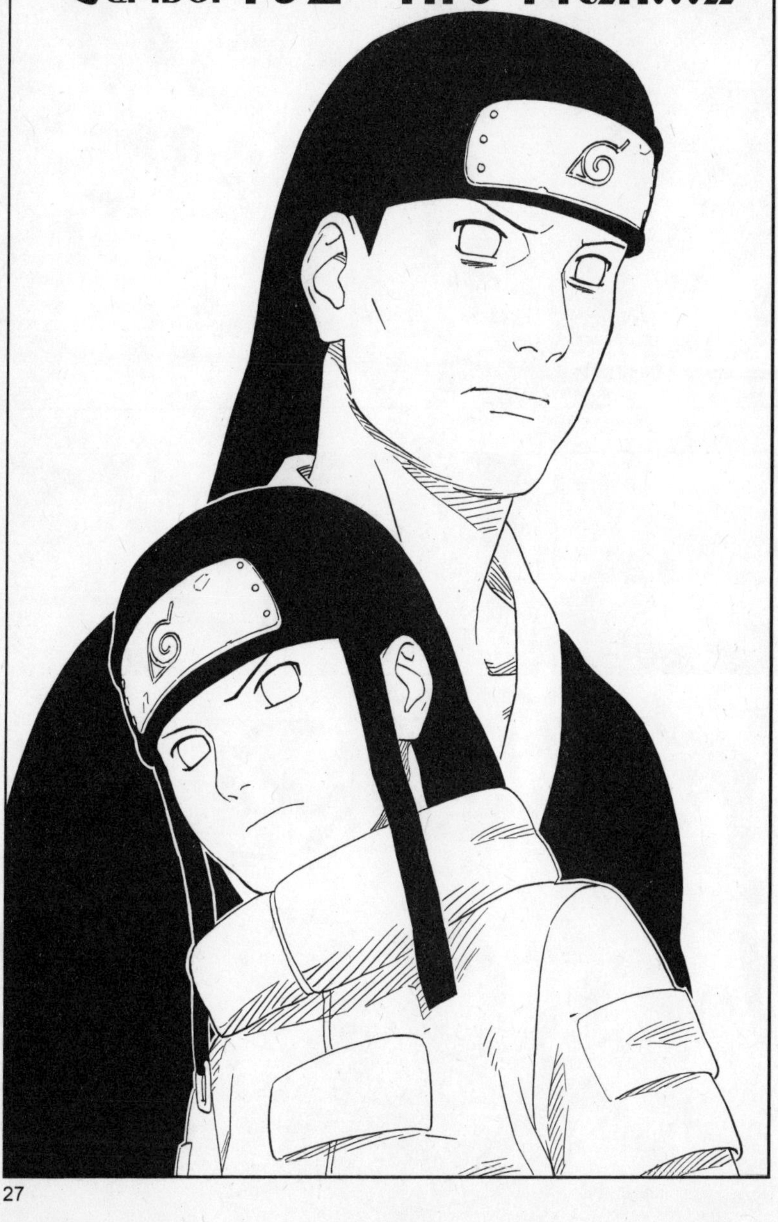

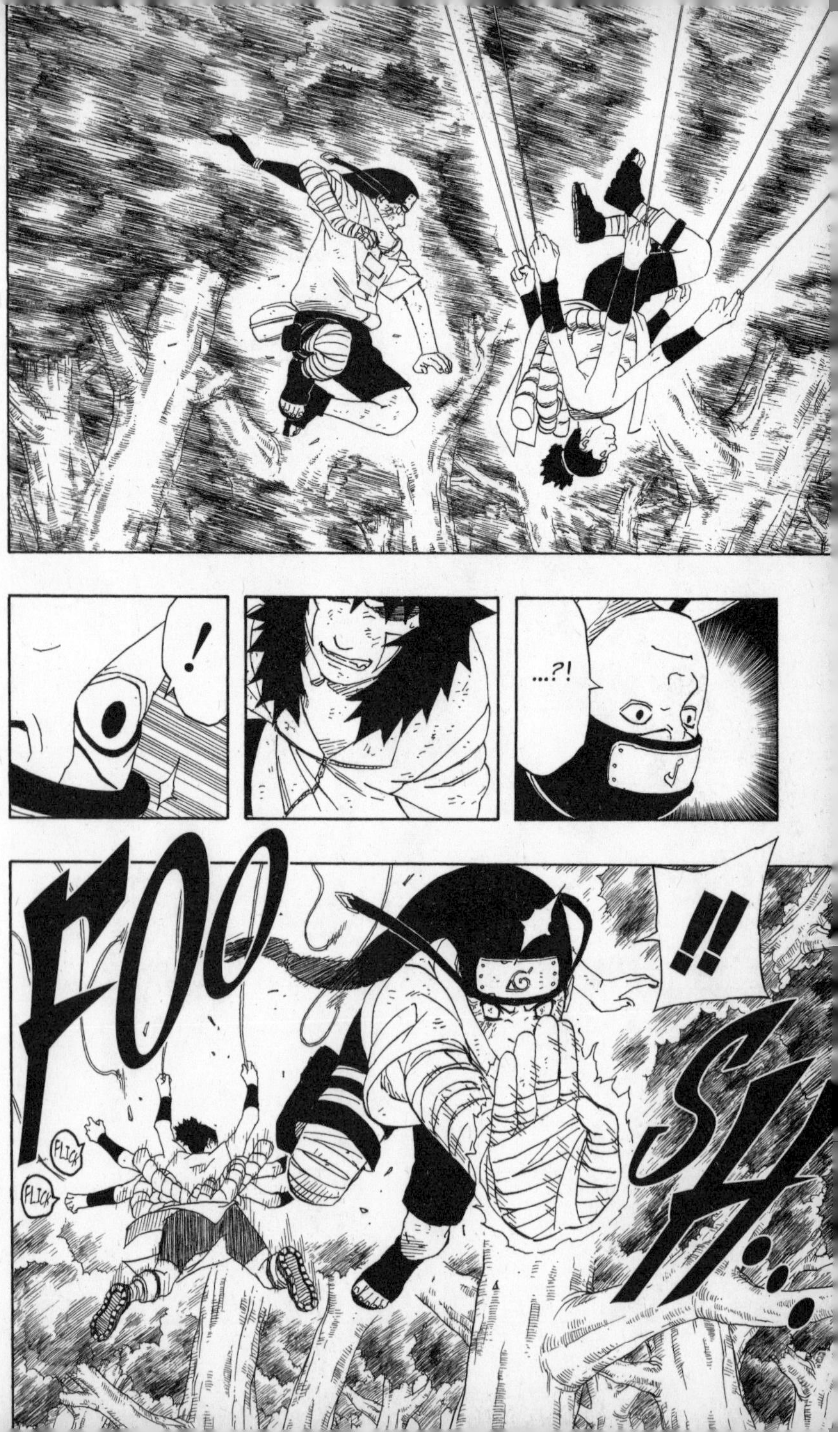
...?!
!
!!
SH...
FOO
FLICK
FLICK

READ THIS WAY

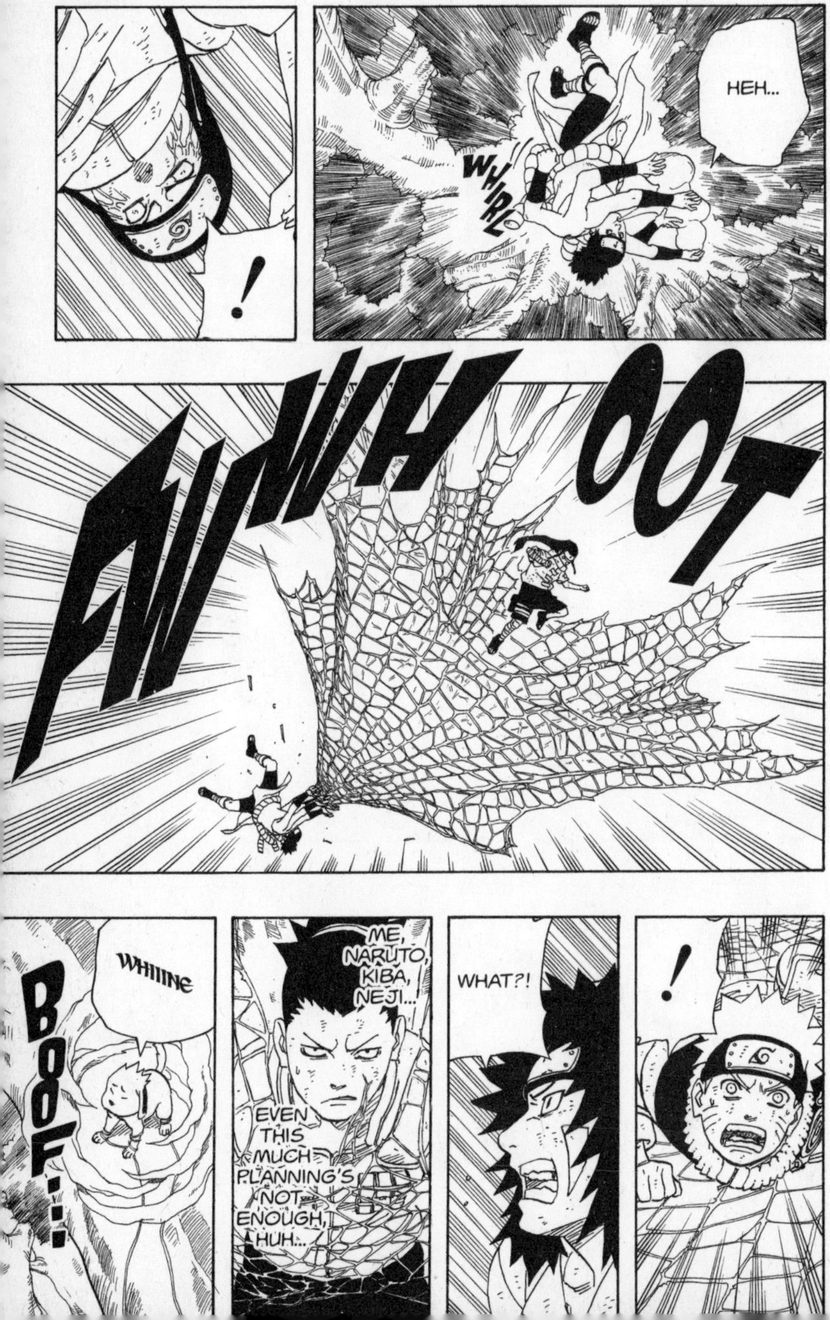
HEH...
WHIRL
!
FWWHOOT
!
WHAT?!
ME, NARUTO, KIBA, NEJI...
EVEN THIS MUCH PLANNING'S NOT ENOUGH, HUH...
WHIIINE
BOOOF....

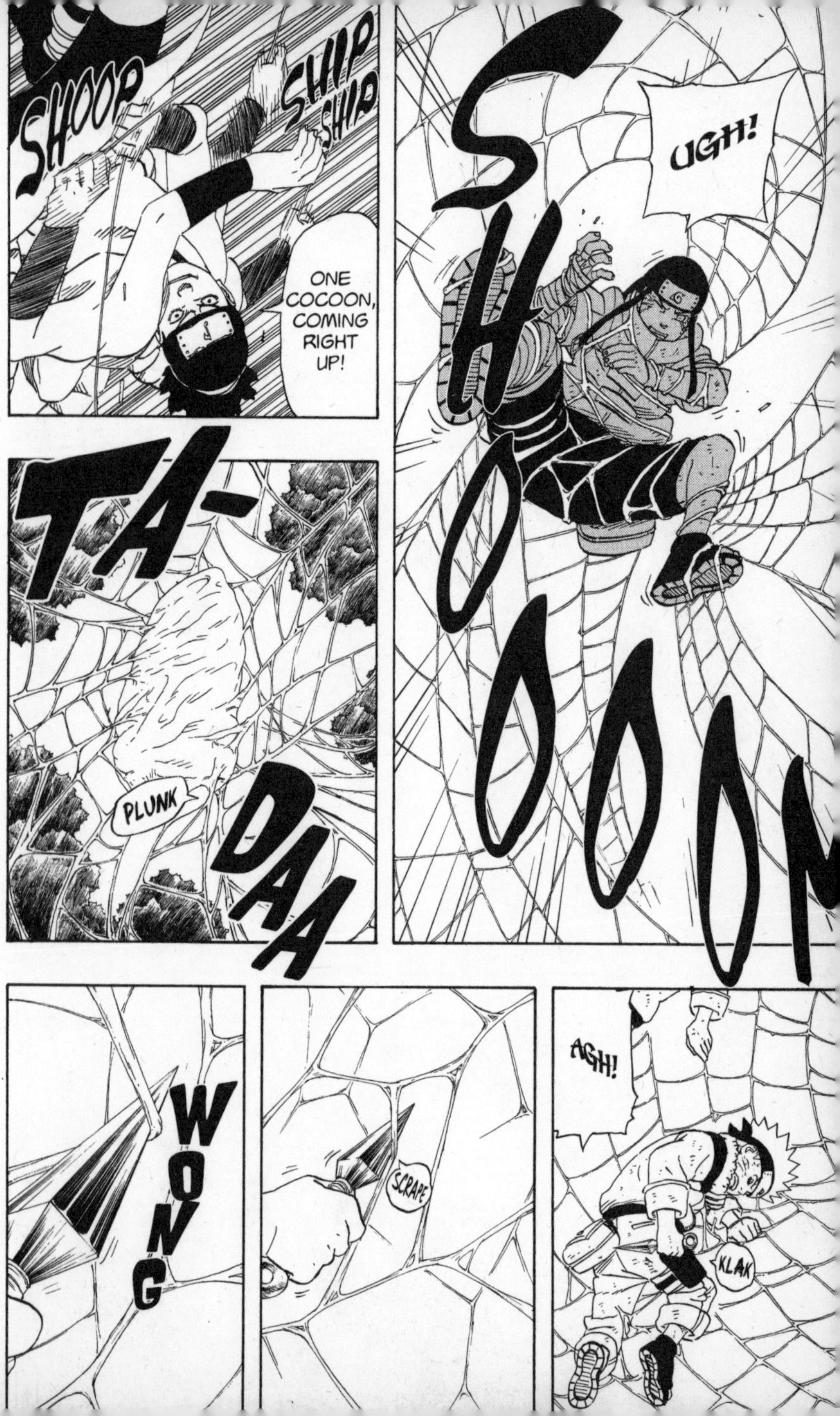
UGH!
SHOOOOOOM
SHIP SHIP
SHOOP
ONE COCOON, COMING RIGHT UP!
TA-DAA
PLUNK
AGH!
KLAK
SCRAPE
WONG

READ THIS WAY

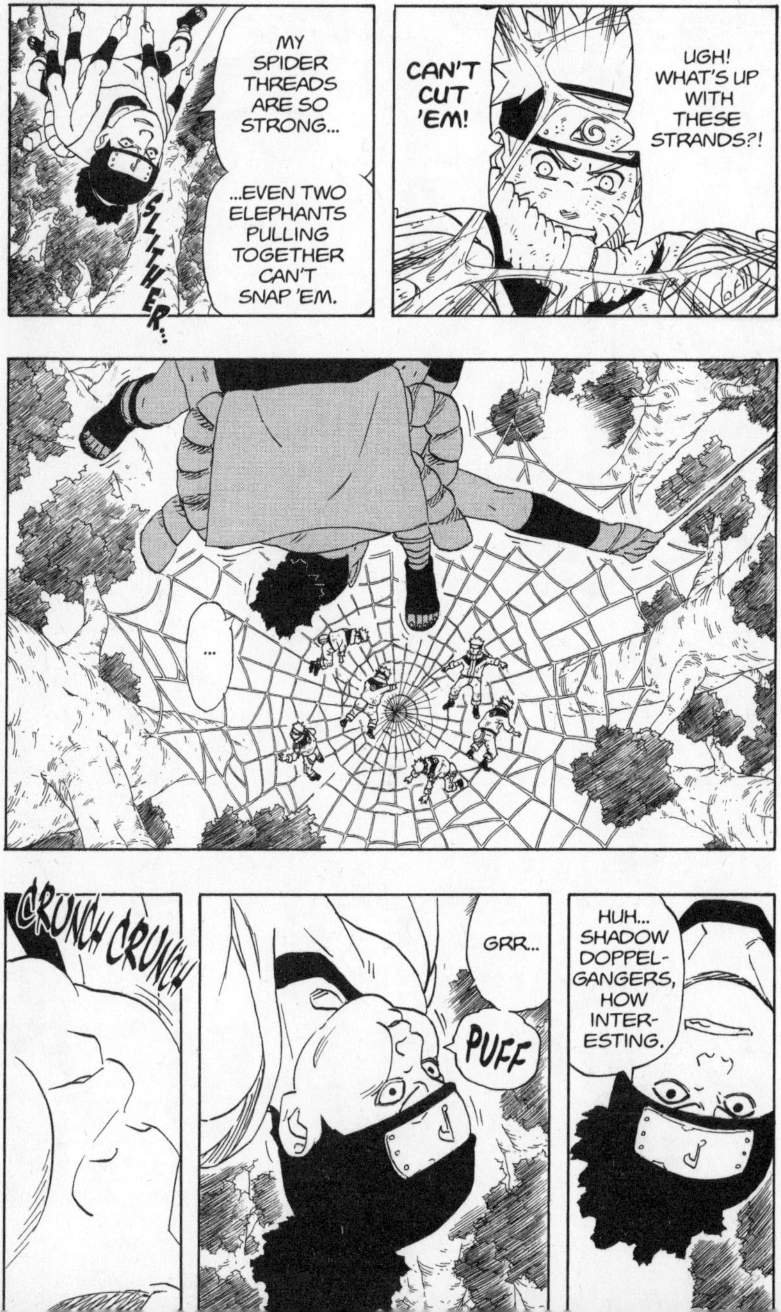
UGH! WHAT'S UP WITH THESE STRANDS?!
CAN'T CUT 'EM!
MY SPIDER THREADS ARE SO STRONG...
...EVEN TWO ELEPHANTS PULLING TOGETHER CAN'T SNAP 'EM.
SLITHER...
...
HUH... SHADOW DOPPEL-GANGERS, HOW INTER-ESTING.
GRR...
PUFF
CRUNCH CRUNCH

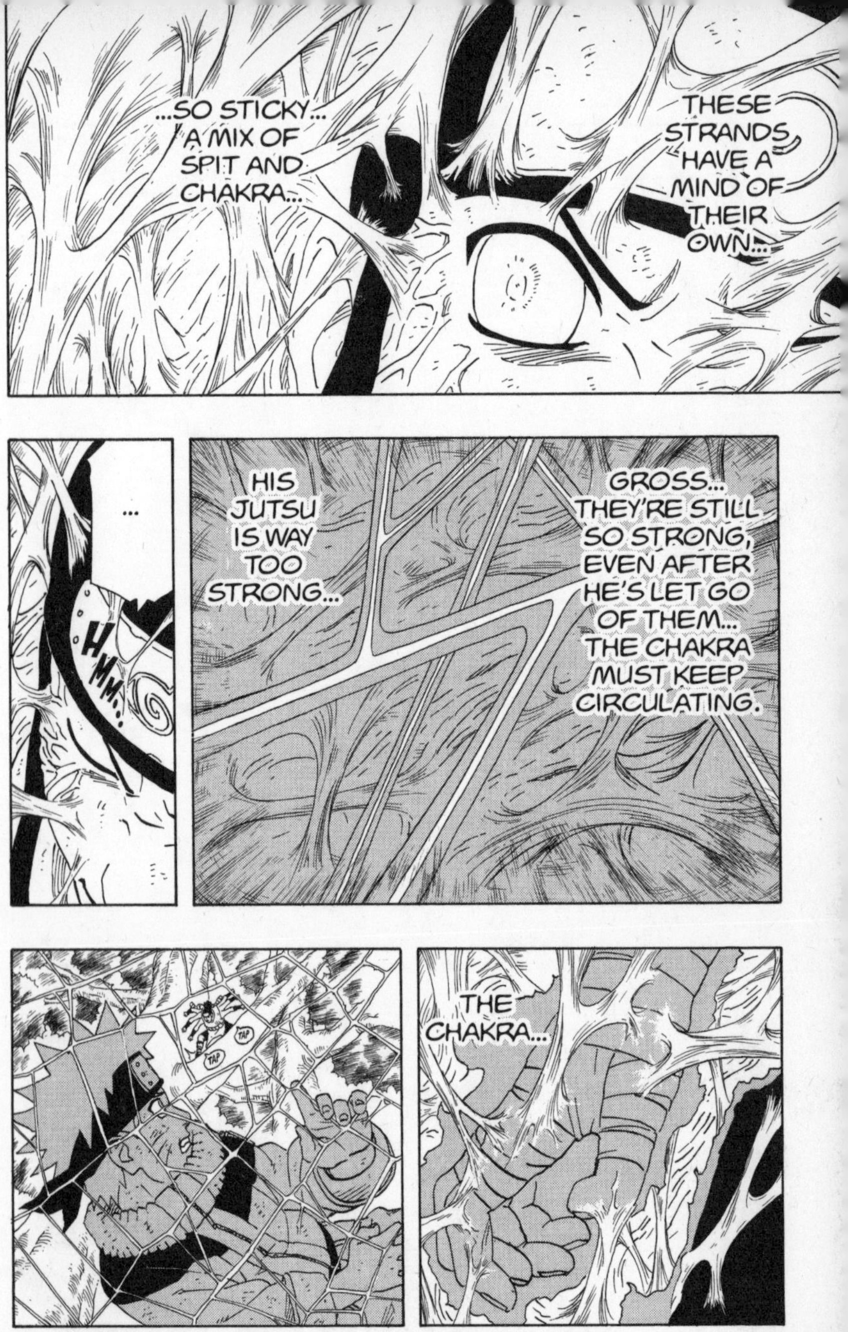
THESE STRANDS HAVE A MIND OF THEIR OWN...
...SO STICKY... A MIX OF SPIT AND CHAKRA...
GROSS... THEY'RE STILL SO STRONG, EVEN AFTER HE'S LET GO OF THEM... THE CHAKRA MUST KEEP CIRCULATING.
HIS JUTSU IS WAY TOO STRONG...
...
HMM...
THE CHAKRA...
TAP
TAP

READ THIS WAY

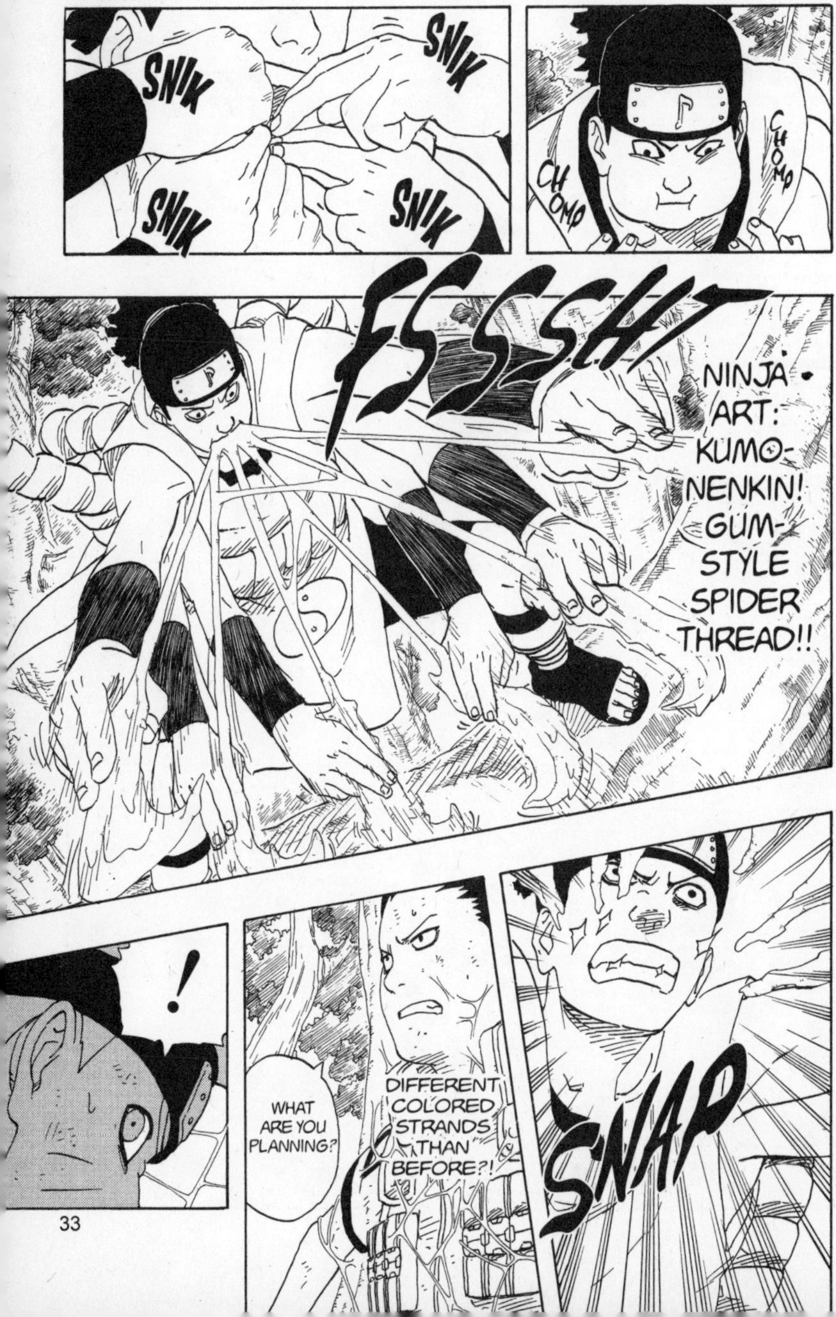
CHOMP
CHOMP
SNIK
SNIK
SNIK
SNIK
FSSSHT
NINJA ART: KUMO-NENKIN! GUM-STYLE SPIDER THREAD!!
SNAP
DIFFERENT COLORED STRANDS THAN BEFORE?!
WHAT ARE YOU PLANNING?
!

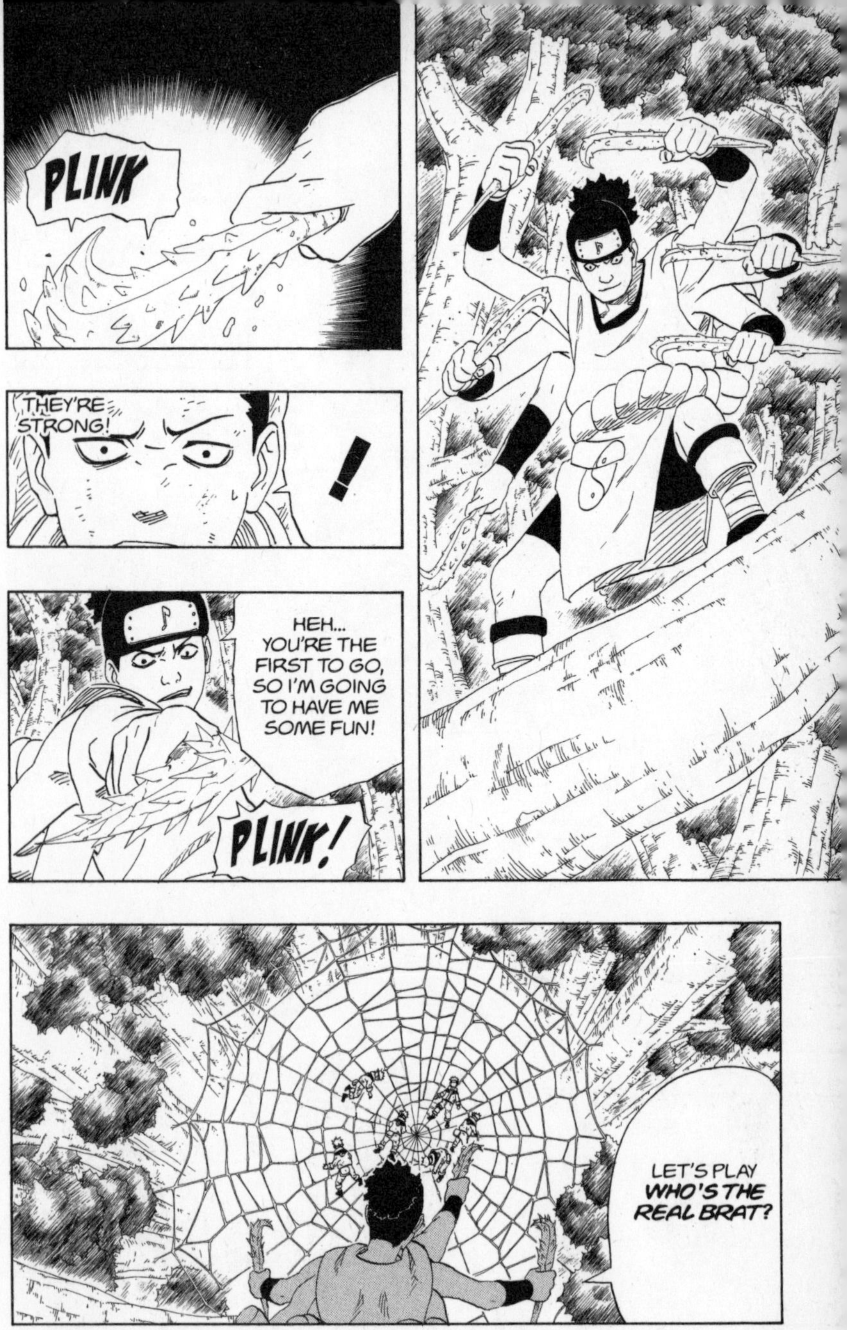
PLINK
THEY'RE STRONG!
!
HEH... YOU'RE THE FIRST TO GO, SO I'M GOING TO HAVE ME SOME FUN!
PLINK!
LET'S PLAY *WHO'S THE REAL BRAT?*

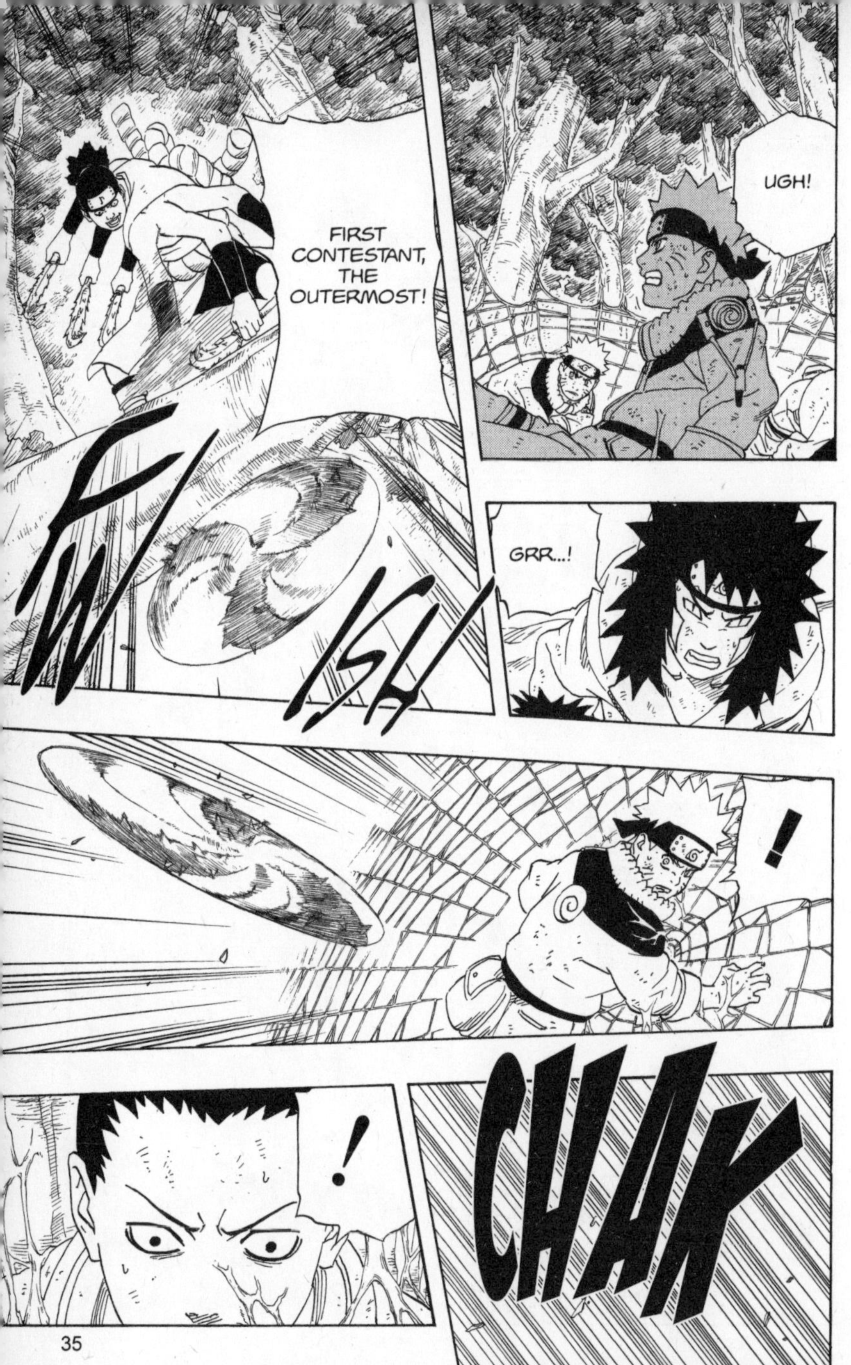
UGH!
FIRST CONTESTANT, THE OUTERMOST!
FWISH
GRR...!
!
CHAK
!

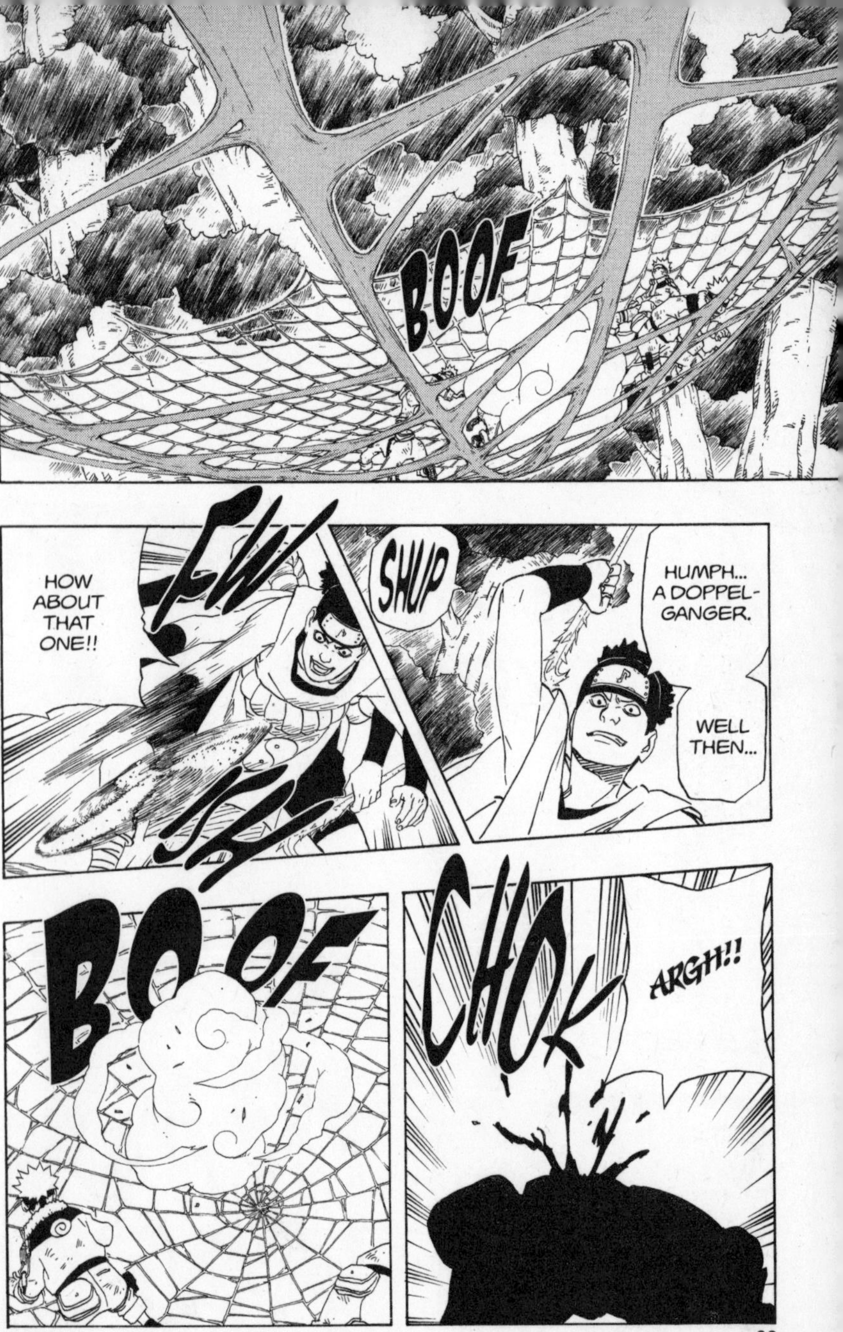
BOOF
SHUP
HUMPH... A DOPPEL-GANGER.
WELL THEN...
HOW ABOUT THAT ONE!!
FWISH
CHOK
ARGH!!
BOOF

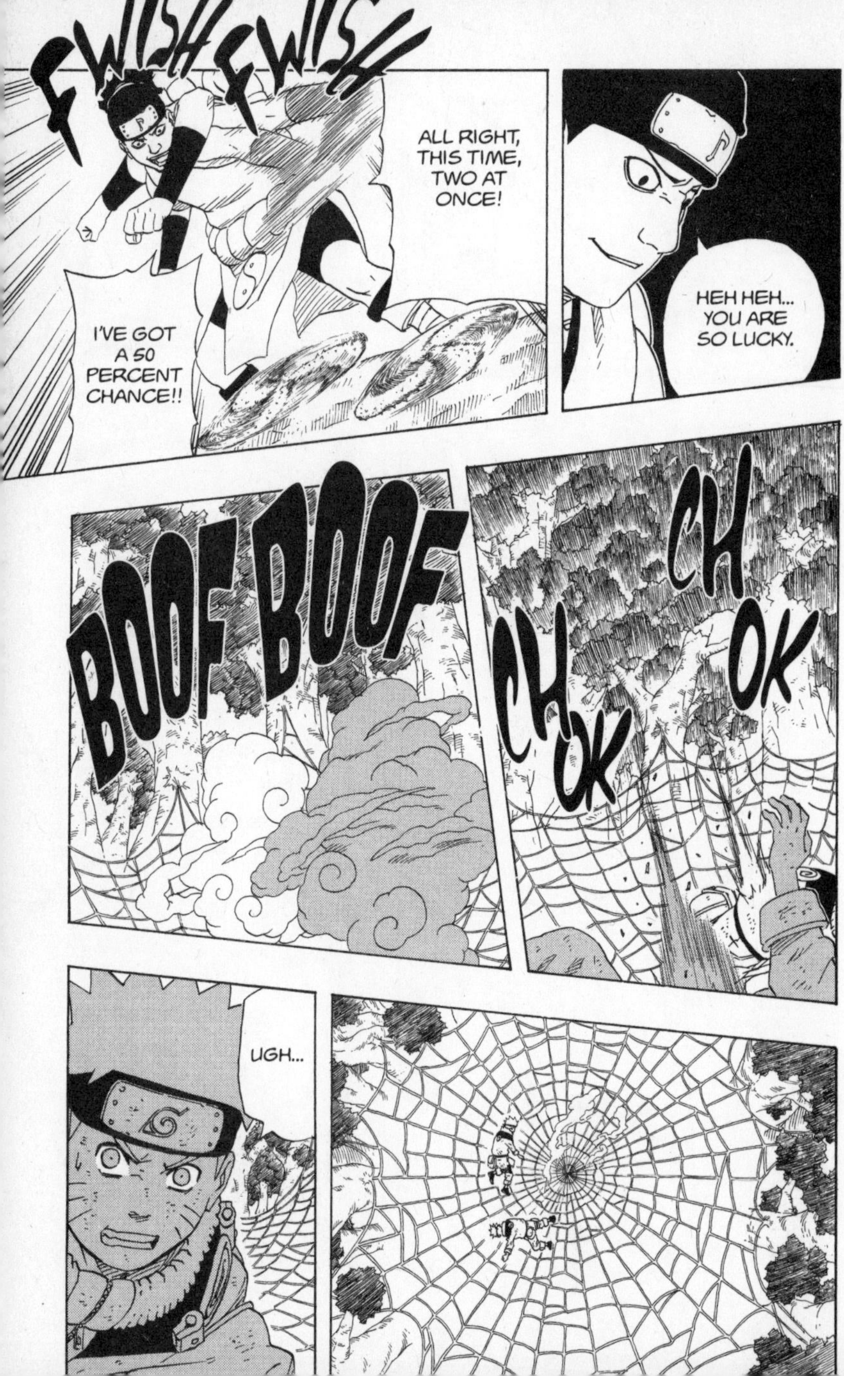
HEH HEH... YOU ARE SO LUCKY.
FWISH FWISH
ALL RIGHT, THIS TIME, TWO AT ONCE!
I'VE GOT A 50 PERCENT CHANCE!!
CHOK CHOK
BOOF BOOF
UGH...

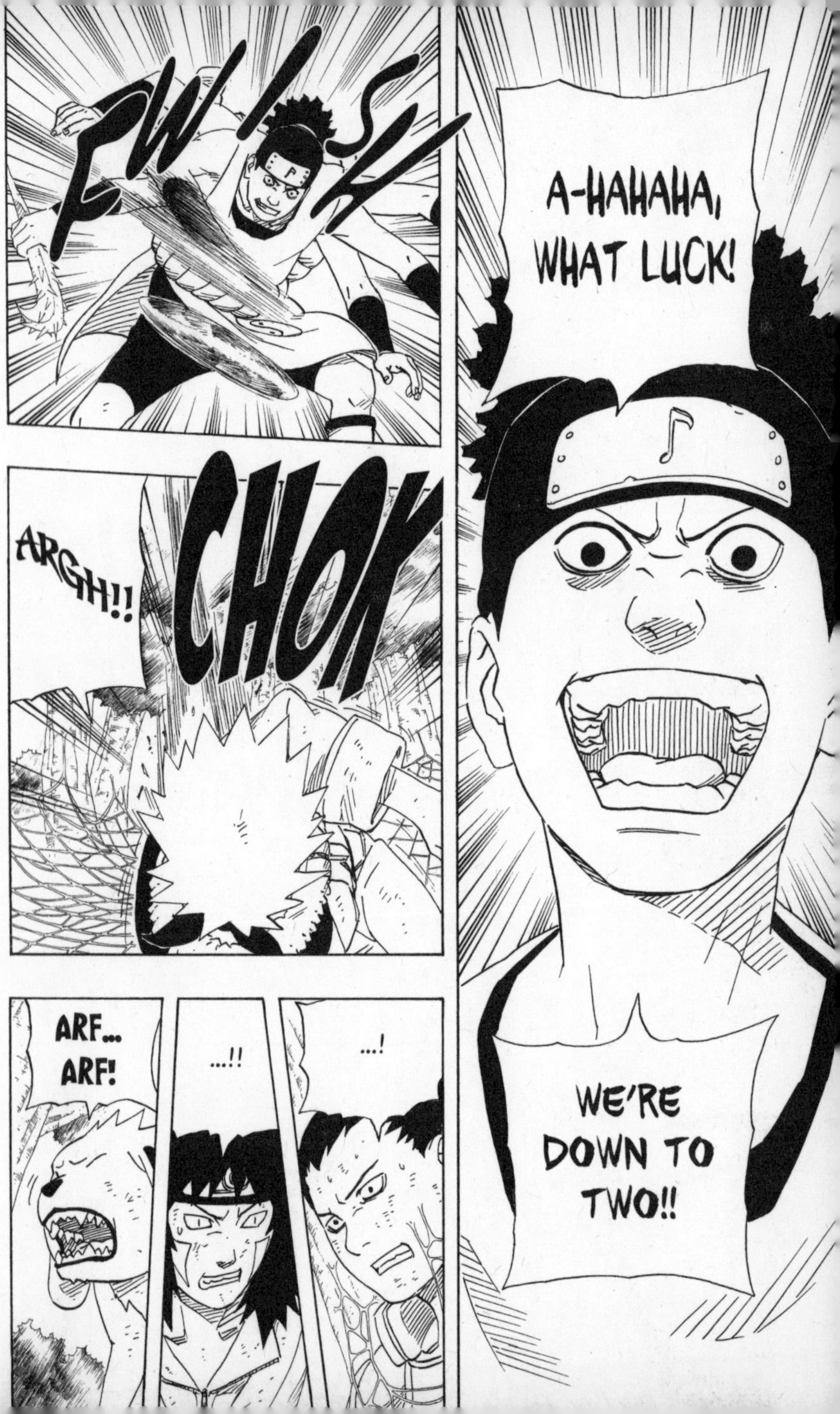
A-HAHAHA, WHAT LUCK!
WE'RE DOWN TO TWO!!
SWISH
CHOK
ARGH!!
...!
...!!
ARF... ARF!

READ THIS WAY

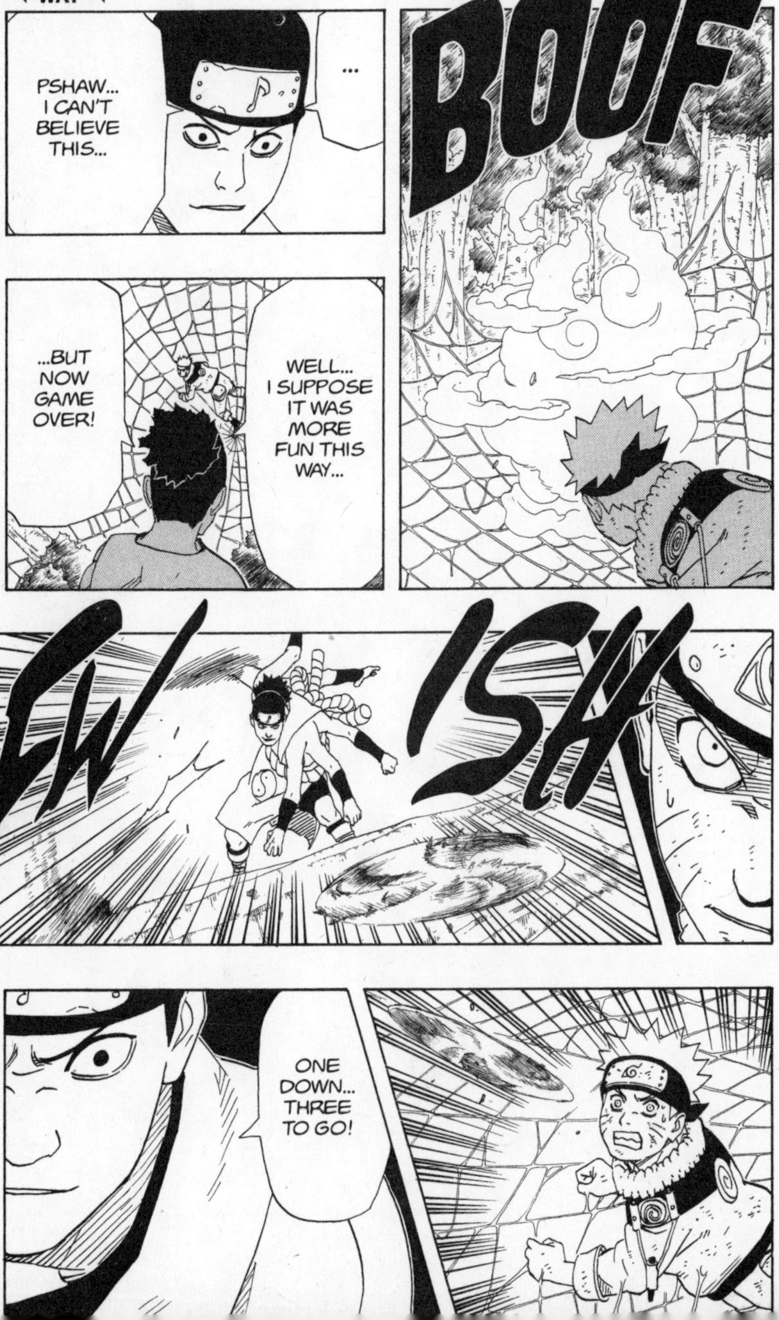
BOOF
...
PSHAW... I CAN'T BELIEVE THIS...
WELL... I SUPPOSE IT WAS MORE FUN THIS WAY...
...BUT NOW GAME OVER!
FWISH
ONE DOWN... THREE TO GO!

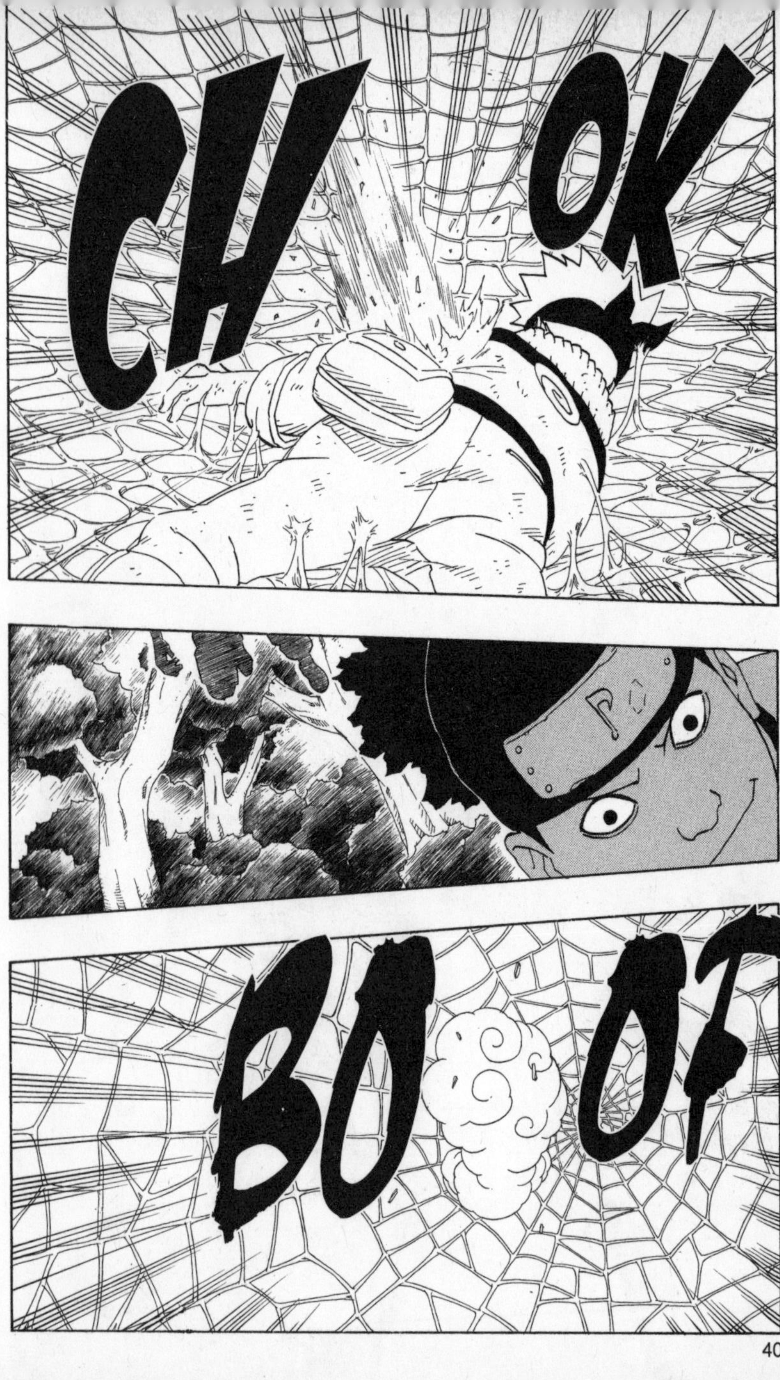
CHOK
BOOF

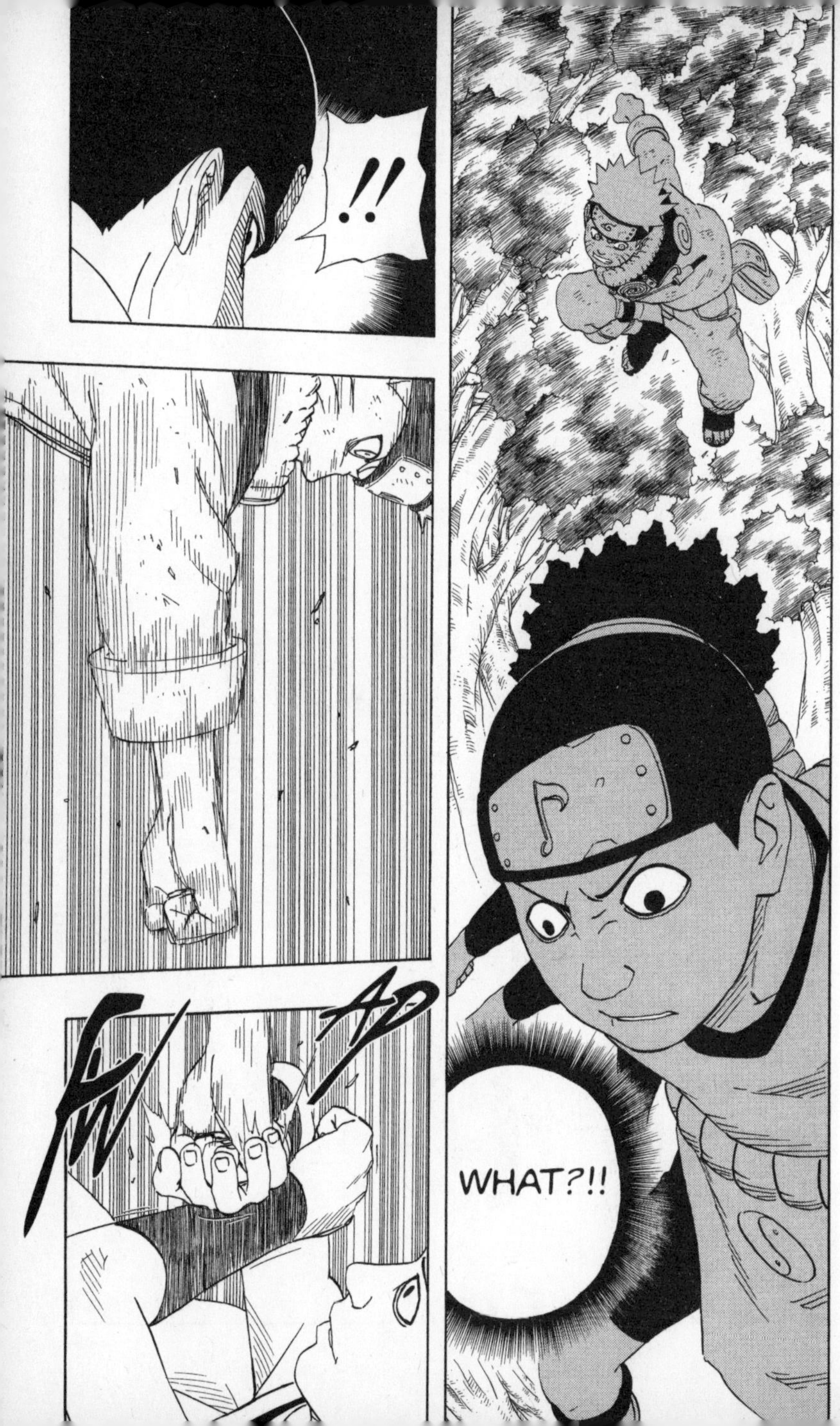
WHAT?!!
!!
FWAP

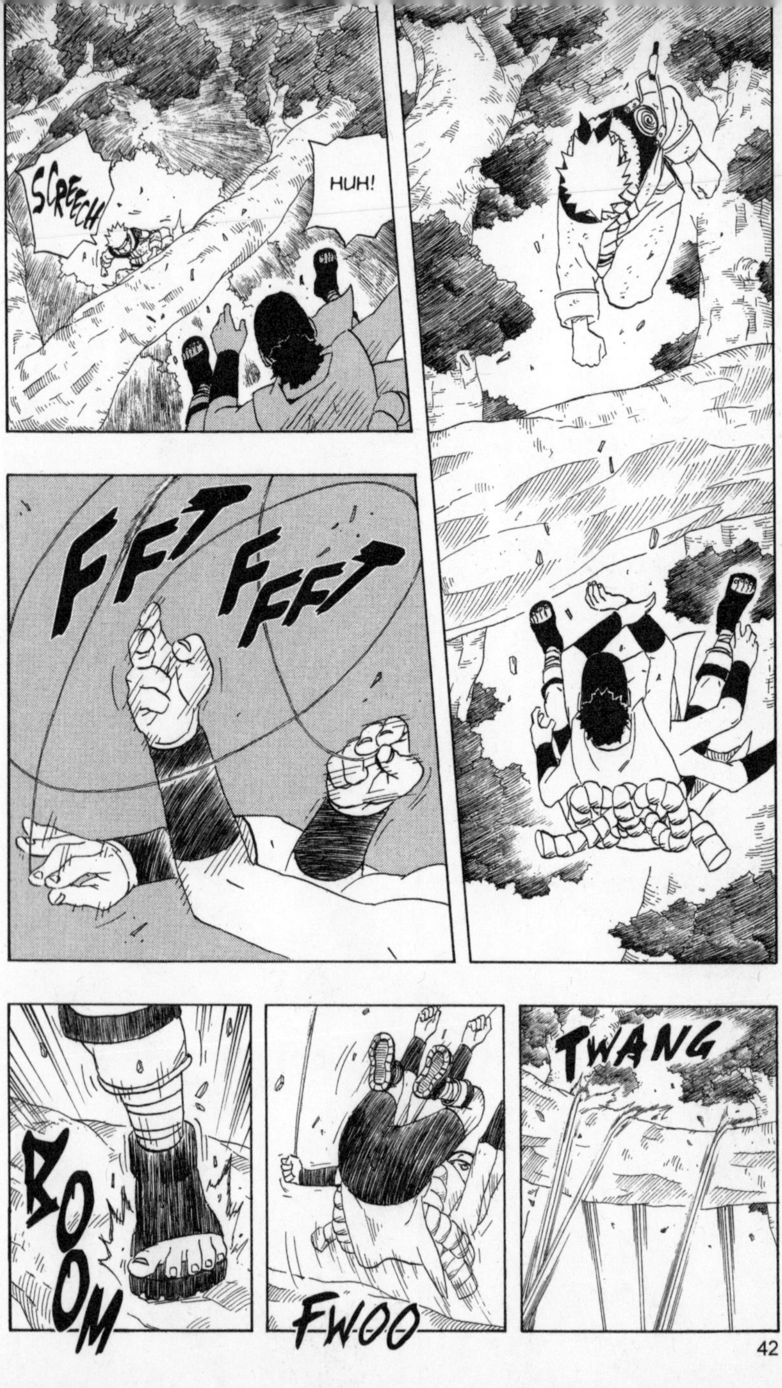
HUH!
SCREECH
FFFT
FFFT
TWANG
FWOO
BOOM

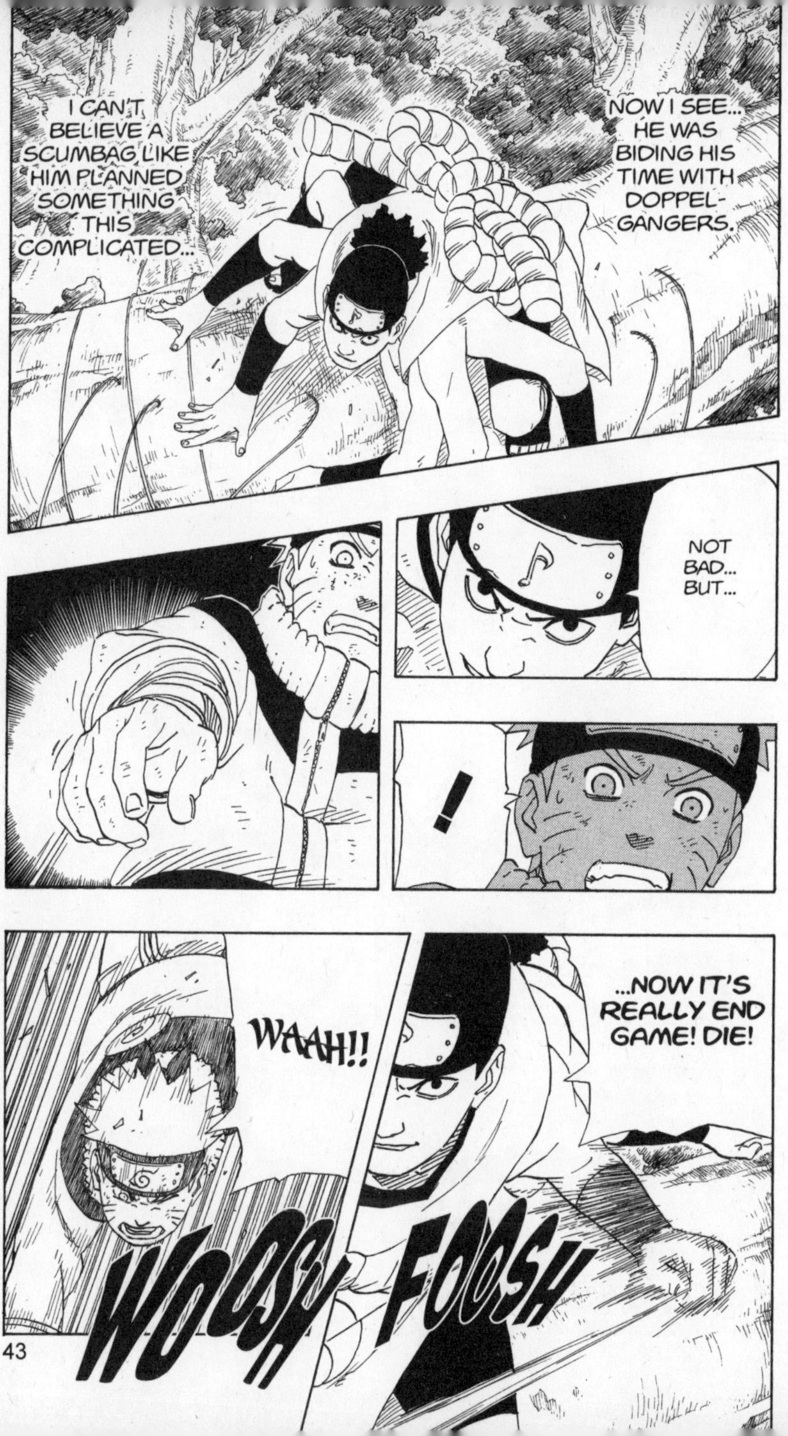
NOW I SEE... HE WAS BIDING HIS TIME WITH DOPPEL-GANGERS.
I CAN'T BELIEVE A SCUMBAG LIKE HIM PLANNED SOMETHING THIS COMPLICATED...
NOT BAD... BUT...
!
...NOW IT'S REALLY END GAME! DIE!
WAAH!!
FOOSH
WOOSH

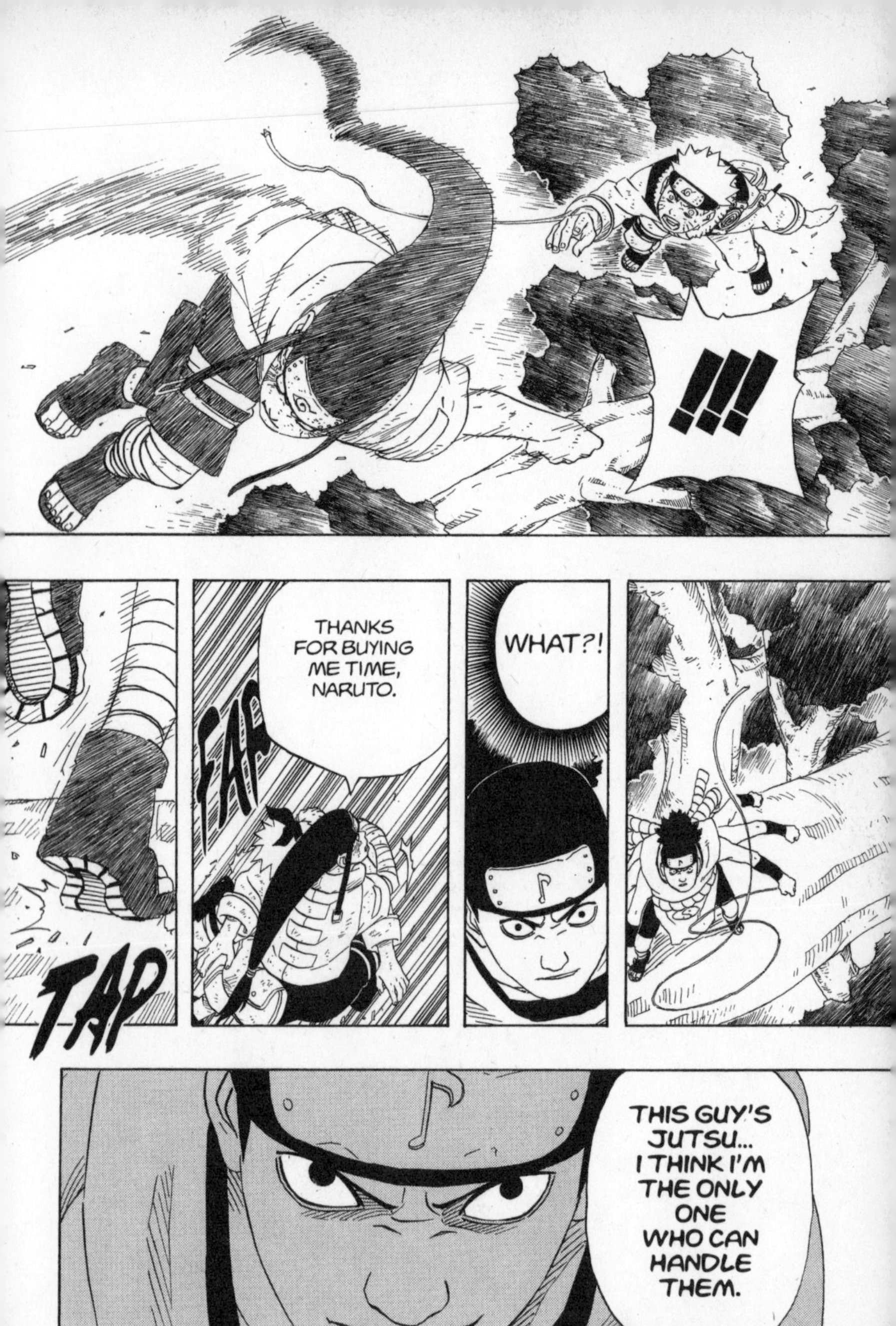
!!!
WHAT?!
THANKS FOR BUYING ME TIME, NARUTO.
FAP
TAP
THIS GUY'S JUTSU... I THINK I'M THE ONLY ONE WHO CAN HANDLE THEM.

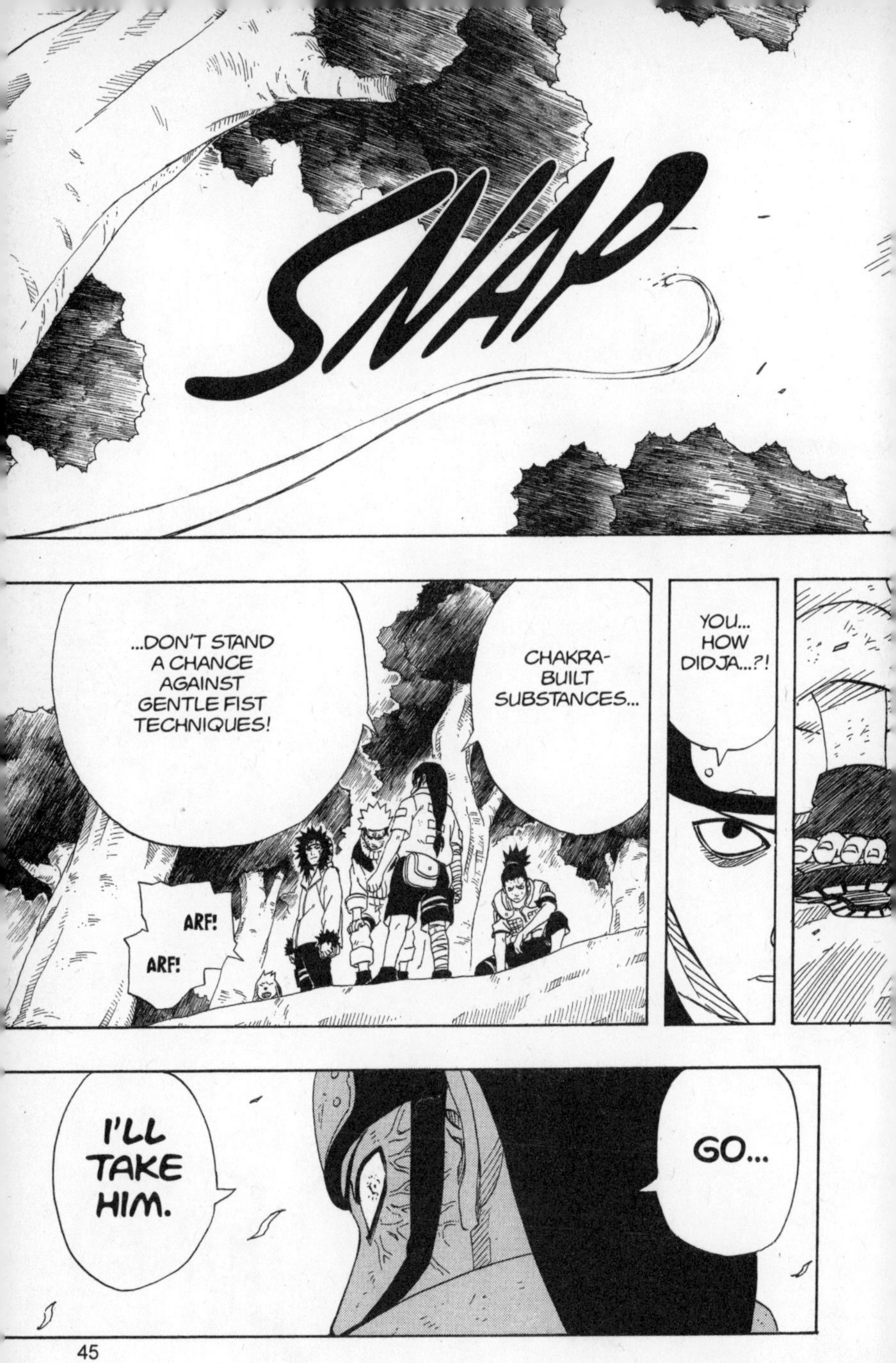
SNAP
YOU... HOW DIDJA...?!
CHAKRA-BUILT SUBSTANCES...
...DON'T STAND A CHANCE AGAINST GENTLE FIST TECHNIQUES!
ARF!
ARF!
GO...
I'LL TAKE HIM.

NARUTO™

Number 193: Game Over

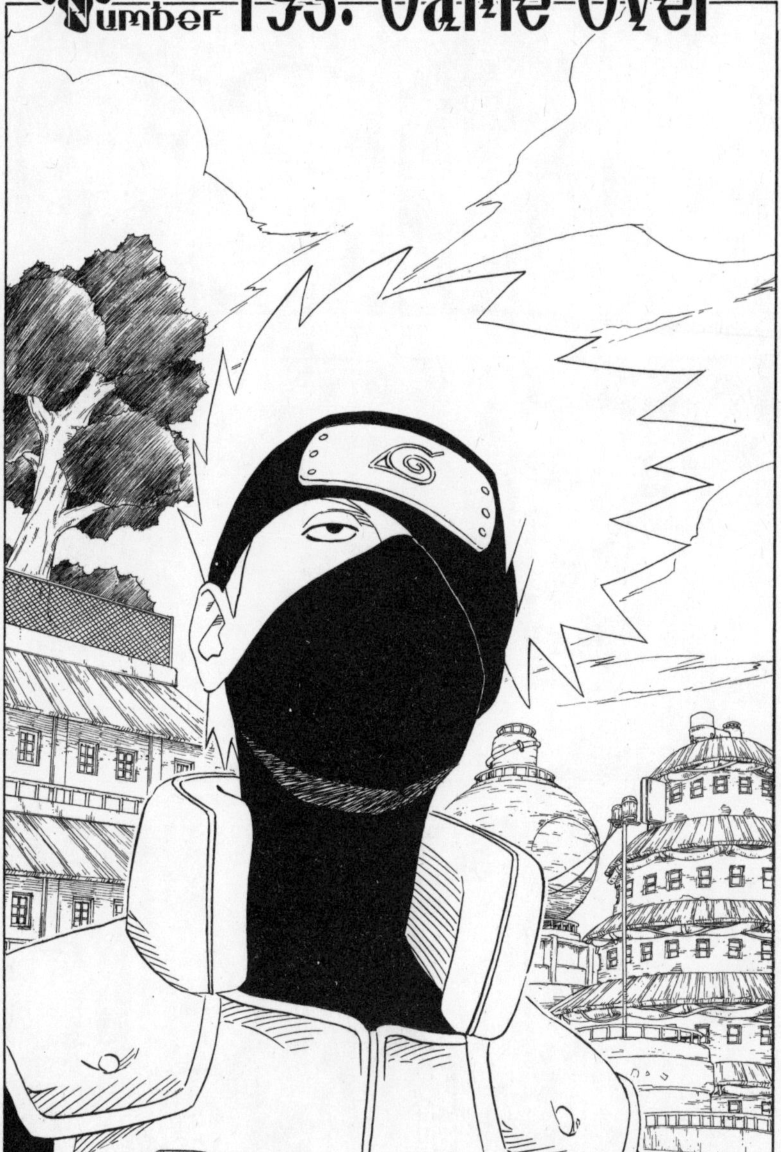

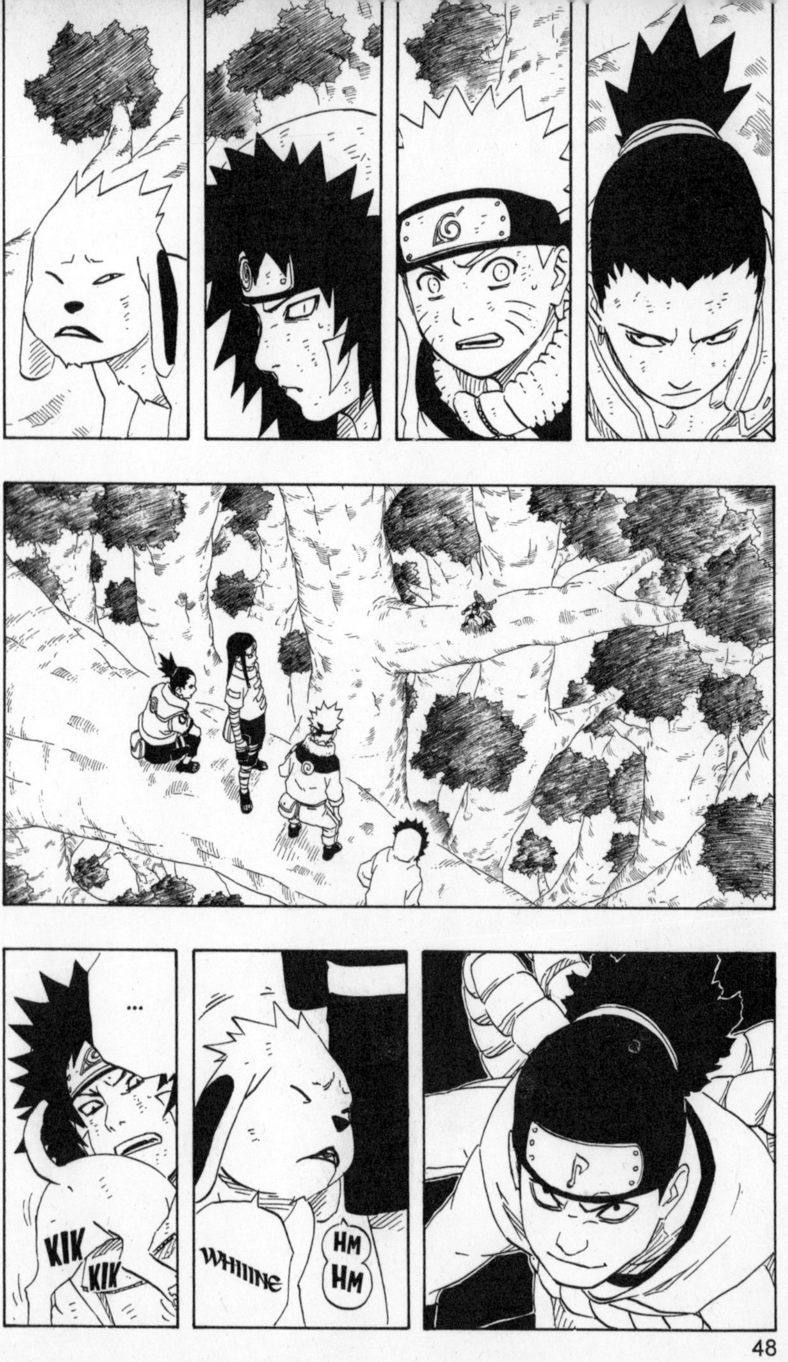
HM
HM
WHIIINE
...
KIK
KIK

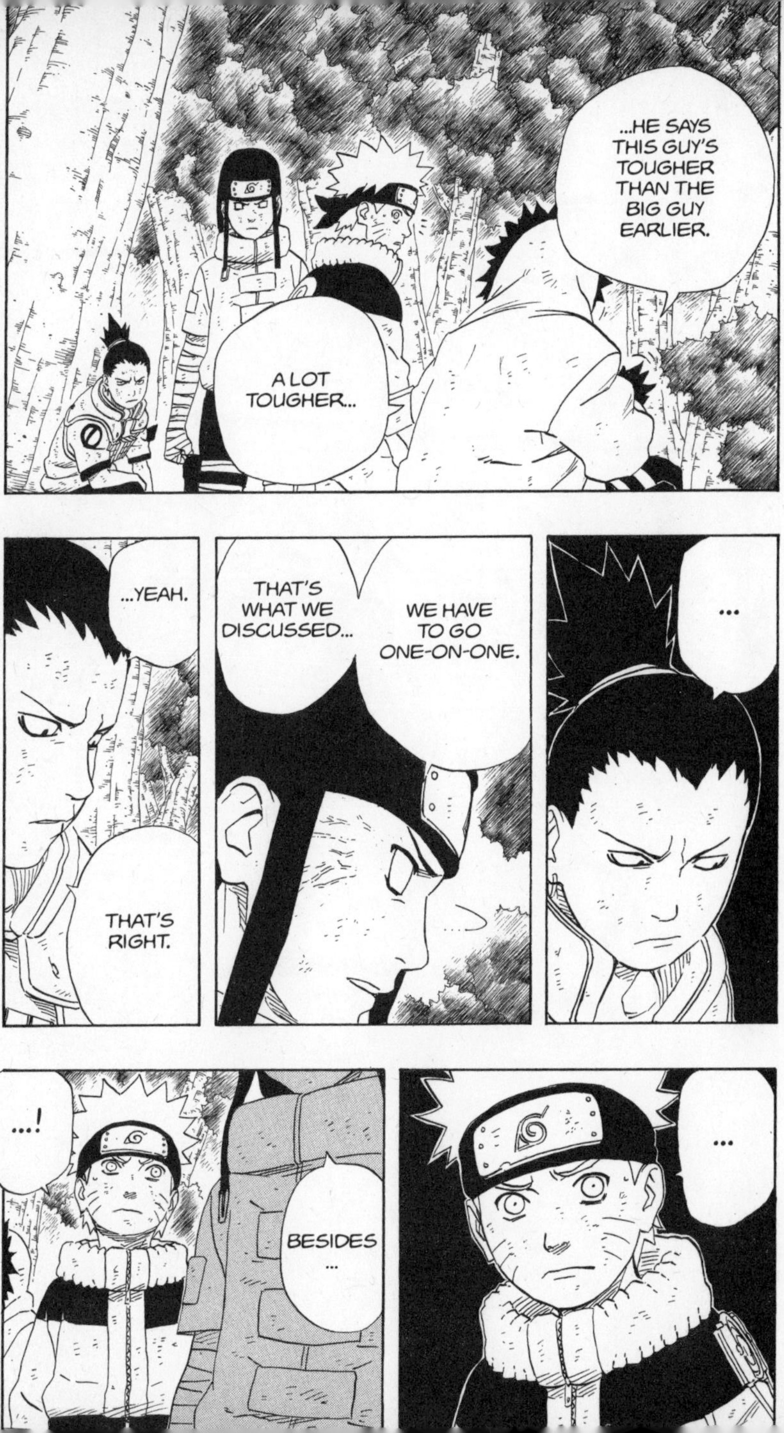
...HE SAYS THIS GUY'S TOUGHER THAN THE BIG GUY EARLIER.
A LOT TOUGHER...
...
WE HAVE TO GO ONE-ON-ONE.
THAT'S WHAT WE DISCUSSED...
...YEAH.
THAT'S RIGHT.
...
...!
BESIDES ...

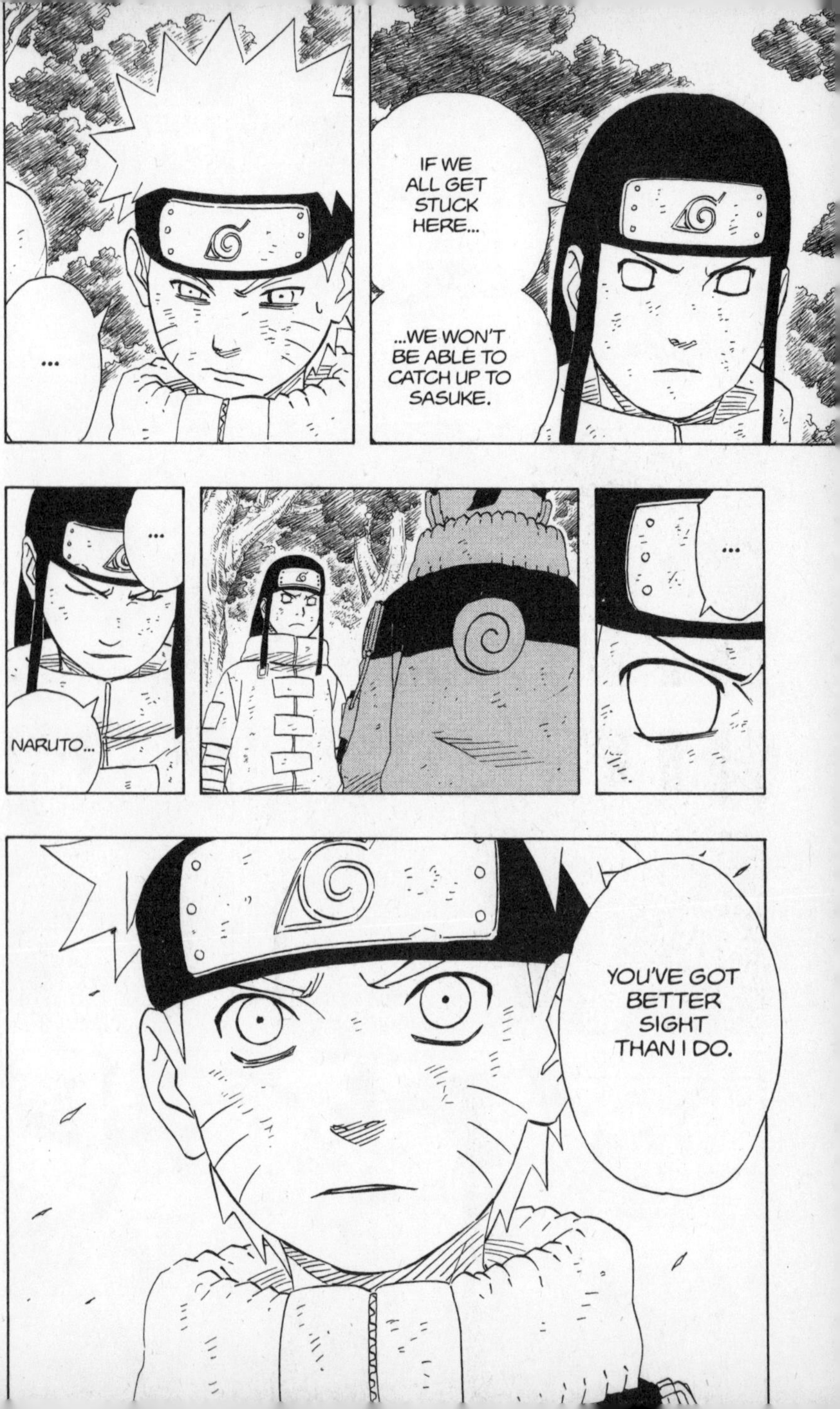
IF WE ALL GET STUCK HERE...
...WE WON'T BE ABLE TO CATCH UP TO SASUKE.
...
...
...
NARUTO...
YOU'VE GOT BETTER SIGHT THAN I DO.

TAP

RIGHT NOW, SASUKE...

?

...IS WRAPPED IN DARKNESS.

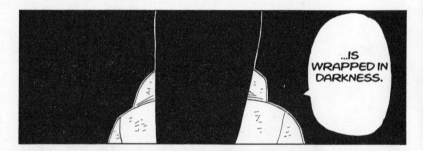

I'LL CATCH UP TO YOU LATER, TOO!!

NOW GO!

...

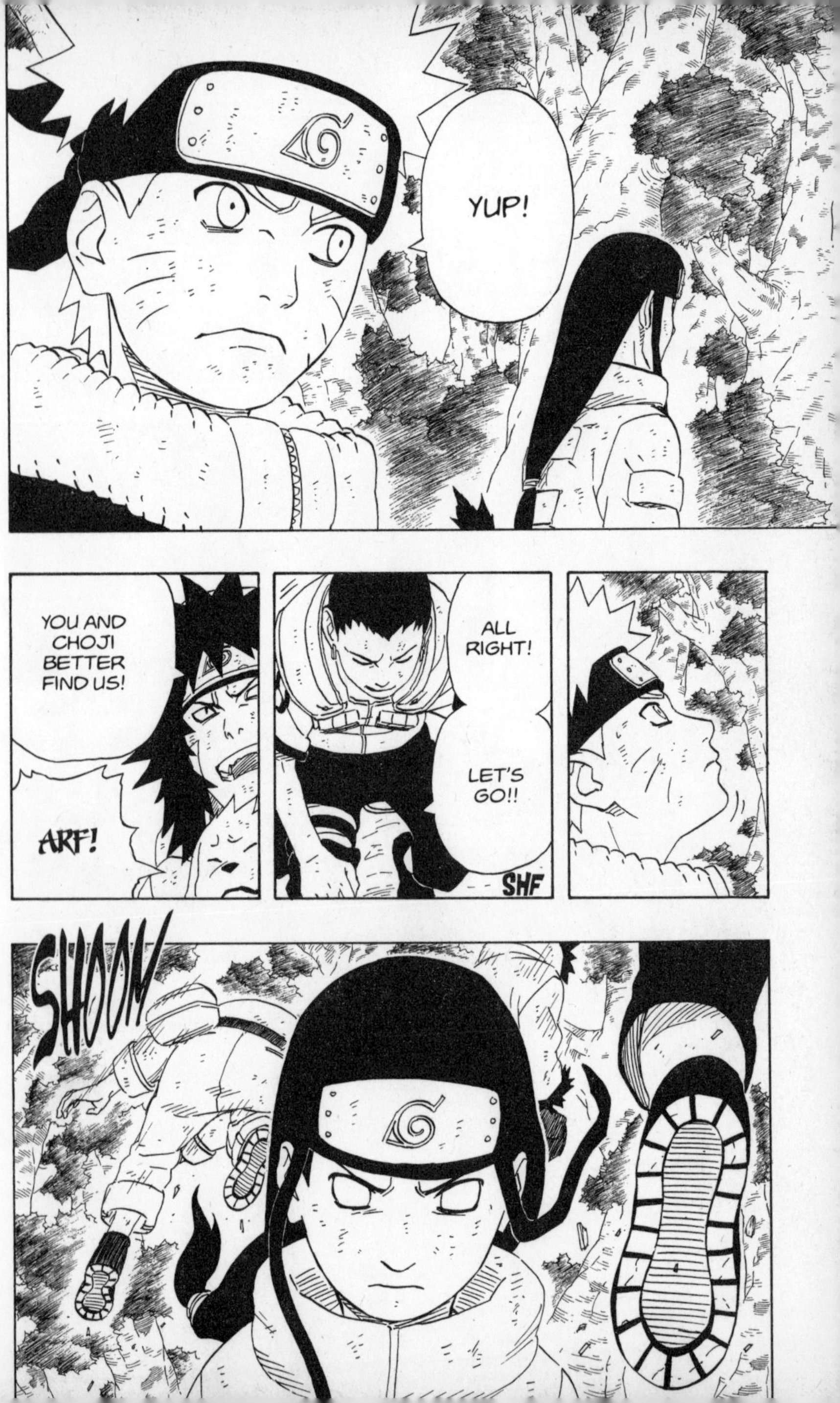
YUP!
ALL RIGHT!
LET'S GO!!
SHF
YOU AND CHOJI BETTER FIND US!
ARF!
SHOOM

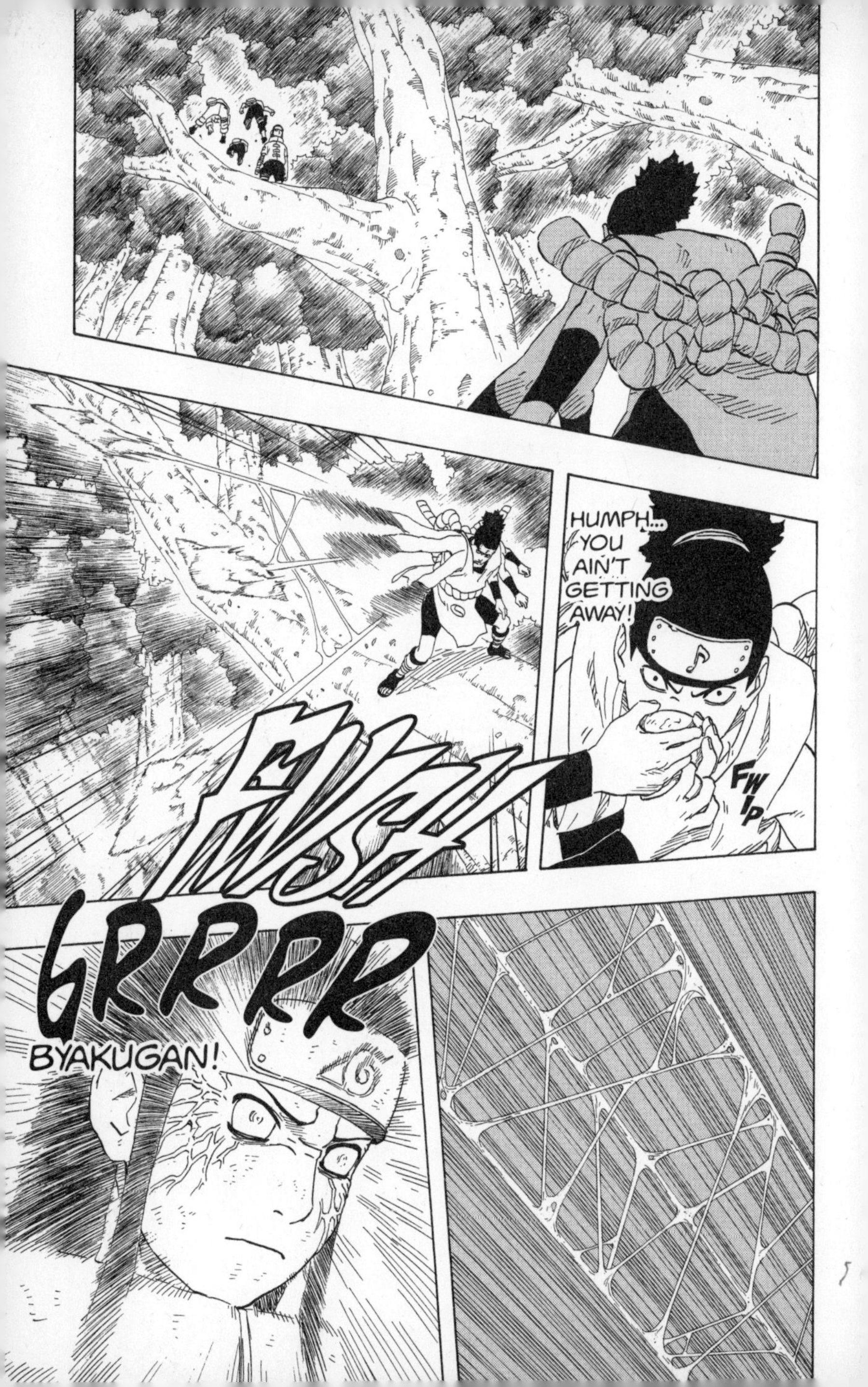
HUMPH... YOU AIN'T GETTING AWAY!
FWIP
FWSH
GRRRR
BYAKUGAN!

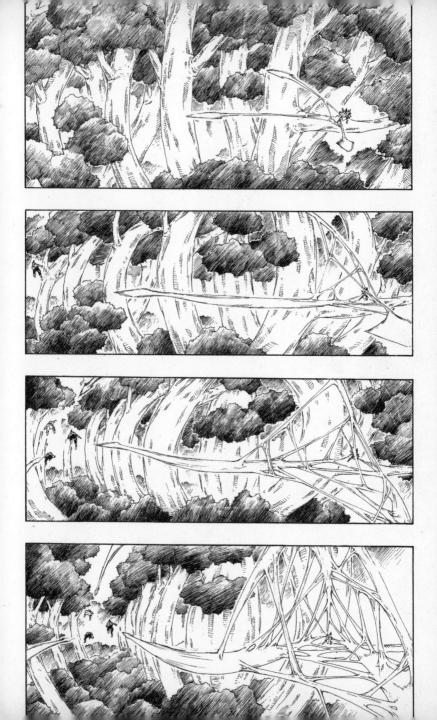

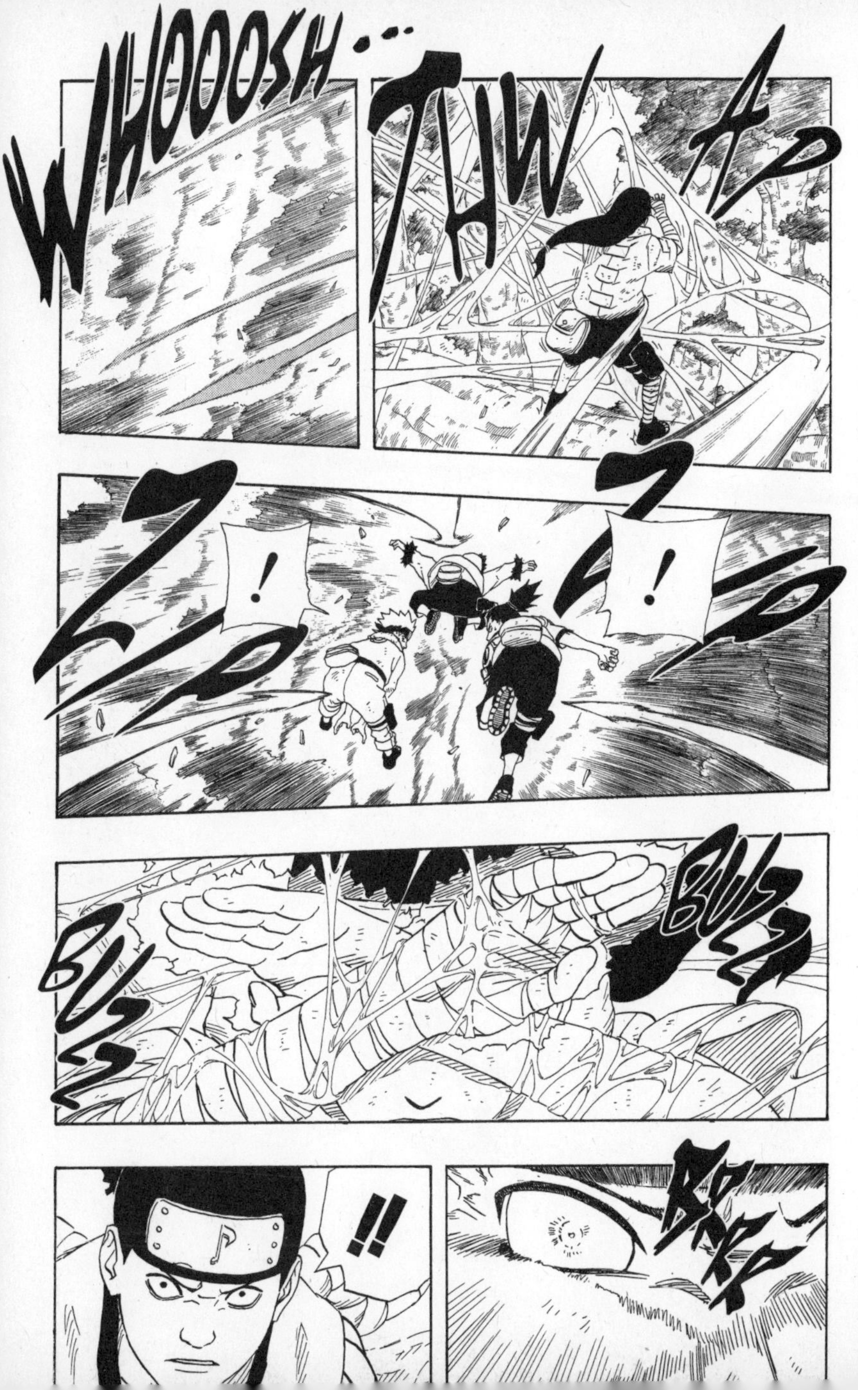
THWAP
WHOOOSH...
ZAP
!
!
ZIP
BUZZ
BUZZ
BRRR
!!

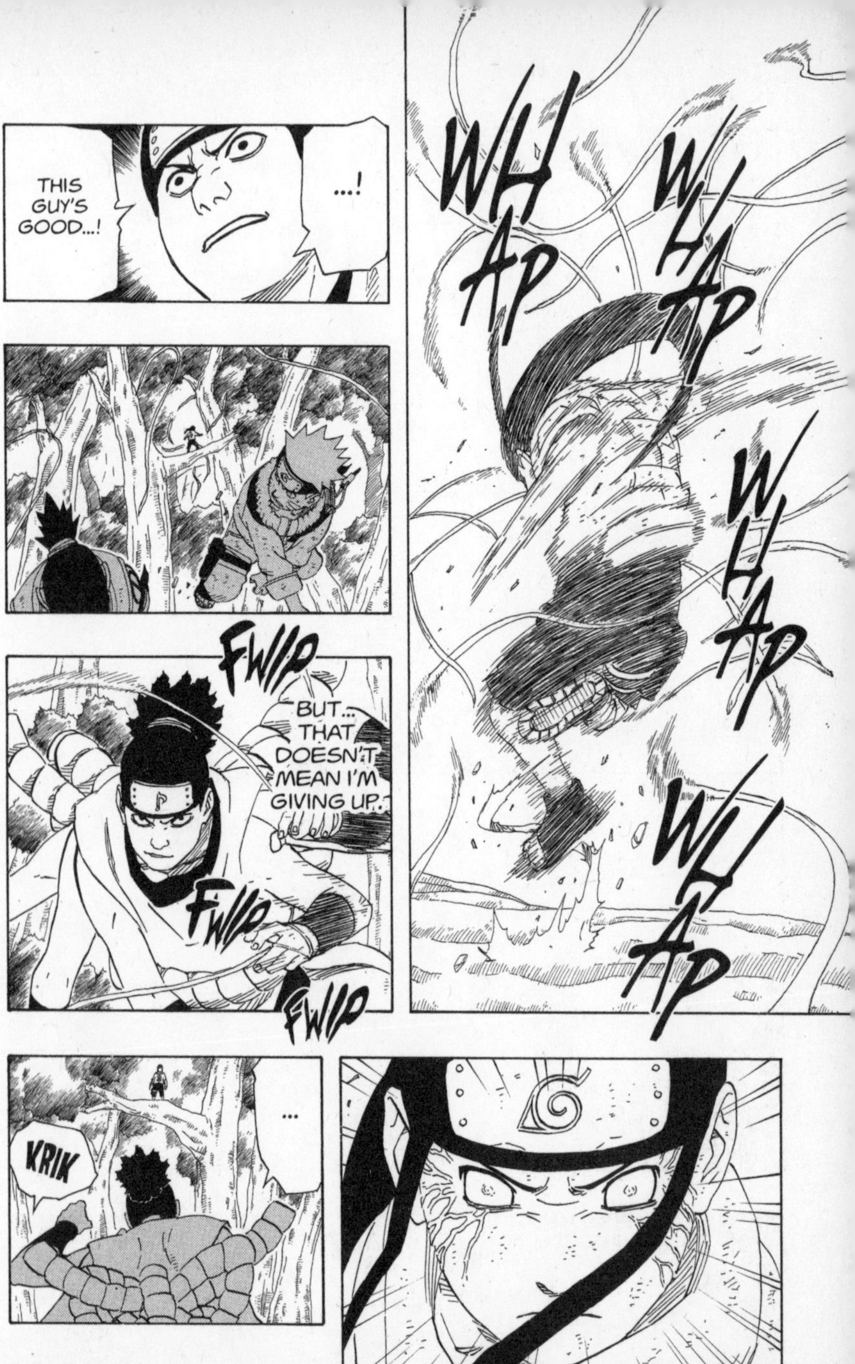
WHAP
WHAP
WHAP
WHAP
...!
THIS GUY'S GOOD...!
FWIP
BUT... THAT DOESN'T MEAN I'M GIVING UP.
FWIP
FWIP
...
KRIK

READ THIS WAY

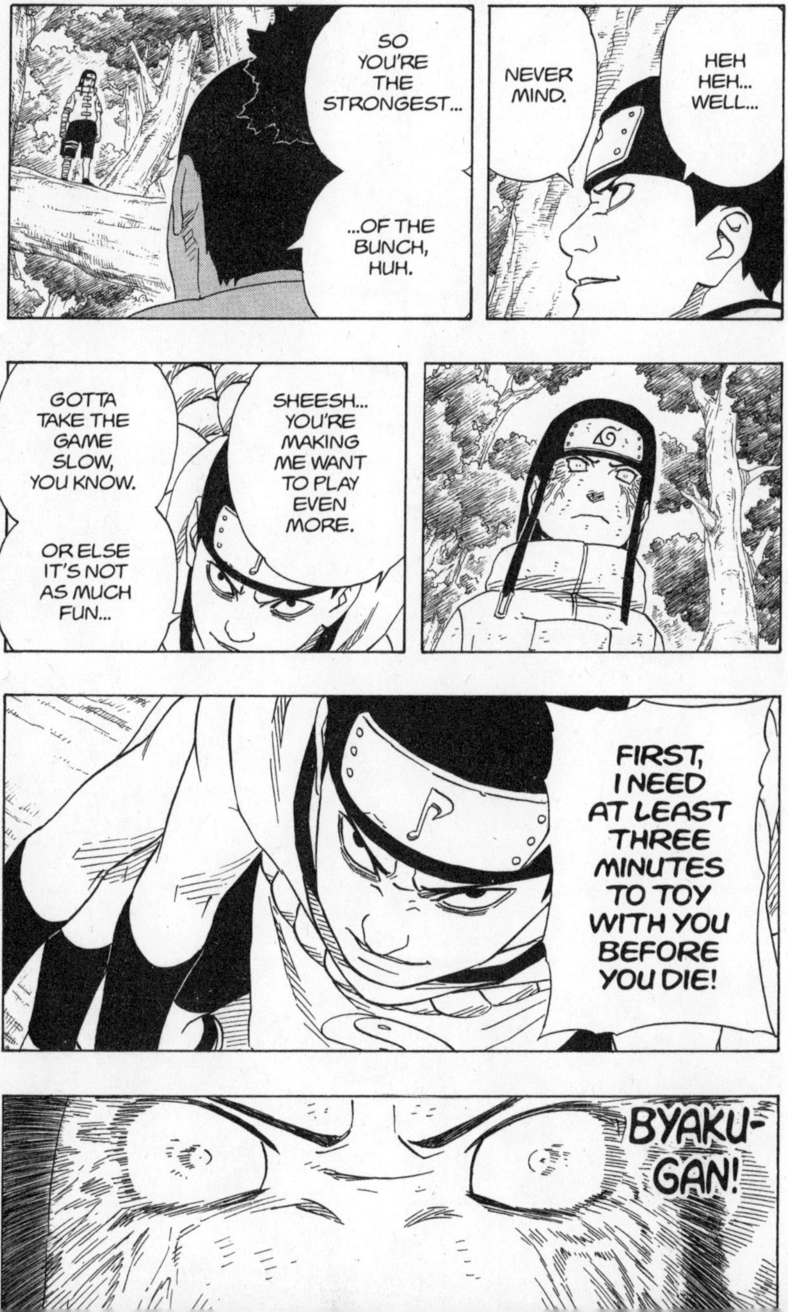
HEH HEH... WELL...
NEVER MIND.
SO YOU'RE THE STRONGEST...
...OF THE BUNCH, HUH.
SHEESH... YOU'RE MAKING ME WANT TO PLAY EVEN MORE.
GOTTA TAKE THE GAME SLOW, YOU KNOW.
OR ELSE IT'S NOT AS MUCH FUN...
FIRST, I NEED AT LEAST THREE MINUTES TO TOY WITH YOU BEFORE YOU DIE!
BYAKU-GAN!

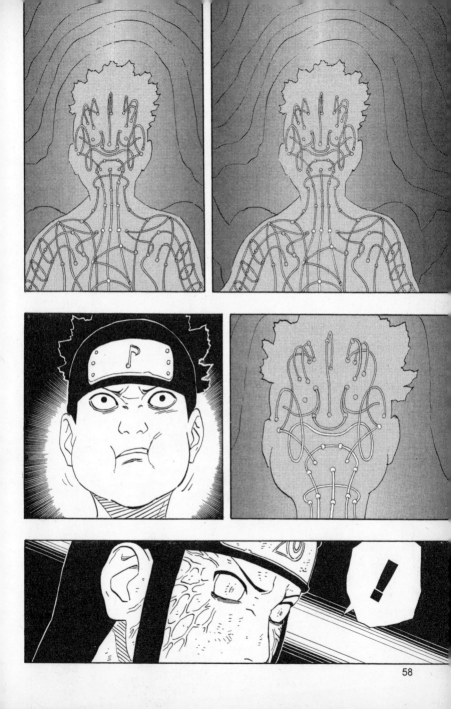

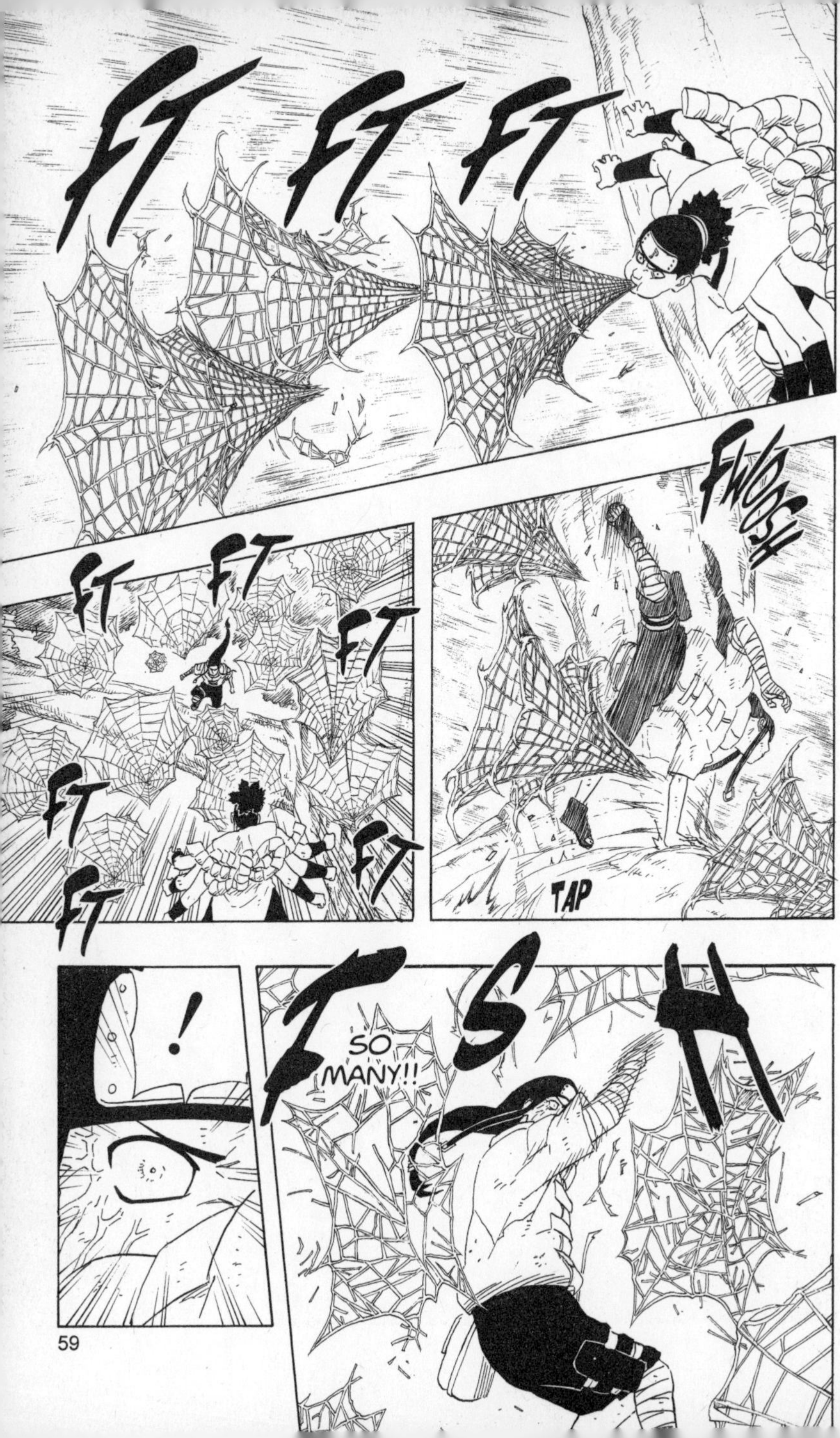
FT FT FT
FWOSH
TAP
FT
FT
FT
FT
FT
FT
TSH
SO MANY!!
!

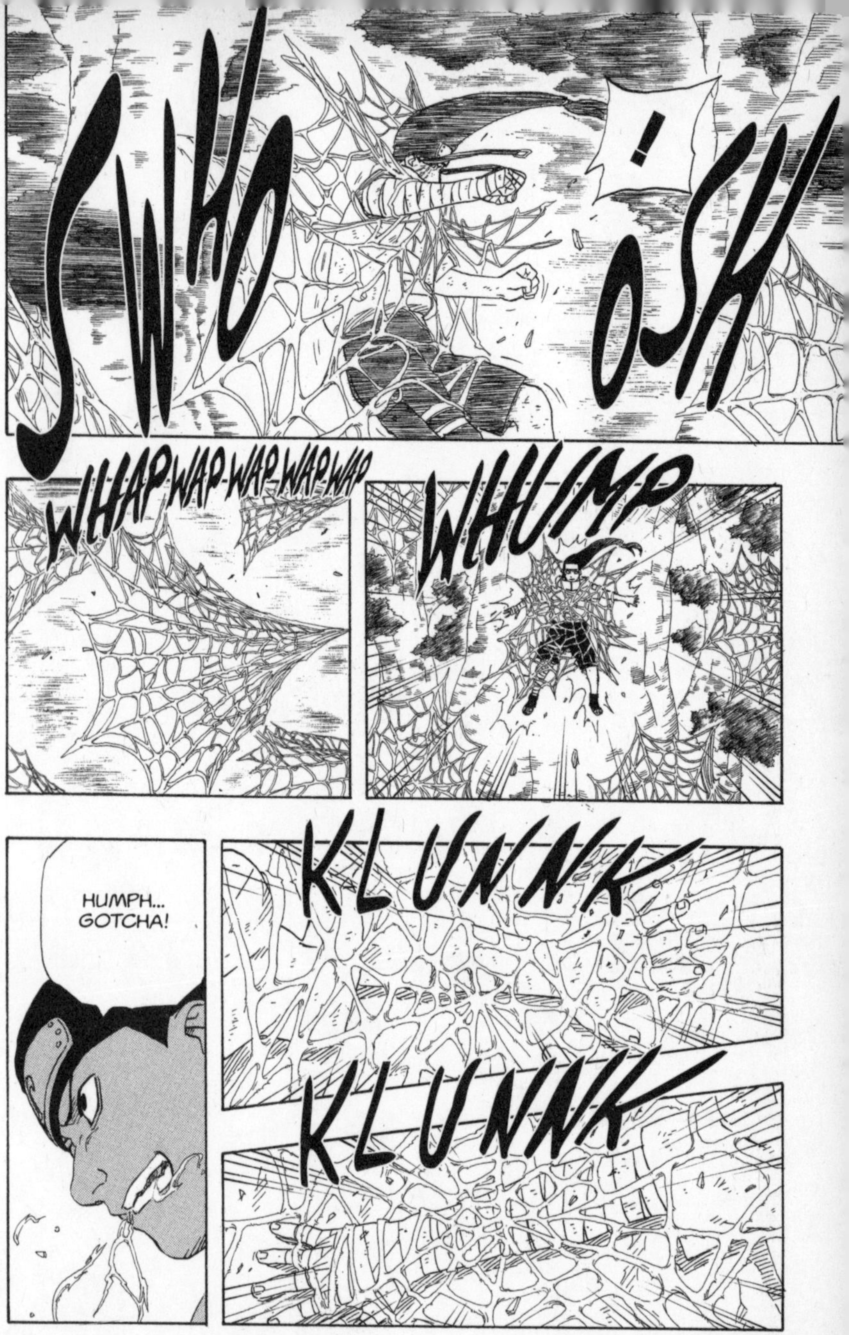
SWHOOSH
!
WHUMP
WHAPWAP-WAP-WAPWAP
KLUNNK
KLUNNK
HUMPH... GOTCHA!

READ THIS WAY

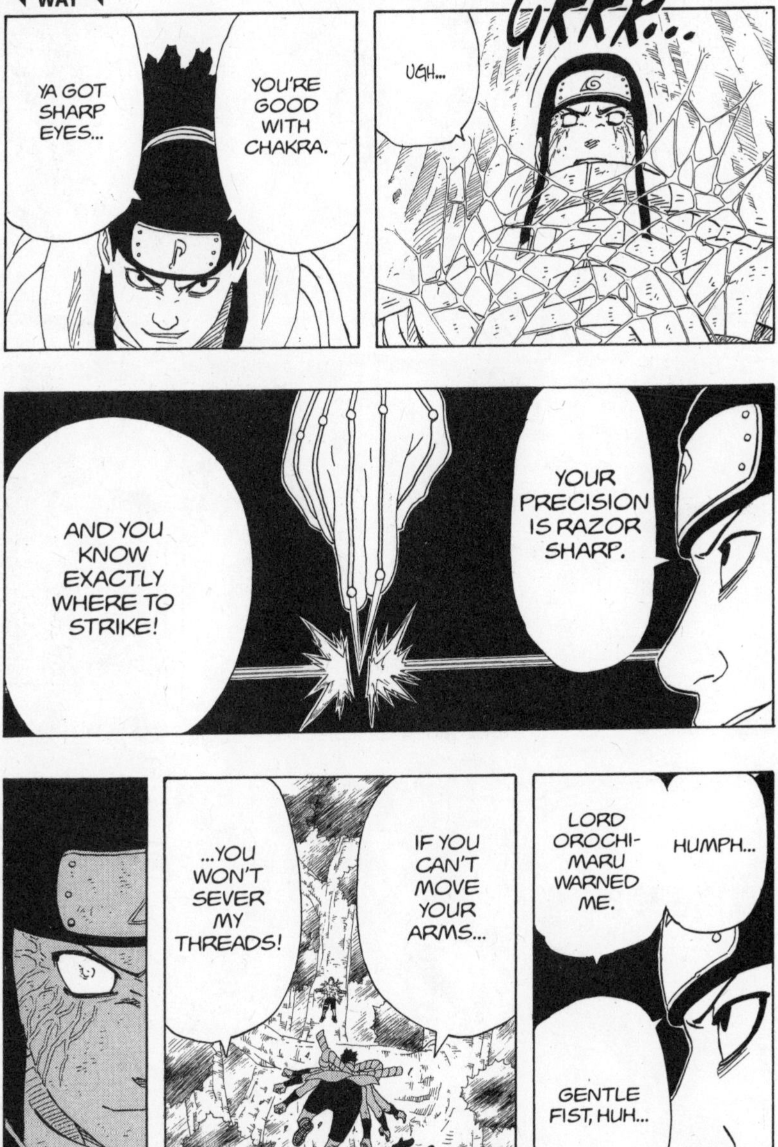
GRRR...
UGH...
YOU'RE GOOD WITH CHAKRA.
YA GOT SHARP EYES...
YOUR PRECISION IS RAZOR SHARP.
AND YOU KNOW EXACTLY WHERE TO STRIKE!
HUMPH...
LORD OROCHIMARU WARNED ME.
GENTLE FIST, HUH...
IF YOU CAN'T MOVE YOUR ARMS...
...YOU WON'T SEVER MY THREADS!

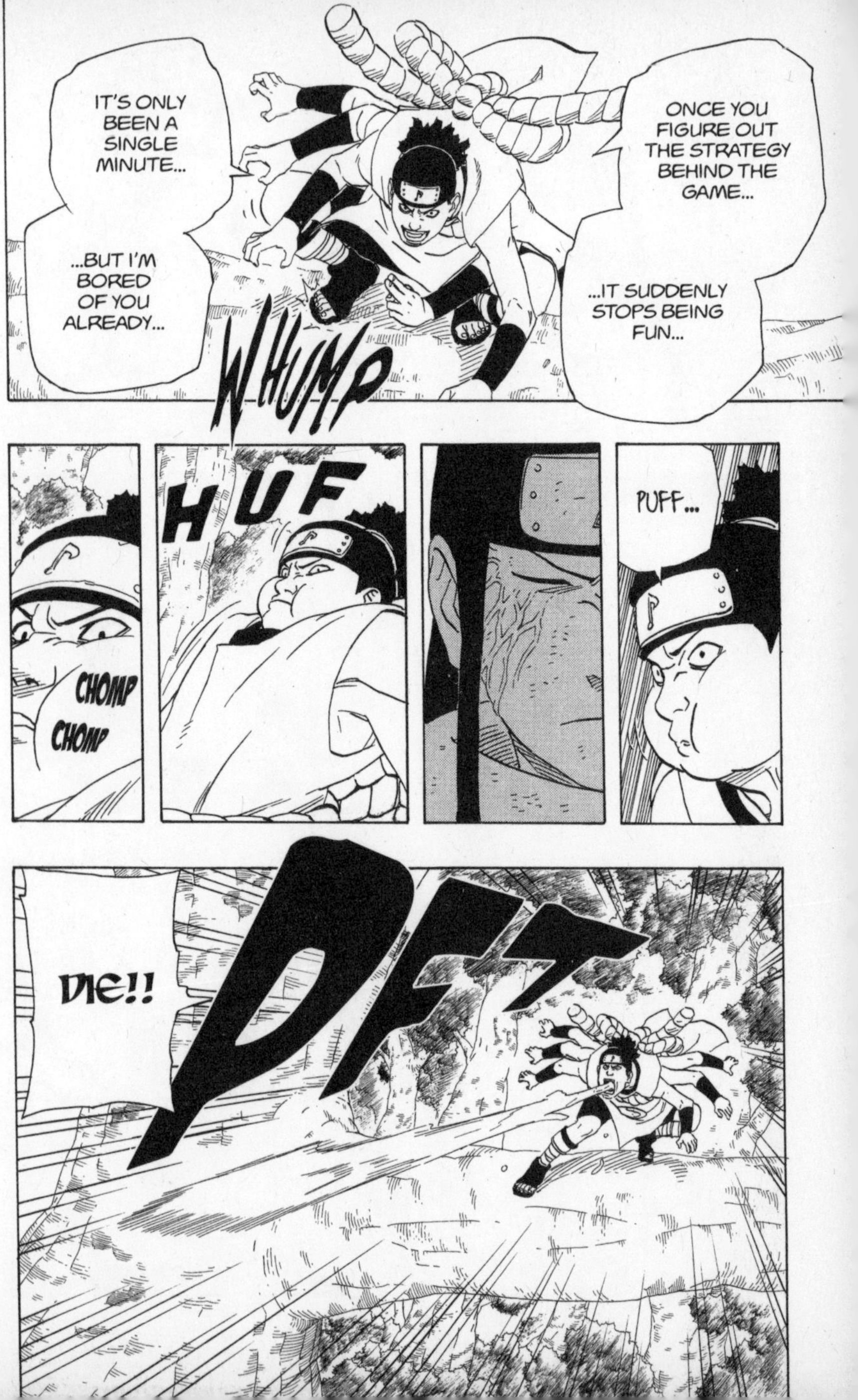
ONCE YOU FIGURE OUT THE STRATEGY BEHIND THE GAME...
...IT SUDDENLY STOPS BEING FUN...
IT'S ONLY BEEN A SINGLE MINUTE...
...BUT I'M BORED OF YOU ALREADY...
WHUMP
PUFF...
HUF
CHOMP
CHOMP
DIE!!
DFT

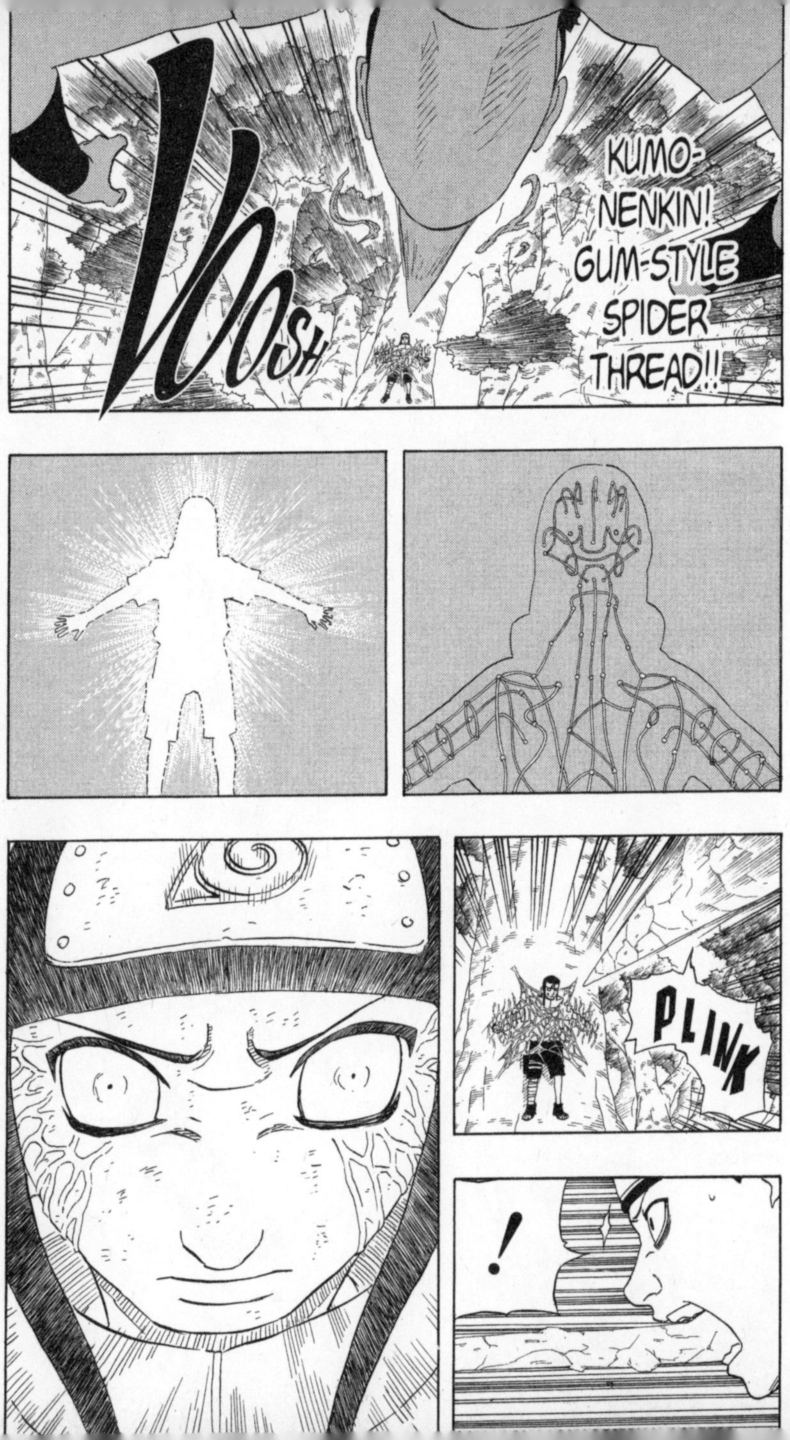
KUMO-NENKIN! GUM-STYLE SPIDER THREAD!!
WOOSH
PLINK
!

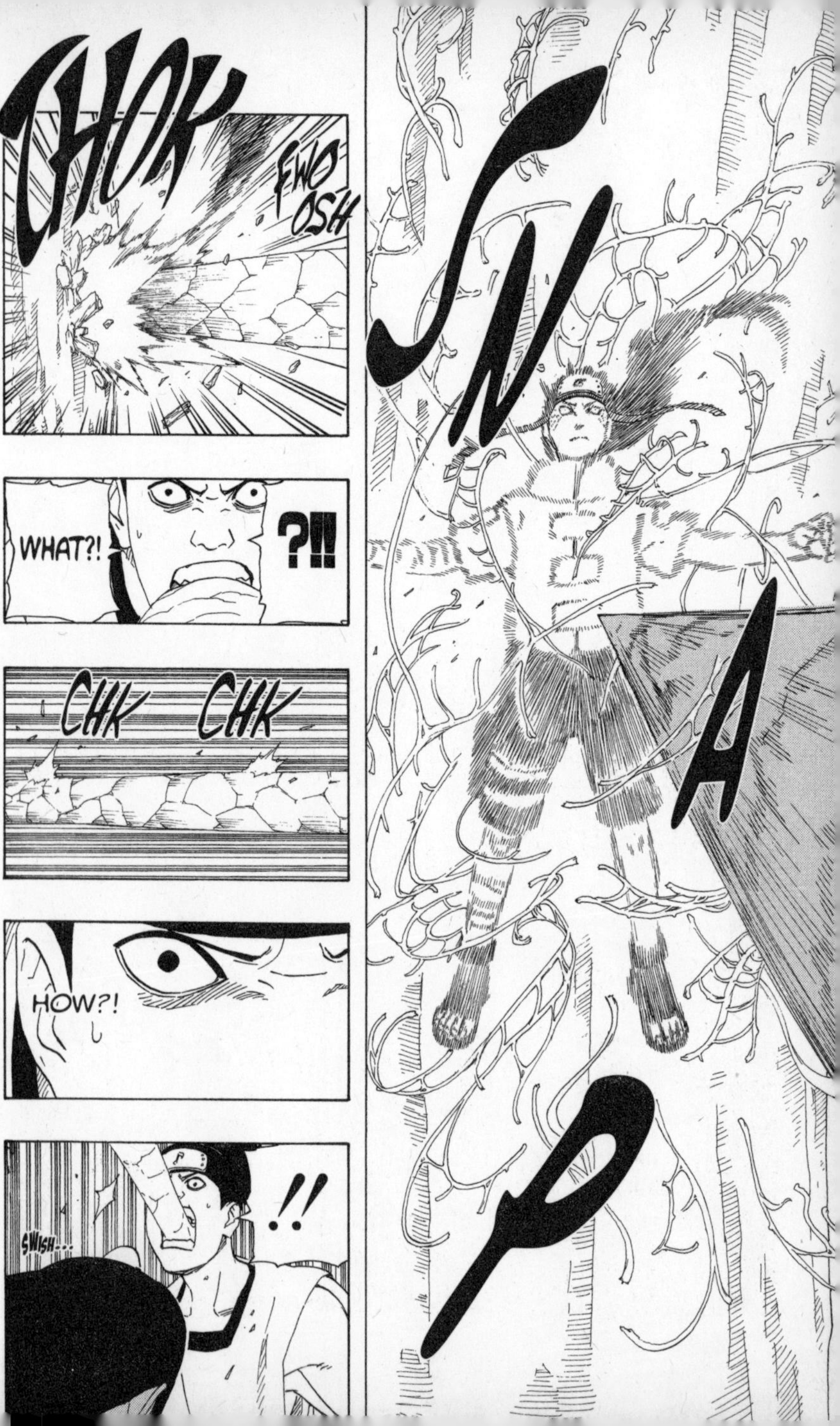

SNAP
CHOK
FWOOSH
WHAT?!
?!!
CHK CHK
HOW?!
!!
SWISH...

READ THIS WAY

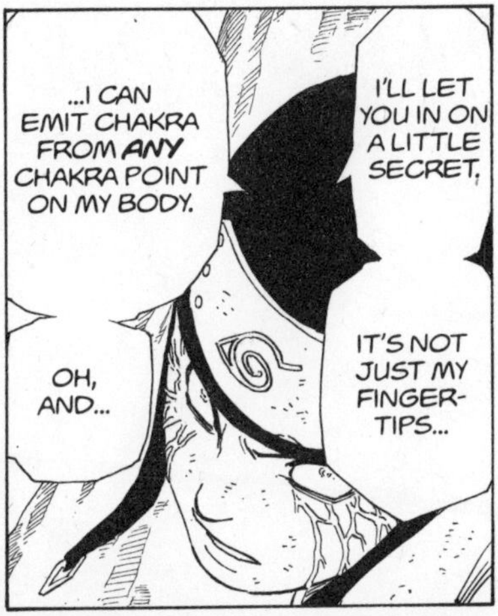
I'LL LET YOU IN ON A LITTLE SECRET.
IT'S NOT JUST MY FINGER-TIPS...
...I CAN EMIT CHAKRA FROM ***ANY*** CHAKRA POINT ON MY BODY.
OH, AND...

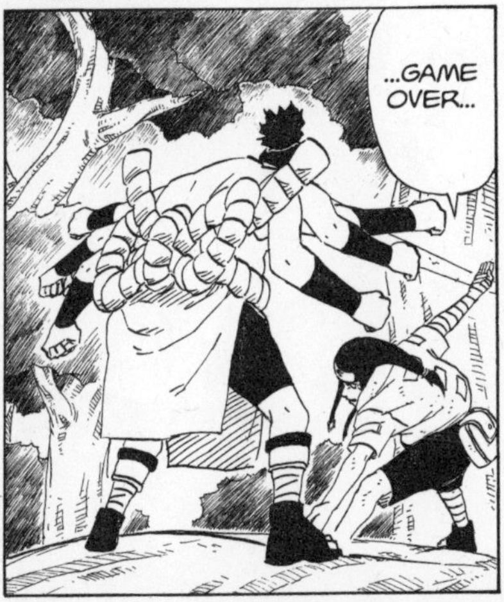
...GAME OVER...

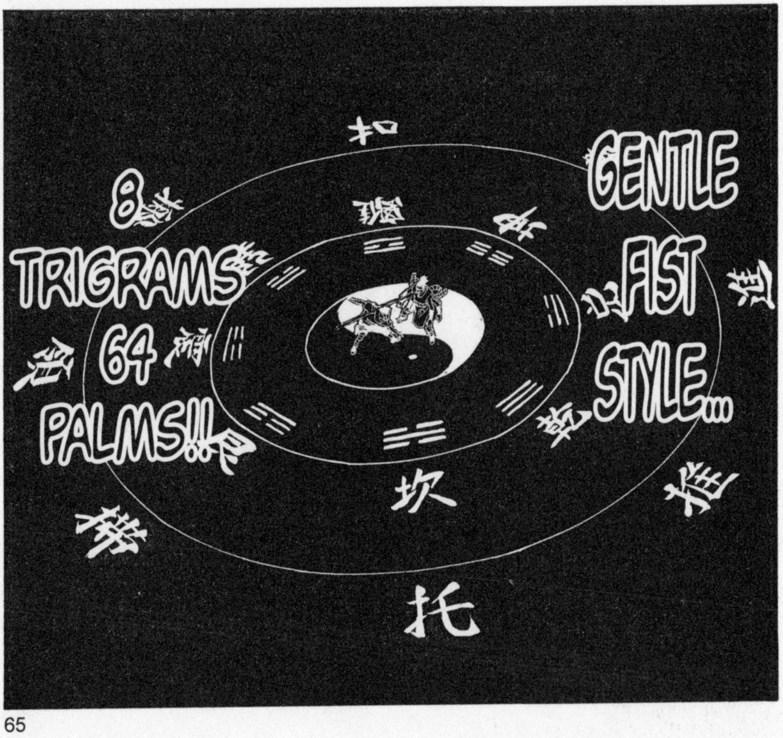
GENTLE FIST STYLE...
8 TRIGRAMS 64 PALMS!!

NARUTO™

Number 194: Taking Stock

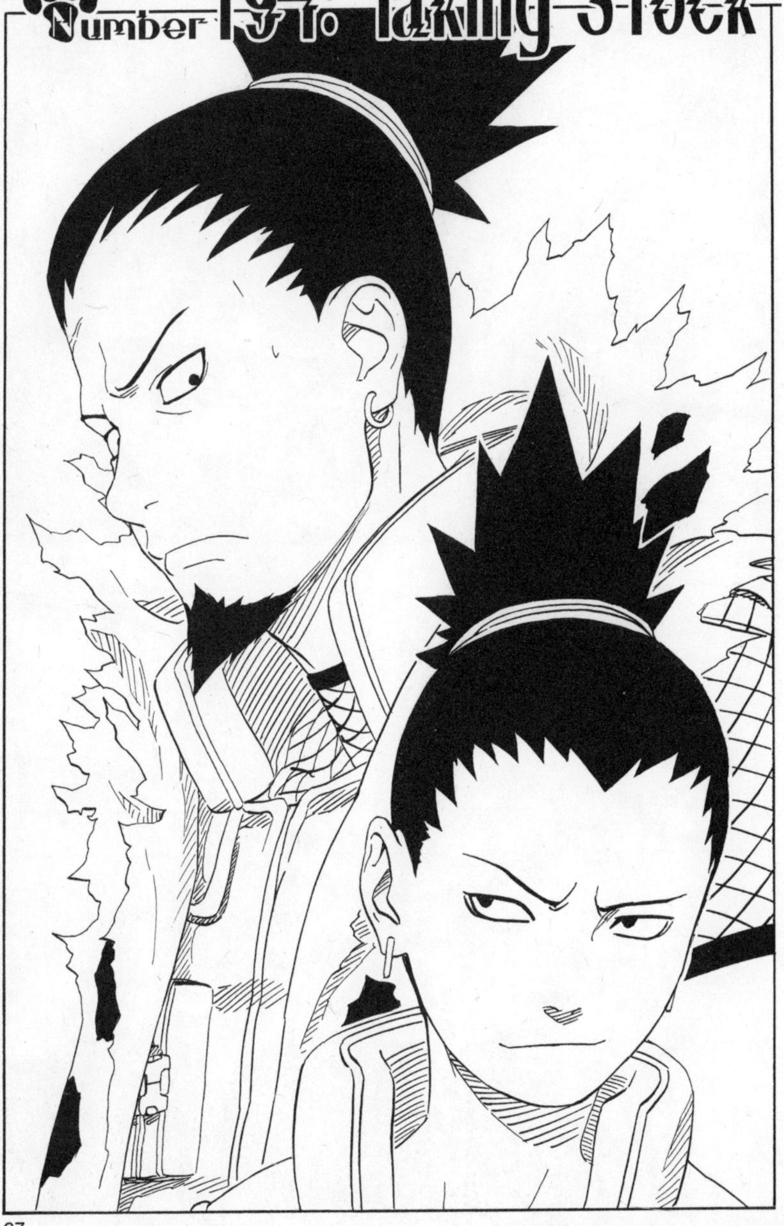

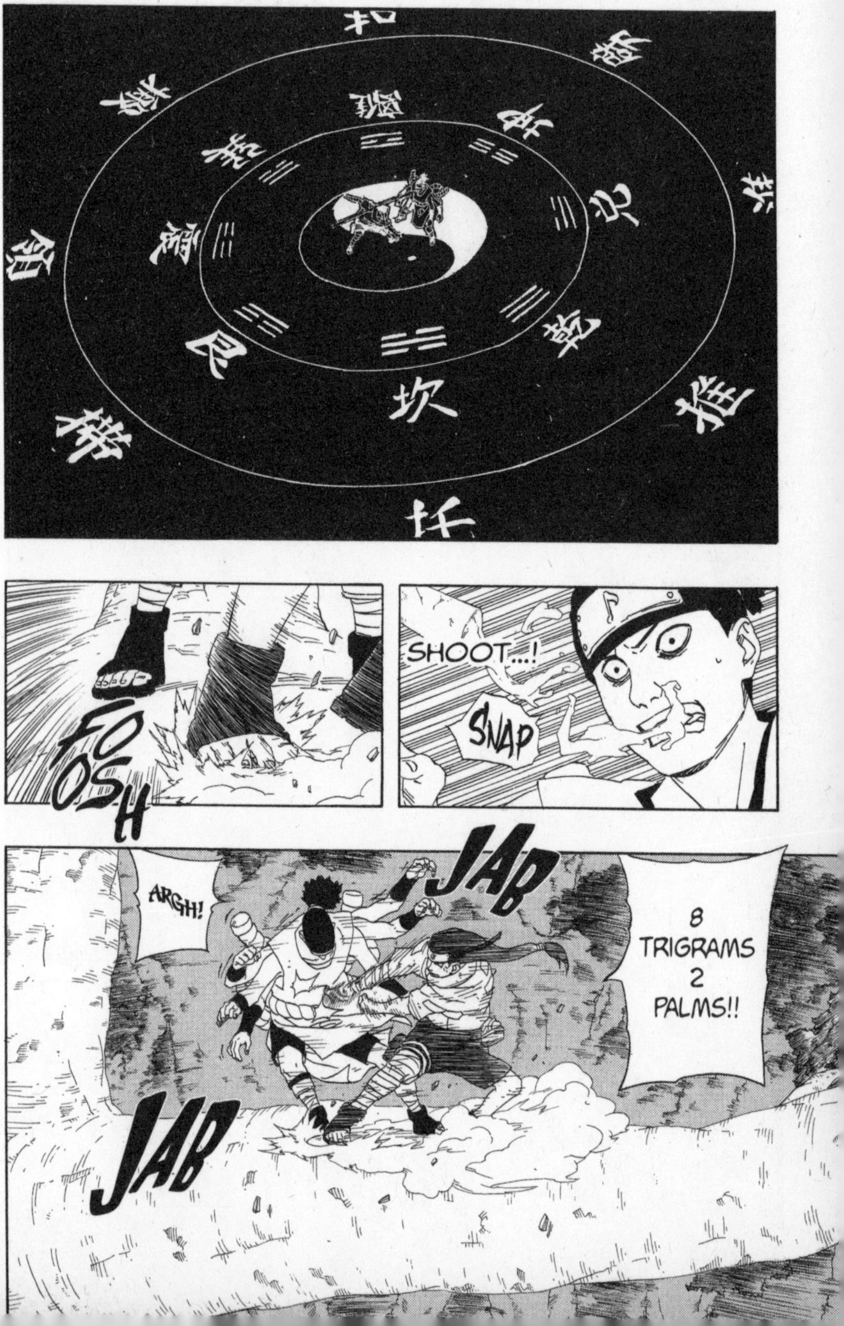
SHOOT...!
SNAP
FOOSH
8 TRIGRAMS 2 PALMS!!
JAB
ARGH!
JAB

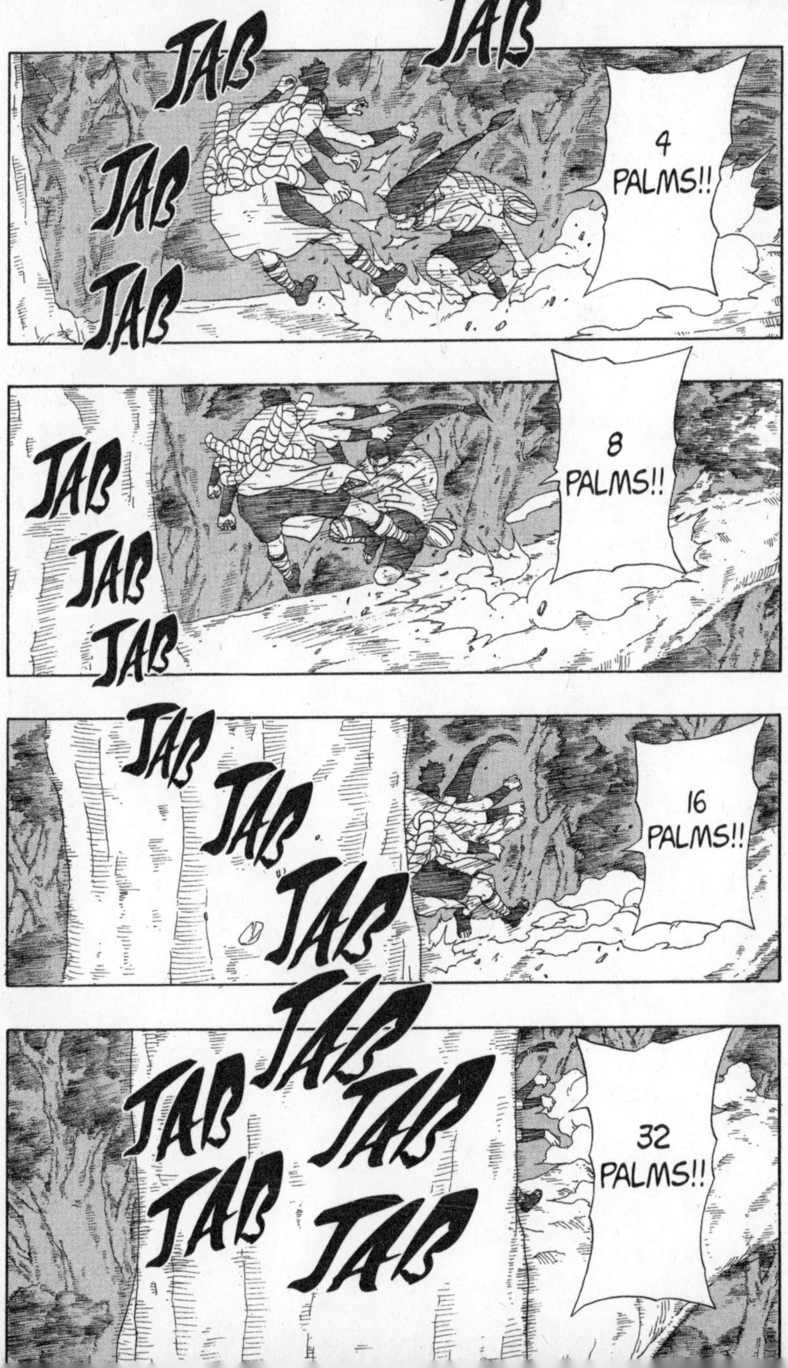
4 PALMS!!
JAB
JAB
JAB
JAB
8 PALMS!!
JAB
JAB
JAB
16 PALMS!!
JAB
JAB
JAB
JAB
32 PALMS!!
JAB
JAB
JAB
JAB
JAB

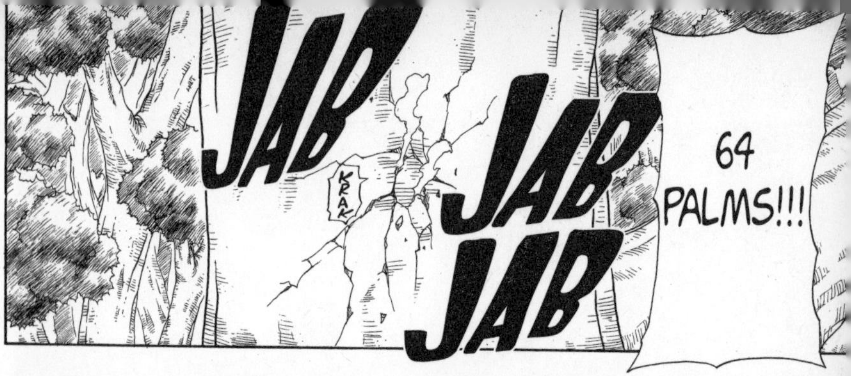
64 PALMS!!!
JAB
JAB
JAB
KRAK

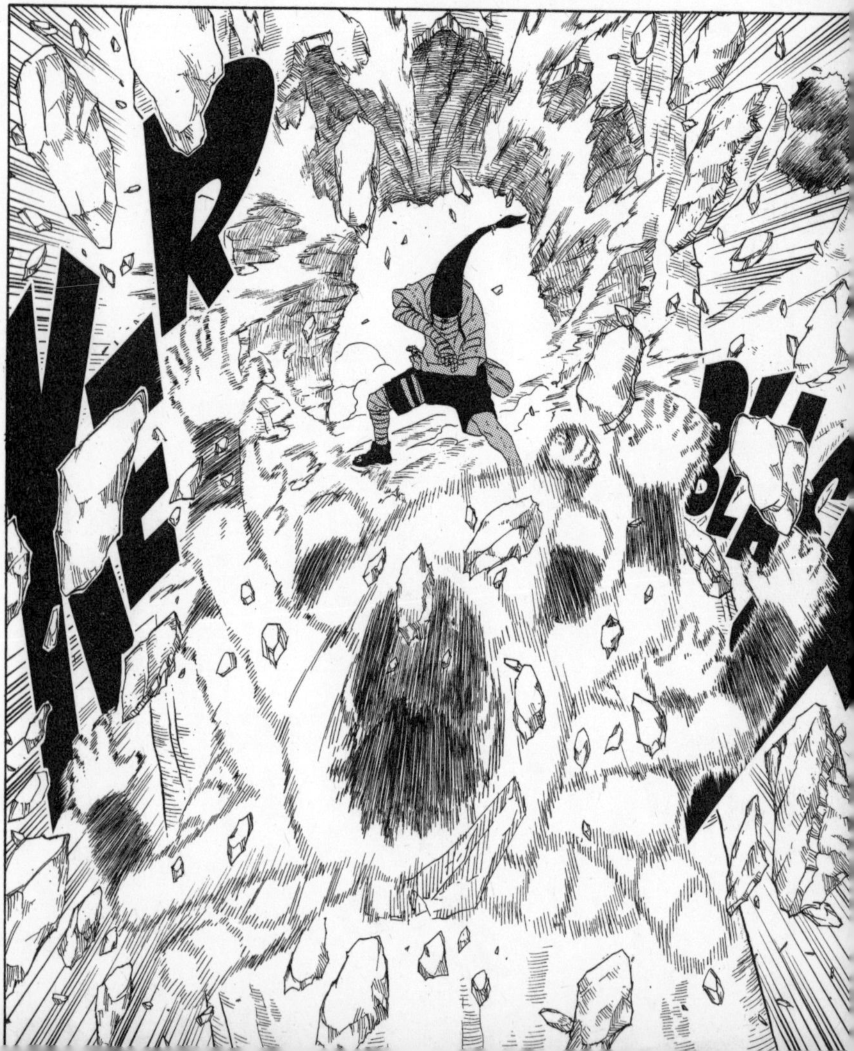

READ THIS WAY

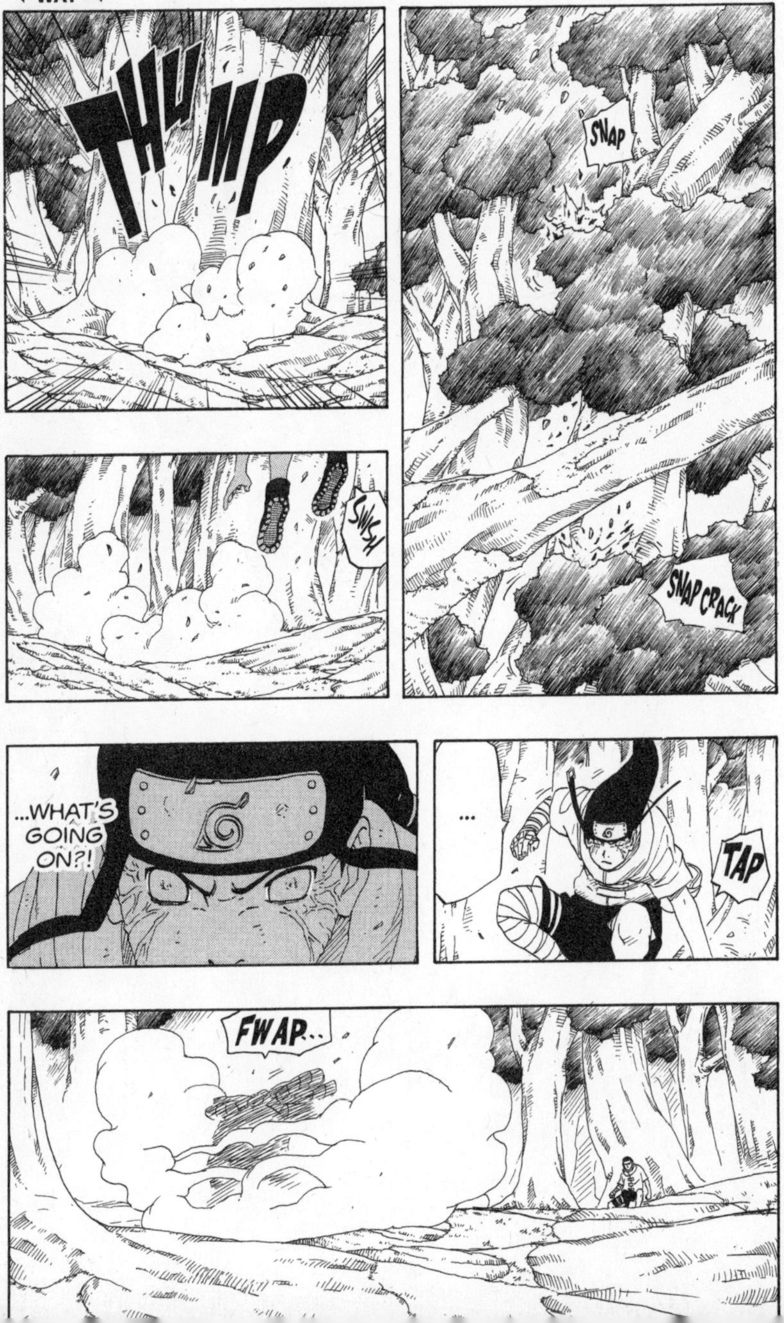
SNAP
SNAP CRACK
THUMP
SWISH
...
TAP
...WHAT'S GOING ON?!
FWAP...

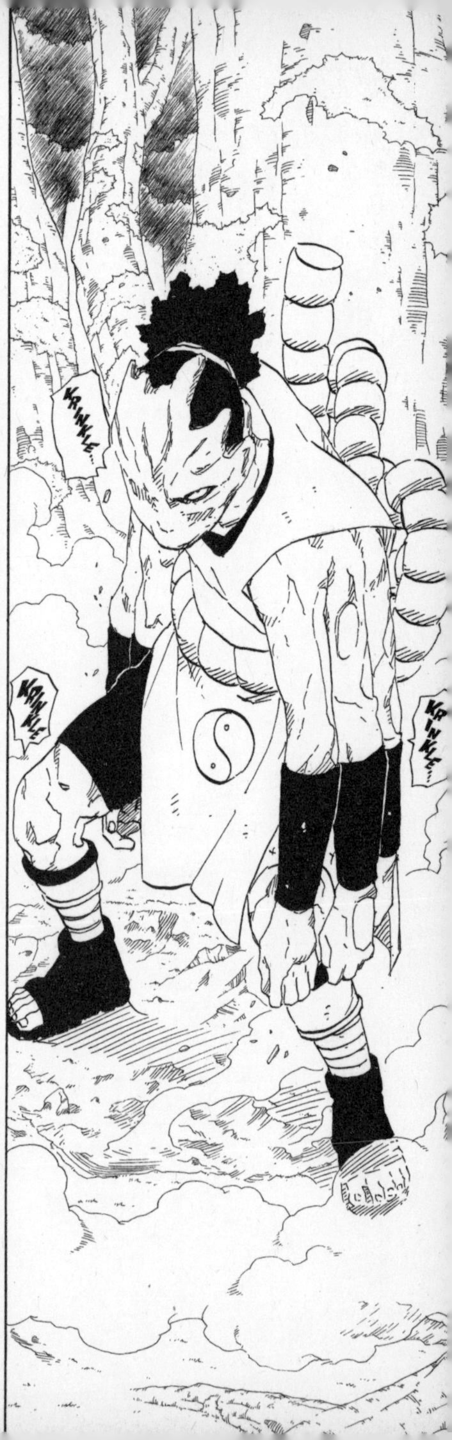
KRINKLE...
KRINKLE...
KRINKLE...
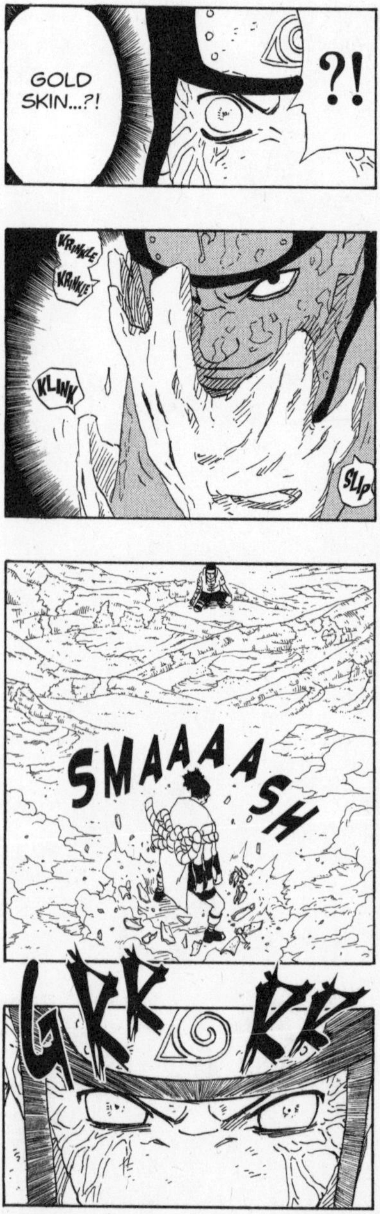
?!
GOLD SKIN...?!
KRINKLE
KRINKLE
KLINK
SLIP
SMAAAASH
GRR RR

READ THIS WAY

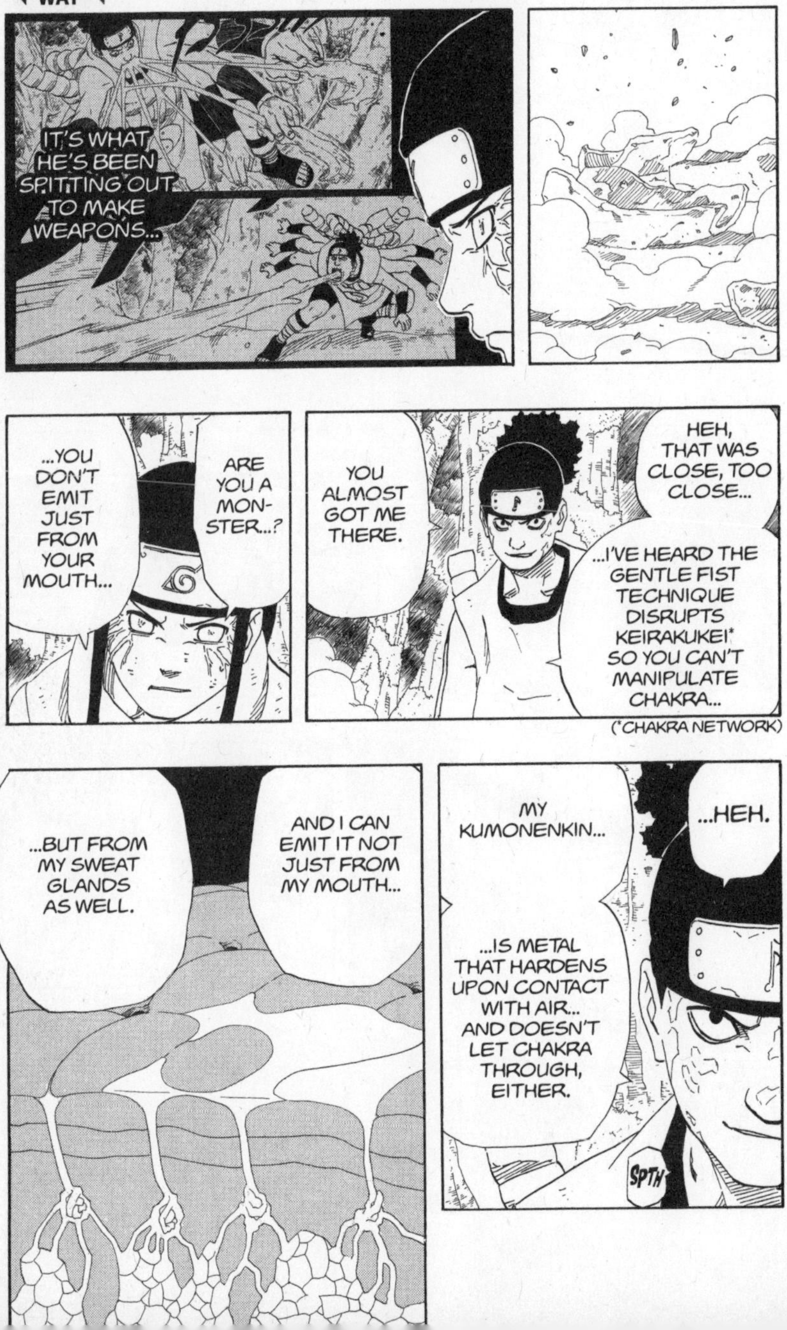
IT'S WHAT HE'S BEEN SPITTING OUT TO MAKE WEAPONS...
HEH, THAT WAS CLOSE, TOO CLOSE...
...I'VE HEARD THE GENTLE FIST TECHNIQUE DISRUPTS KEIRAKUKEI* SO YOU CAN'T MANIPULATE CHAKRA...
YOU ALMOST GOT ME THERE.
ARE YOU A MON-STER...?
...YOU DON'T EMIT JUST FROM YOUR MOUTH...
(*CHAKRA NETWORK)
...HEH.
MY KUMONENKIN...
...IS METAL THAT HARDENS UPON CONTACT WITH AIR... AND DOESN'T LET CHAKRA THROUGH, EITHER.
SPTH
AND I CAN EMIT IT NOT JUST FROM MY MOUTH...
...BUT FROM MY SWEAT GLANDS AS WELL.

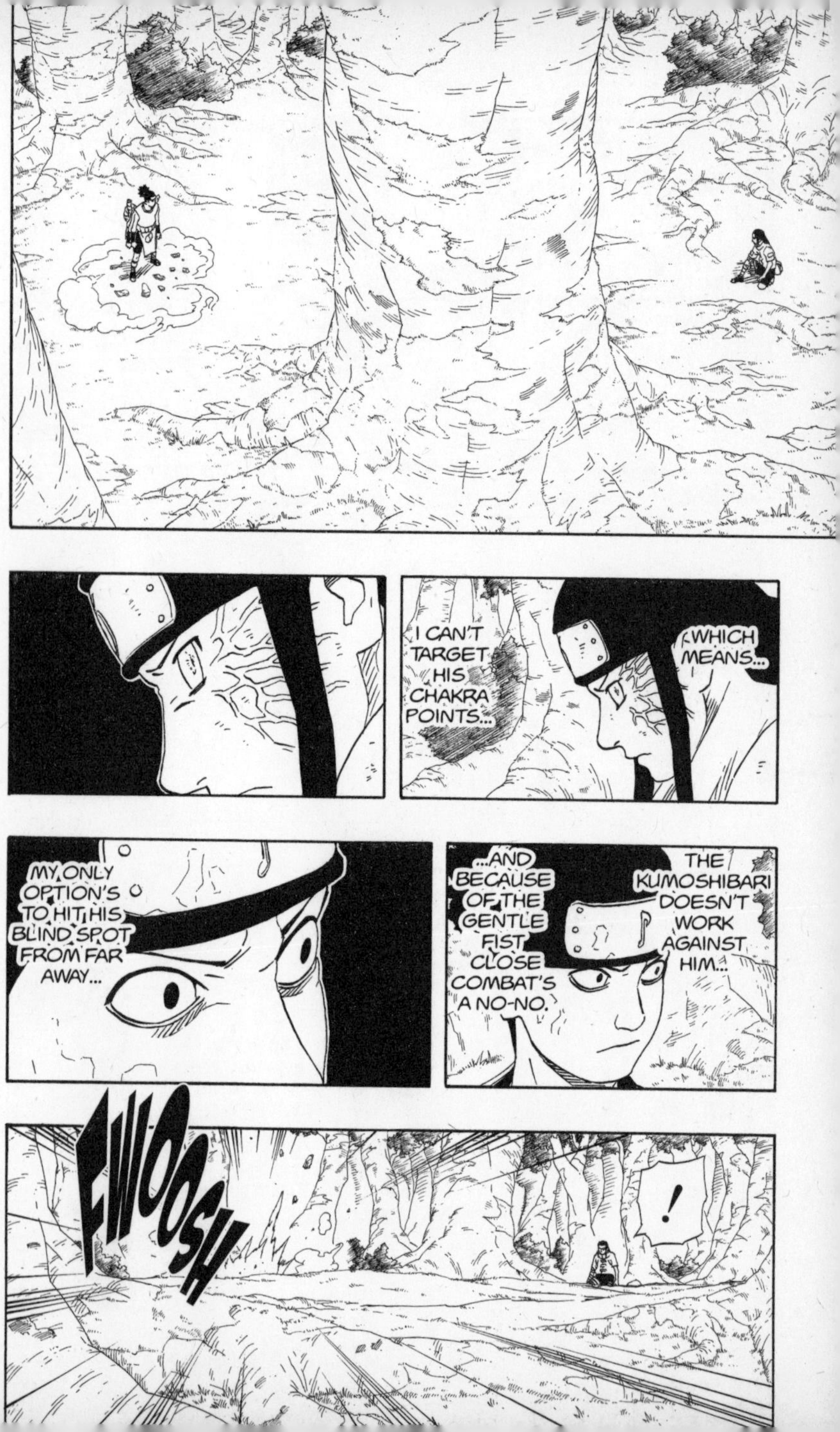
I CAN'T TARGET HIS CHAKRA POINTS...
...WHICH MEANS...
THE KUMOSHIBARI DOESN'T WORK AGAINST HIM...
...AND BECAUSE OF THE GENTLE FIST CLOSE COMBAT'S A NO-NO.
MY ONLY OPTION'S TO HIT HIS BLIND SPOT FROM FAR AWAY...
!
FWOOSH

READ THIS WAY

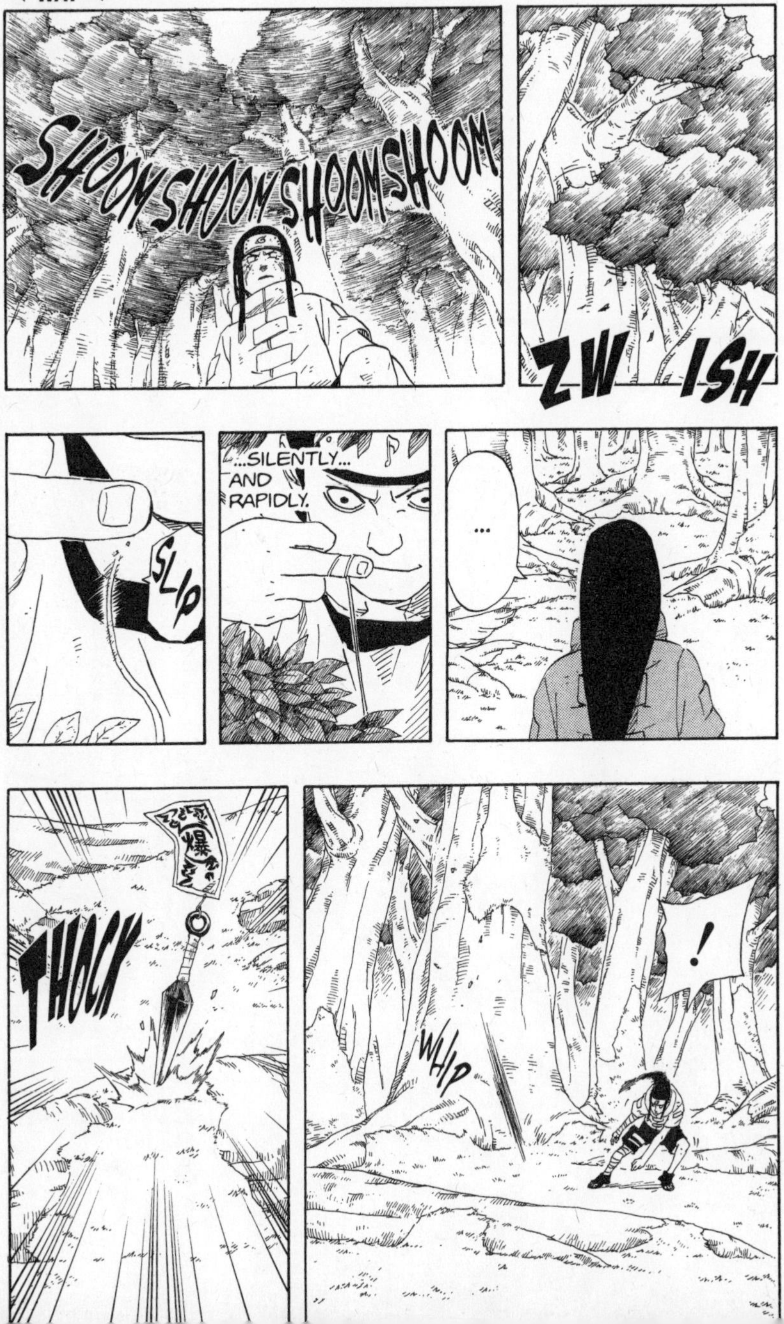
ZW ISH
SHOOM SHOOM SHOOM SHOOM
...
...SILENTLY... AND RAPIDLY.
SLIP
!
WHIP
THOCK

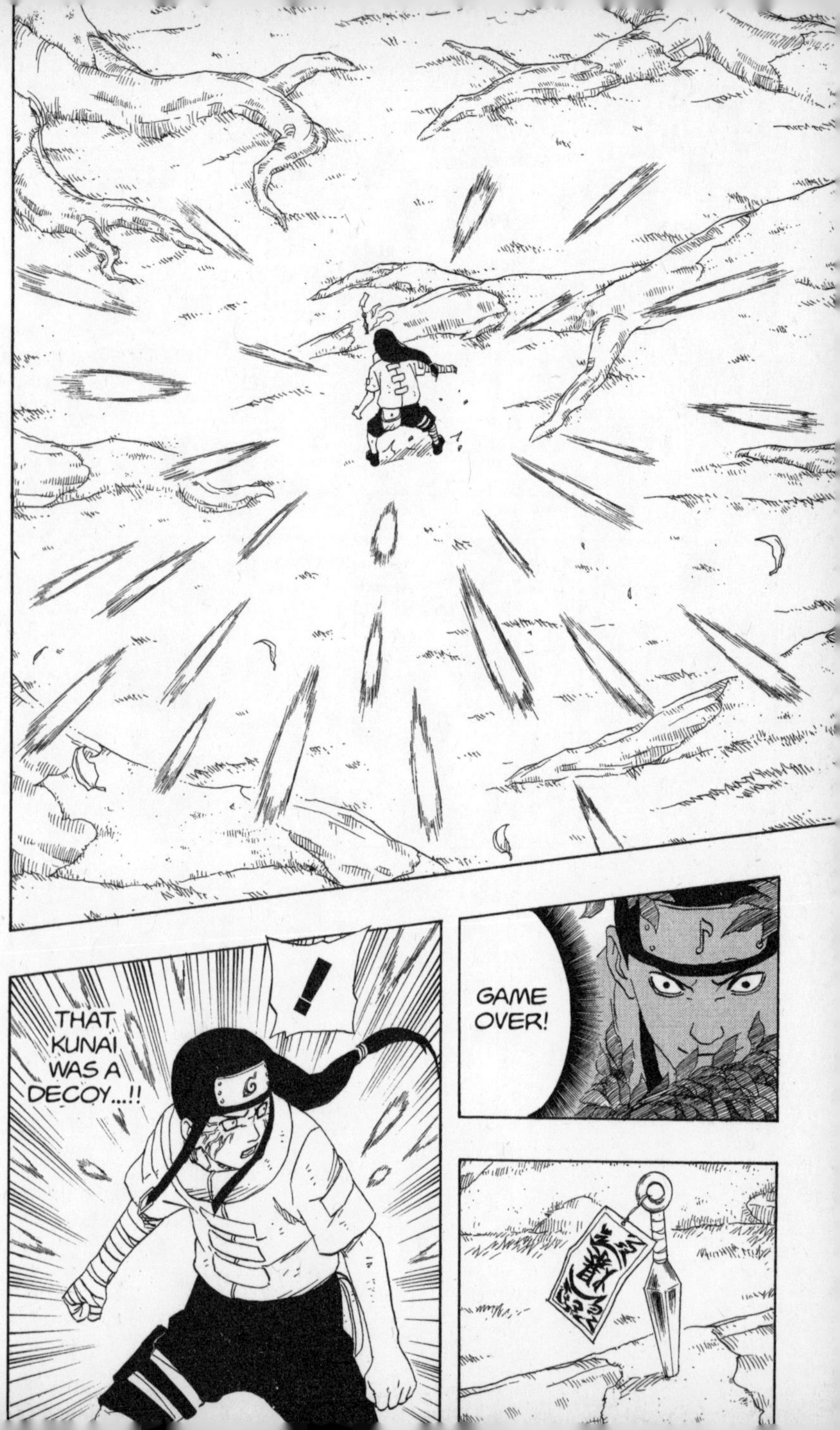
GAME OVER!
!
THAT KUNAI WAS A DECOY...!!

READ THIS WAY

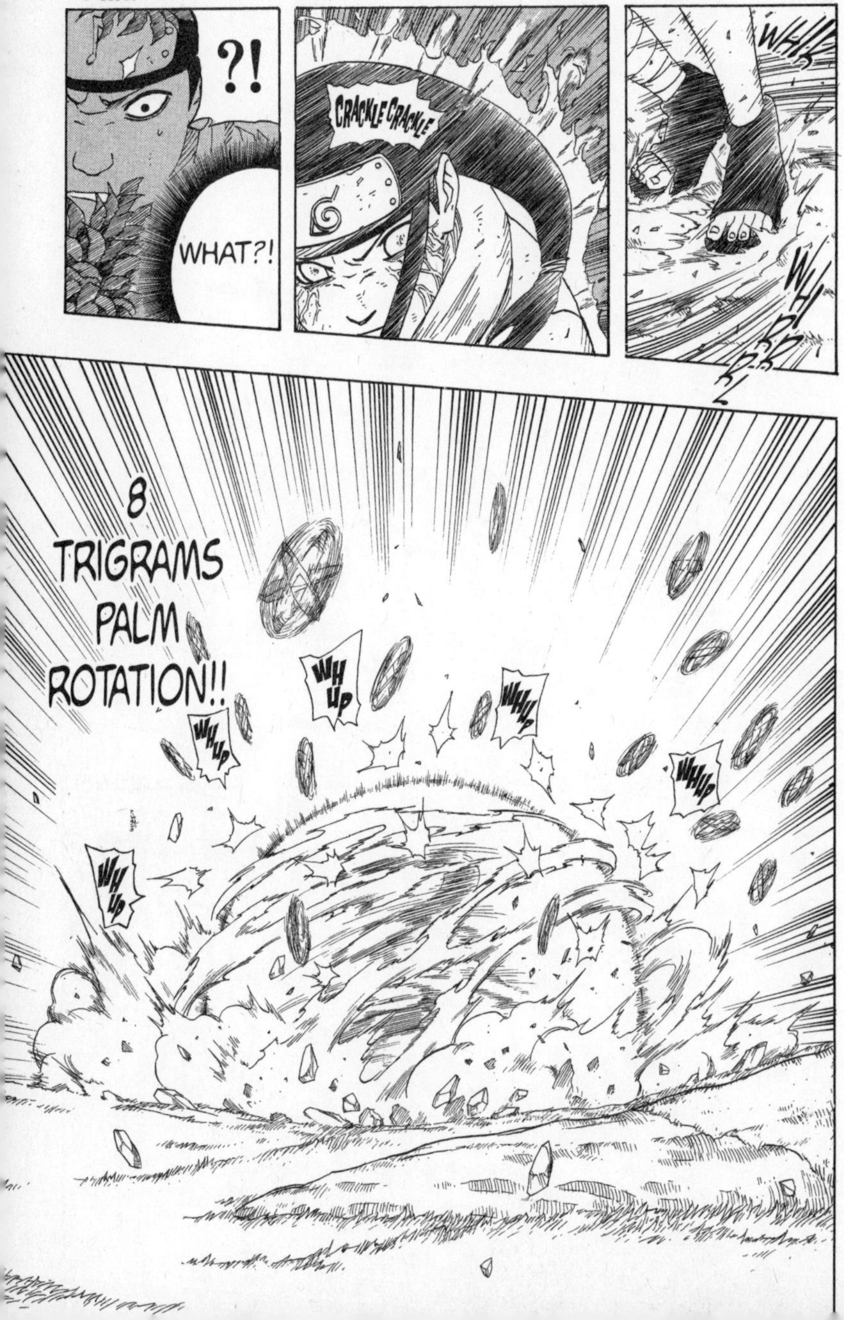
WHK
CRACKLE CRACKLE
?!
WHAT?!
8 TRIGRAMS PALM ROTATION!!
WHUP
WHUP
WHUP
WHUP
WHUP

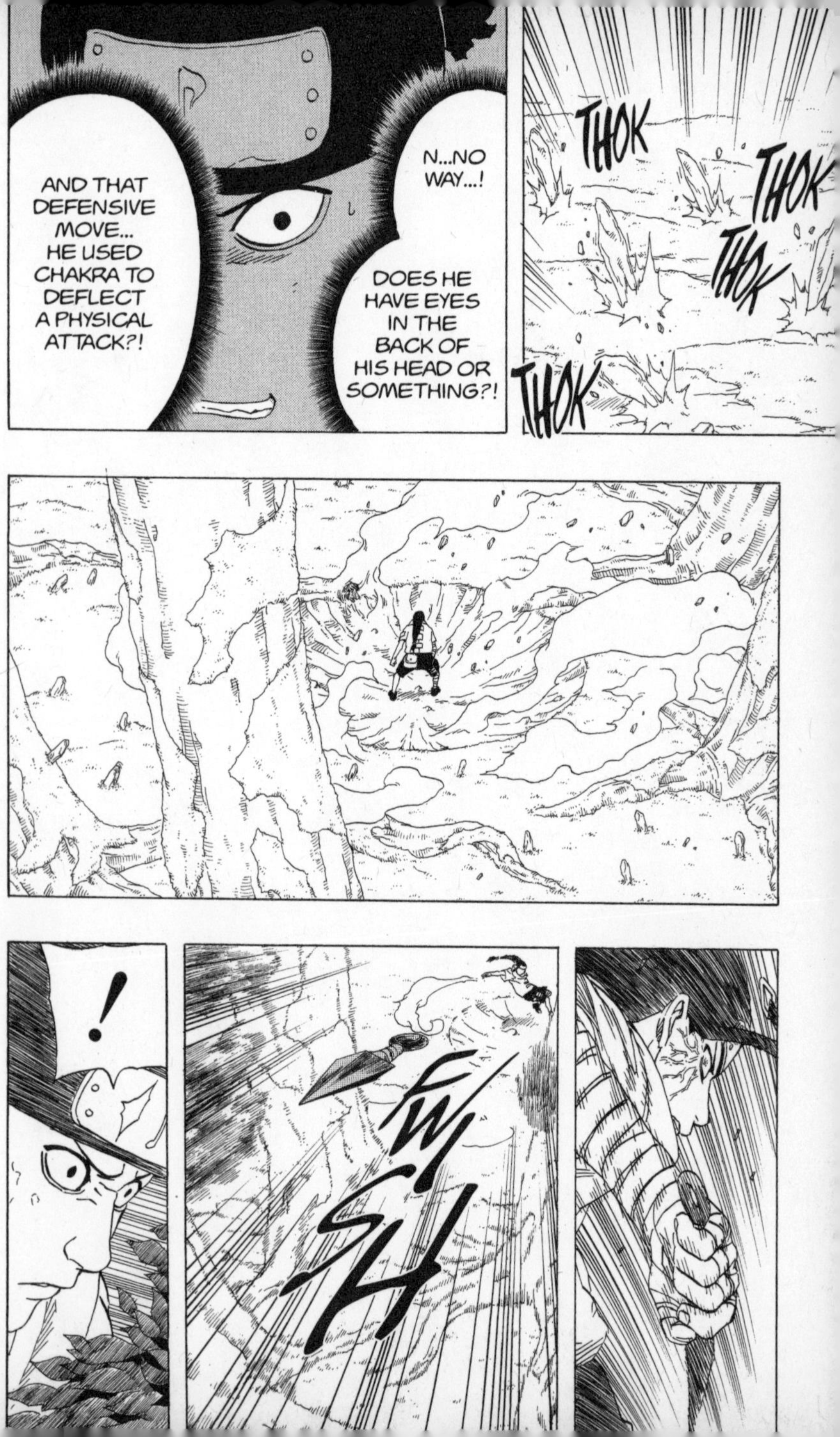
THOK
THOK
THOK
THOK
N...NO WAY...!
DOES HE HAVE EYES IN THE BACK OF HIS HEAD OR SOMETHING?!
AND THAT DEFENSIVE MOVE... HE USED CHAKRA TO DEFLECT A PHYSICAL ATTACK?!
FWISH
!

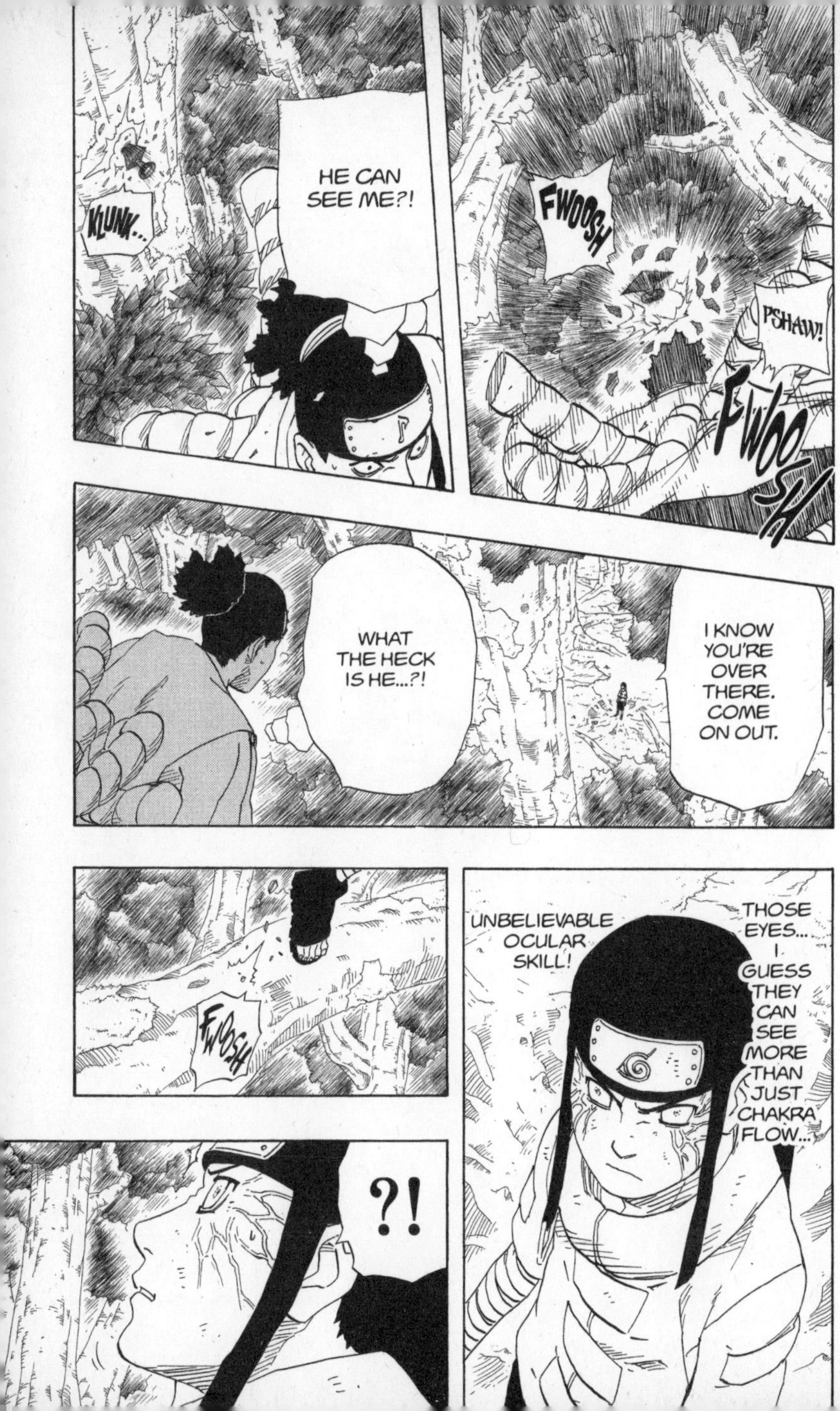
FWOOSH
PSHAW!
FWOOSH
HE CAN SEE ME?!
KLUNK...
I KNOW YOU'RE OVER THERE. COME ON OUT.
WHAT THE HECK IS HE...?!
THOSE EYES... I GUESS THEY CAN SEE MORE THAN JUST CHAKRA FLOW...
UNBELIEVABLE OCULAR SKILL!
FWOOSH
?!

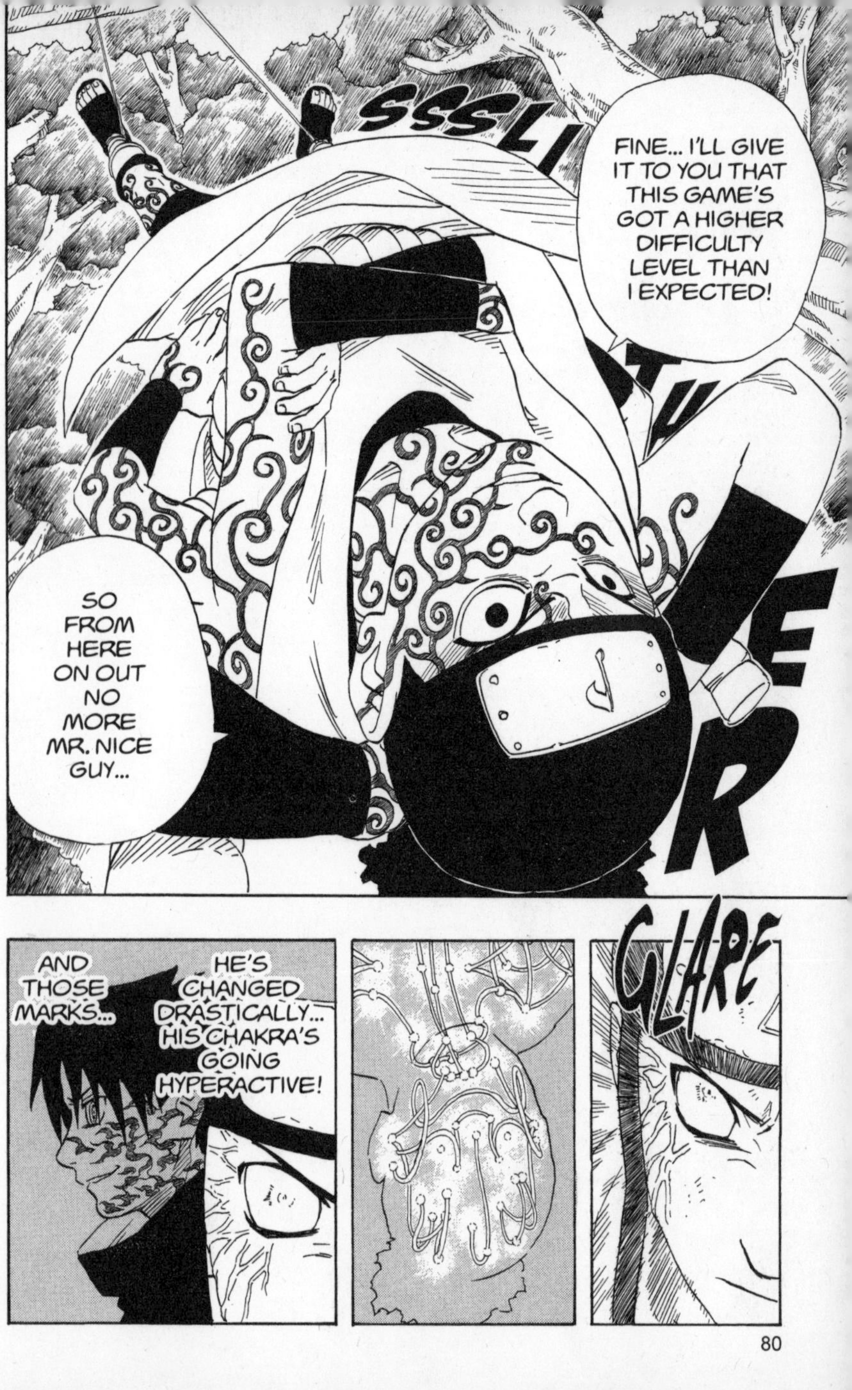

SSSLI
FINE... I'LL GIVE IT TO YOU THAT THIS GAME'S GOT A HIGHER DIFFICULTY LEVEL THAN I EXPECTED!
SO FROM HERE ON OUT NO MORE MR. NICE GUY...
GLARE
HE'S CHANGED DRASTICALLY... HIS CHAKRA'S GOING HYPERACTIVE!
AND THOSE MARKS...

READ THIS WAY

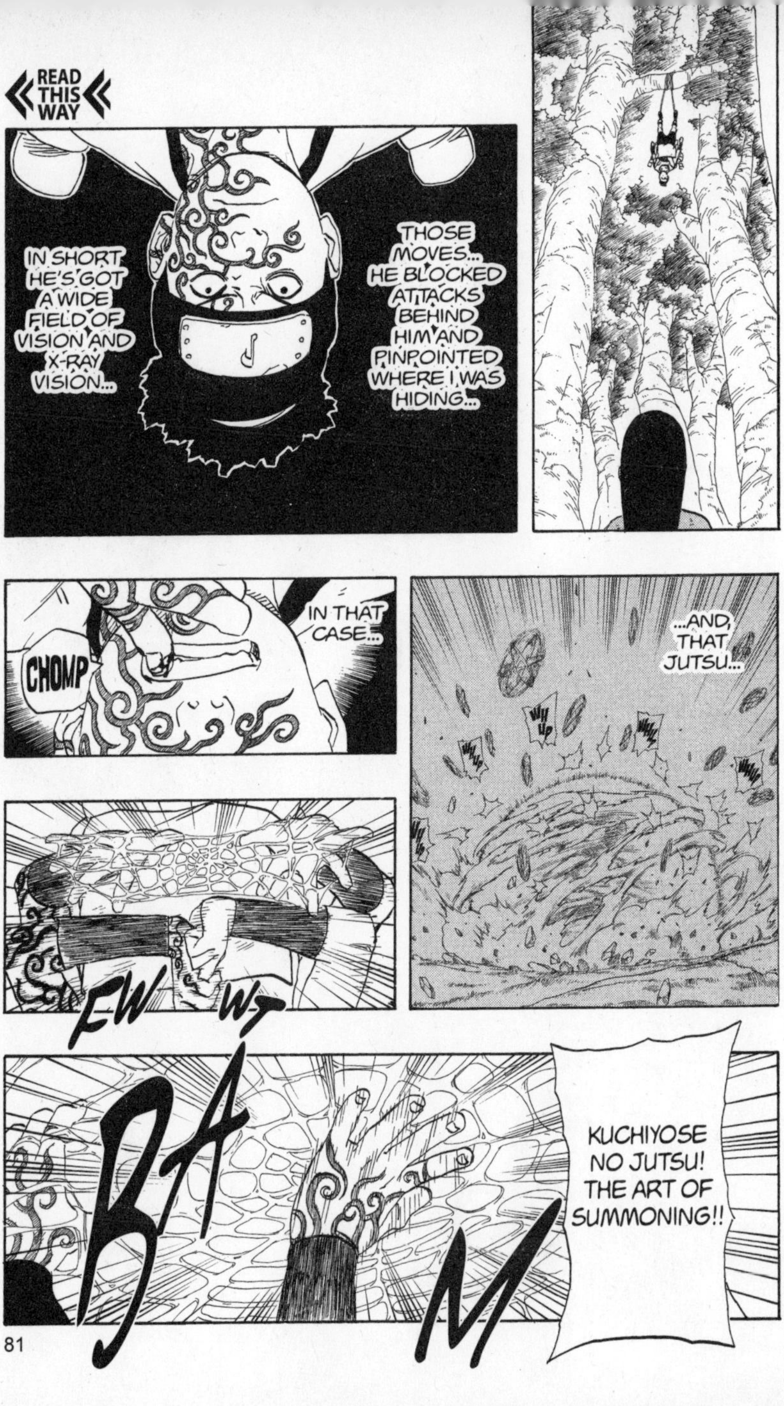
THOSE MOVES... HE BLOCKED ATTACKS BEHIND HIM AND PINPOINTED WHERE I WAS HIDING...
IN SHORT HE'S GOT A WIDE FIELD OF VISION AND X-RAY VISION...
...AND, THAT JUTSU...
IN THAT CASE...
CHOMP
KUCHIYOSE NO JUTSU! THE ART OF SUMMONING!!
BAM

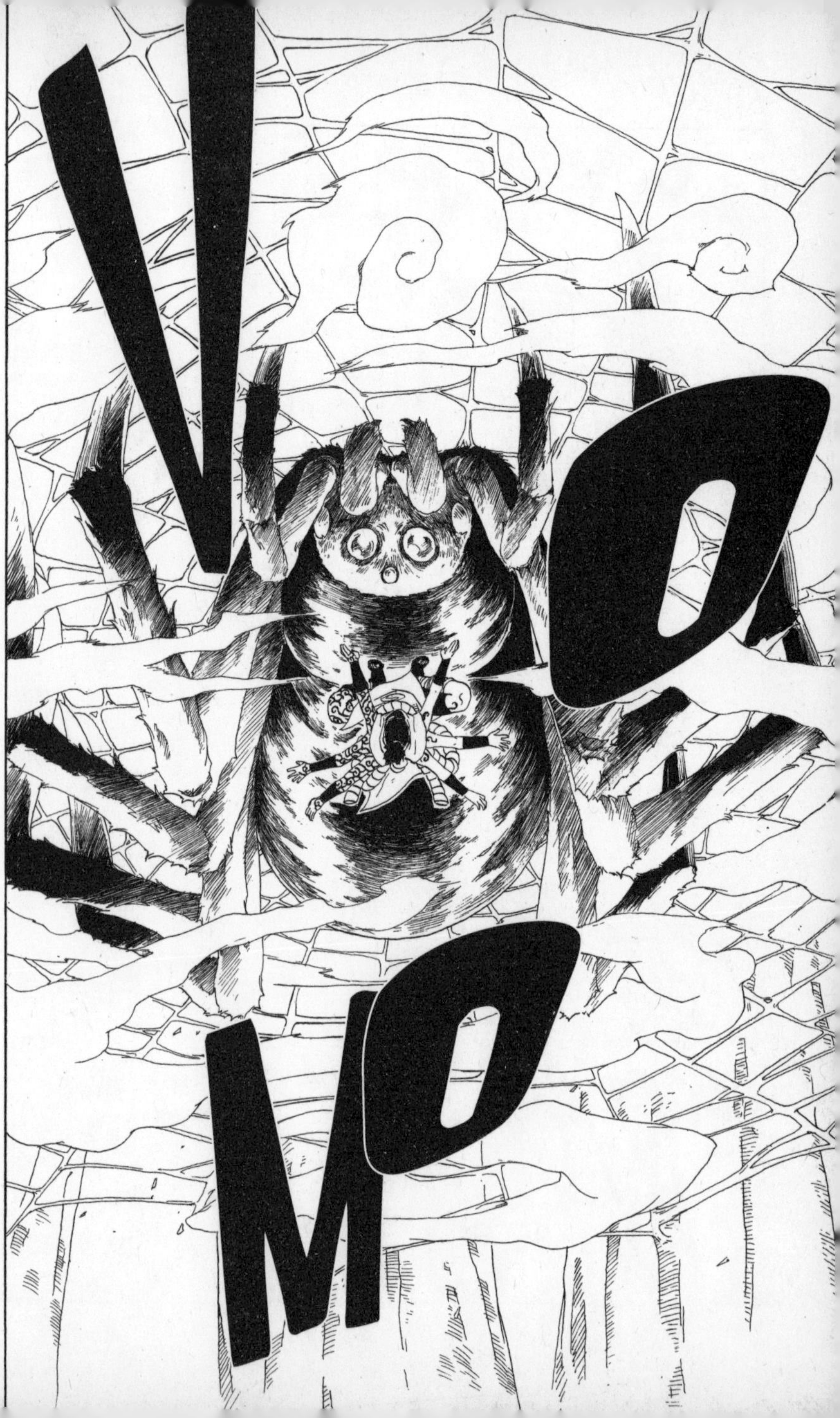
VOOM

READ THIS WAY

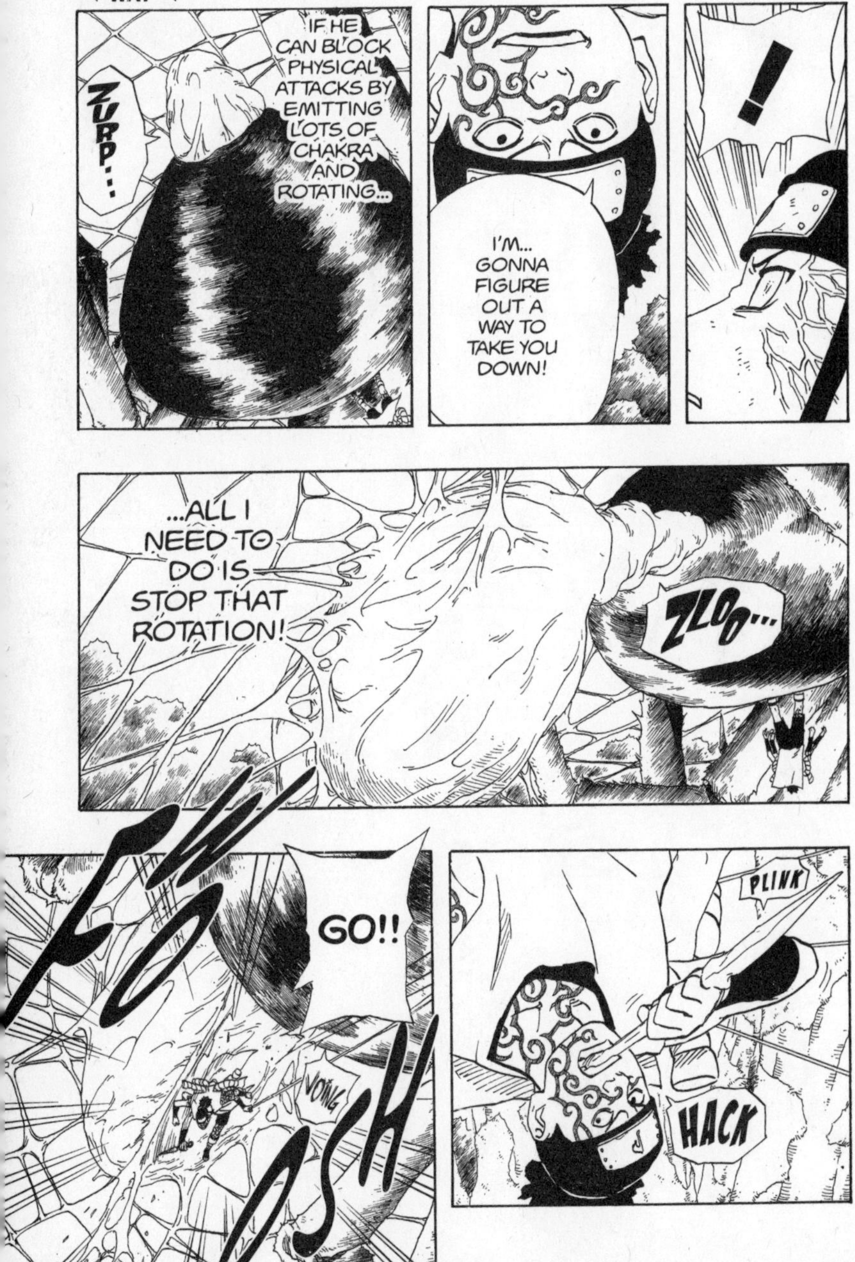
!
I'M... GONNA FIGURE OUT A WAY TO TAKE YOU DOWN!
IF HE CAN BLOCK PHYSICAL ATTACKS BY EMITTING LOTS OF CHAKRA AND ROTATING...
ZURP...
...ALL I NEED TO DO IS STOP THAT ROTATION!
ZLOO...
PLINK
HACK
GO!!
FWOOSH
VOING

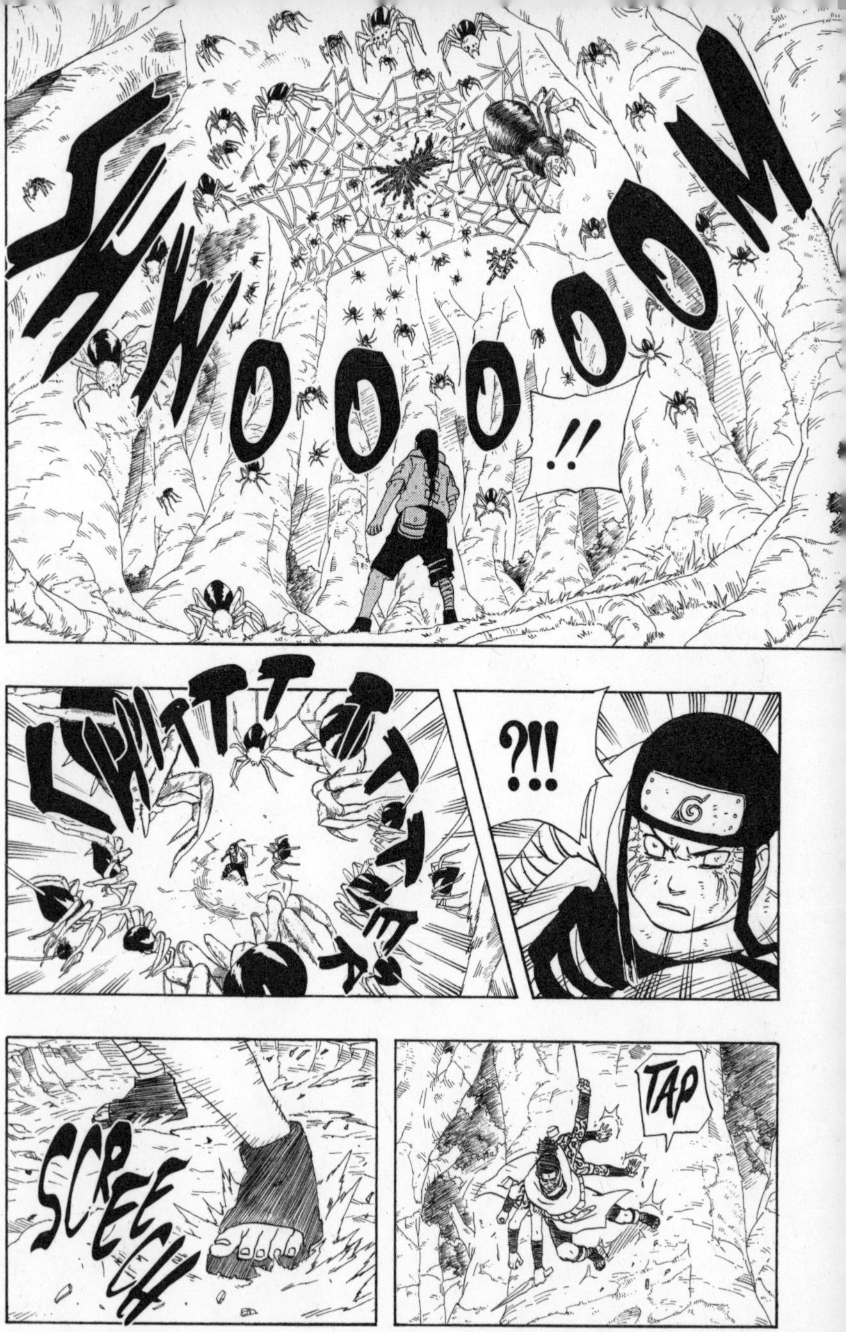
SHWOOOOOOM
!!
?!!
TAP
SCREECH

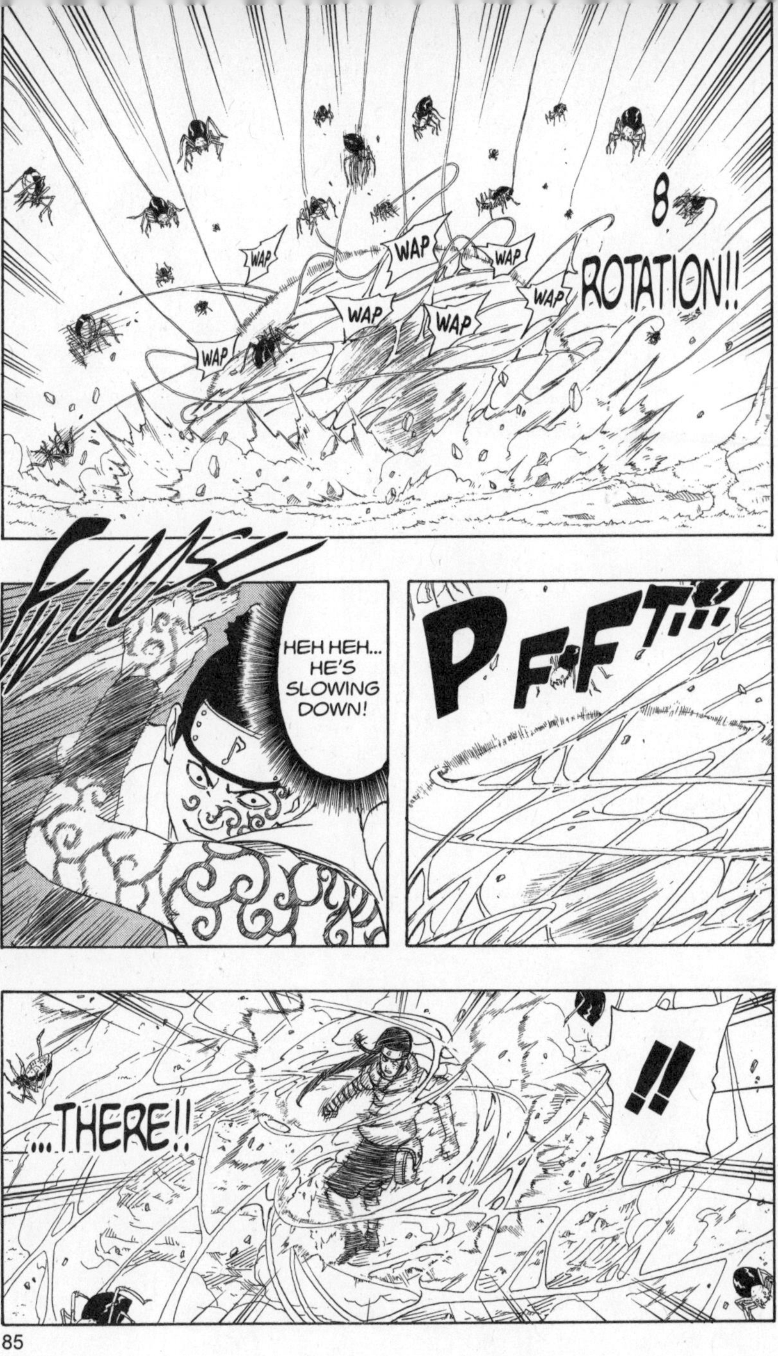

8
ROTATION!!
WAP
WAP
WAP
WAP
WAP
WAP
WAP
PFFT...
HEH HEH... HE'S SLOWING DOWN!
!!
...THERE!!

NARUTO™

Number 195: Capture...!!

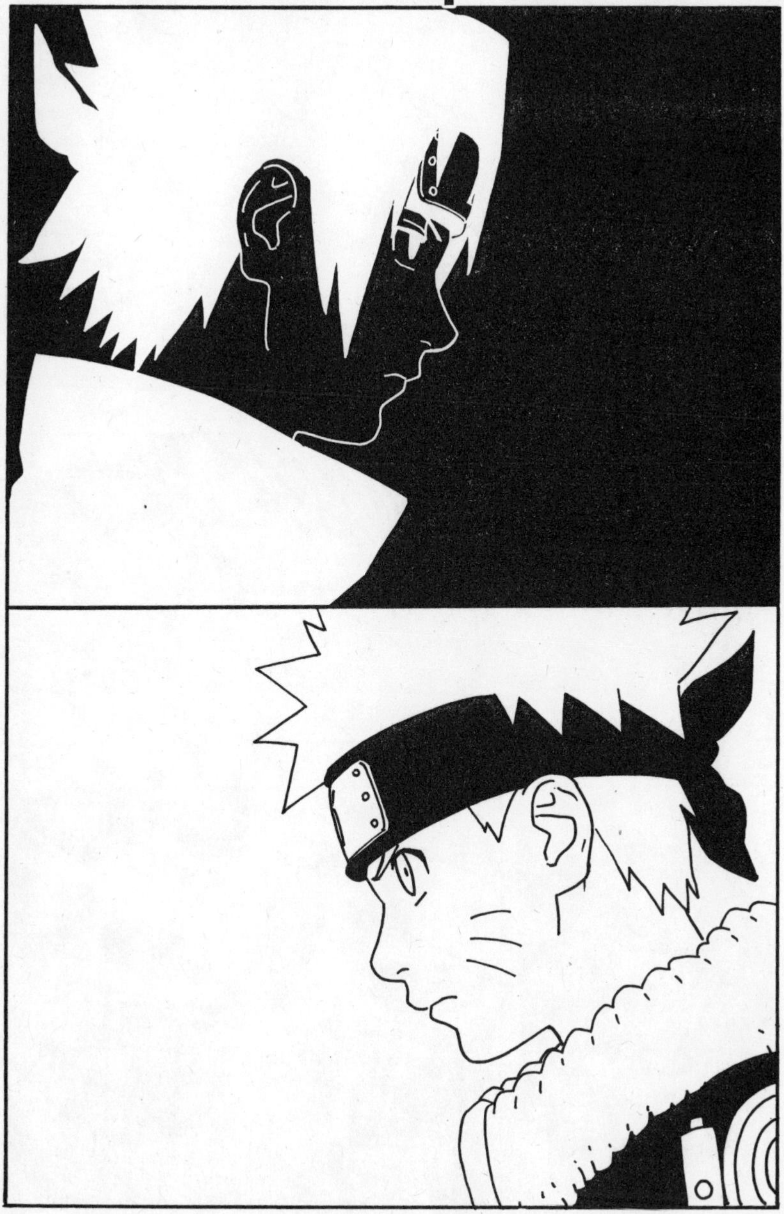

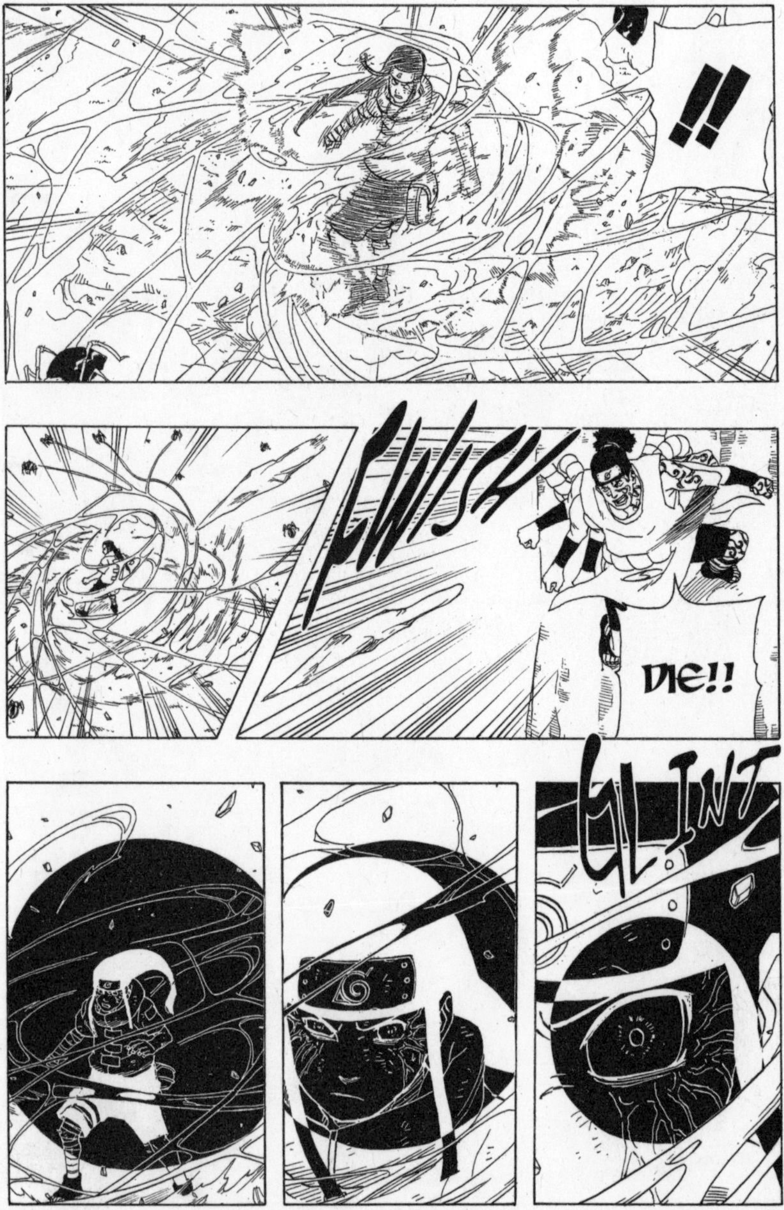
!!
DIE!!
FWISH
GLINT

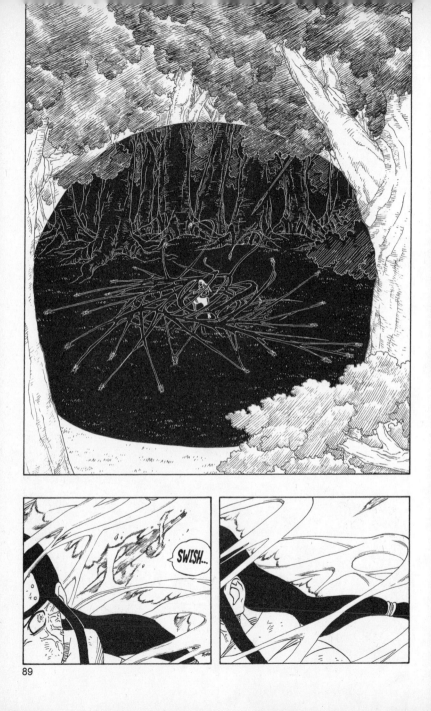

SWISH...

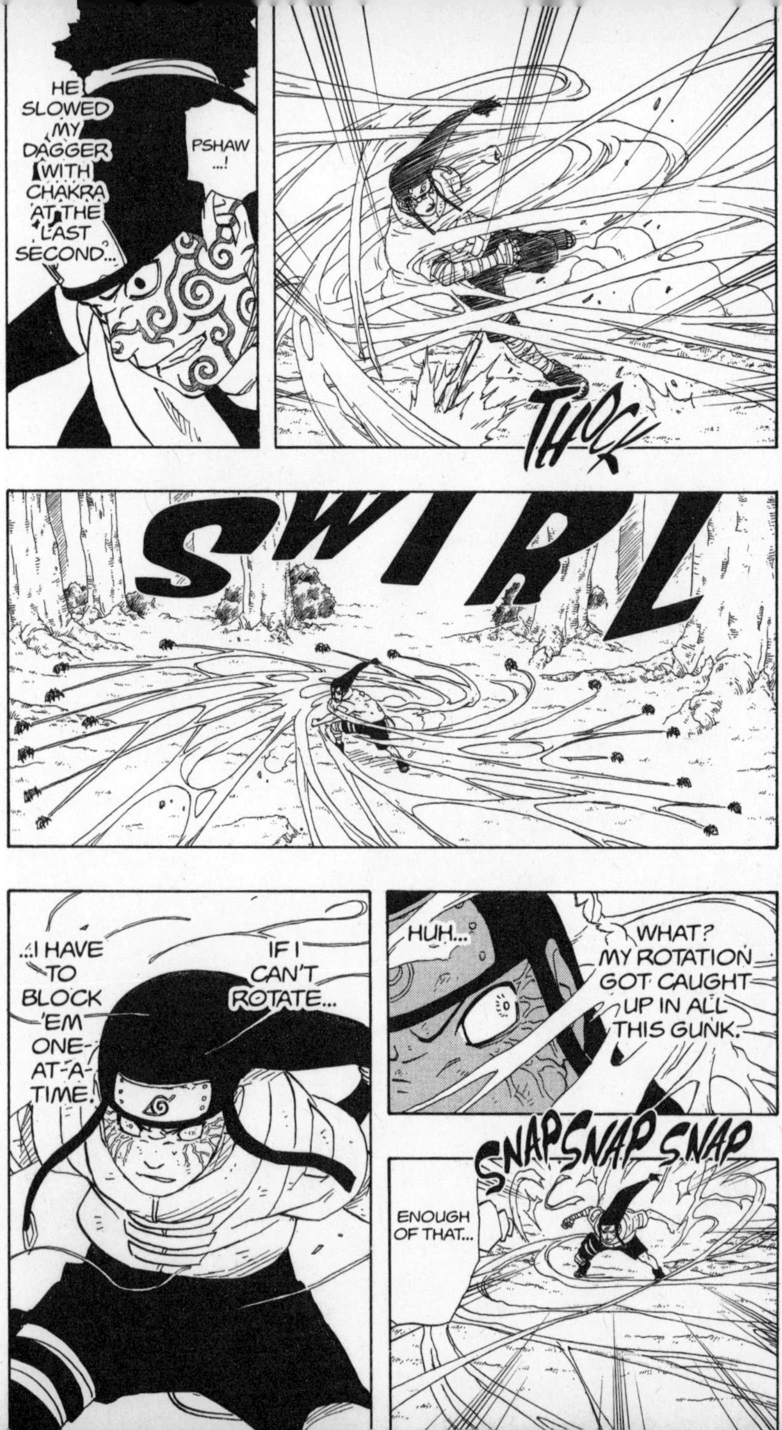
THOCK
PSHAW ...!
HE SLOWED MY DAGGER WITH CHAKRA AT THE LAST SECOND...
SWIRL
WHAT? MY ROTATION GOT CAUGHT UP IN ALL THIS GUNK.
HUH...
SNAP SNAP SNAP
ENOUGH OF THAT...
IF I CAN'T ROTATE...
...I HAVE TO BLOCK 'EM ONE-AT-A-TIME.

READ THIS WAY

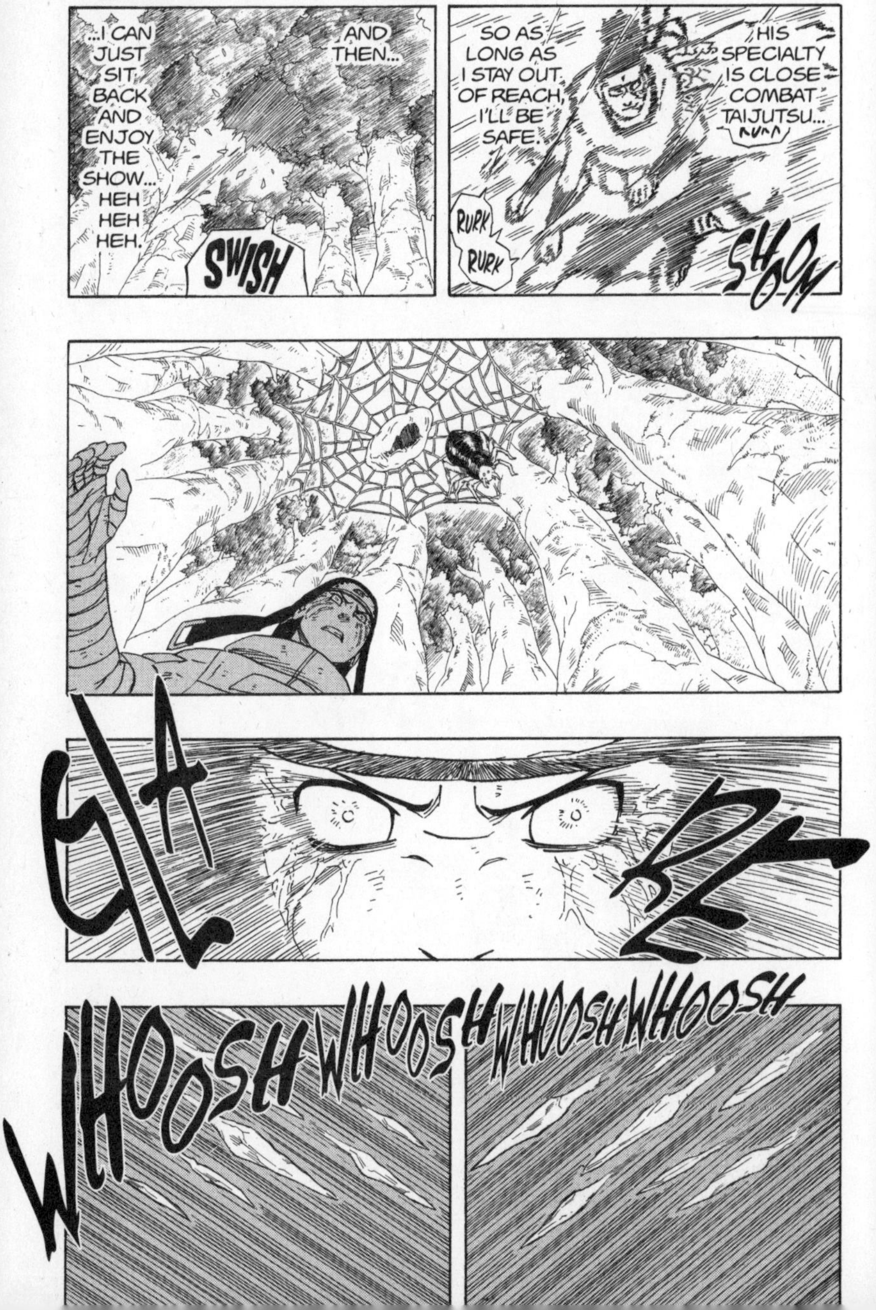

HIS SPECIALTY IS CLOSE COMBAT TAIJUTSU...
SO AS LONG AS I STAY OUT OF REACH, I'LL BE SAFE.
RURK RURK
SHOOM
AND THEN...
...I CAN JUST SIT BACK AND ENJOY THE SHOW... HEH HEH HEH.
SWISH
WHOOSH WHOOSH WHOOSH WHOOSH

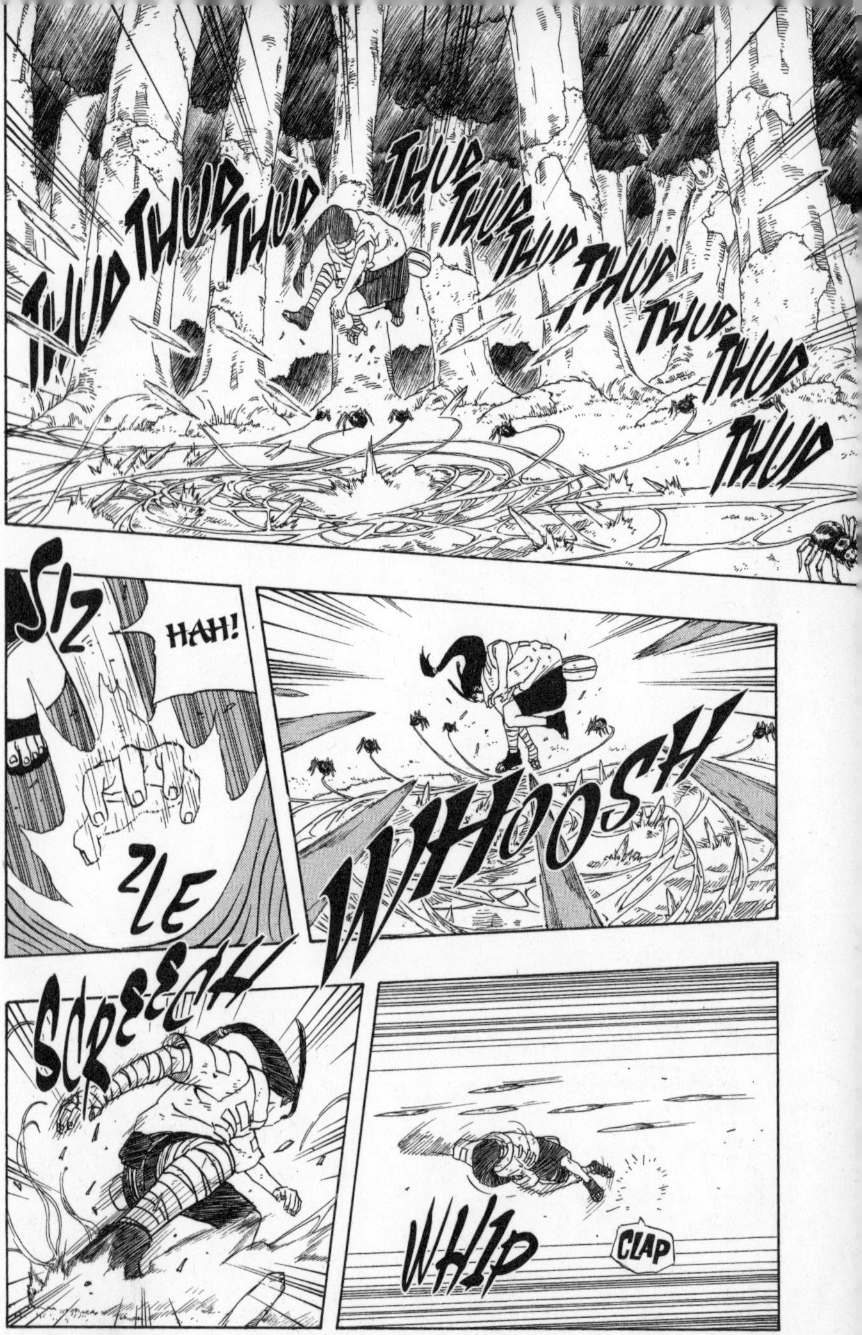
THUD THUD THUD THUD THUD THUD THUD THUD THUD THUD
WHOOSH
HAH!
SIZZLE
WHIP
CLAP
SCREECH

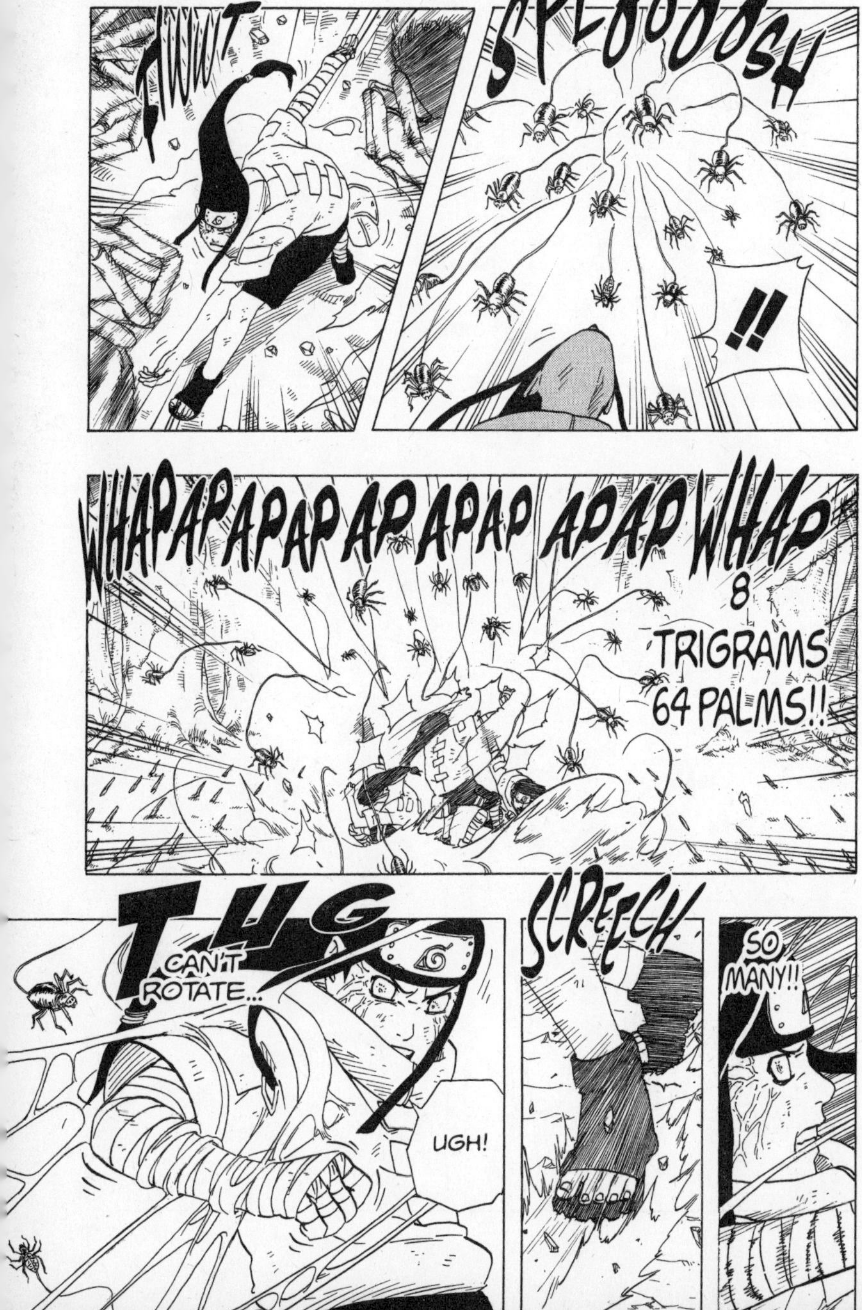
SPLOOOOSH
!!
FWUT
WHAPAPAPAPAPAPAPAPAPAPAPAPWHAP
8 TRIGRAMS 64 PALMS!!
SO MANY!!
SCREECH
TUG
CAN'T ROTATE...
UGH!

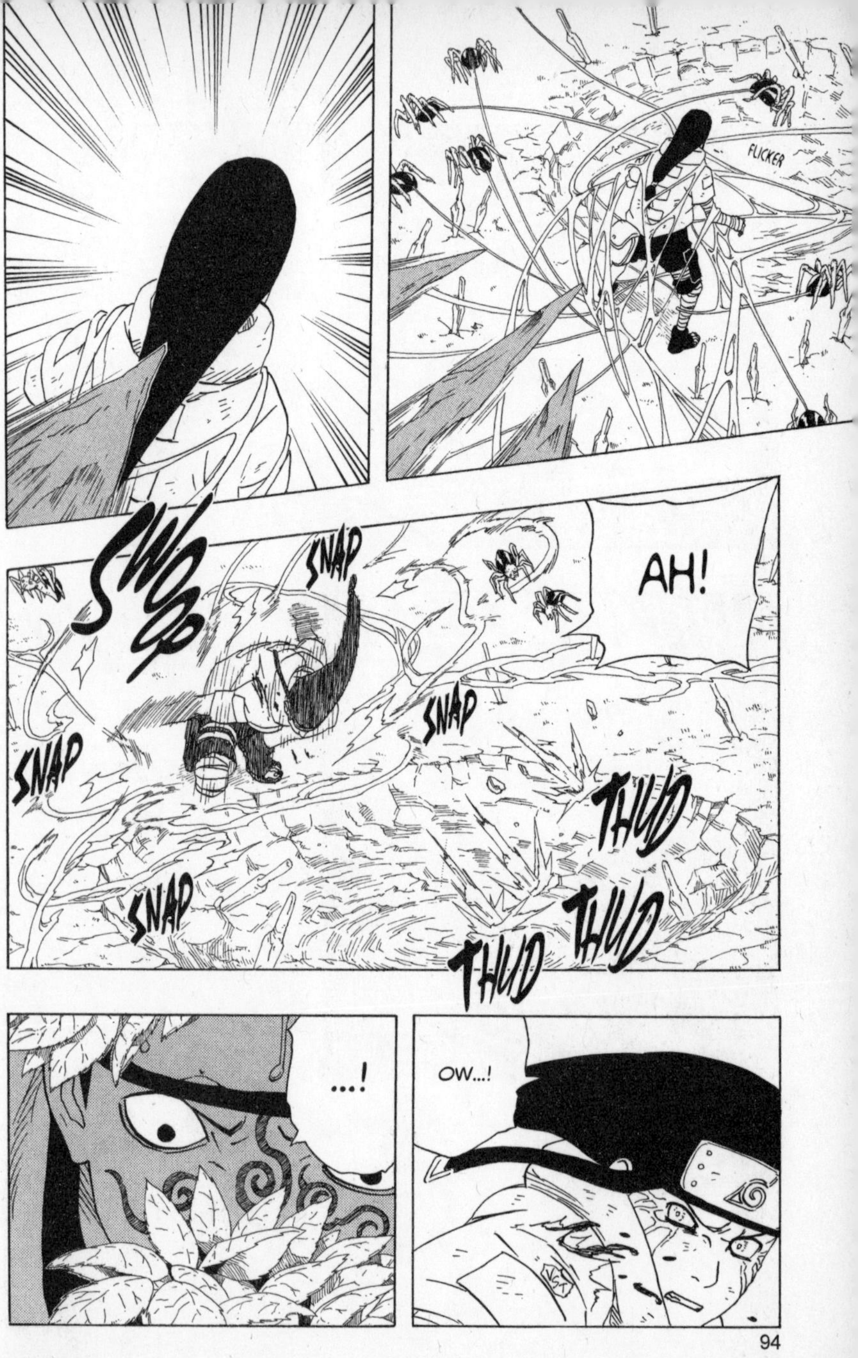
FLICKER
SWOOP
AH!
SNAP
SNAP
SNAP
SNAP
THUD
THUD
THUD
OW...!
...!

READ THIS WAY

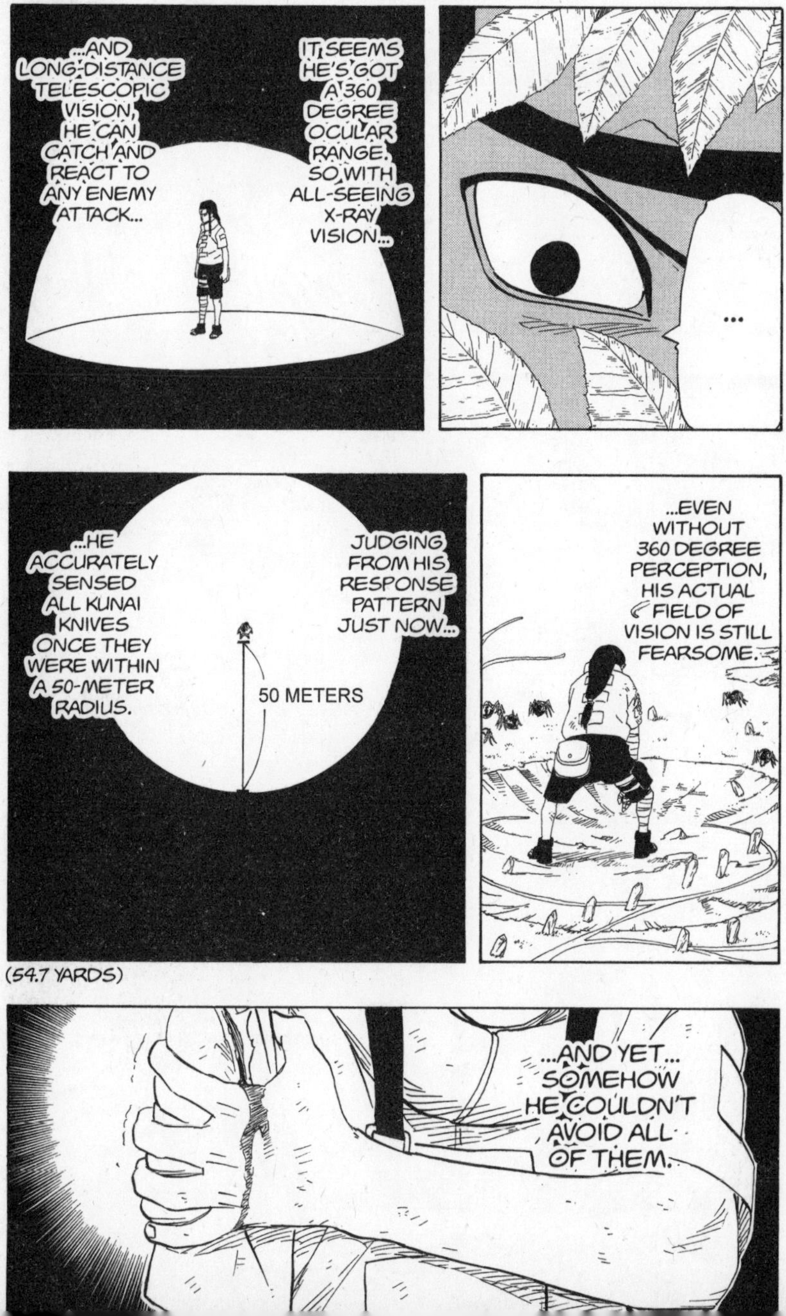
...
IT SEEMS HE'S GOT A 360 DEGREE OCULAR RANGE. SO WITH ALL-SEEING X-RAY VISION...
...AND LONG-DISTANCE TELESCOPIC VISION, HE CAN CATCH AND REACT TO ANY ENEMY ATTACK...
...EVEN WITHOUT 360 DEGREE PERCEPTION, HIS ACTUAL FIELD OF VISION IS STILL FEARSOME.
JUDGING FROM HIS RESPONSE PATTERN JUST NOW...
...HE ACCURATELY SENSED ALL KUNAI KNIVES ONCE THEY WERE WITHIN A 50-METER RADIUS.
50 METERS
(54.7 YARDS)
...AND YET... SOMEHOW HE COULDN'T AVOID ALL OF THEM.

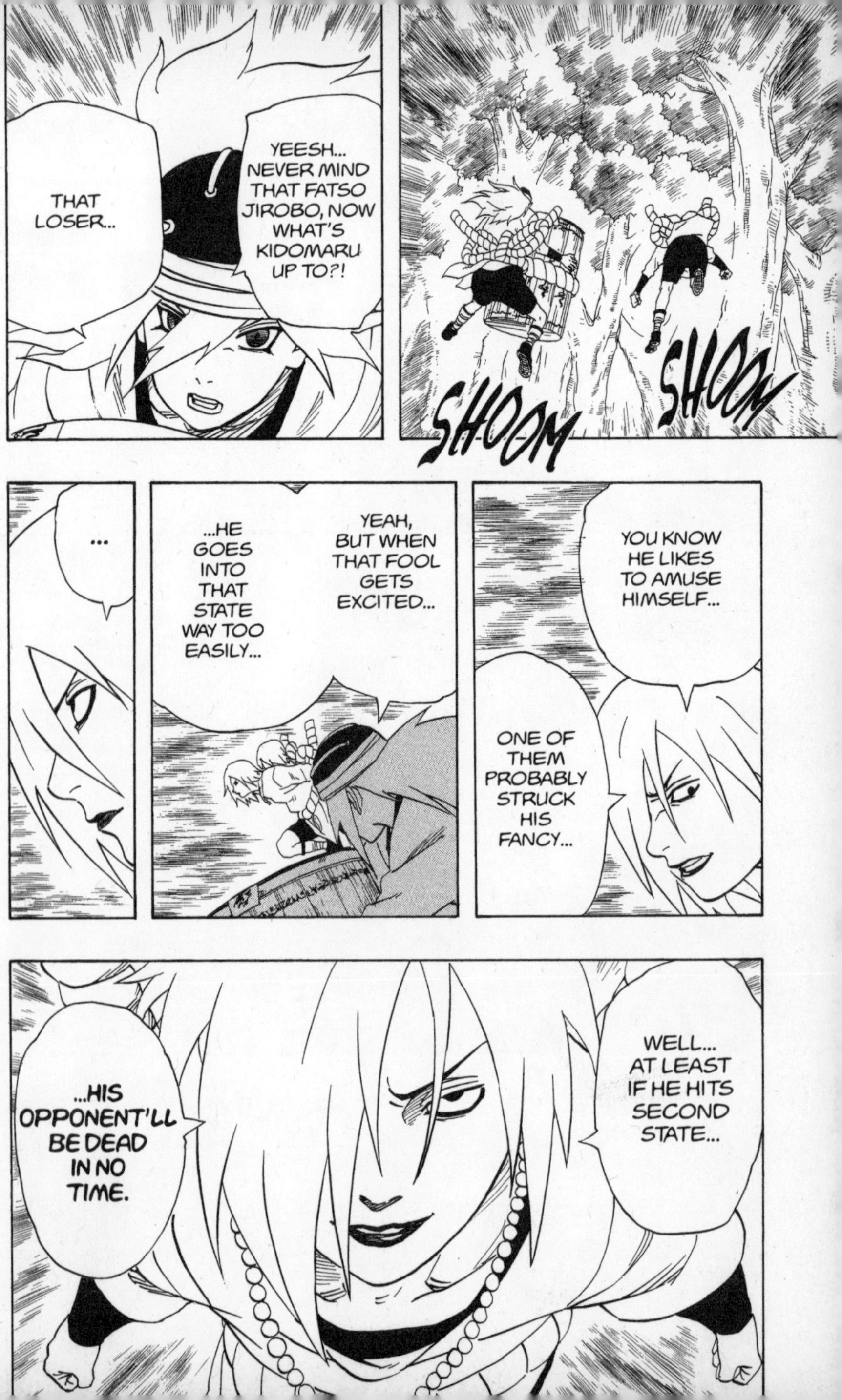
SHOOM
SHOOM
YEESH... NEVER MIND THAT FATSO JIROBO, NOW WHAT'S KIDOMARU UP TO?!
THAT LOSER...
YOU KNOW HE LIKES TO AMUSE HIMSELF...
ONE OF THEM PROBABLY STRUCK HIS FANCY...
YEAH, BUT WHEN THAT FOOL GETS EXCITED...
...HE GOES INTO THAT STATE WAY TOO EASILY...
...
WELL... AT LEAST IF HE HITS SECOND STATE...
...HIS OPPONENT'LL BE DEAD IN NO TIME.

READ THIS WAY

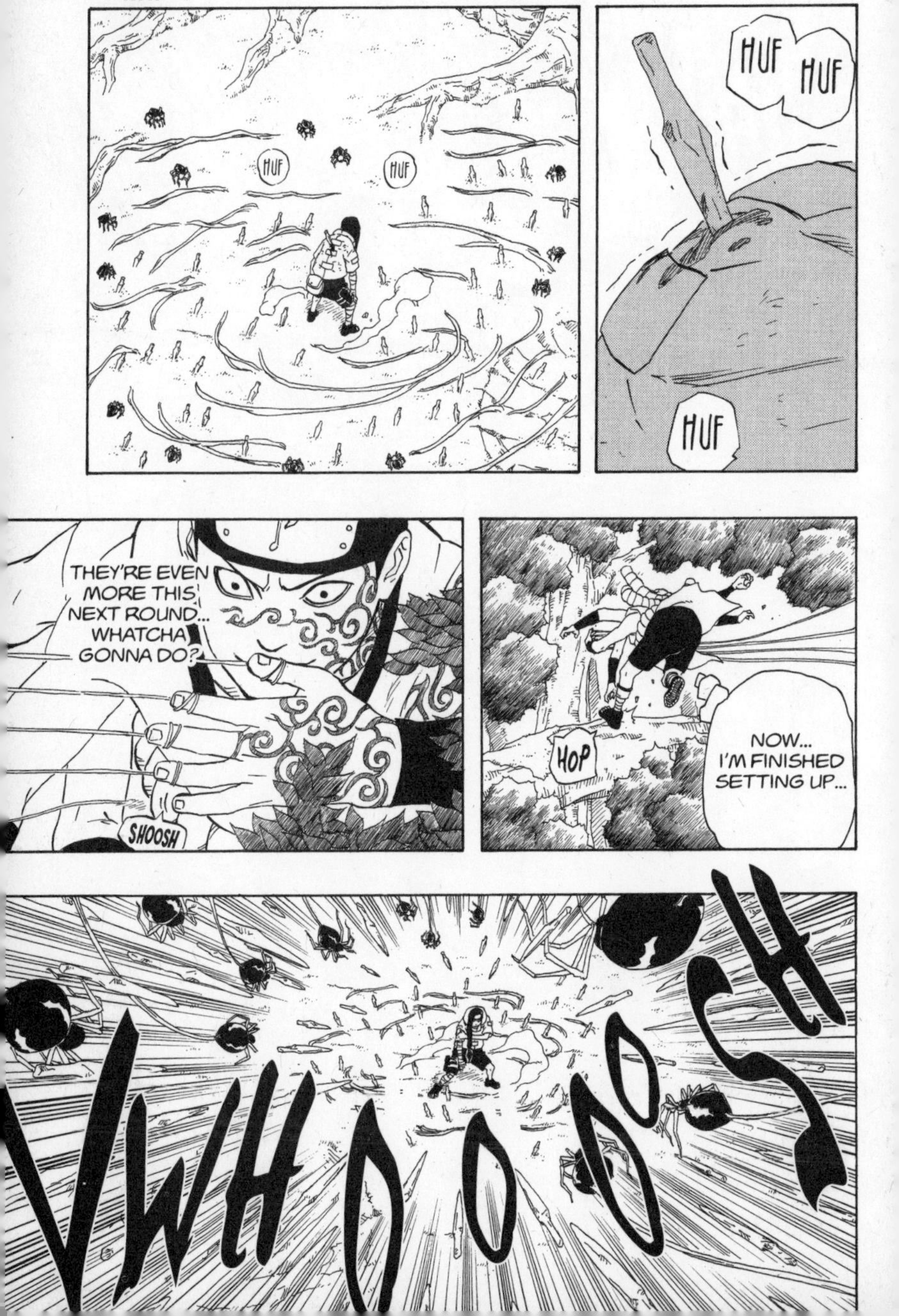
HUF HUF
HUF
HUF
HUF
NOW... I'M FINISHED SETTING UP...
HOP
THEY'RE EVEN MORE THIS NEXT ROUND... WHATCHA GONNA DO?
SHOOSH
VWHOOOSH

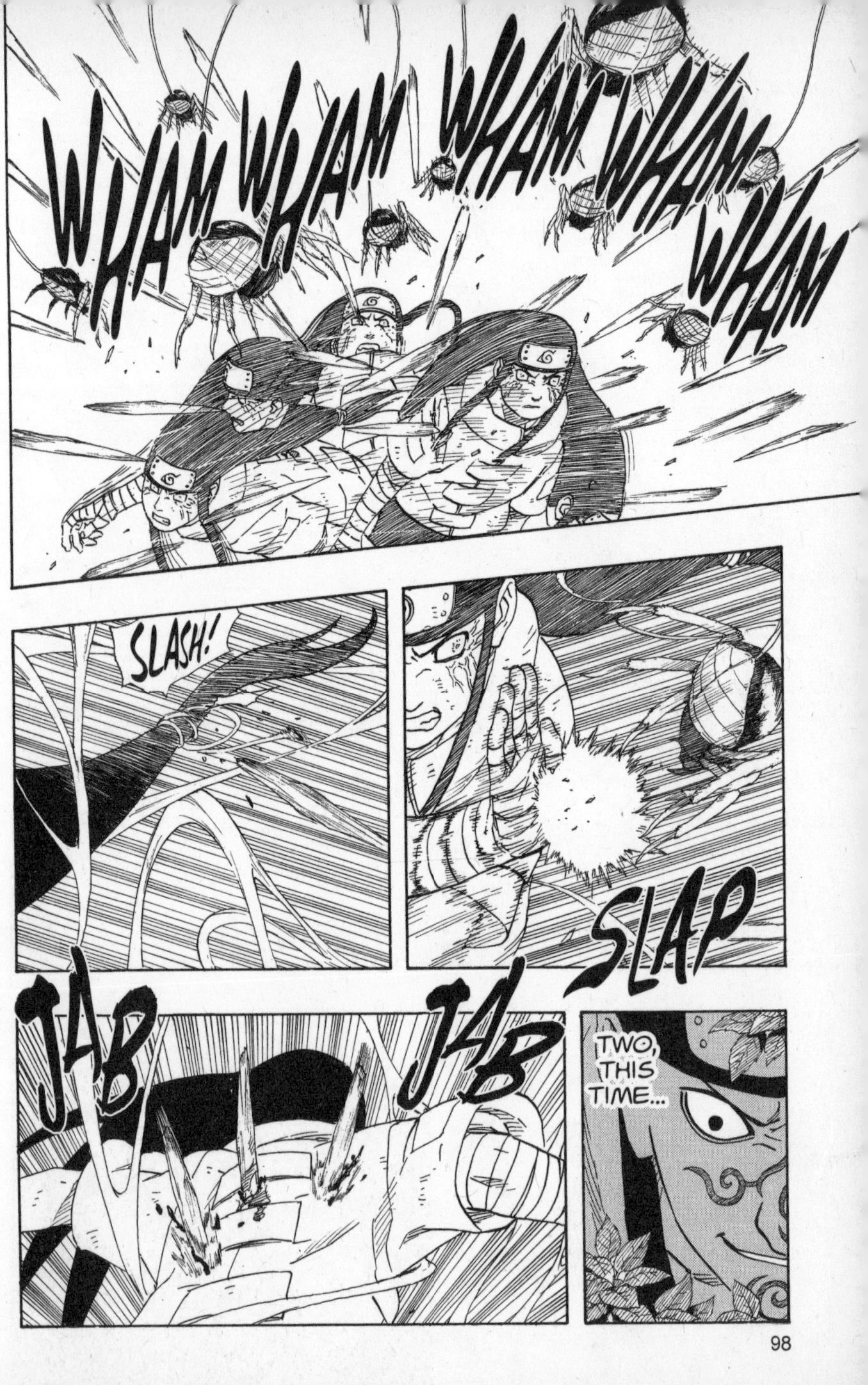
WHAM WHAM WHAM WHAM WHAM
SLAP
SLASH!
TWO, THIS TIME...
JAB JAB

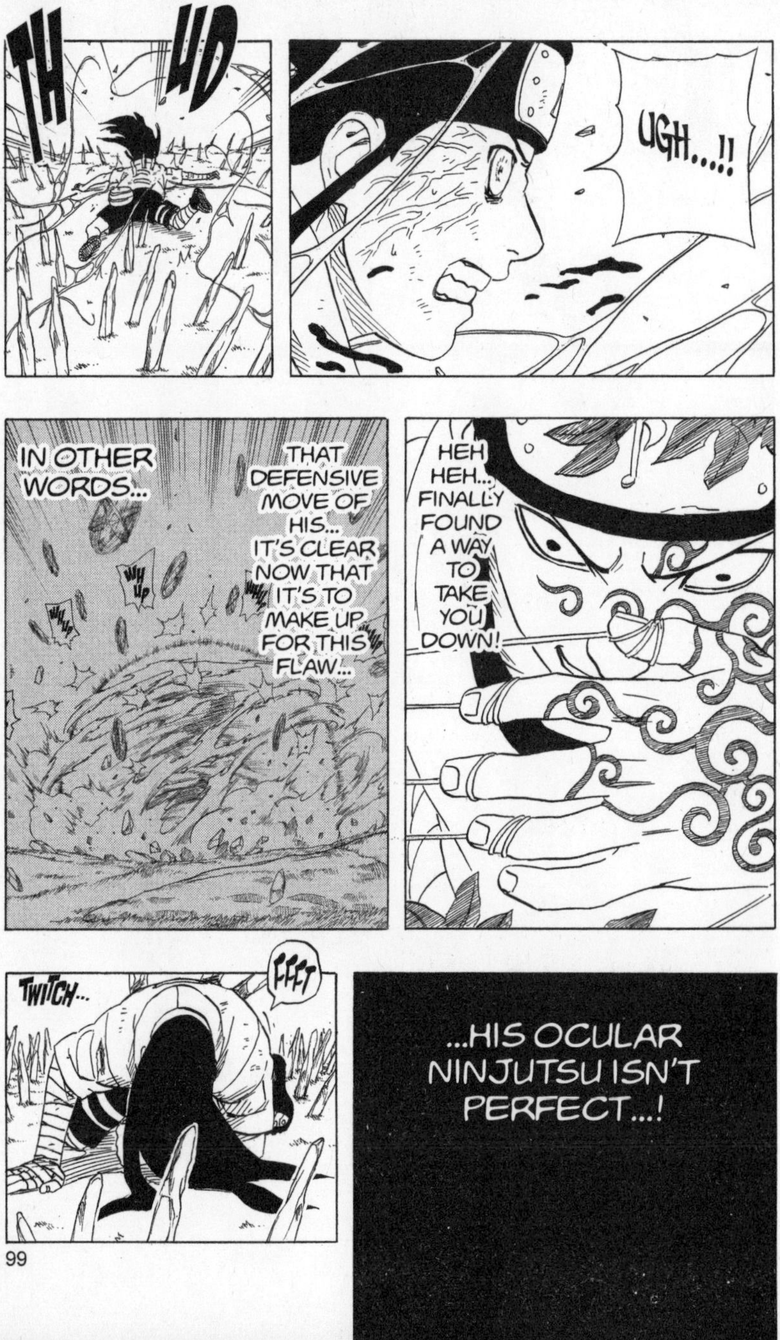
UGH...!!
TH
UD
HEH HEH... FINALLY FOUND A WAY TO TAKE YOU DOWN!
THAT DEFENSIVE MOVE OF HIS... IT'S CLEAR NOW THAT IT'S TO MAKE UP FOR THIS FLAW...
WHUP
WHUP
WHUP
WHUP
IN OTHER WORDS...
...HIS OCULAR NINJUTSU ISN'T PERFECT...!
FFFT
TWITCH...

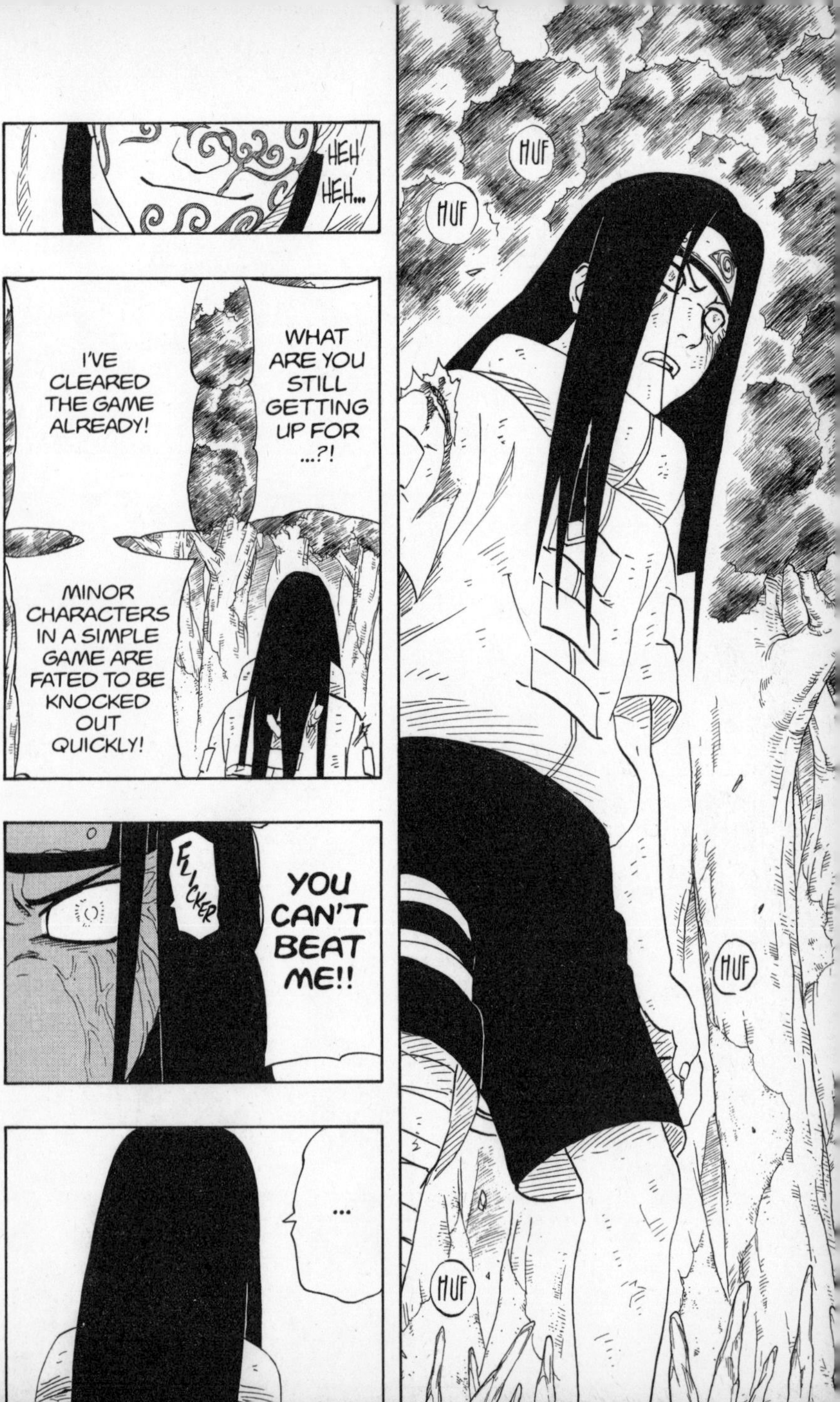
HUF
HUF
HUF
HUF
HEH HEH...
WHAT ARE YOU STILL GETTING UP FOR ...?!
I'VE CLEARED THE GAME ALREADY!
MINOR CHARACTERS IN A SIMPLE GAME ARE FATED TO BE KNOCKED OUT QUICKLY!
YOU CAN'T BEAT ME!!
FLICKER
...

READ THIS WAY

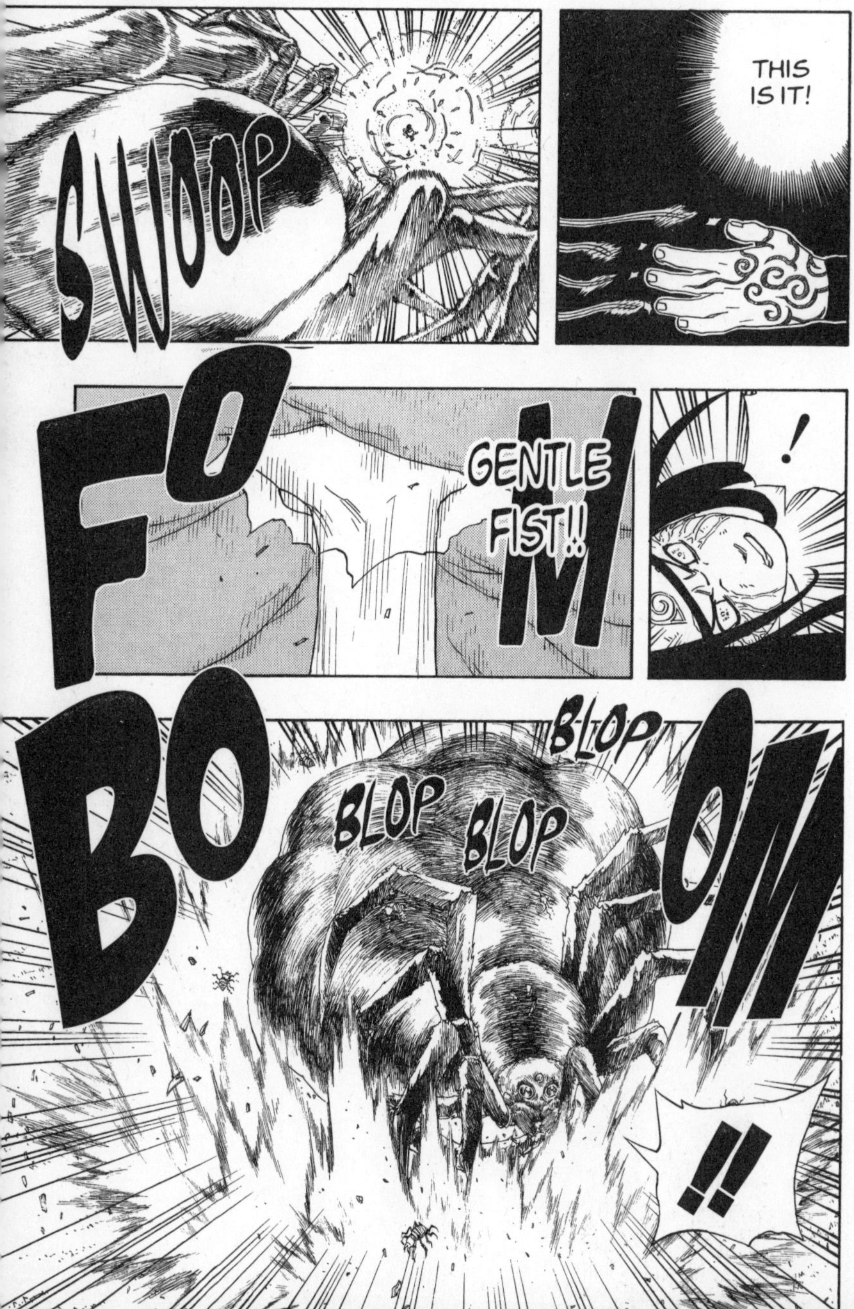
THIS IS IT!
SWOOP
!
FOOM
GENTLE FIST!!
BOOM!!
BLOP
BLOP
BLOP
BLOP

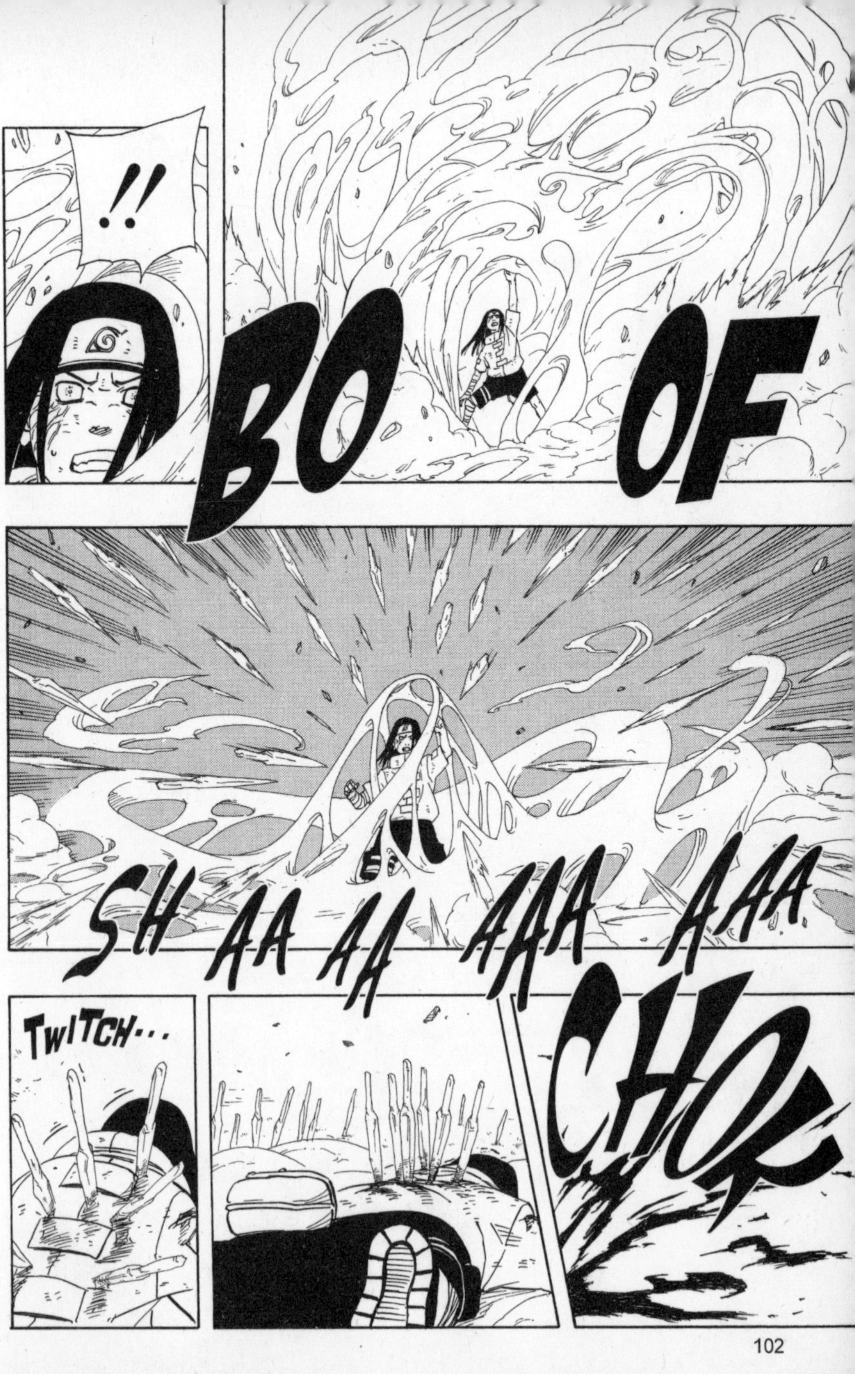
BOOF
!!
SHAAAAAAAAAA
CHOK
TWITCH...

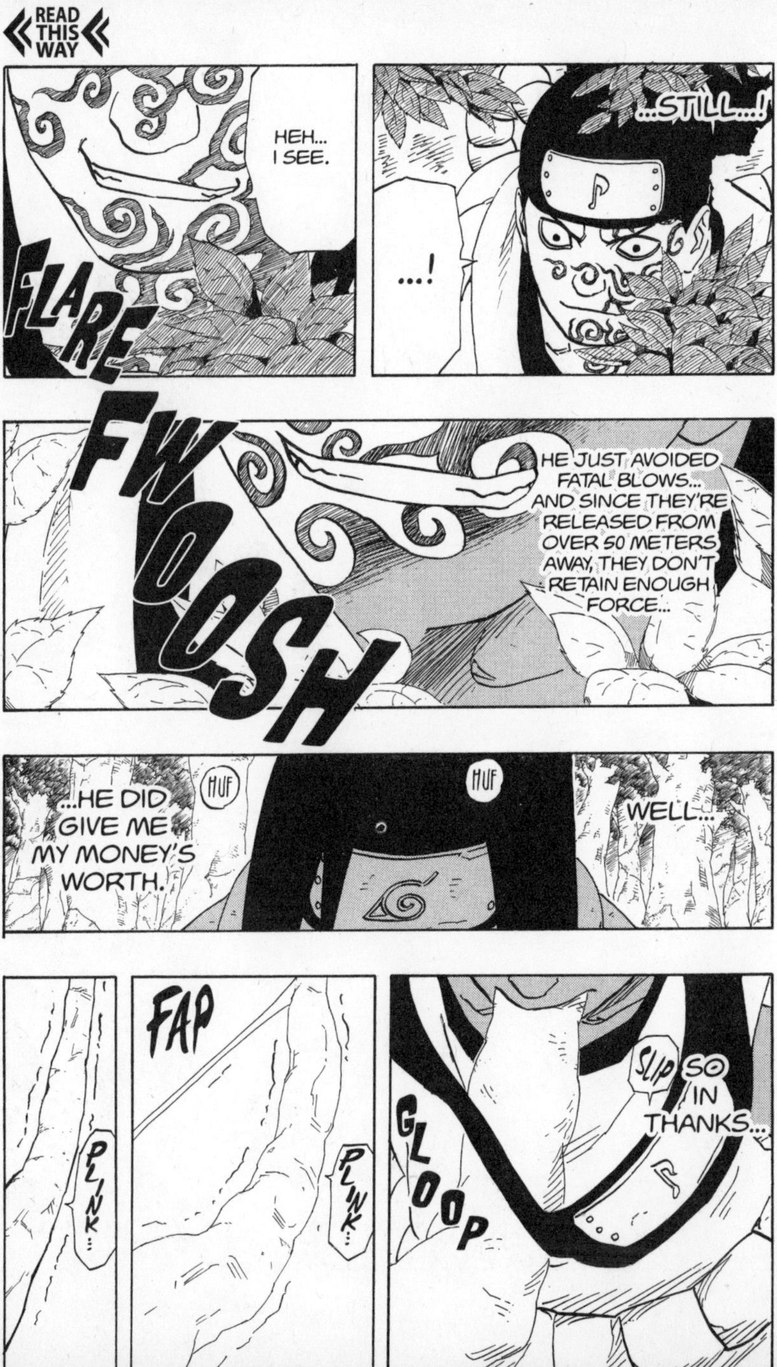
READ THIS WAY
...STILL...!
...!
HEH... I SEE.
FLARE
FWOOSH
HE JUST AVOIDED FATAL BLOWS... AND SINCE THEY'RE RELEASED FROM OVER 50 METERS AWAY, THEY DON'T RETAIN ENOUGH FORCE...
WELL...
HUF
HUF
...HE DID GIVE ME MY MONEY'S WORTH.
SLIP
SO IN THANKS...
GLOOP
FAP
PLINK...
PLINK...

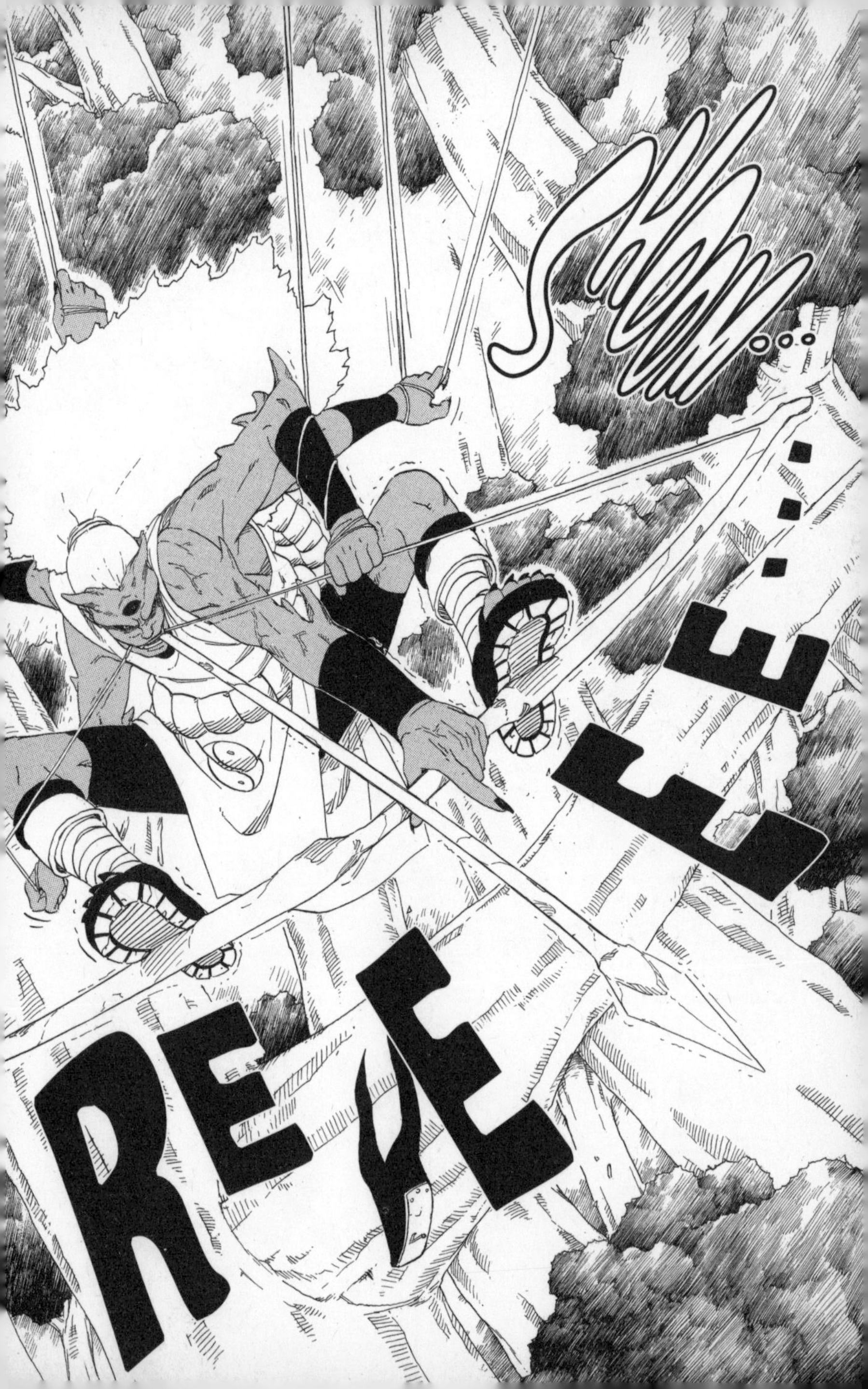
REEEEE...

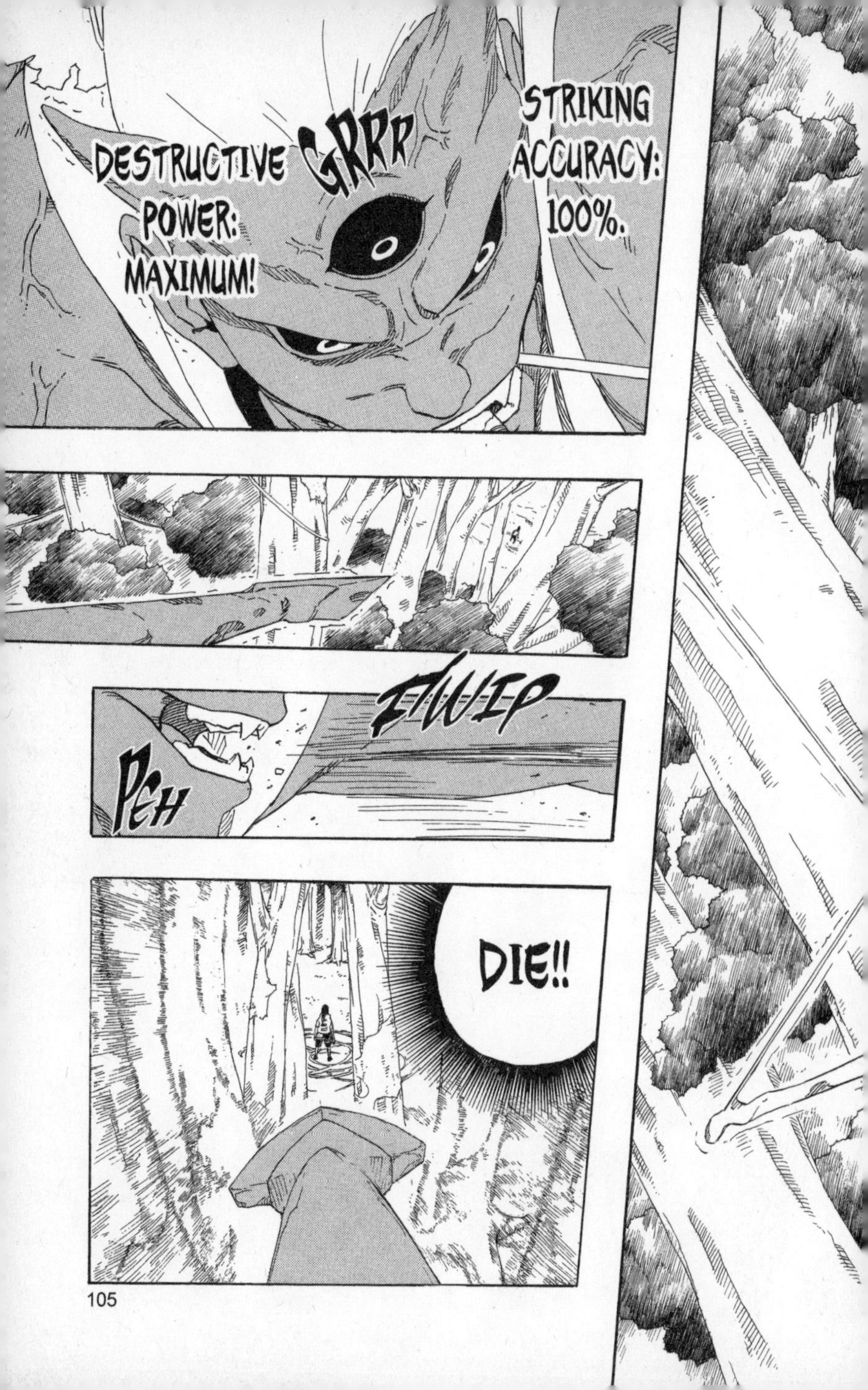
STRIKING ACCURACY: 100%.
GRRR
DESTRUCTIVE POWER: MAXIMUM!
FWIP
PCH
DIE!!

NARUTO™

Number 196: The Strongest Enemy!!

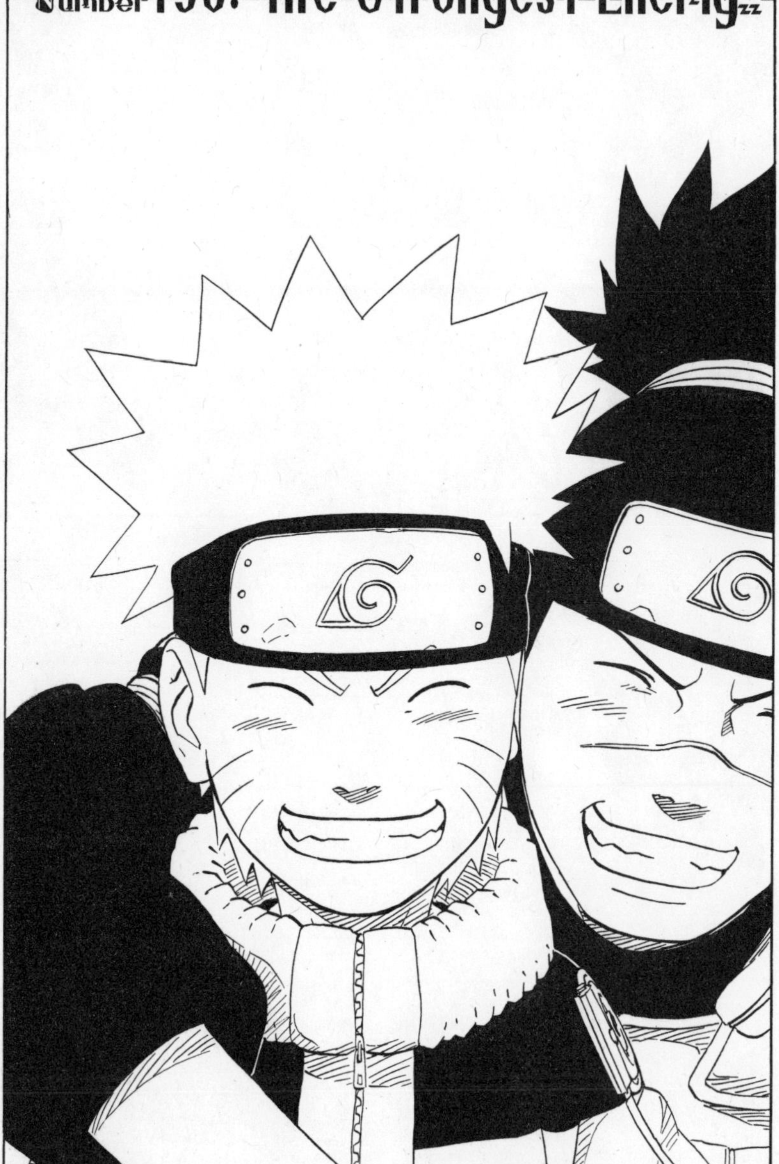

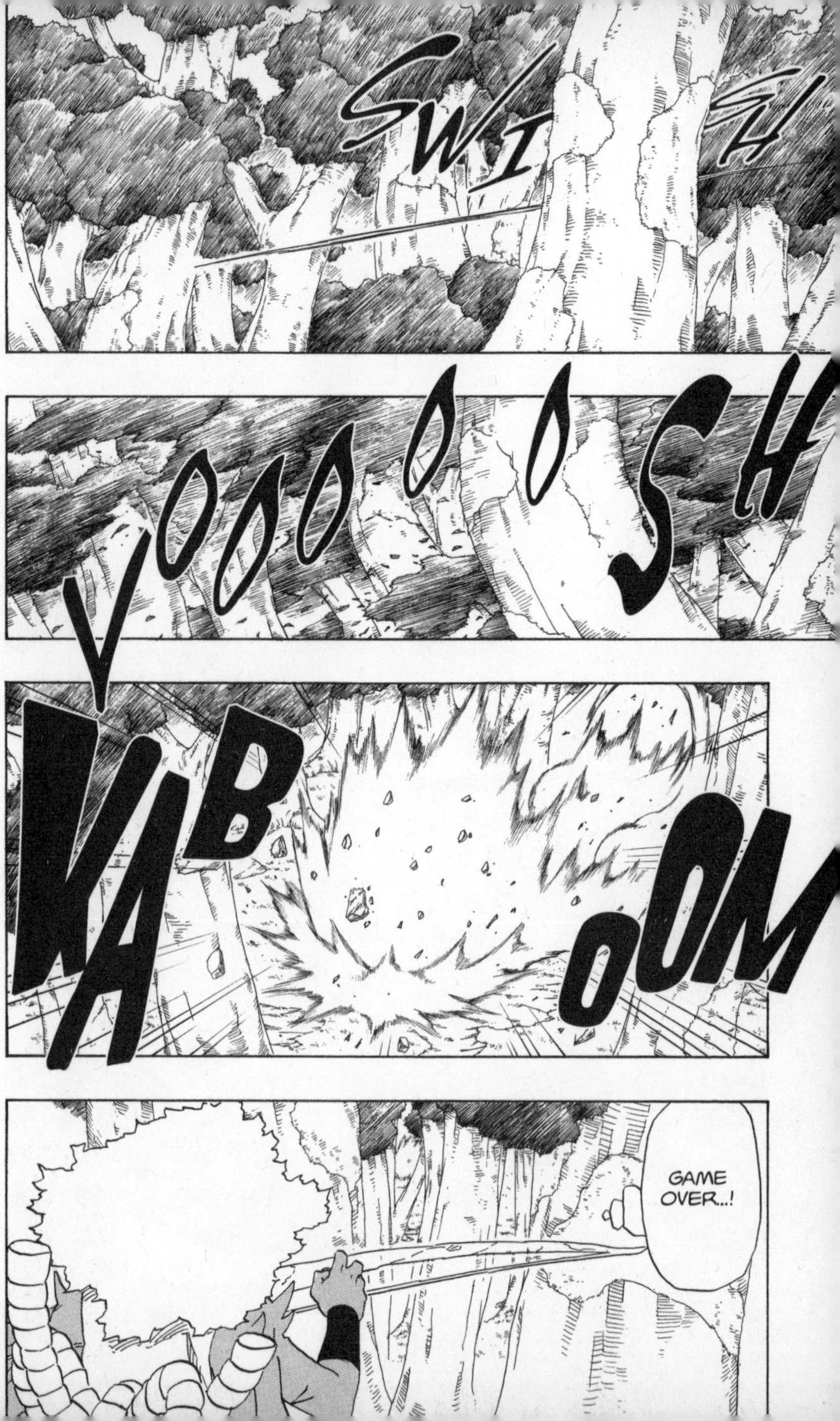
SWISH
VOOOOOOSH
KABOOOM
GAME OVER...!

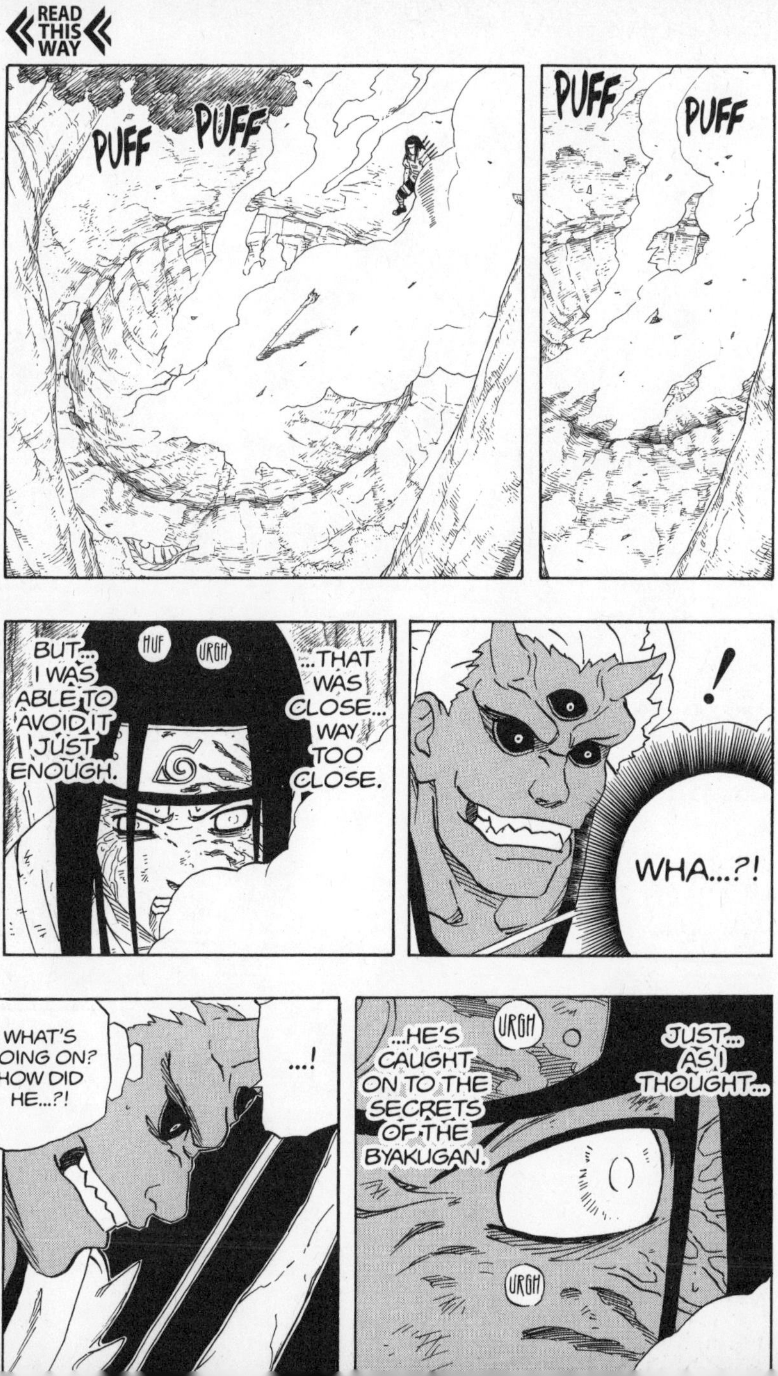
READ THIS WAY
PUFF
PUFF
PUFF
PUFF
!
WHA...?!
...THAT WAS CLOSE... WAY TOO CLOSE.
HUF
URGH
BUT... I WAS ABLE TO AVOID IT JUST ENOUGH.
JUST... AS I THOUGHT...
URGH
...HE'S CAUGHT ON TO THE SECRETS OF THE BYAKUGAN.
URGH
...!
WHAT'S GOING ON? HOW DID HE...?!

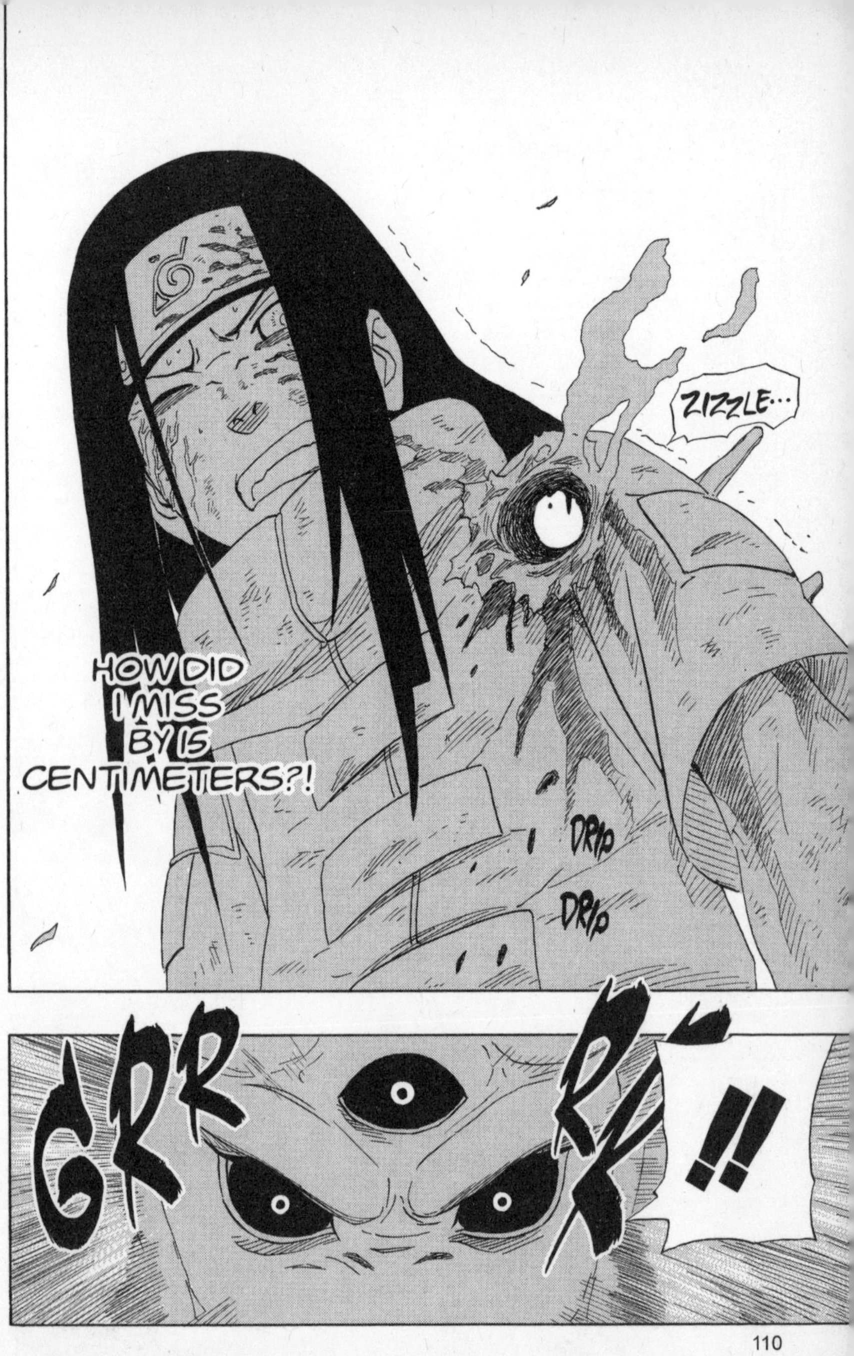
ZIZZLE...
HOW DID I MISS BY 15 CENTIMETERS?!
DRIP
DRIP
GRR
RR!!

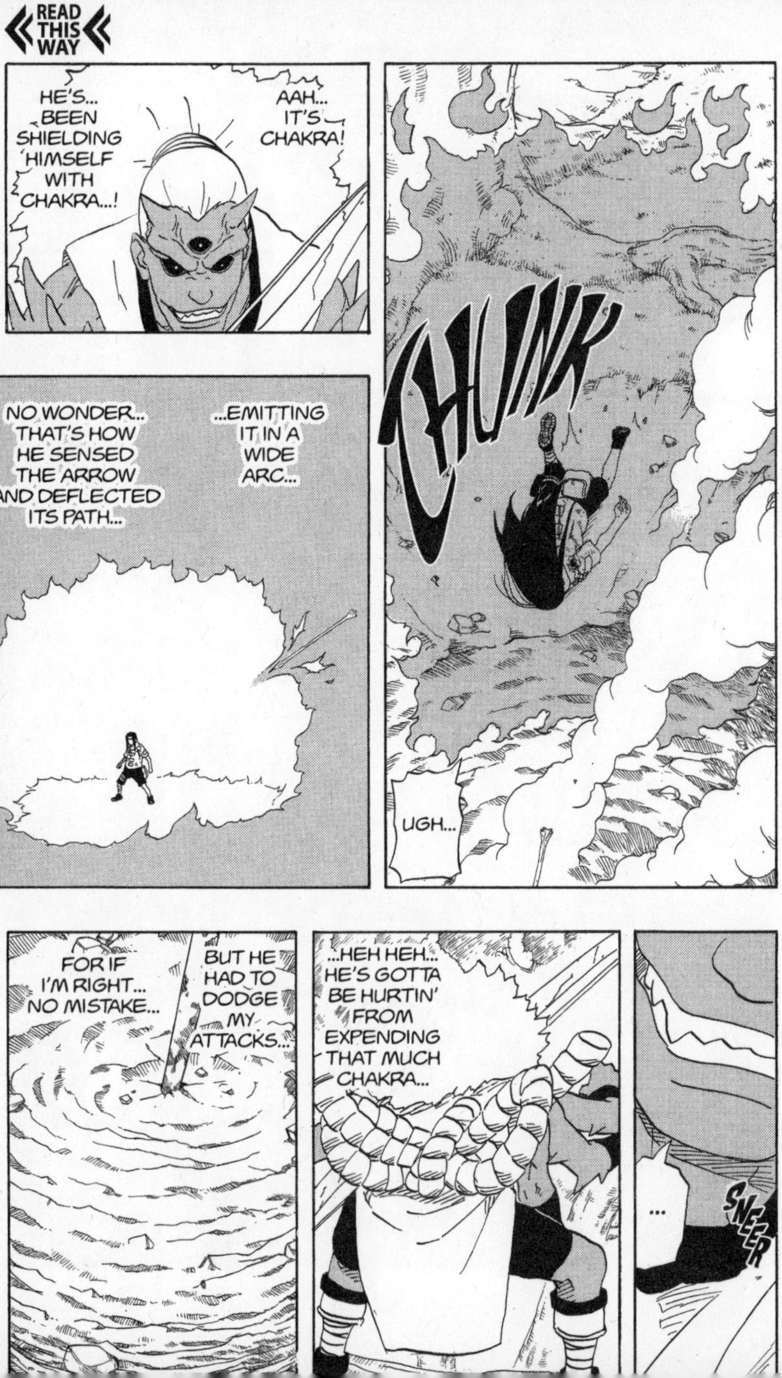
READ THIS WAY
THUNK
UGH...
AAH... IT'S CHAKRA!
HE'S... BEEN SHIELDING HIMSELF WITH CHAKRA...!
...EMITTING IT IN A WIDE ARC...
NO WONDER... THAT'S HOW HE SENSED THE ARROW AND DEFLECTED ITS PATH...
...
SNEER
...HEH HEH... HE'S GOTTA BE HURTIN' FROM EXPENDING THAT MUCH CHAKRA...
BUT HE HAD TO DODGE MY ATTACKS...
FOR IF I'M RIGHT... NO MISTAKE...

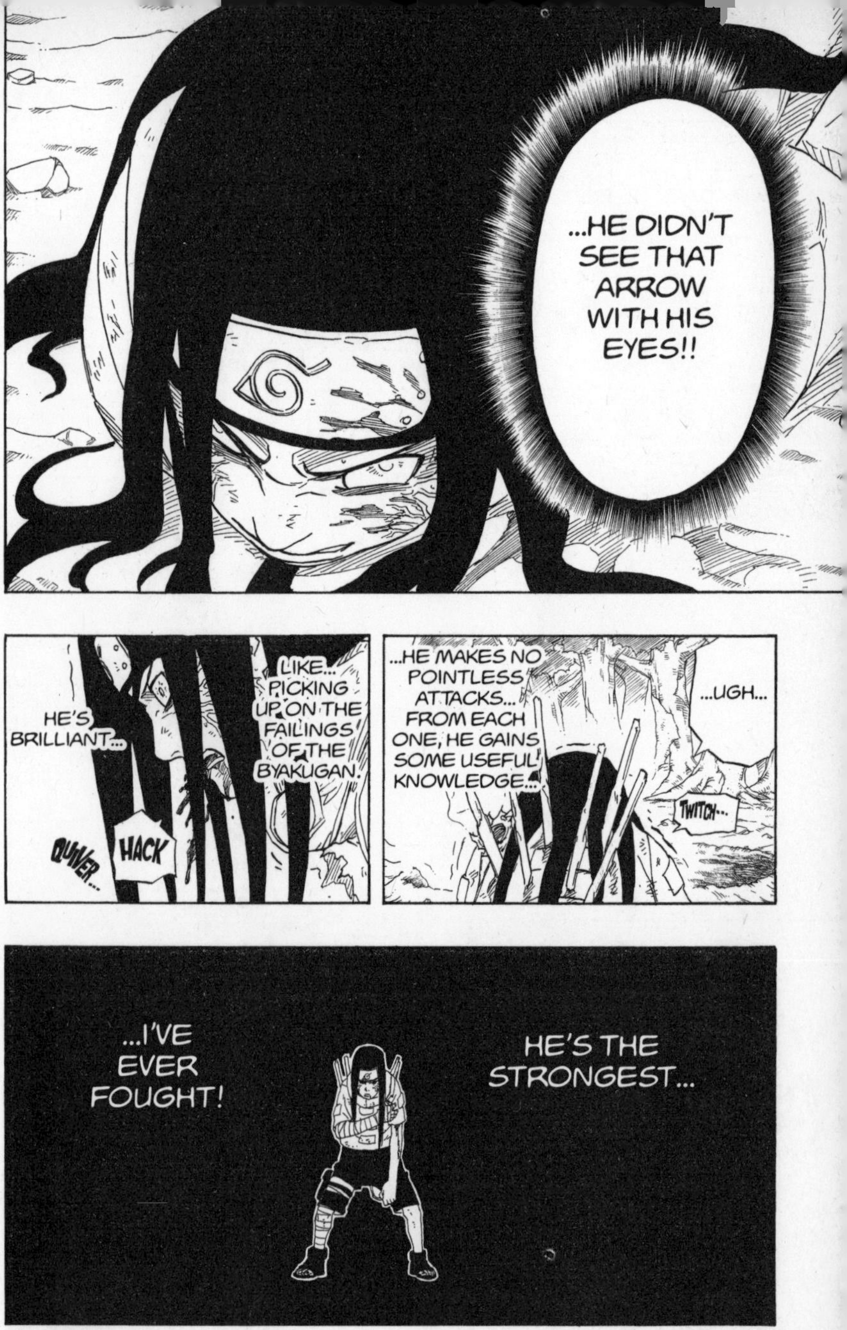
...HE DIDN'T SEE THAT ARROW WITH HIS EYES!!
...UGH...
...HE MAKES NO POINTLESS ATTACKS... FROM EACH ONE, HE GAINS SOME USEFUL KNOWLEDGE...
TWITCH...
LIKE... PICKING UP ON THE FAILINGS OF THE BYAKUGAN.
HE'S BRILLIANT...
HACK
QUIVER...
HE'S THE STRONGEST...
...I'VE EVER FOUGHT!

READ THIS WAY

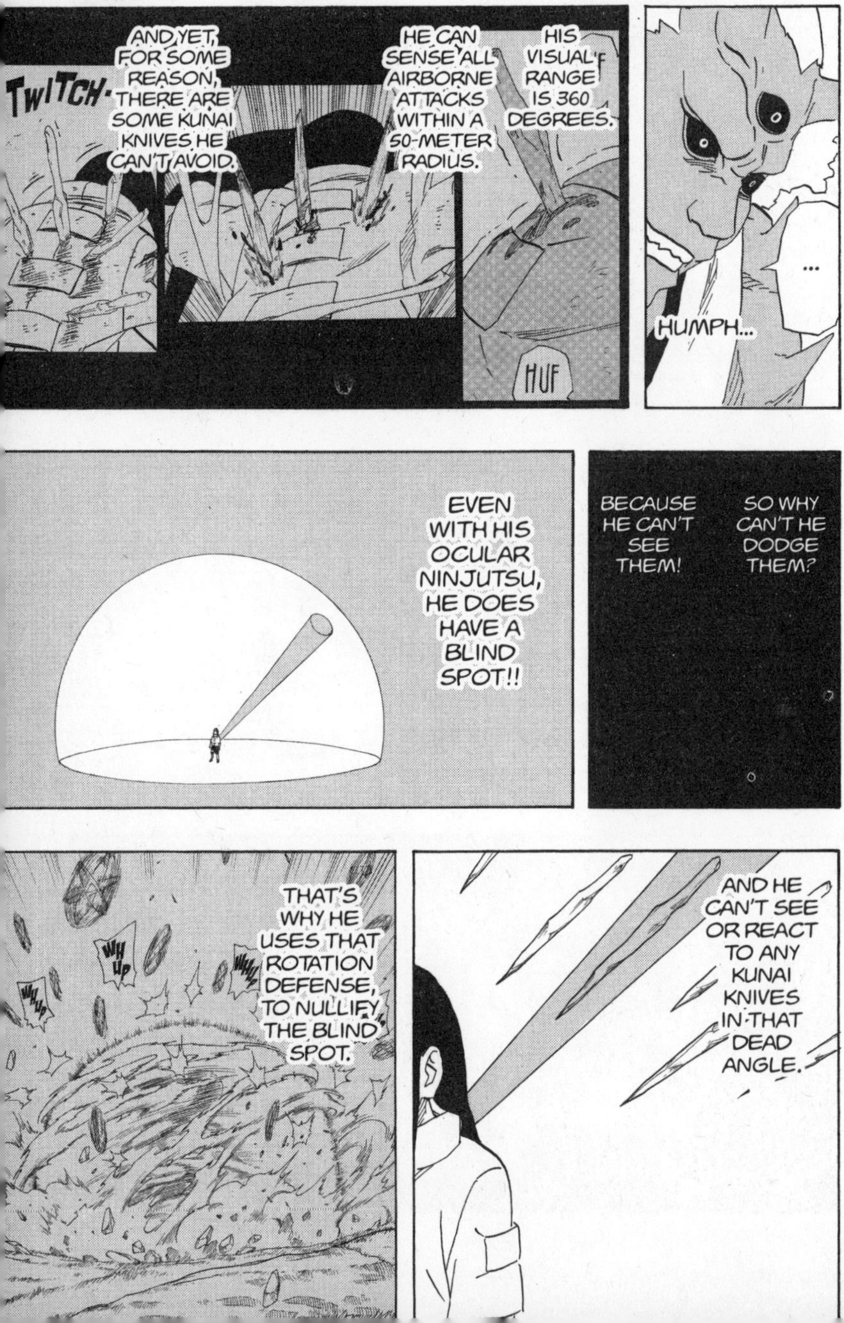
...
HUMPH...
HIS VISUAL RANGE IS 360 DEGREES.
HUF
HE CAN SENSE ALL AIRBORNE ATTACKS WITHIN A 50-METER RADIUS.
AND YET, FOR SOME REASON, THERE ARE SOME KUNAI KNIVES HE CAN'T AVOID.
TWITCH
SO WHY CAN'T HE DODGE THEM?
BECAUSE HE CAN'T SEE THEM!
EVEN WITH HIS OCULAR NINJUTSU, HE DOES HAVE A BLIND SPOT!!
AND HE CAN'T SEE OR REACT TO ANY KUNAI KNIVES IN THAT DEAD ANGLE.
THAT'S WHY HE USES THAT ROTATION DEFENSE, TO NULLIFY THE BLIND SPOT.

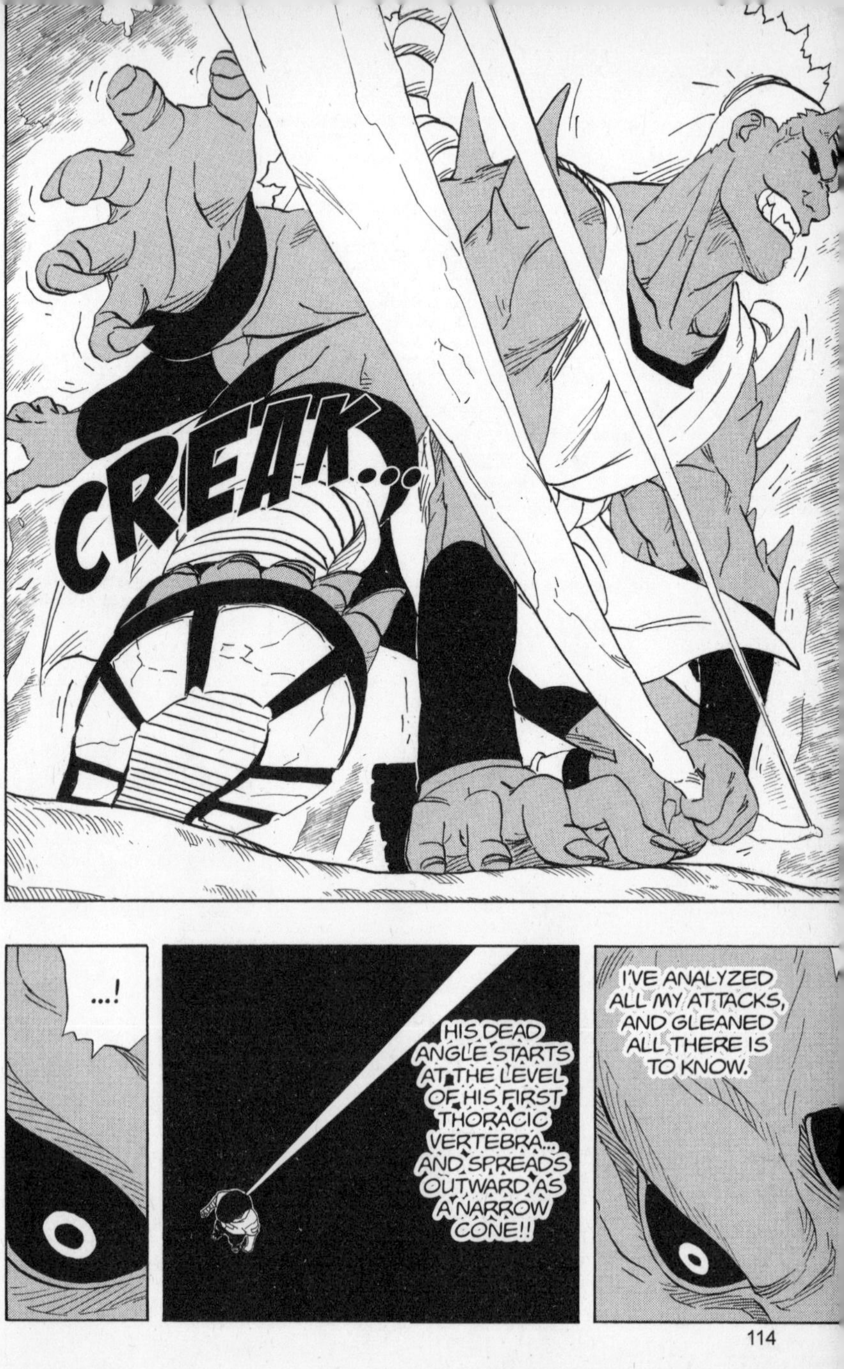
CREAK...
I'VE ANALYZED ALL MY ATTACKS, AND GLEANED ALL THERE IS TO KNOW.
HIS DEAD ANGLE STARTS AT THE LEVEL OF HIS FIRST THORACIC VERTEBRA... AND SPREADS OUTWARD AS A NARROW CONE!!
...!

READ THIS WAY

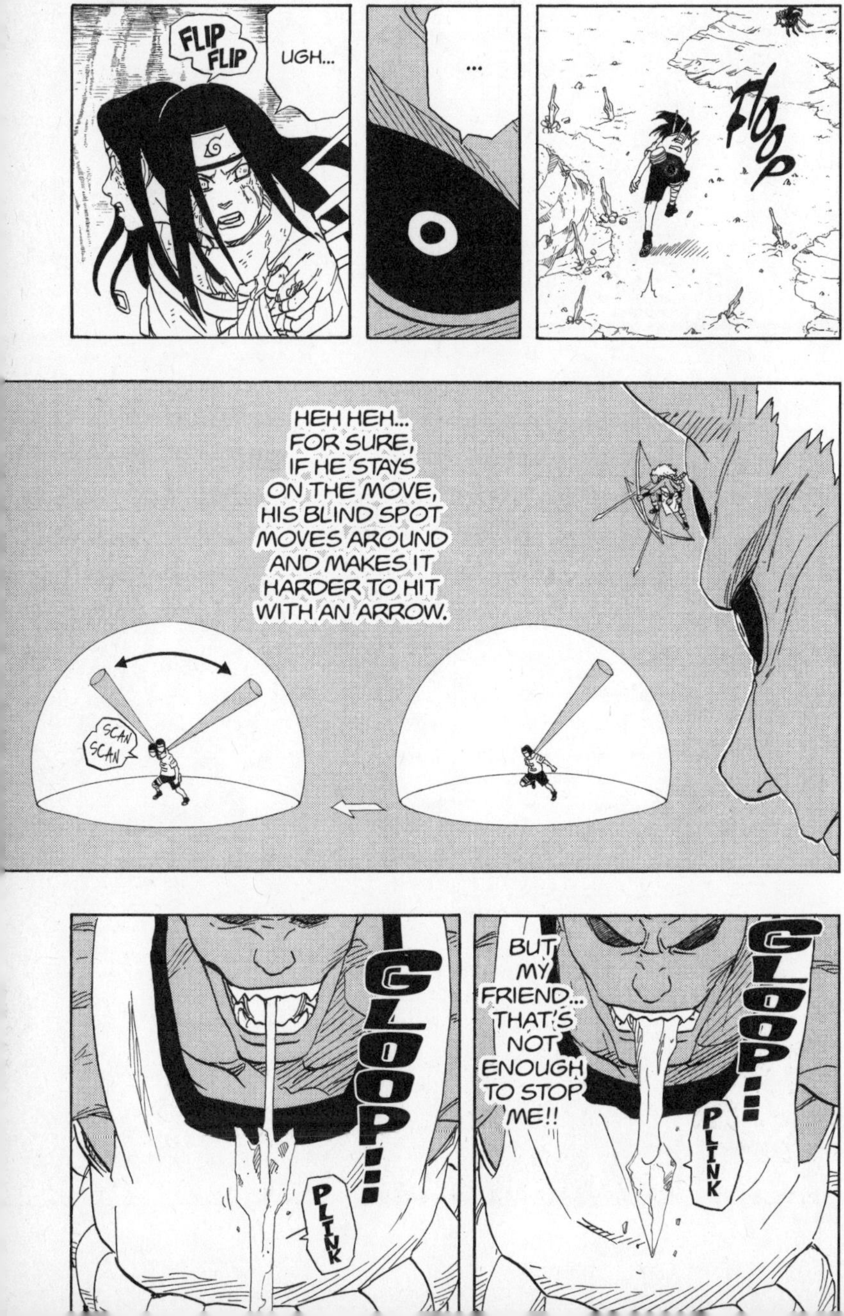
FLOOP
...
UGH...
FLIP FLIP
HEH HEH... FOR SURE, IF HE STAYS ON THE MOVE, HIS BLIND SPOT MOVES AROUND AND MAKES IT HARDER TO HIT WITH AN ARROW.
SCAN SCAN
GLOOP!!
BUT MY FRIEND... THAT'S NOT ENOUGH TO STOP ME!!
PLINK
GLOOP!!!
PLINK

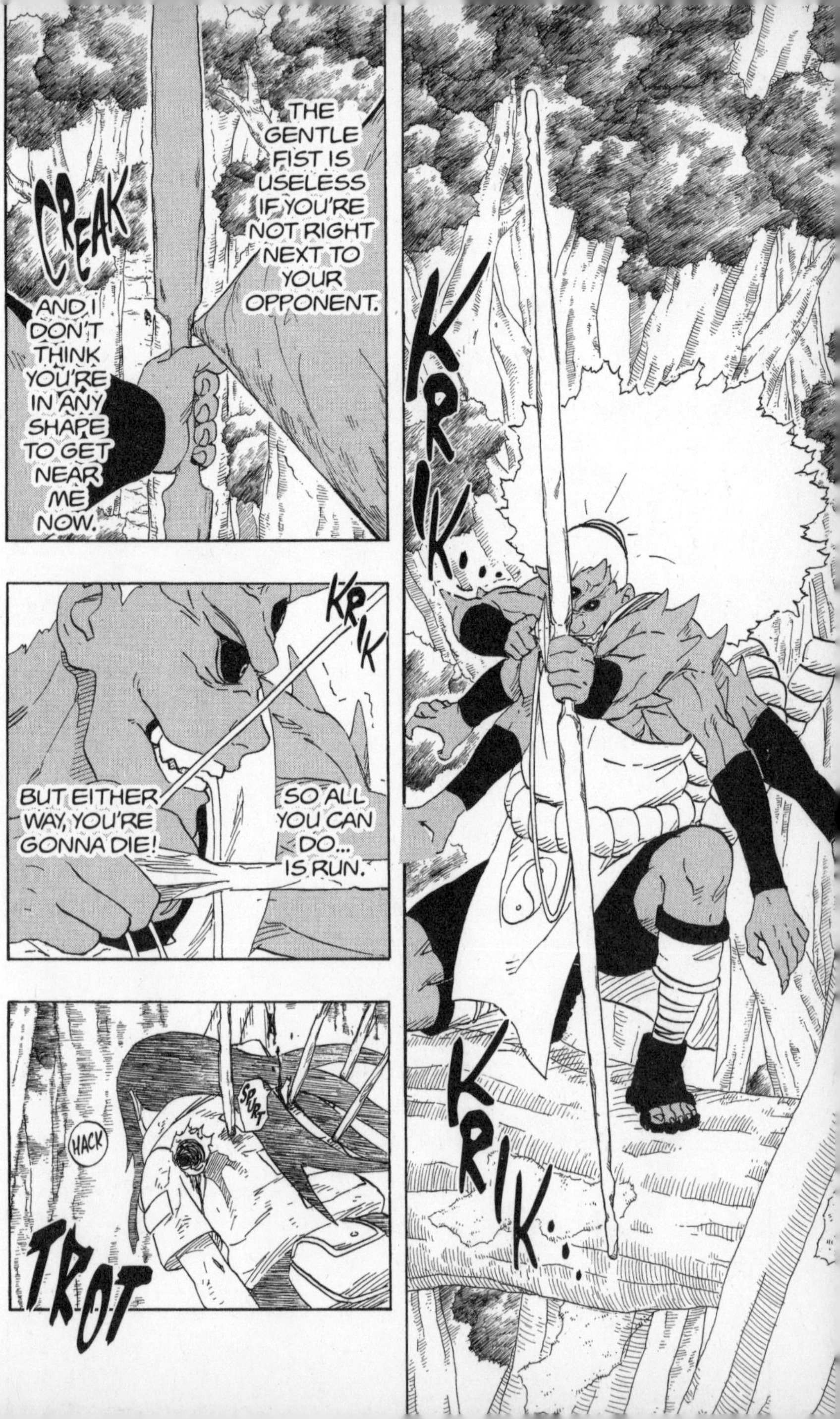
KRIK...
KRIK...
THE GENTLE FIST IS USELESS IF YOU'RE NOT RIGHT NEXT TO YOUR OPPONENT.
CREAK
AND I DON'T THINK YOU'RE IN ANY SHAPE TO GET NEAR ME NOW.
KRIK
SO ALL YOU CAN DO... IS RUN.
BUT EITHER WAY, YOU'RE GONNA DIE!
SPURT
HACK
TROT

READ THIS WAY

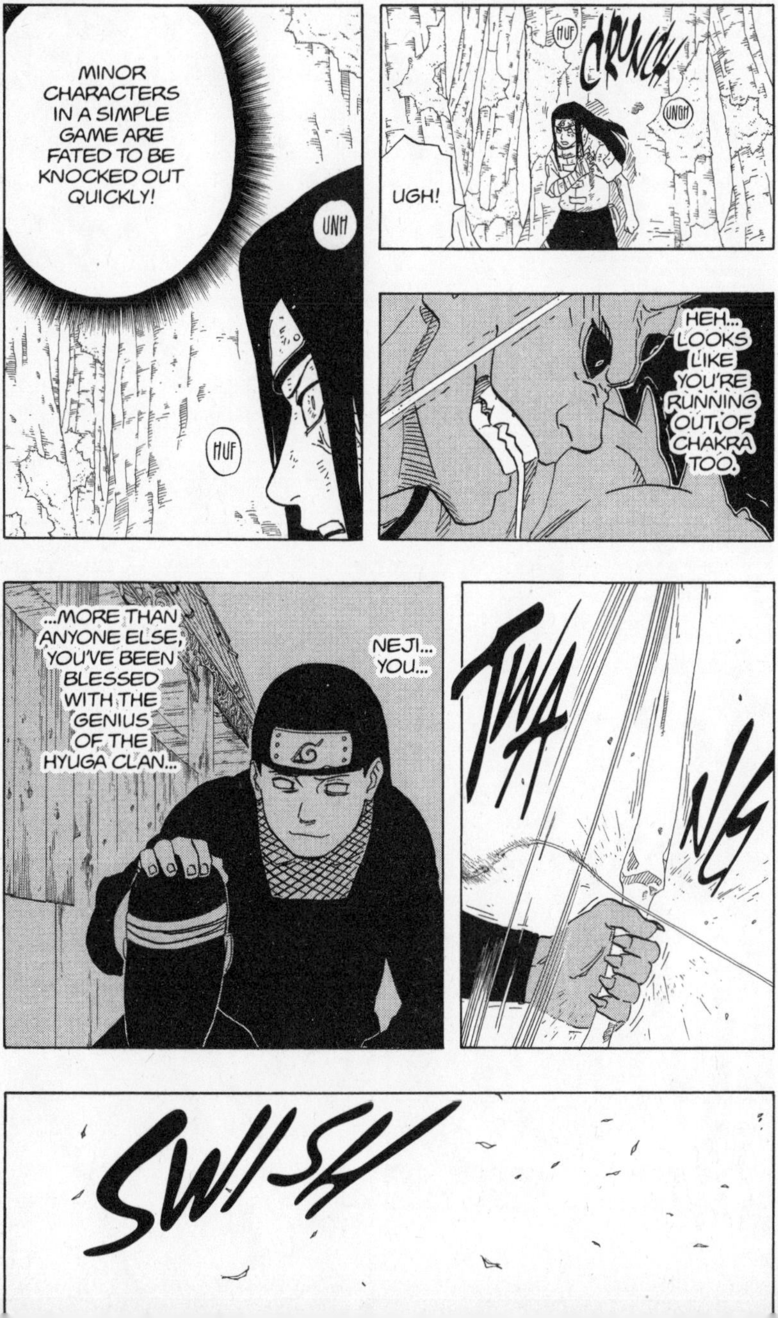
HUF
CRUNCH
UNGH
UGH!
HEH... LOOKS LIKE YOU'RE RUNNING OUT OF CHAKRA TOO.
MINOR CHARACTERS IN A SIMPLE GAME ARE FATED TO BE KNOCKED OUT QUICKLY!
UNH
HUF
TWANG
NEJI... YOU...
...MORE THAN ANYONE ELSE, YOU'VE BEEN BLESSED WITH THE GENIUS OF THE HYUGA CLAN...
SWISH

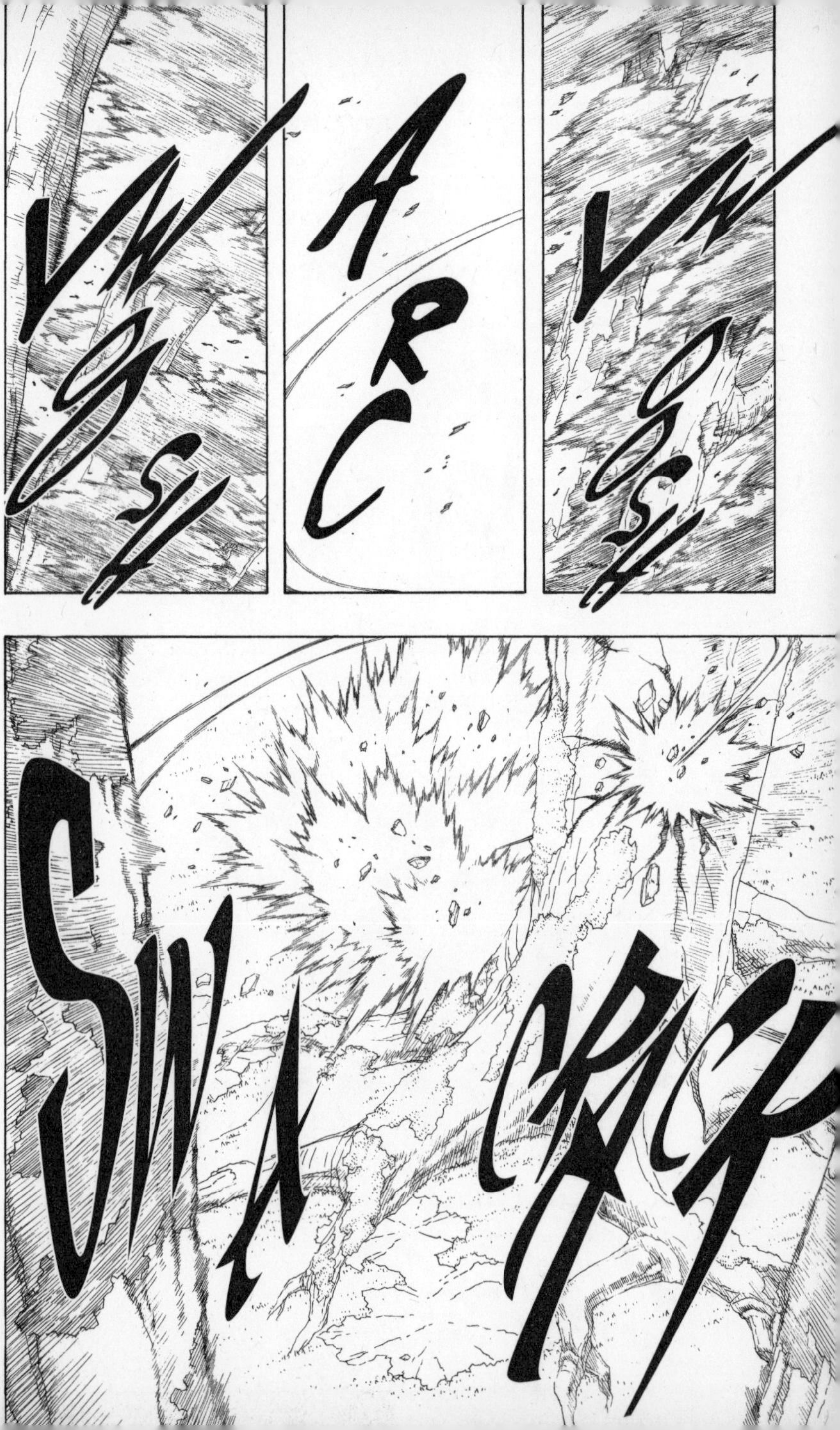
VWOOSH
ARC
VWOOSH
CRACK
SWAA

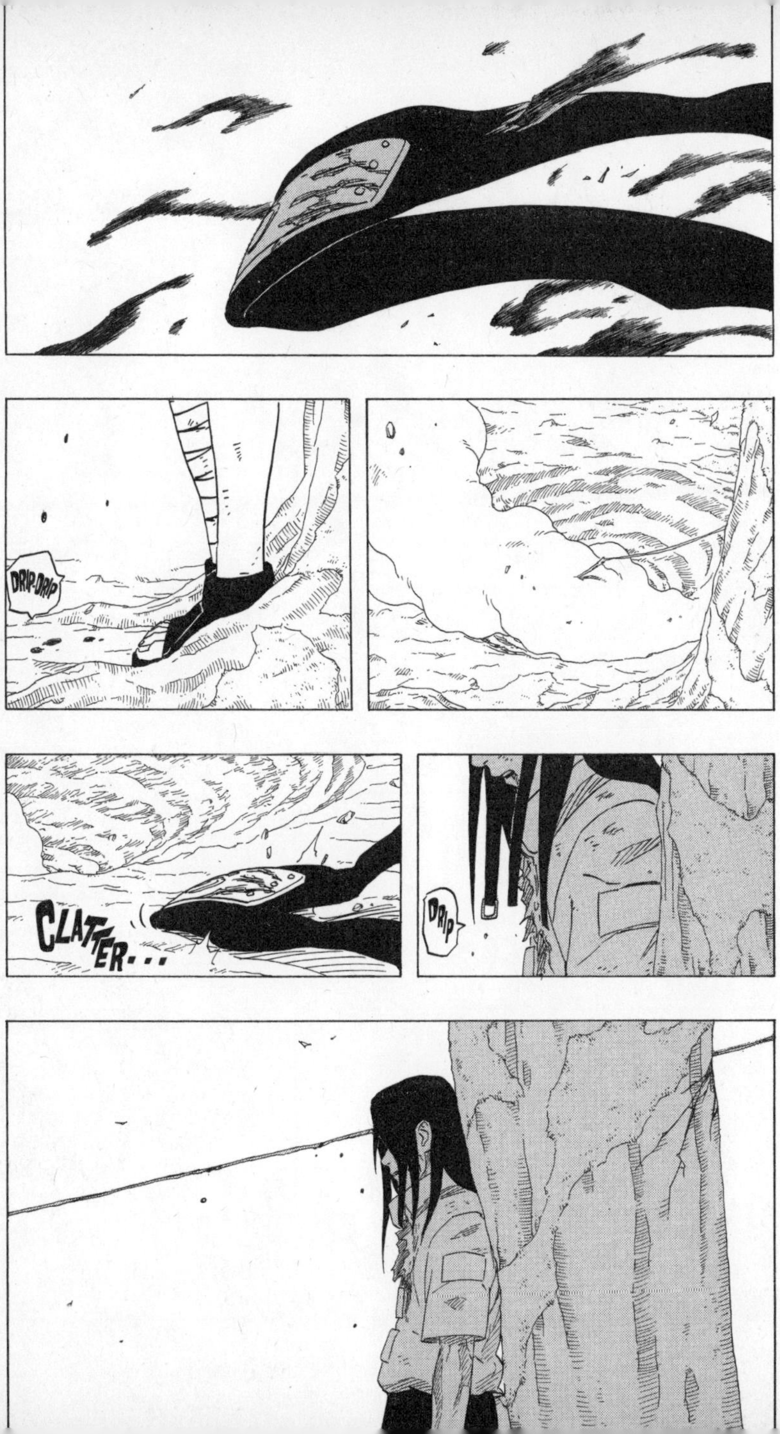
DRIP-DRIP
DRIP
CLATTER...

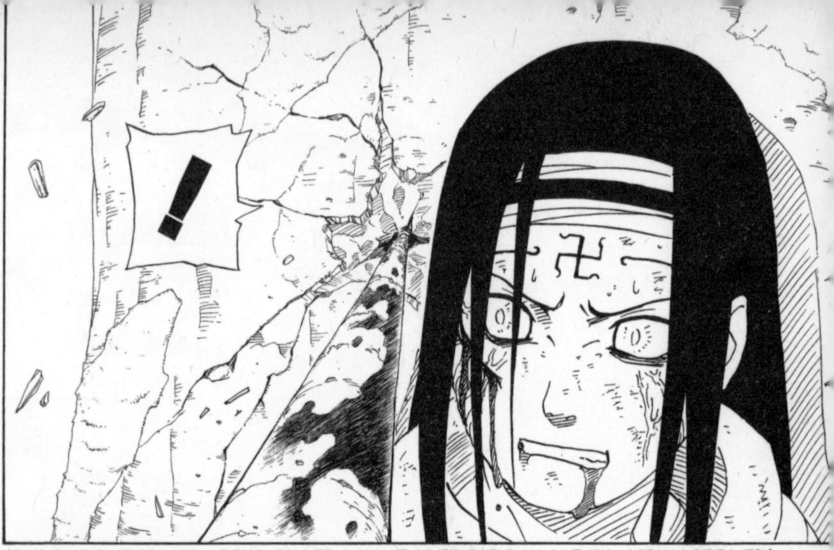
!

(THE SYMBOL PICTURED ABOVE, CALLED A MANJI, IS TRADITIONAL IN BUDDHIST IMAGERY -ED.)

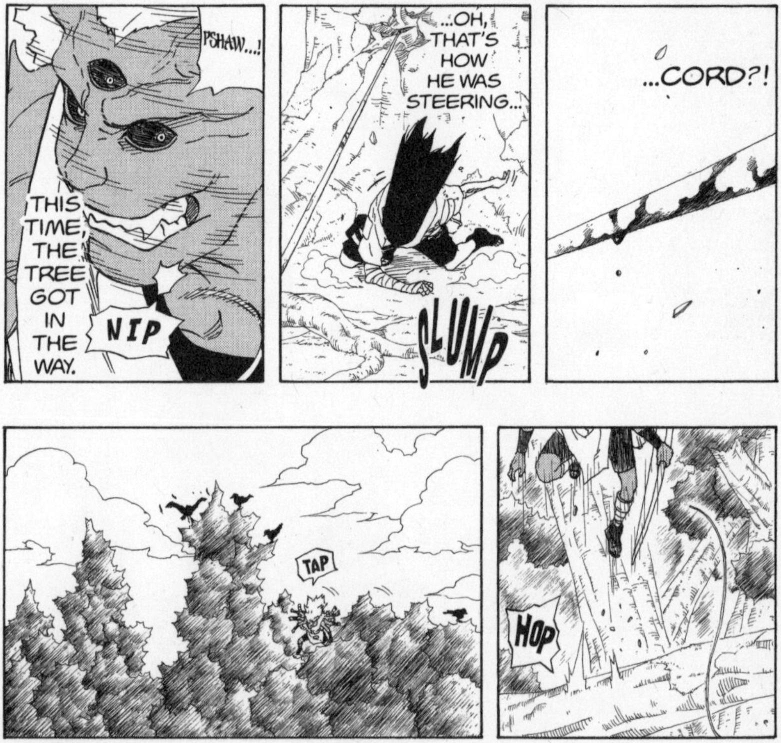
...CORD?!
...OH, THAT'S HOW HE WAS STEERING...
SLUMP
PSHAW...!
THIS TIME, THE TREE GOT IN THE WAY.
NIP
HOP
TAP

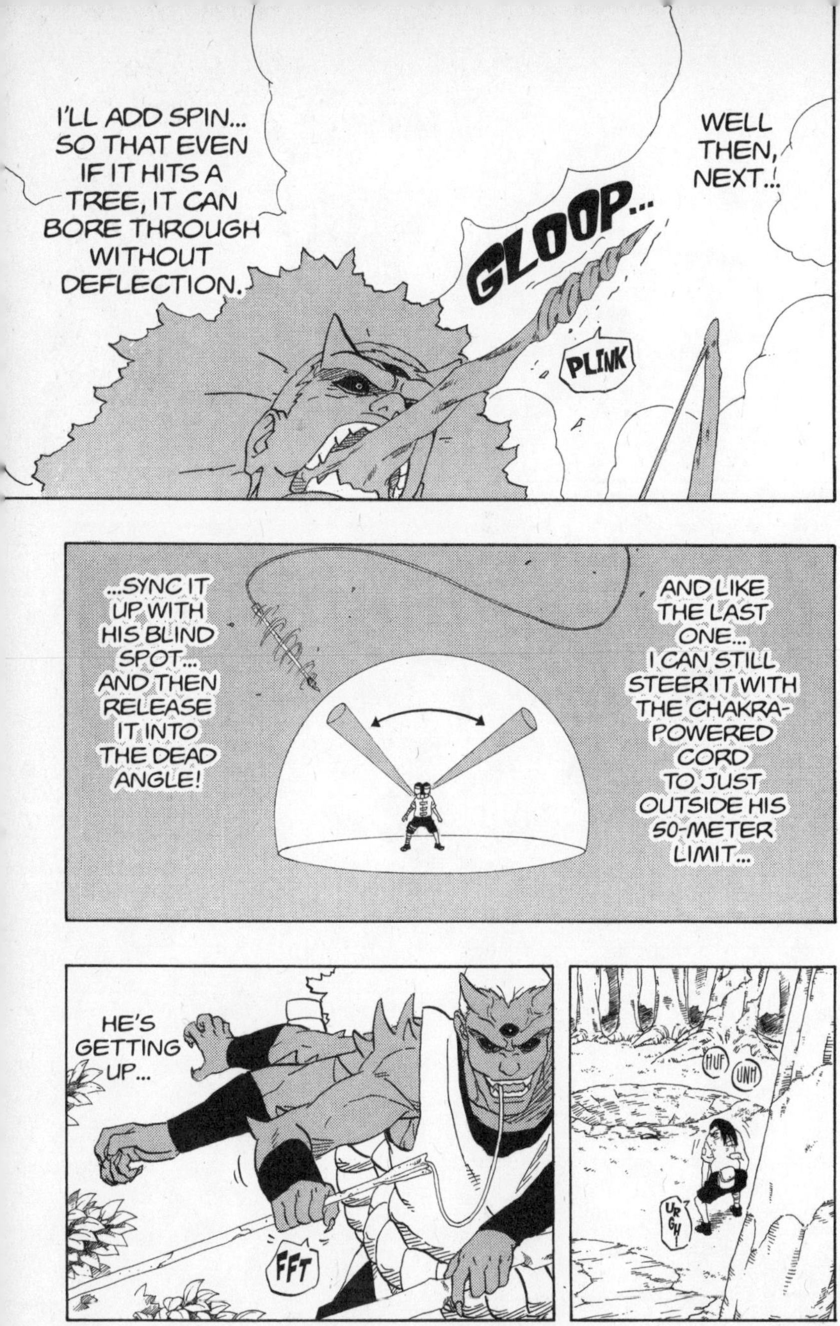
WELL THEN, NEXT...!
I'LL ADD SPIN... SO THAT EVEN IF IT HITS A TREE, IT CAN BORE THROUGH WITHOUT DEFLECTION.
GLOOP...
PLINK
AND LIKE THE LAST ONE... I CAN STILL STEER IT WITH THE CHAKRA-POWERED CORD TO JUST OUTSIDE HIS 50-METER LIMIT...
...SYNC IT UP WITH HIS BLIND SPOT... AND THEN RELEASE IT INTO THE DEAD ANGLE!
HUF
UNH
URGH!
HE'S GETTING UP...
FFT

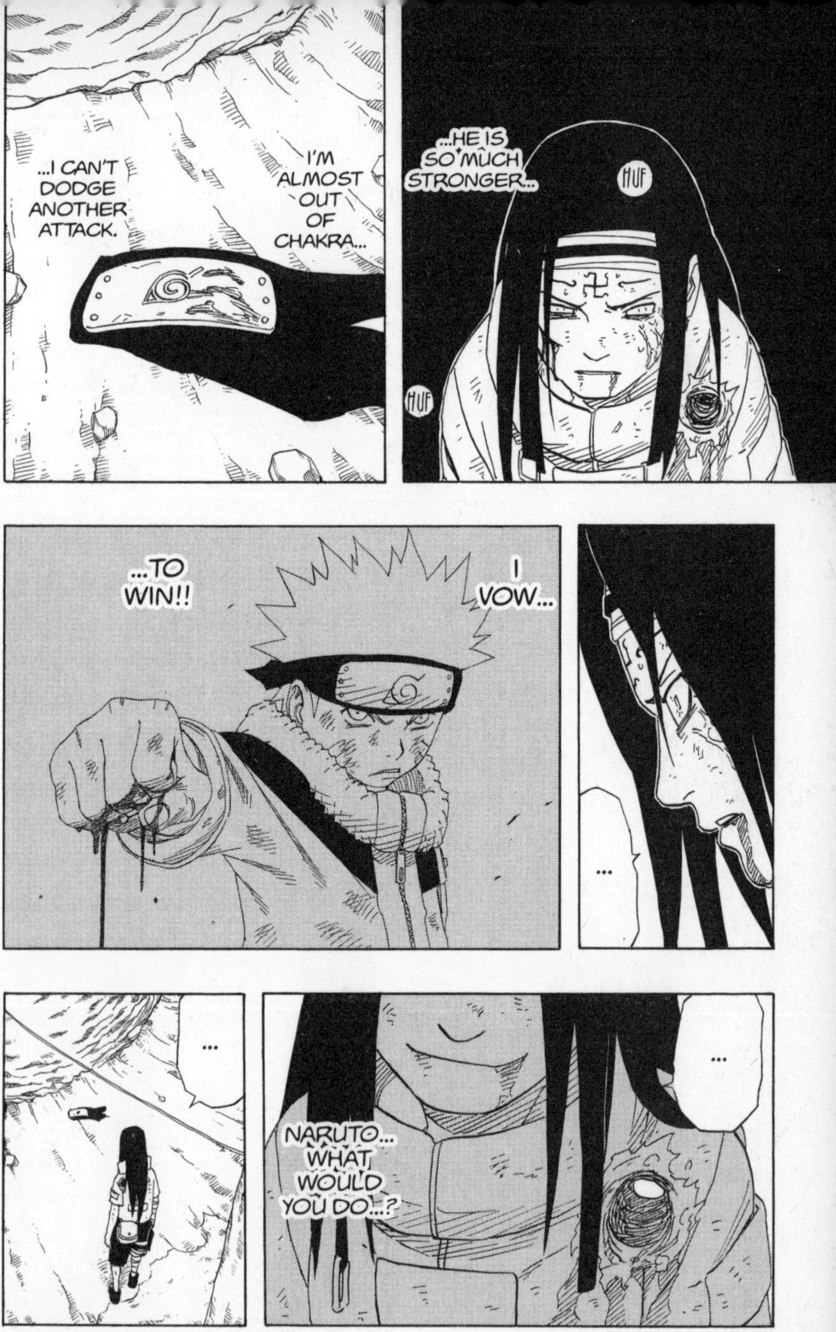
...HE IS SO MUCH STRONGER...
HUF
HUF
I'M ALMOST OUT OF CHAKRA...
...I CAN'T DODGE ANOTHER ATTACK.
...
I VOW...
...TO WIN!!
...
NARUTO... WHAT WOULD YOU DO...?
...

READ THIS WAY

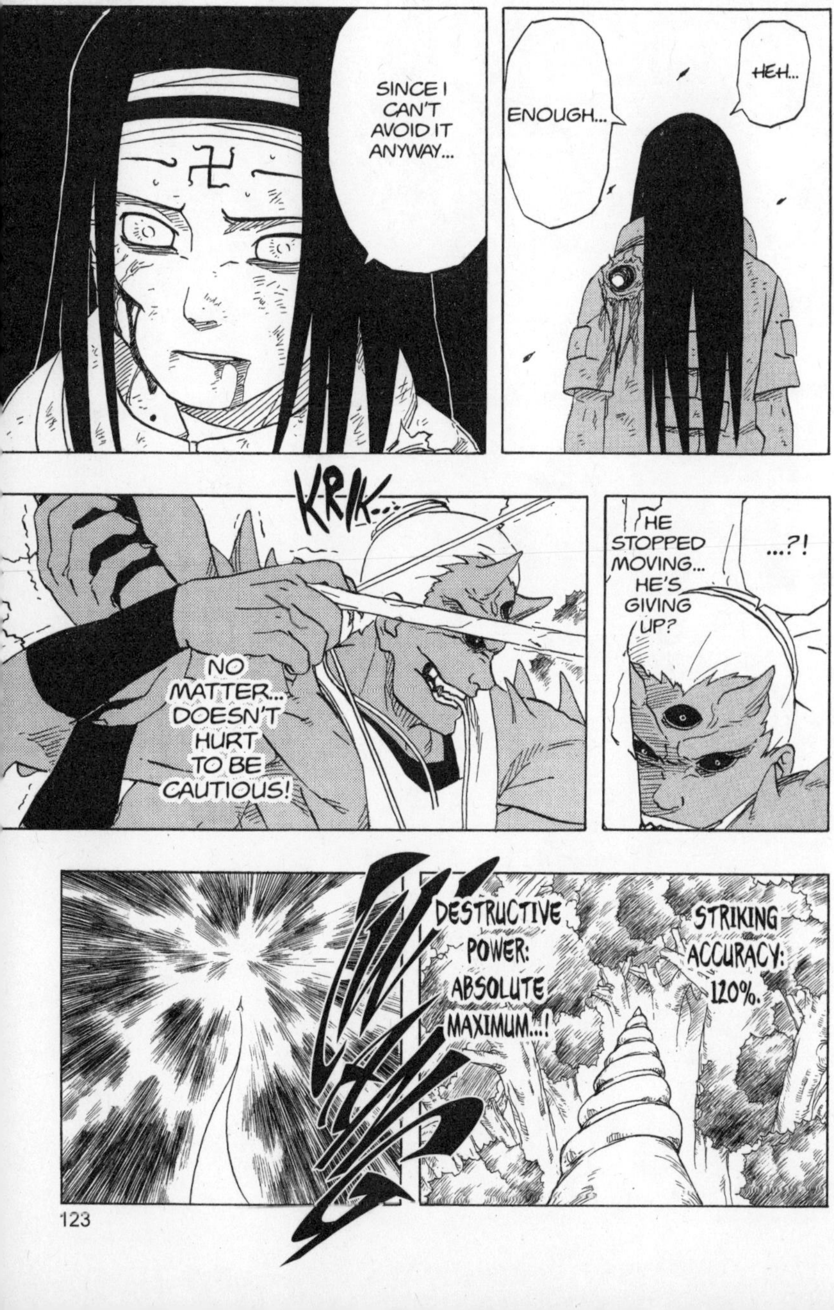
HEH...
ENOUGH...
SINCE I CAN'T AVOID IT ANYWAY...
...?!
HE STOPPED MOVING... HE'S GIVING UP?
KRIK...
NO MATTER... DOESN'T HURT TO BE CAUTIOUS!
STRIKING ACCURACY: 120%.
DESTRUCTIVE POWER: ABSOLUTE MAXIMUM...!

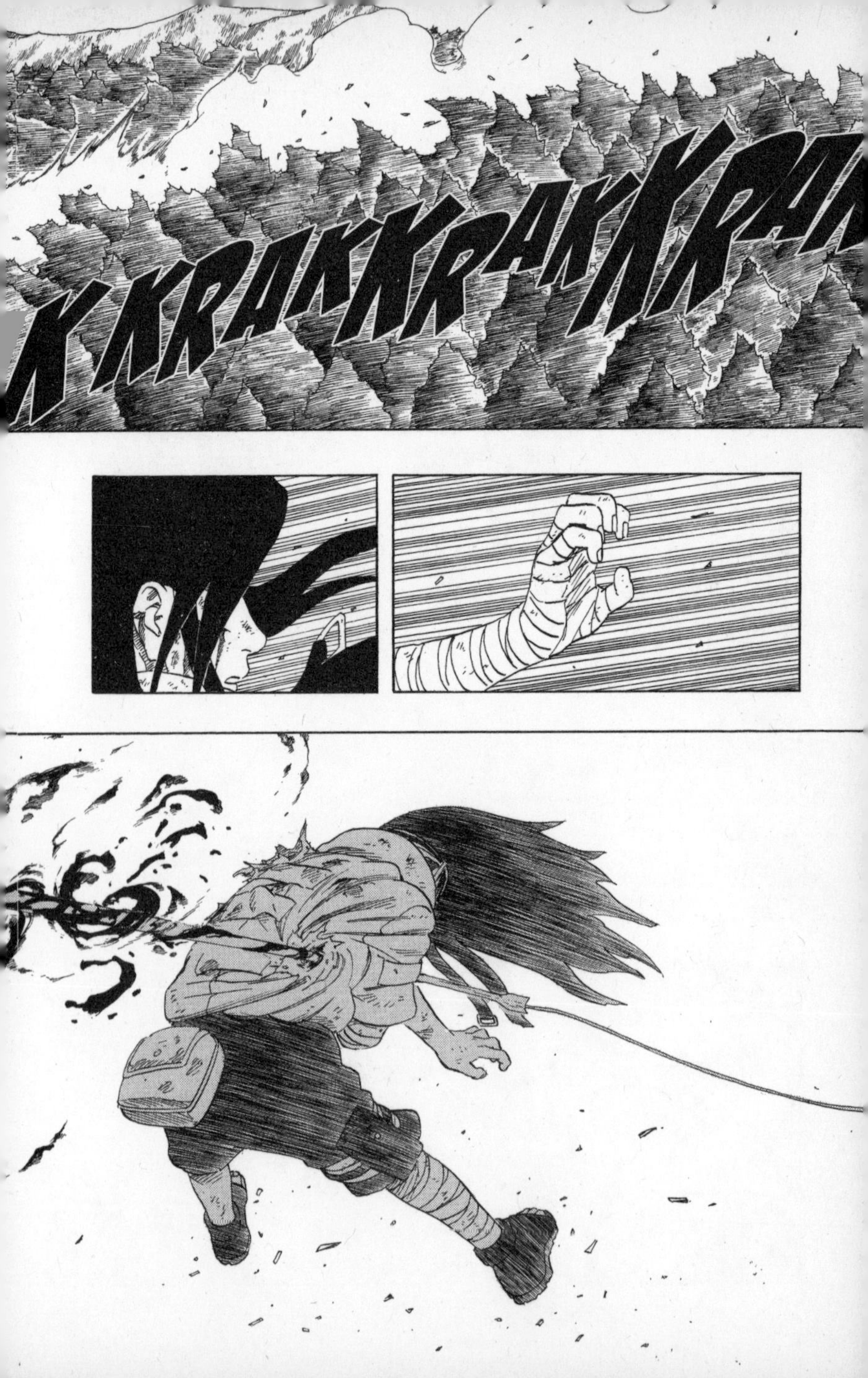
K KRAKKRAKKRAKKRA

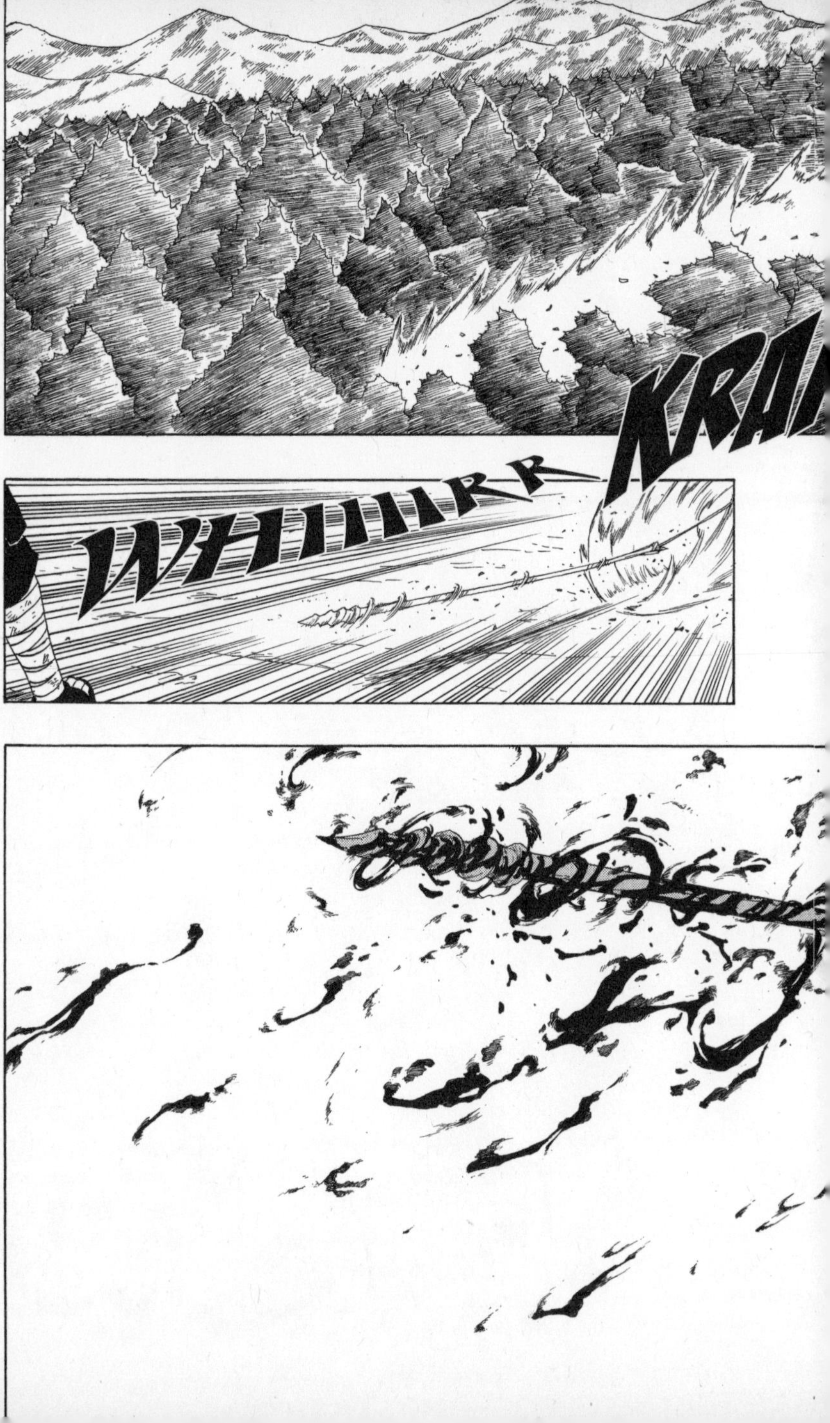
KRA
WHIIIIIRR

NARUTO™

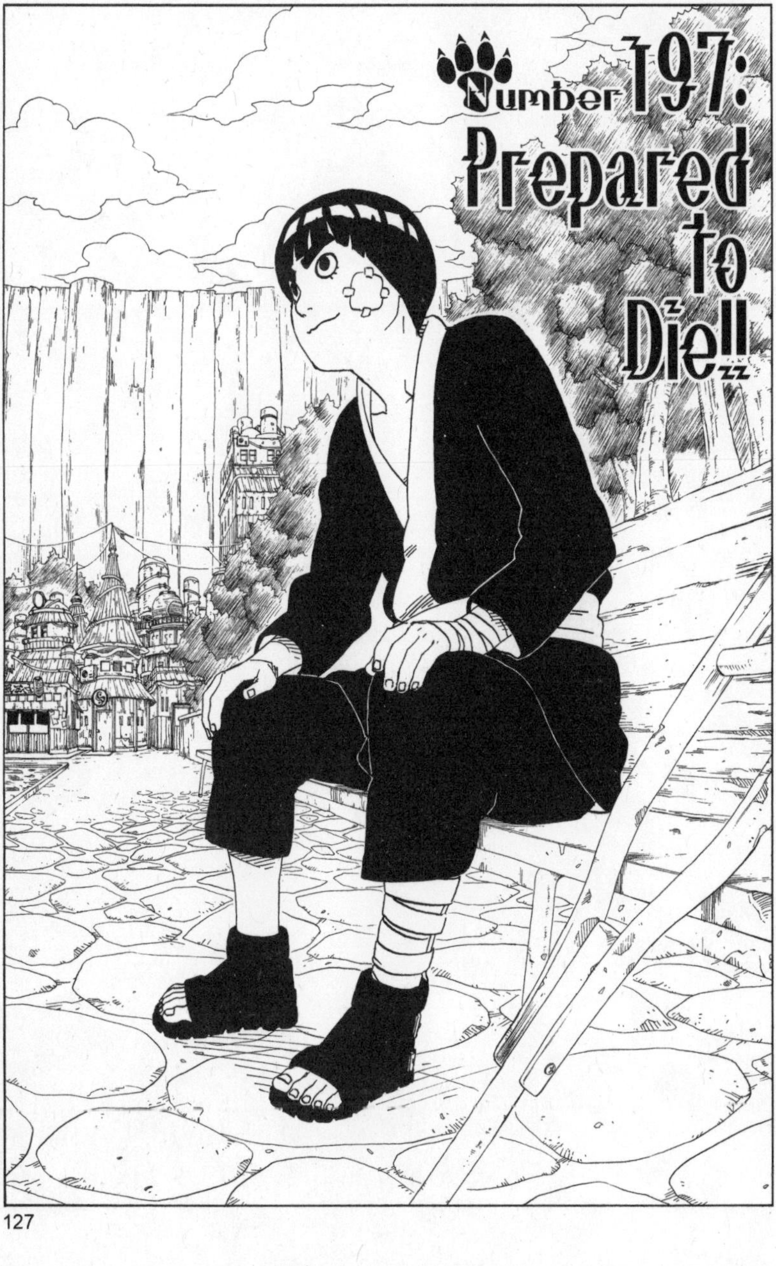
Number 197: Prepared to Die!!

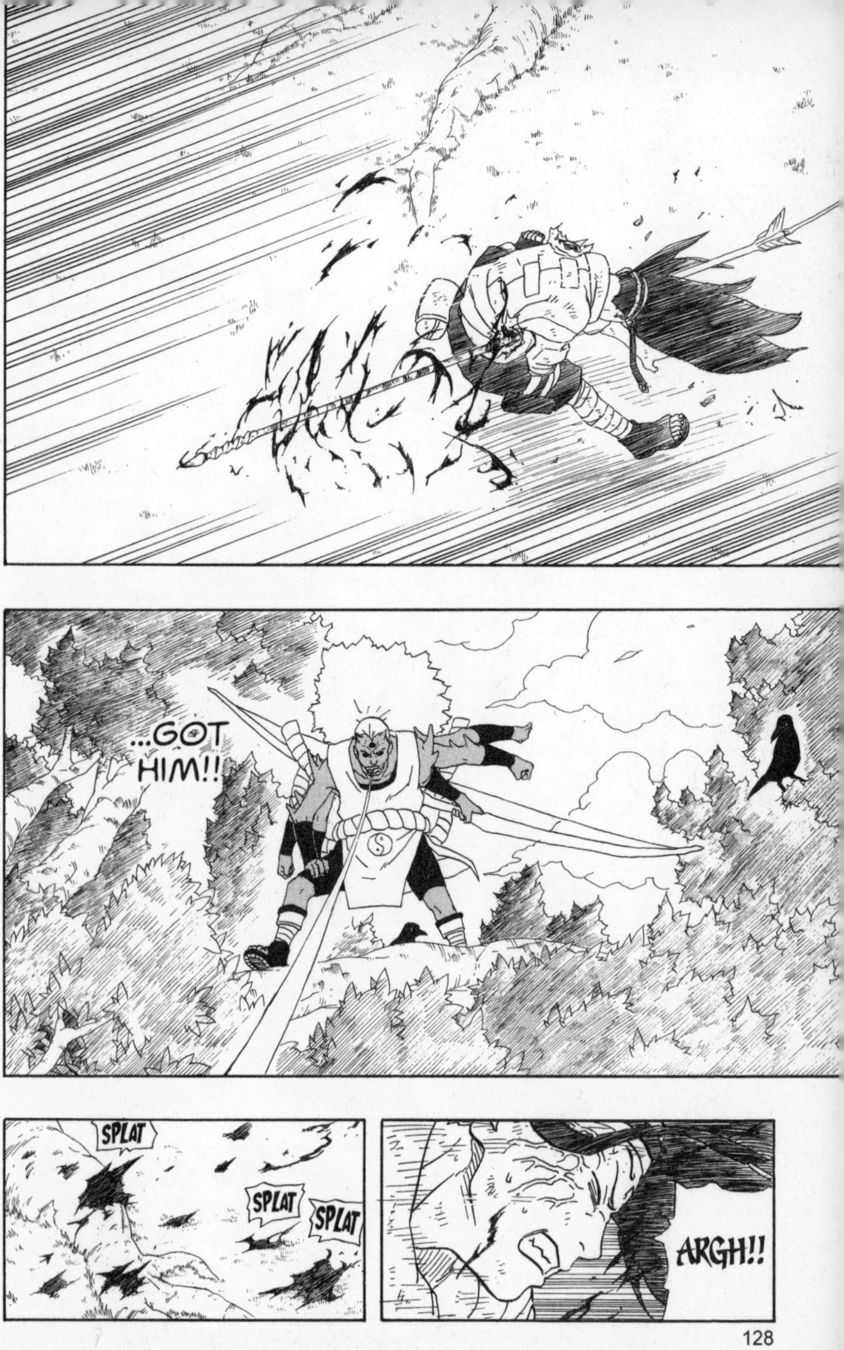
...GOT HIM!!
ARGH!!
SPLAT
SPLAT
SPLAT

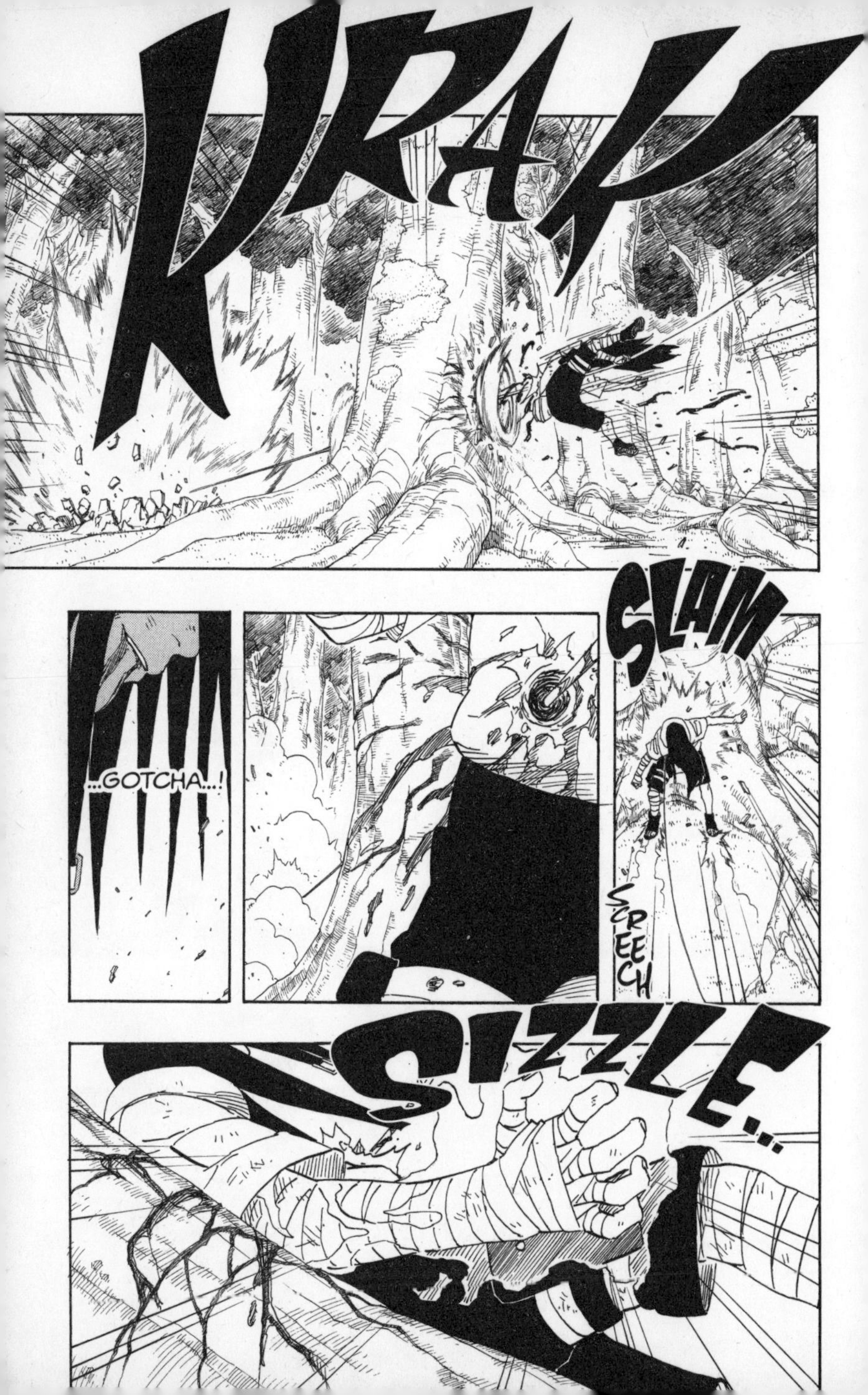
KRAK
SLAM
SCREECH
...GOTCHA...!
SIZZLE...

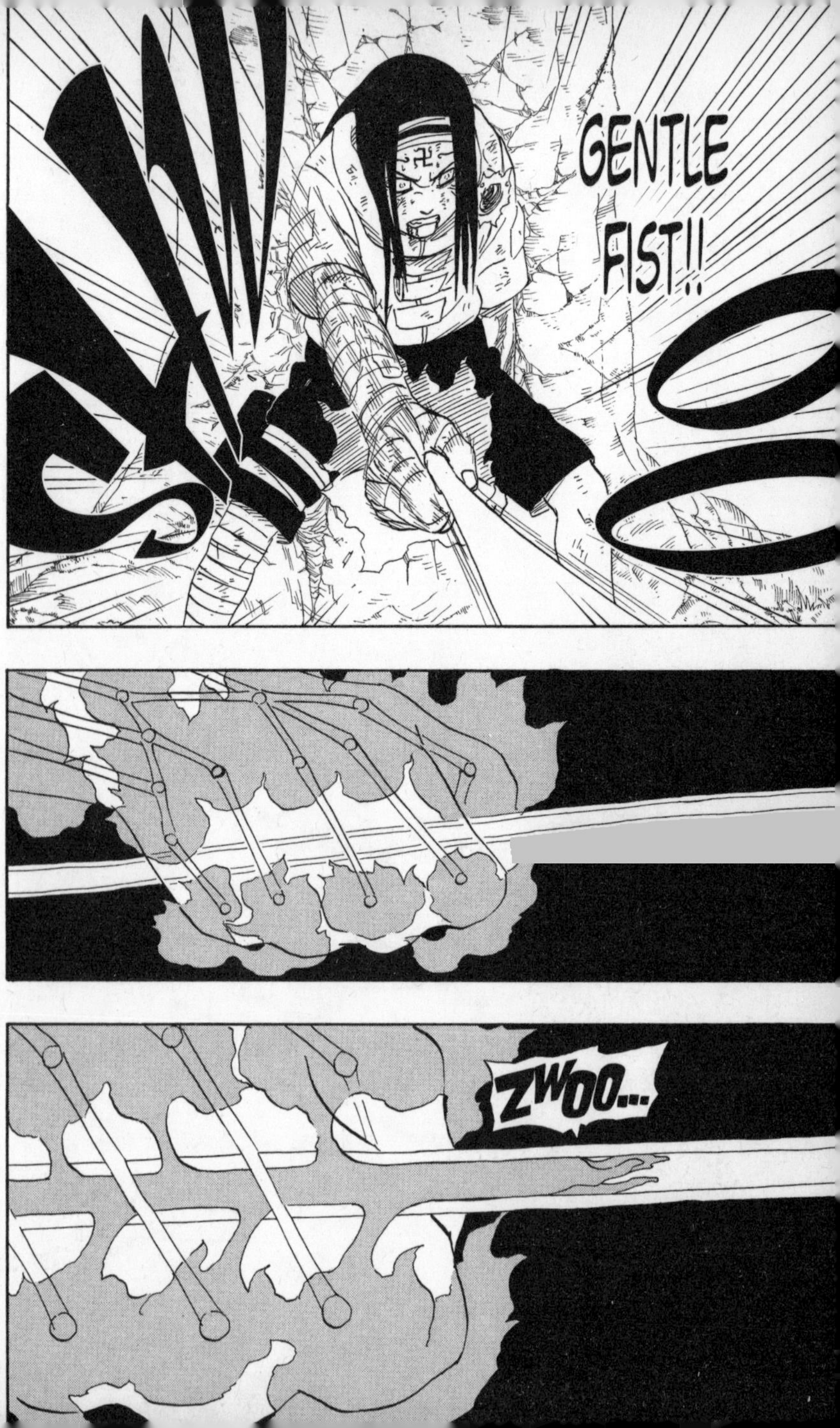
GENTLE FIST!!
ZWOO...

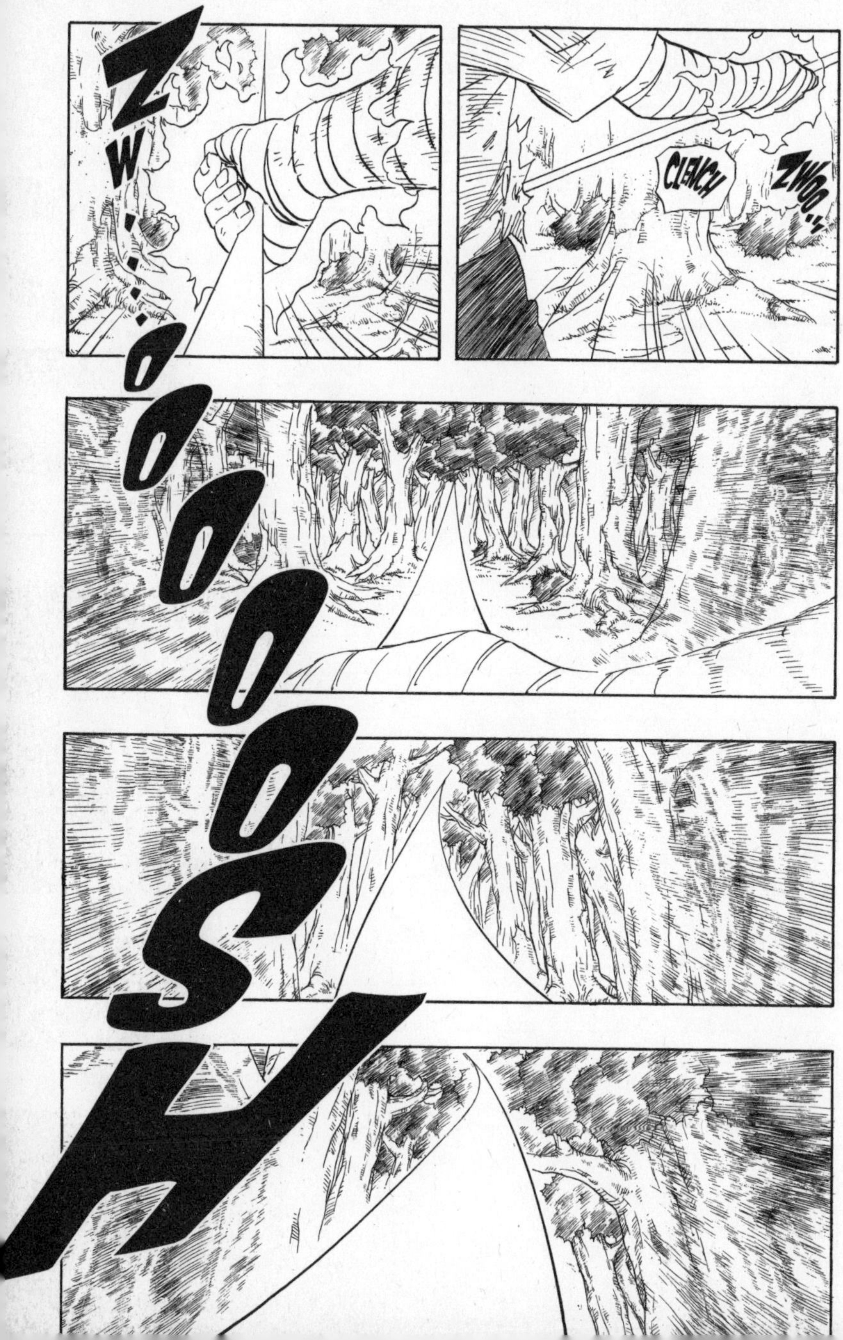
CLENCH
ZWOO...
ZW....OOOOOOOSH

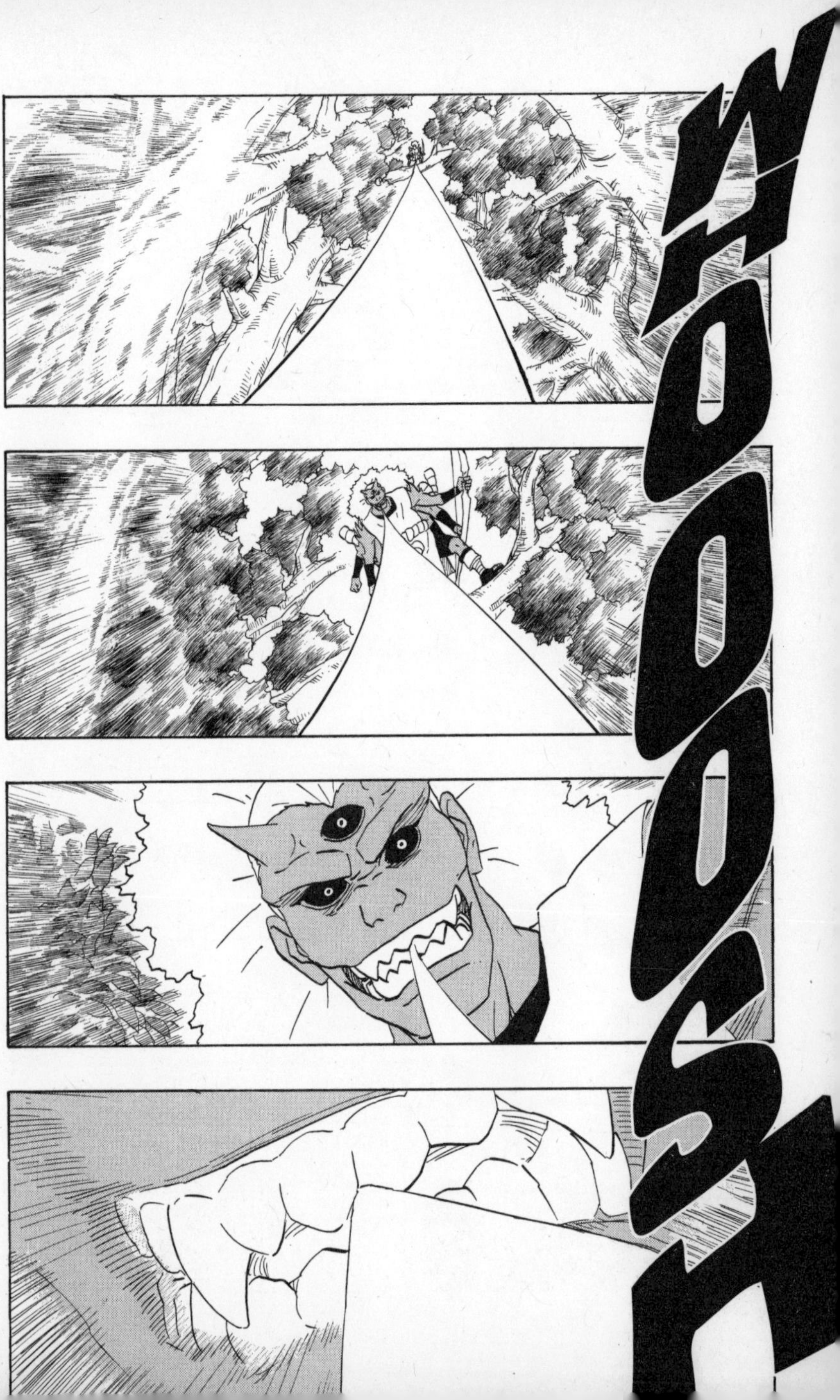
WHOOOSH

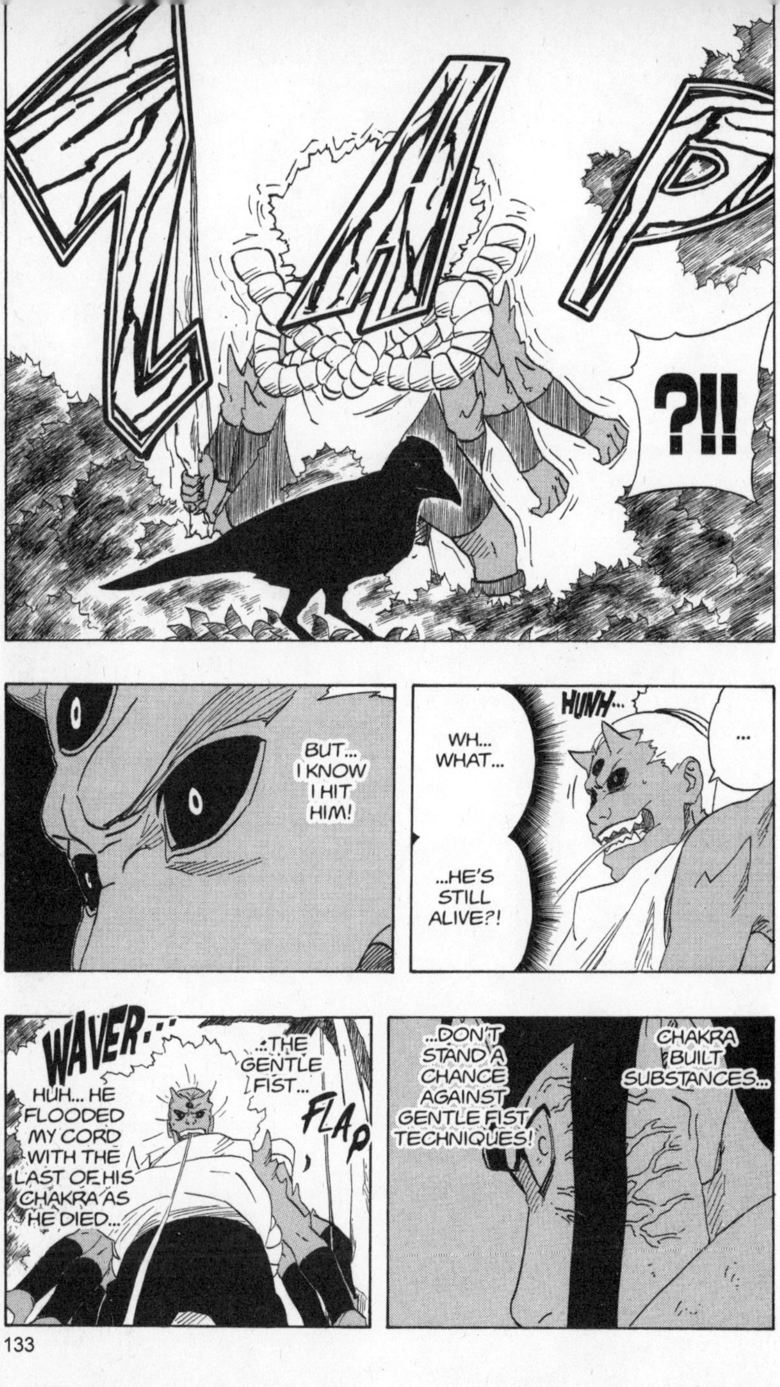
ZAP
?!!
HUNH...
...
WH... WHAT...
...HE'S STILL ALIVE?!
BUT... I KNOW I HIT HIM!
CHAKRA BUILT SUBSTANCES...
...DON'T STAND A CHANCE AGAINST GENTLE FIST TECHNIQUES!
...THE GENTLE FIST...
FLAP
WAVER...
HUH... HE FLOODED MY CORD WITH THE LAST OF HIS CHAKRA AS HE DIED...

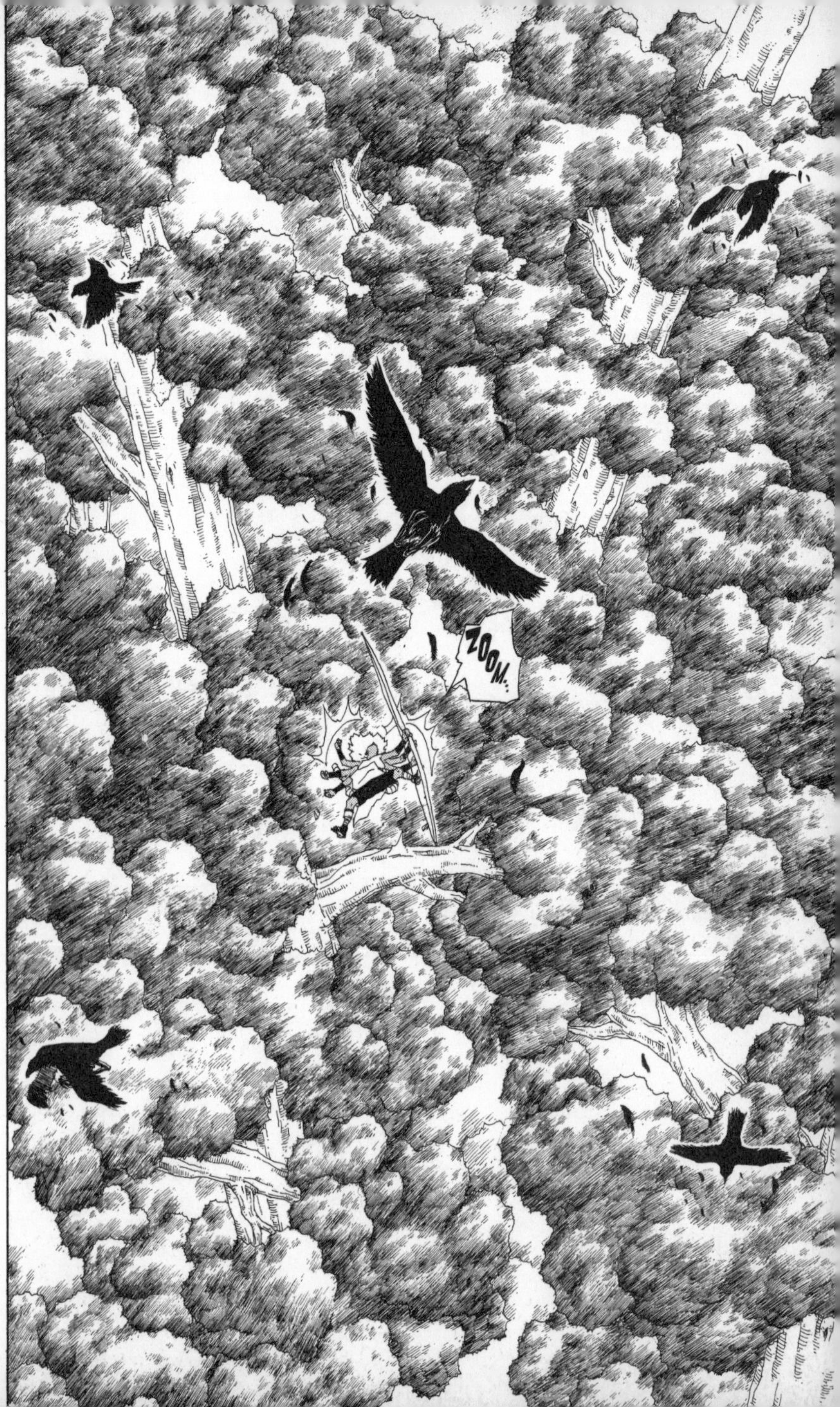
ZOOM...

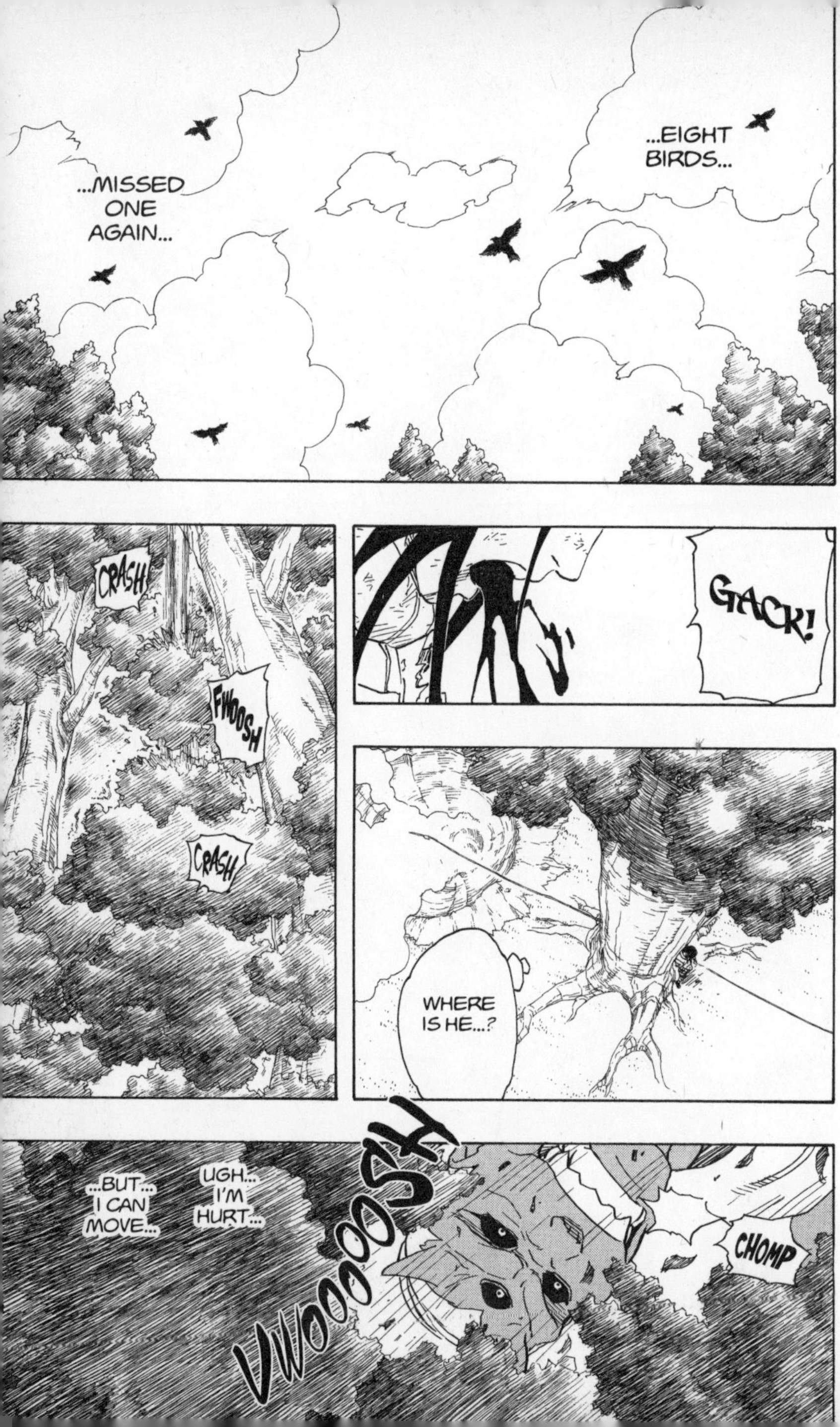
...EIGHT BIRDS...
...MISSED ONE AGAIN...
GACK!
WHERE IS HE...?
CRASH!
FWOOSH
CRASH
CHOMP
VWOOOOOSH
UGH... I'M HURT...
...BUT... I CAN MOVE...

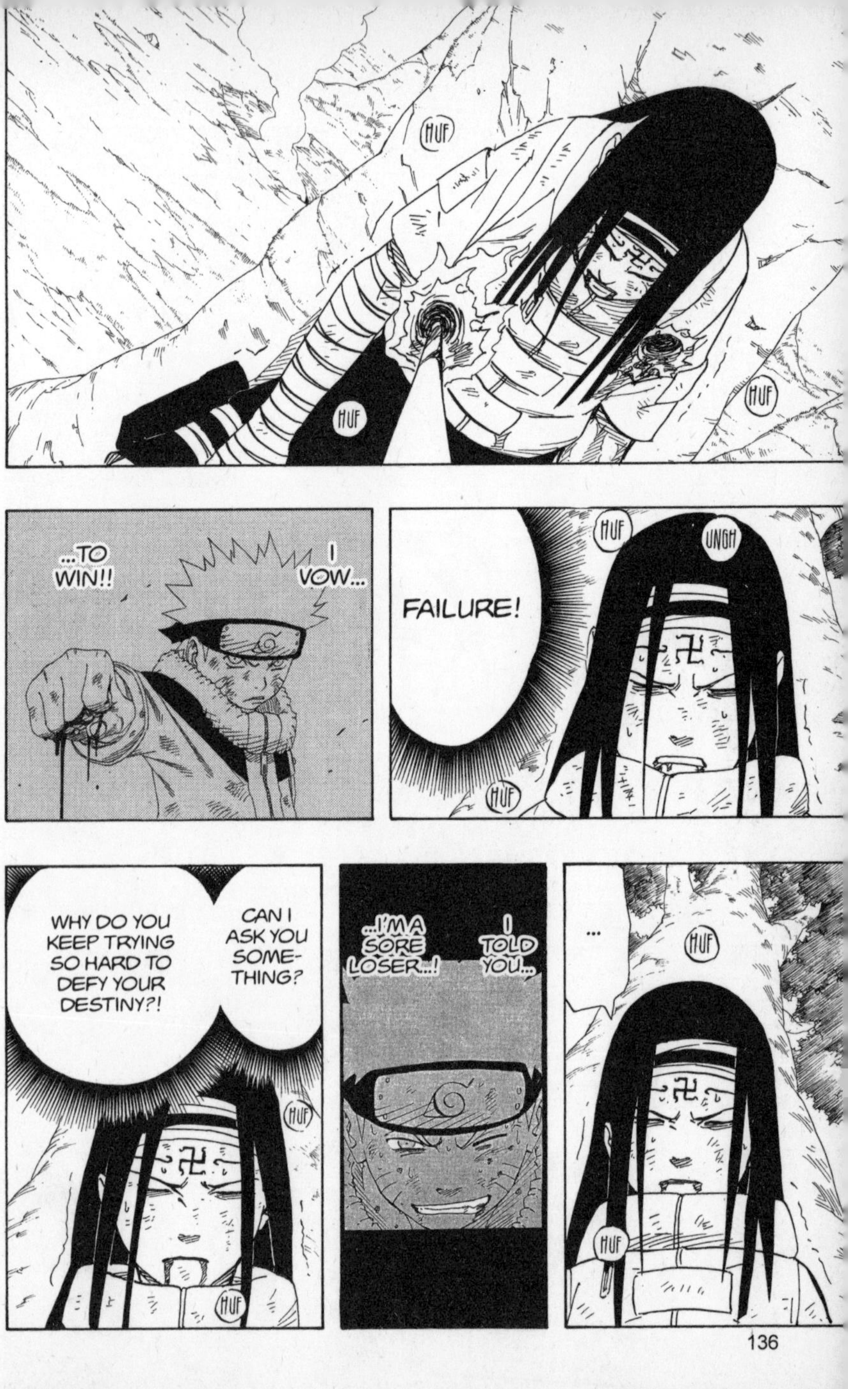
HUF
HUF
HUF
HUF
UNGH
FAILURE!
HUF
I VOW...
...TO WIN!!
...
HUF
HUF
I TOLD YOU...
...I'M A SORE LOSER...!
CAN I ASK YOU SOME-THING?
WHY DO YOU KEEP TRYING SO HARD TO DEFY YOUR DESTINY?!
HUF
HUF

READ THIS WAY

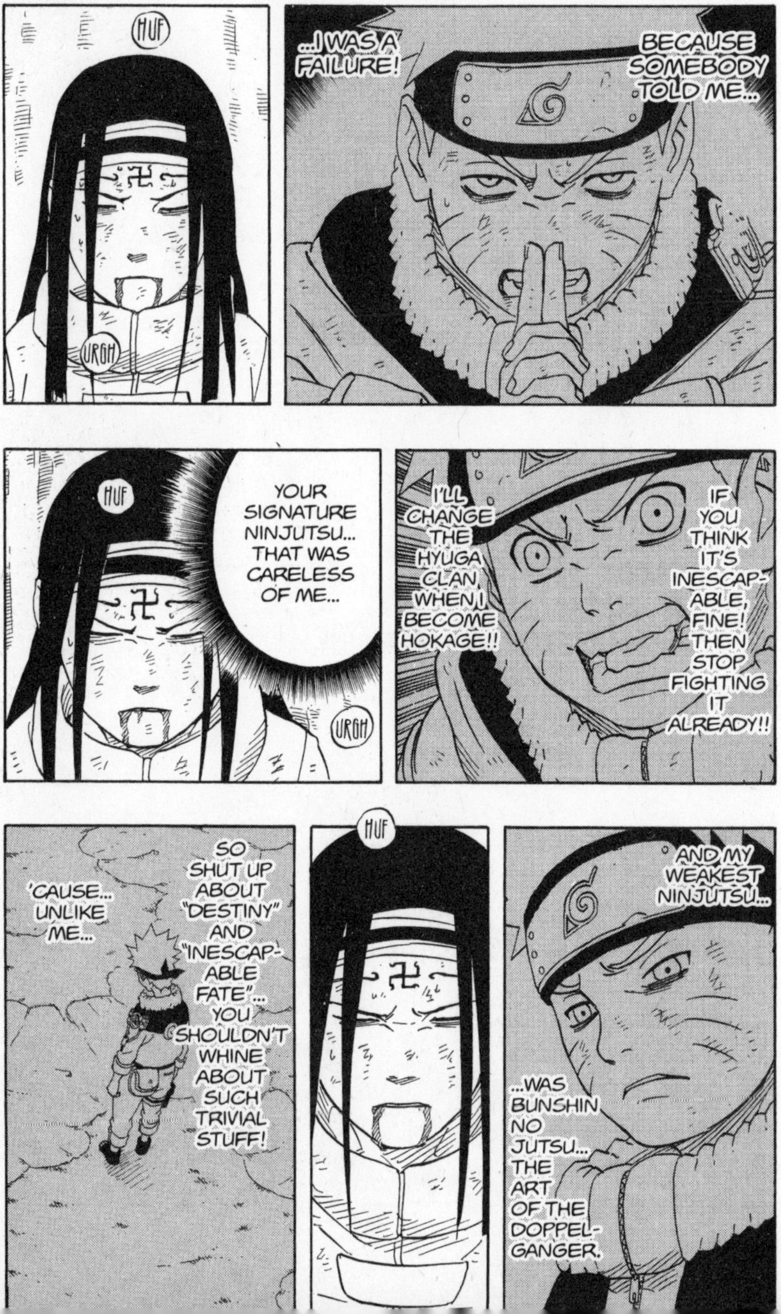
BECAUSE SOMEBODY TOLD ME...
...I WAS A FAILURE!
HUF
URGH
IF YOU THINK IT'S INESCAPABLE, FINE! THEN STOP FIGHTING IT ALREADY!!
I'LL CHANGE THE HYUGA CLAN WHEN I BECOME HOKAGE!!
HUF
YOUR SIGNATURE NINJUTSU... THAT WAS CARELESS OF ME...
URGH
AND MY WEAKEST NINJUTSU...
...WAS BUNSHIN NO JUTSU... THE ART OF THE DOPPELGANGER.
HUF
SO SHUT UP ABOUT "DESTINY" AND "INESCAPABLE FATE"... YOU SHOULDN'T WHINE ABOUT SUCH TRIVIAL STUFF!
'CAUSE... UNLIKE ME...

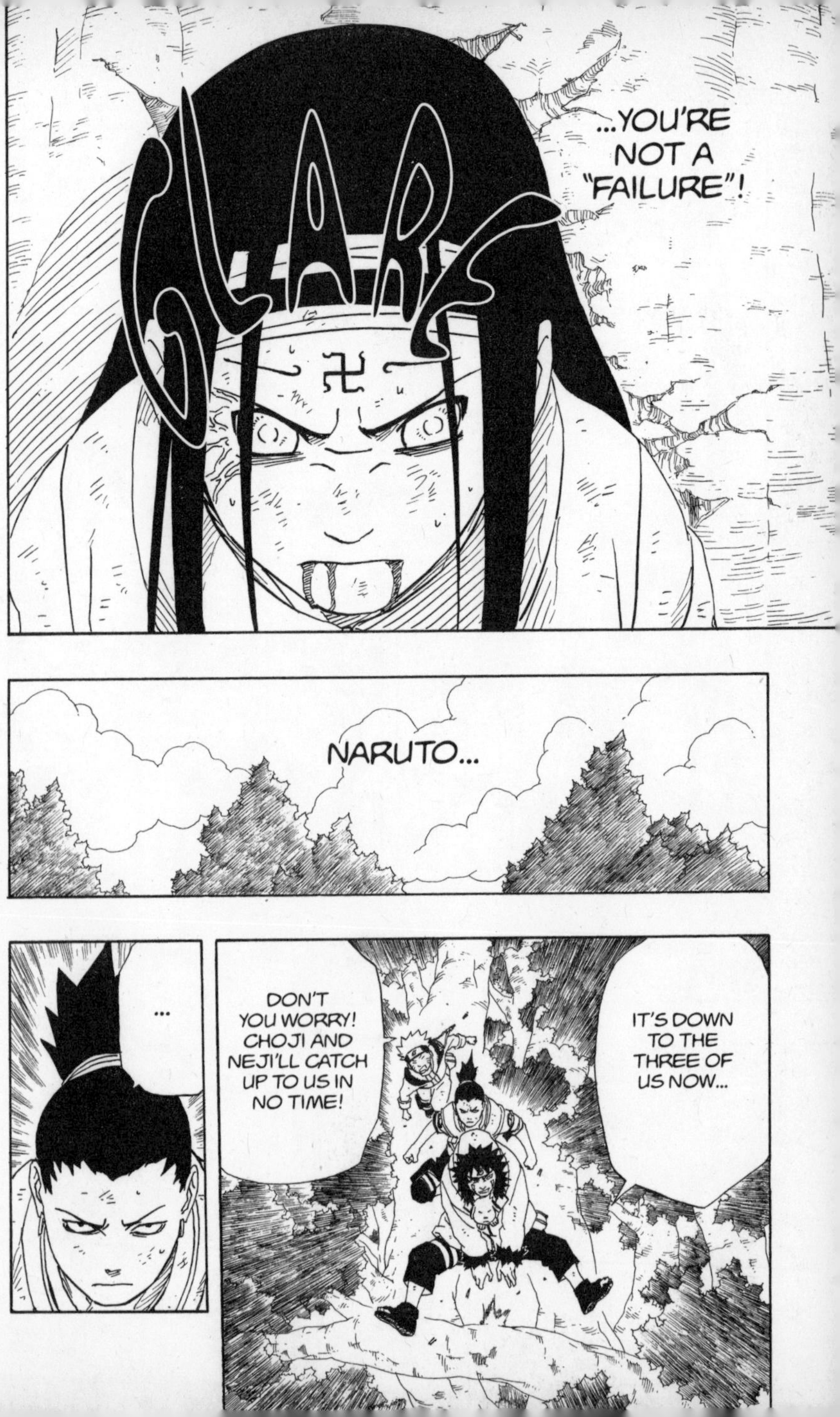
GLARE
...YOU'RE NOT A "FAILURE"!
NARUTO...
IT'S DOWN TO THE THREE OF US NOW...
DON'T YOU WORRY! CHOJI AND NEJI'LL CATCH UP TO US IN NO TIME!
...

READ THIS WAY

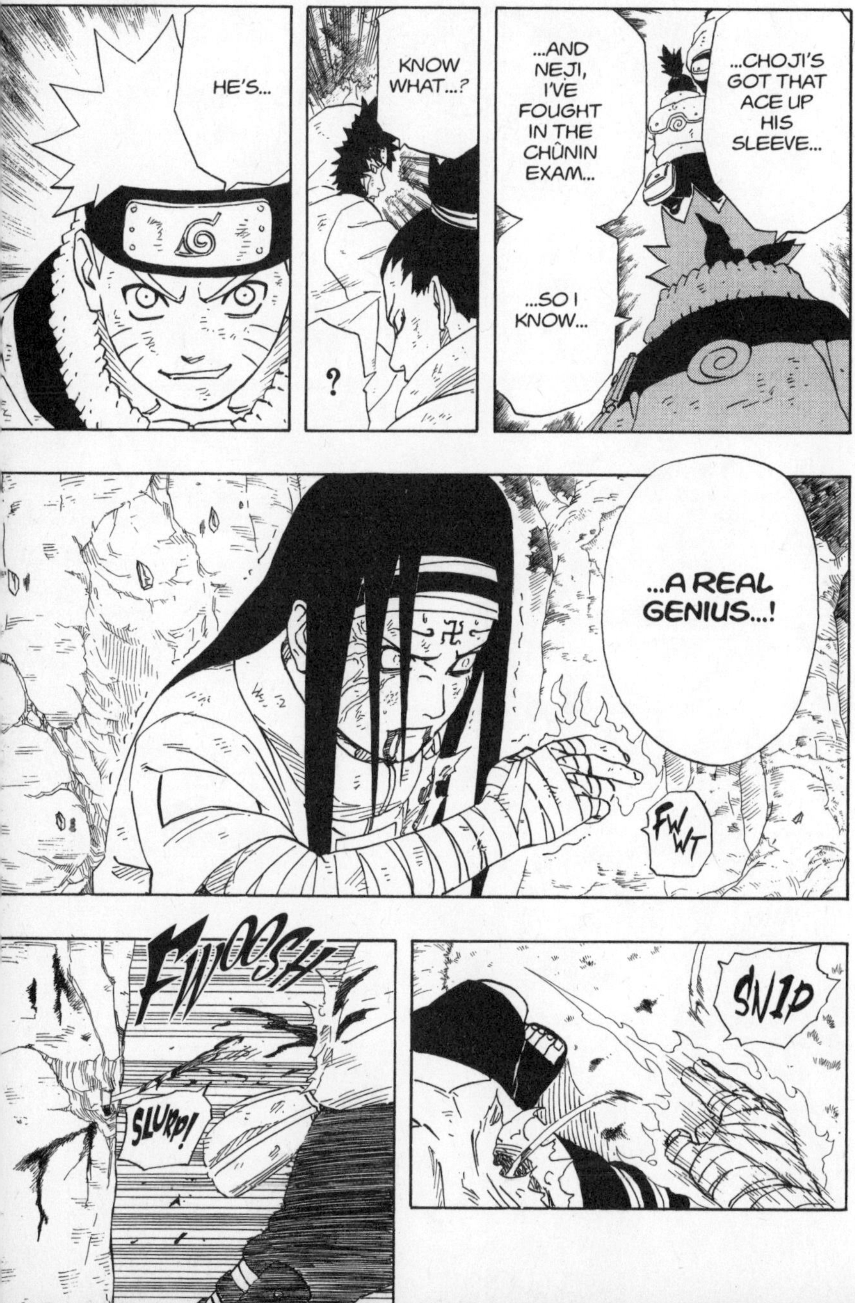
...CHOJI'S GOT THAT ACE UP HIS SLEEVE...
...AND NEJI, I'VE FOUGHT IN THE CHÛNIN EXAM...
...SO I KNOW...
KNOW WHAT...?
?
HE'S...
...A REAL GENIUS...!
FWWT
SNIP
FWOOSH
SLURP!

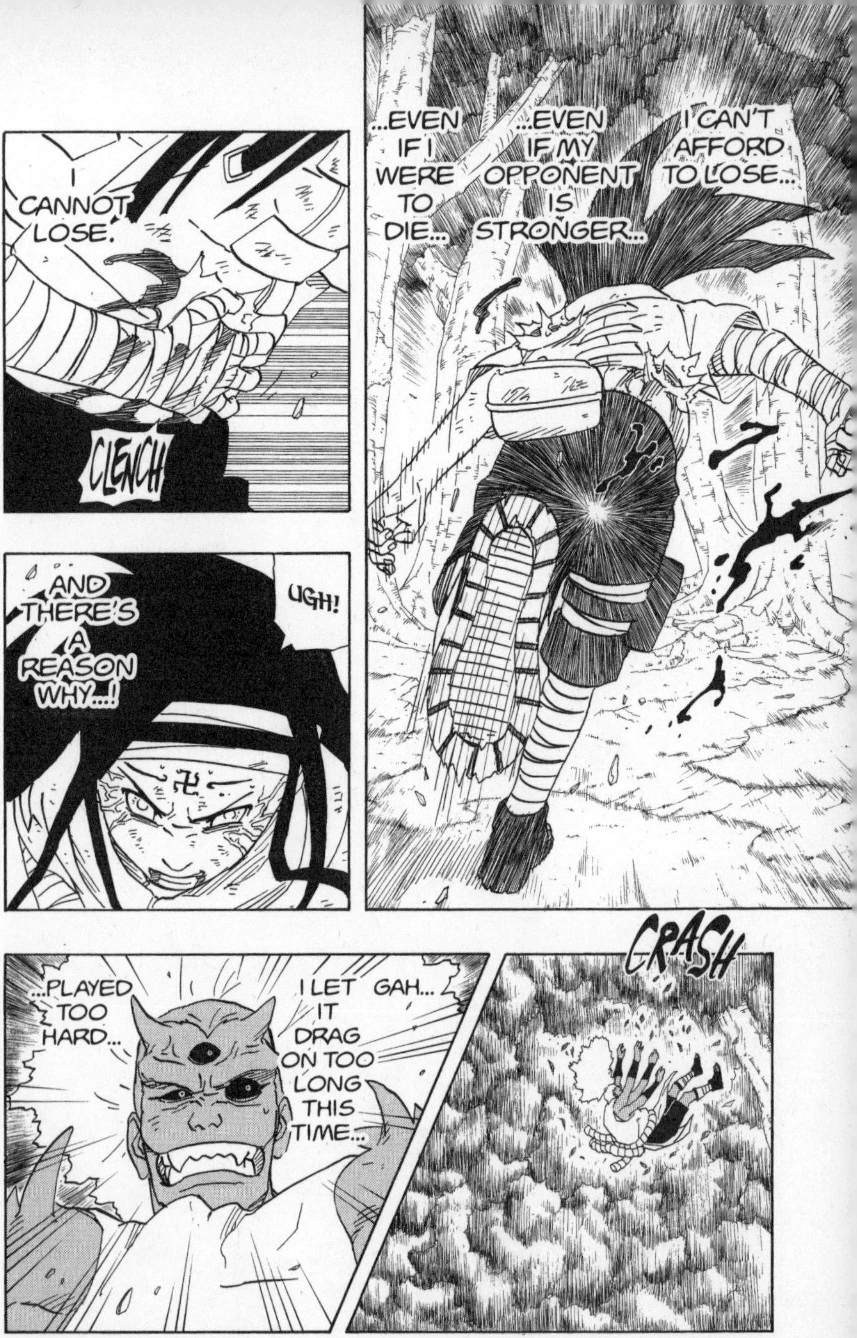
I CAN'T AFFORD TO LOSE...
...EVEN IF MY OPPONENT IS STRONGER...
...EVEN IF I WERE TO DIE...
I CANNOT LOSE.
CLENCH
UGH!
AND THERE'S A REASON WHY...!
CRASH
GAH...
I LET IT DRAG ON TOO LONG THIS TIME...
...PLAYED TOO HARD...

READ THIS WAY

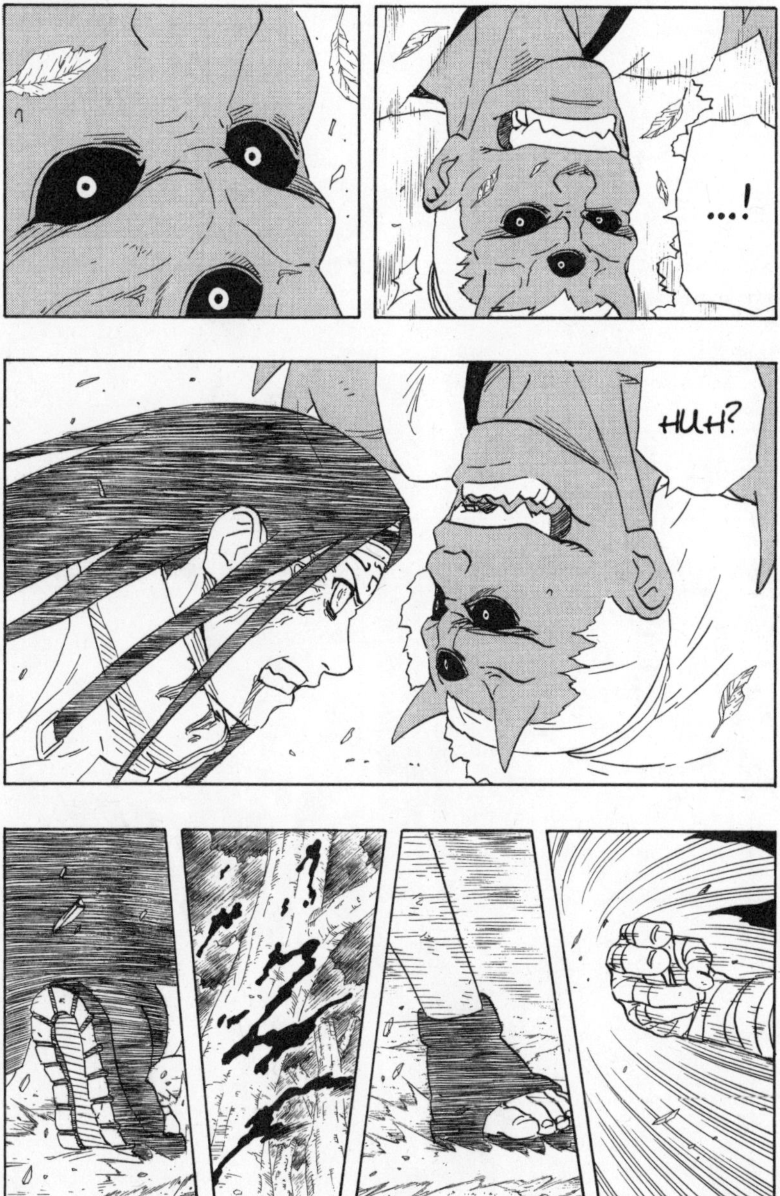
...!
HUH?

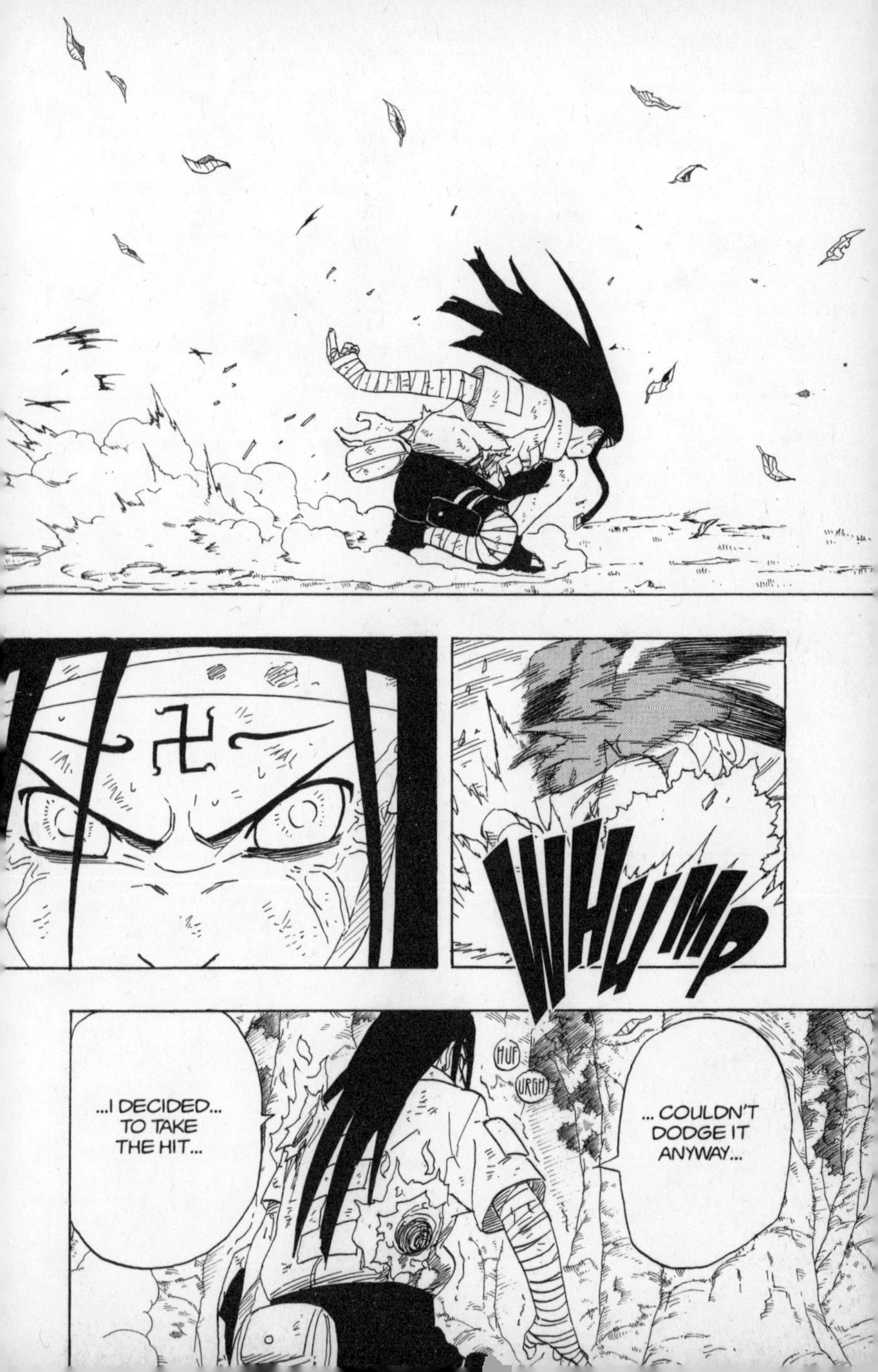
WHUMP
HUF
URGH
... COULDN'T DODGE IT ANYWAY...
...I DECIDED... TO TAKE THE HIT...

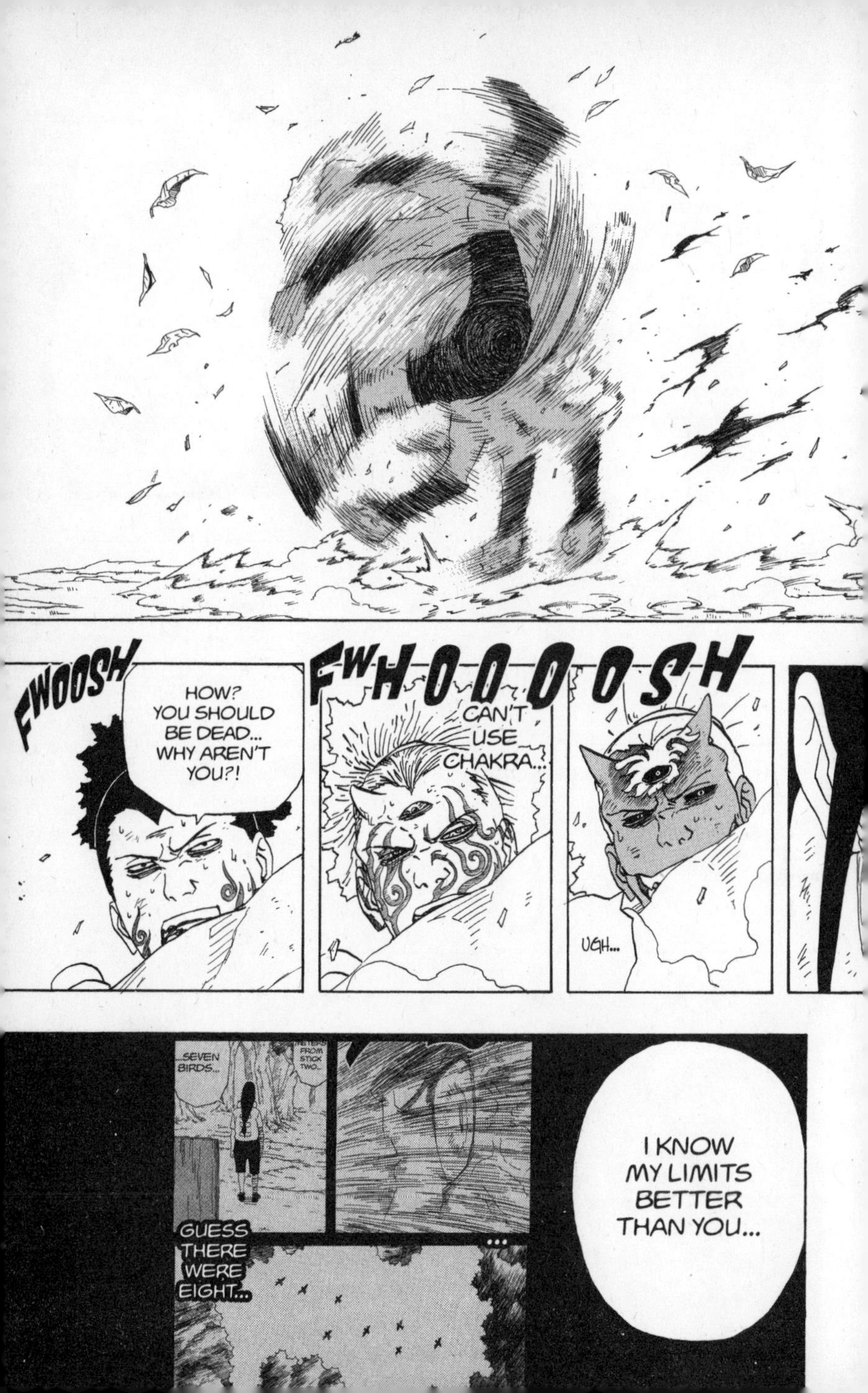
FWHOOOOSH
UGH...
CAN'T USE CHAKRA...
FWOOSH
HOW? YOU SHOULD BE DEAD... WHY AREN'T YOU?!
I KNOW MY LIMITS BETTER THAN YOU...
FROM STICK TWO...
...SEVEN BIRDS...
...
GUESS THERE WERE EIGHT...

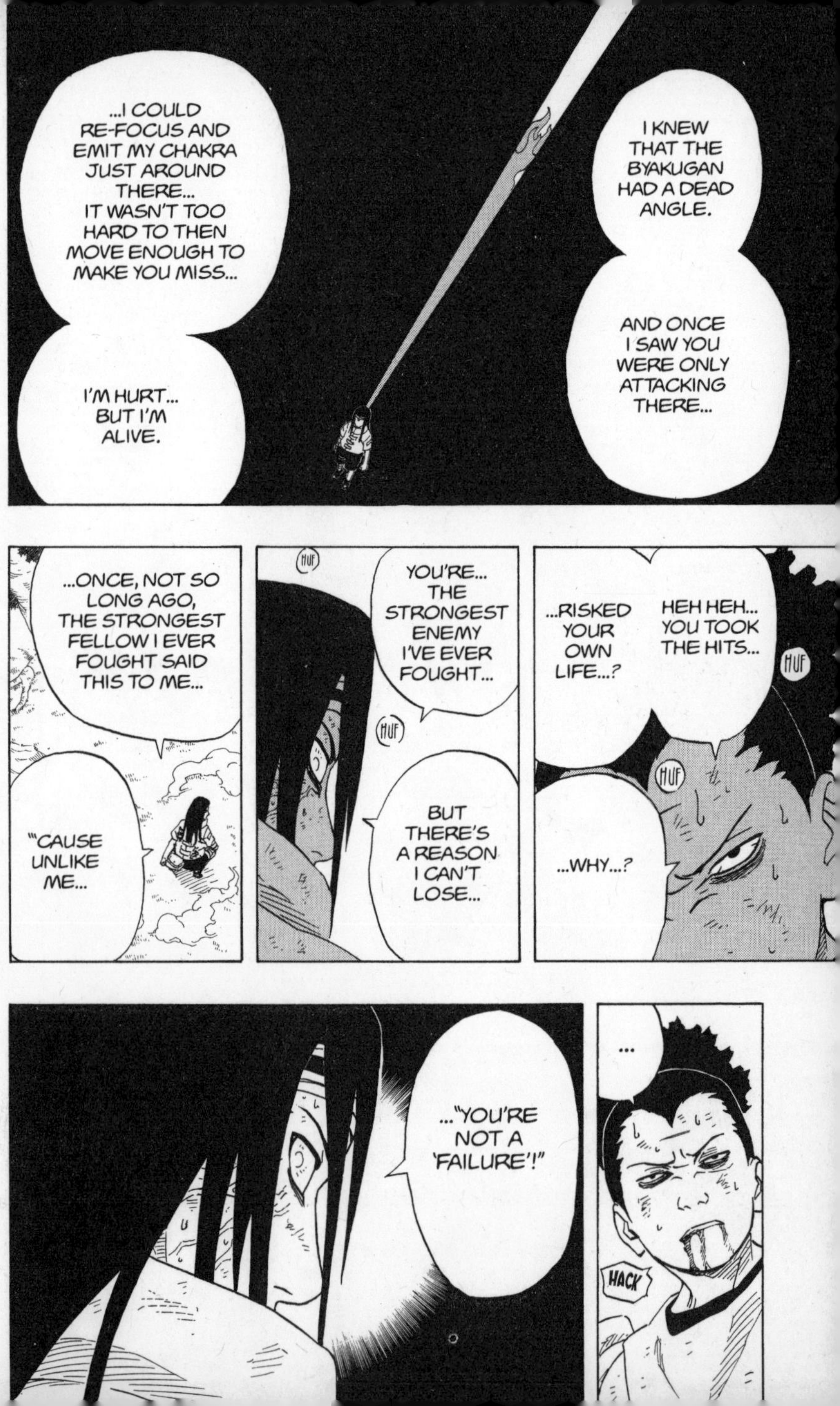
I KNEW THAT THE BYAKUGAN HAD A DEAD ANGLE.
AND ONCE I SAW YOU WERE ONLY ATTACKING THERE...
...I COULD RE-FOCUS AND EMIT MY CHAKRA JUST AROUND THERE... IT WASN'T TOO HARD TO THEN MOVE ENOUGH TO MAKE YOU MISS...
I'M HURT... BUT I'M ALIVE.
HEH HEH... YOU TOOK THE HITS...
...RISKED YOUR OWN LIFE...?
HUF
HUF
...WHY...?
HUF
YOU'RE... THE STRONGEST ENEMY I'VE EVER FOUGHT...
HUF
BUT THERE'S A REASON I CAN'T LOSE...
...ONCE, NOT SO LONG AGO, THE STRONGEST FELLOW I EVER FOUGHT SAID THIS TO ME...
"'CAUSE UNLIKE ME...
...
HACK
..."YOU'RE NOT A 'FAILURE'!"

READ THIS WAY

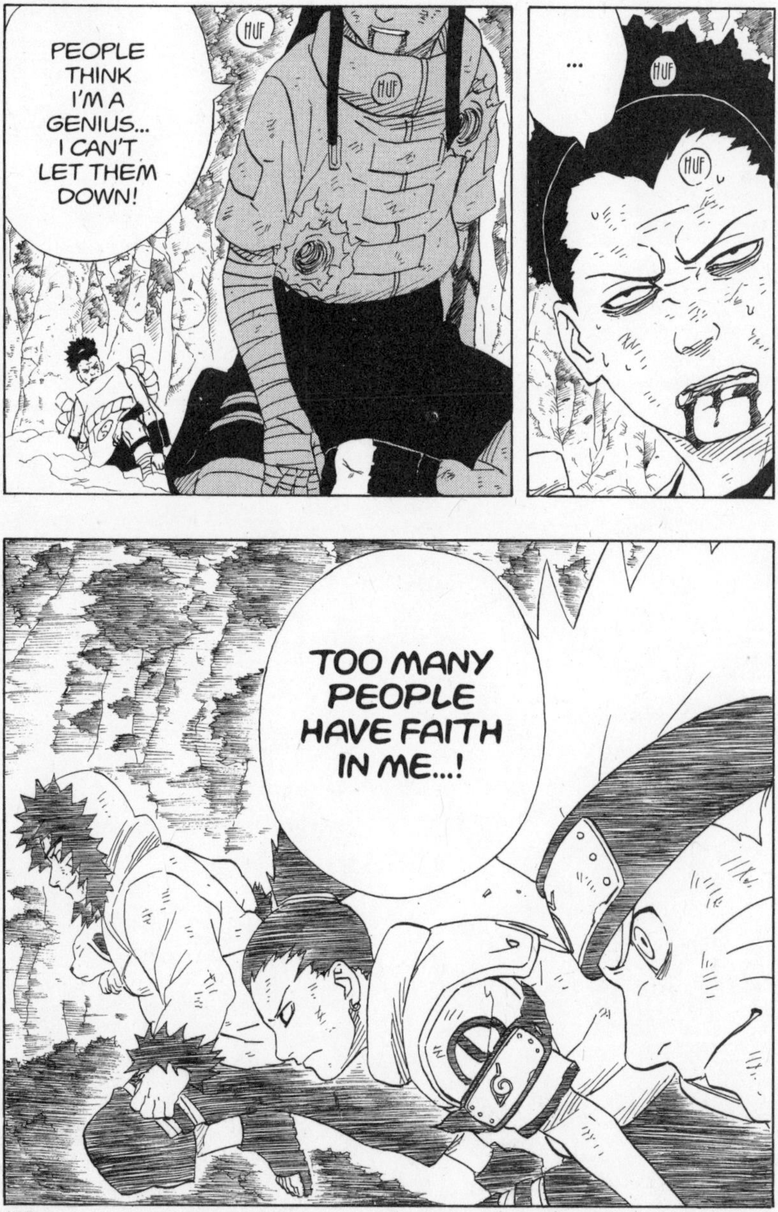
...
HUF
HUF
HUF
HUF
PEOPLE THINK I'M A GENIUS... I CAN'T LET THEM DOWN!
TOO MANY PEOPLE HAVE FAITH IN ME...!

NARUTO™

Number 198: Transference...!!

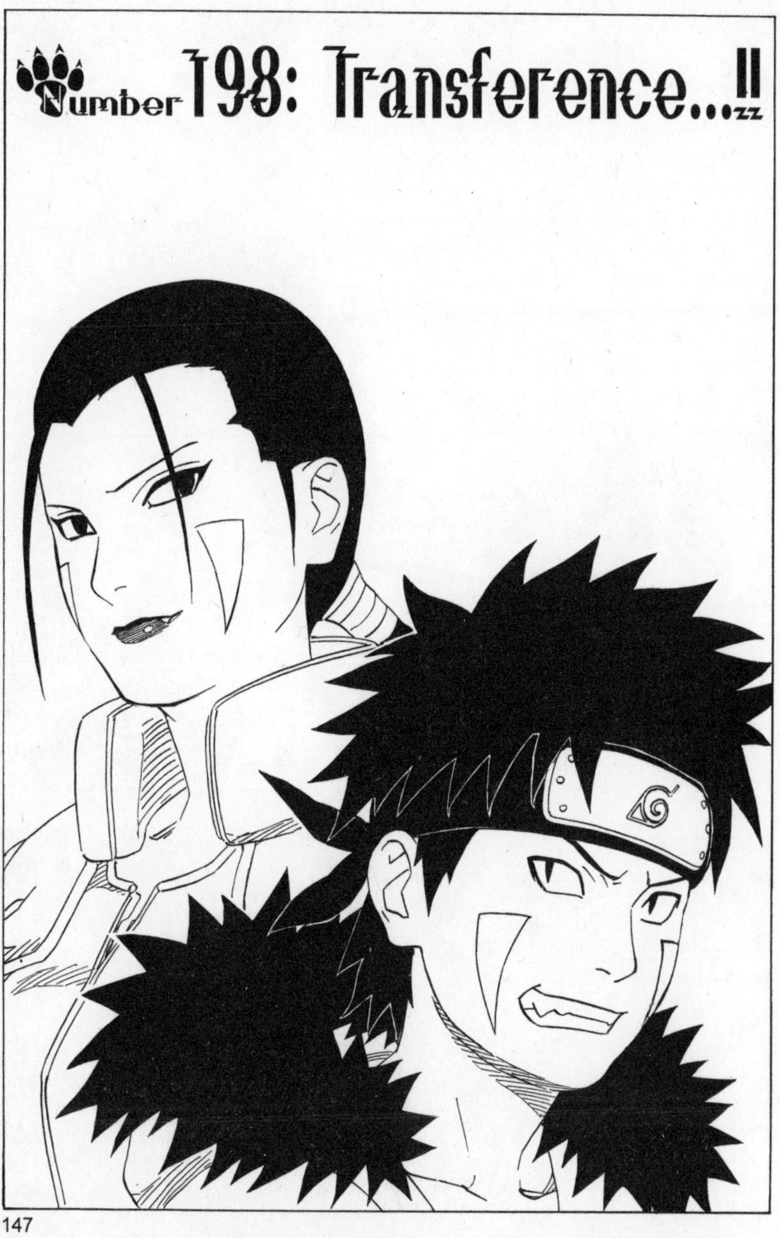

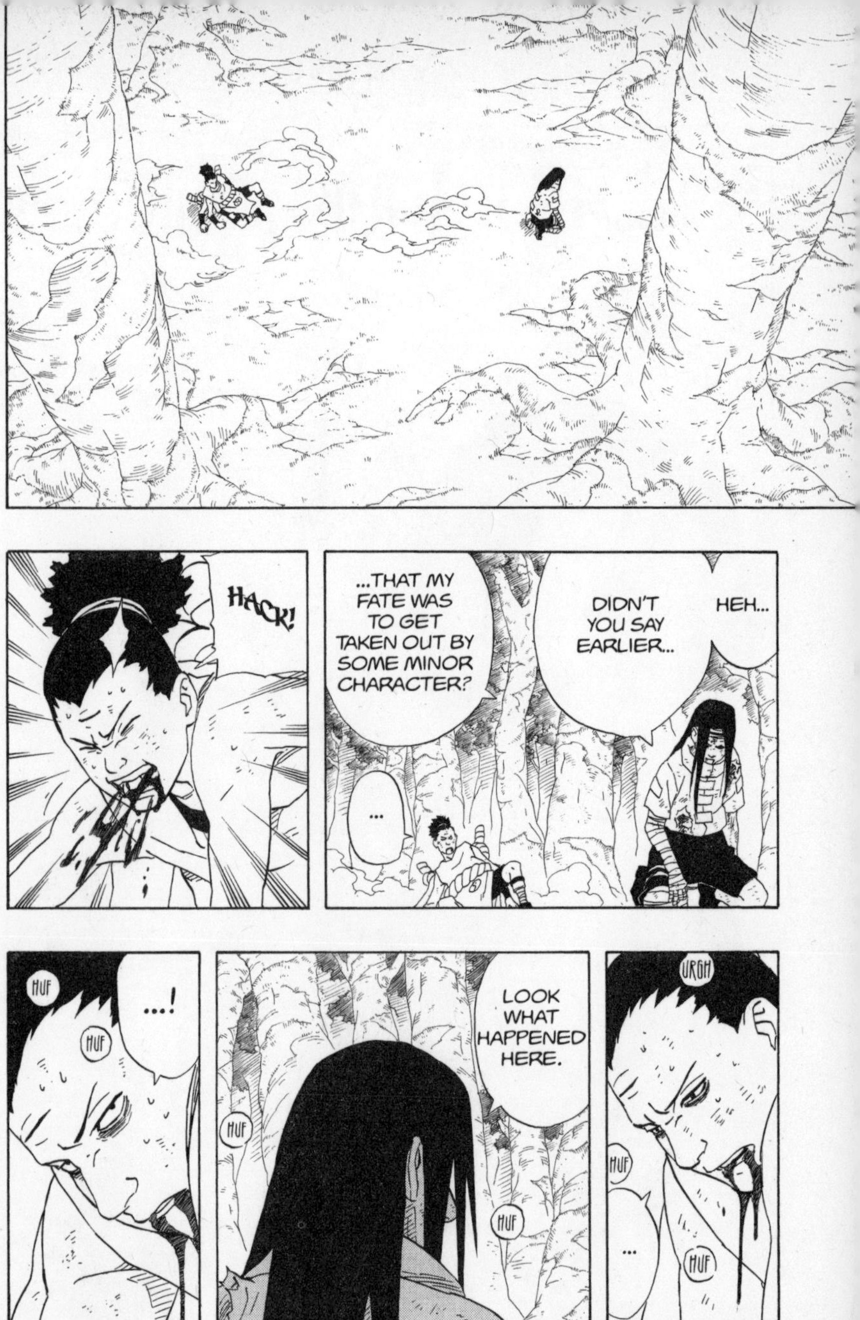
HEH...
DIDN'T YOU SAY EARLIER...
...THAT MY FATE WAS TO GET TAKEN OUT BY SOME MINOR CHARACTER?
...
HACK!
URGH
HUF
...
HUF
LOOK WHAT HAPPENED HERE.
HUF
HUF
HUF
...!
HUF

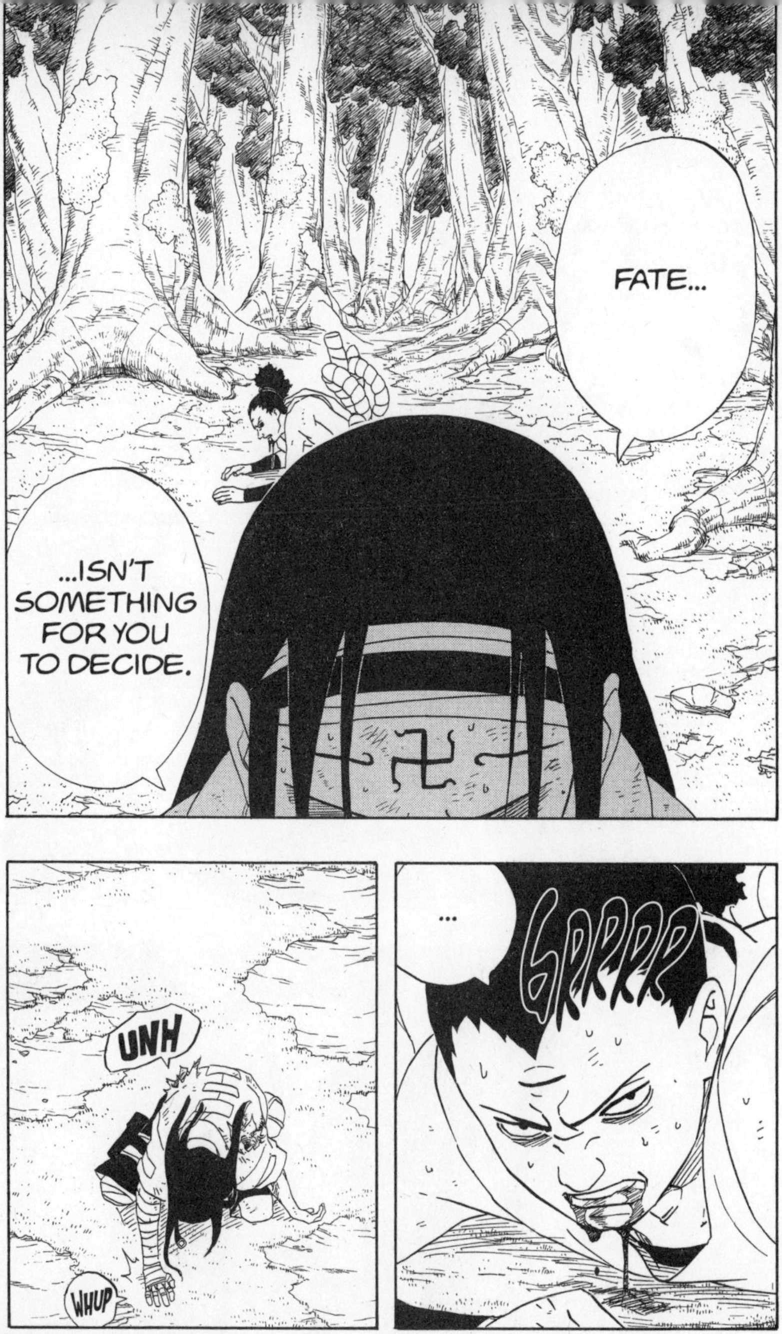
FATE...
...ISN'T SOMETHING FOR YOU TO DECIDE.
...
GRRRR
UNH
WHUP

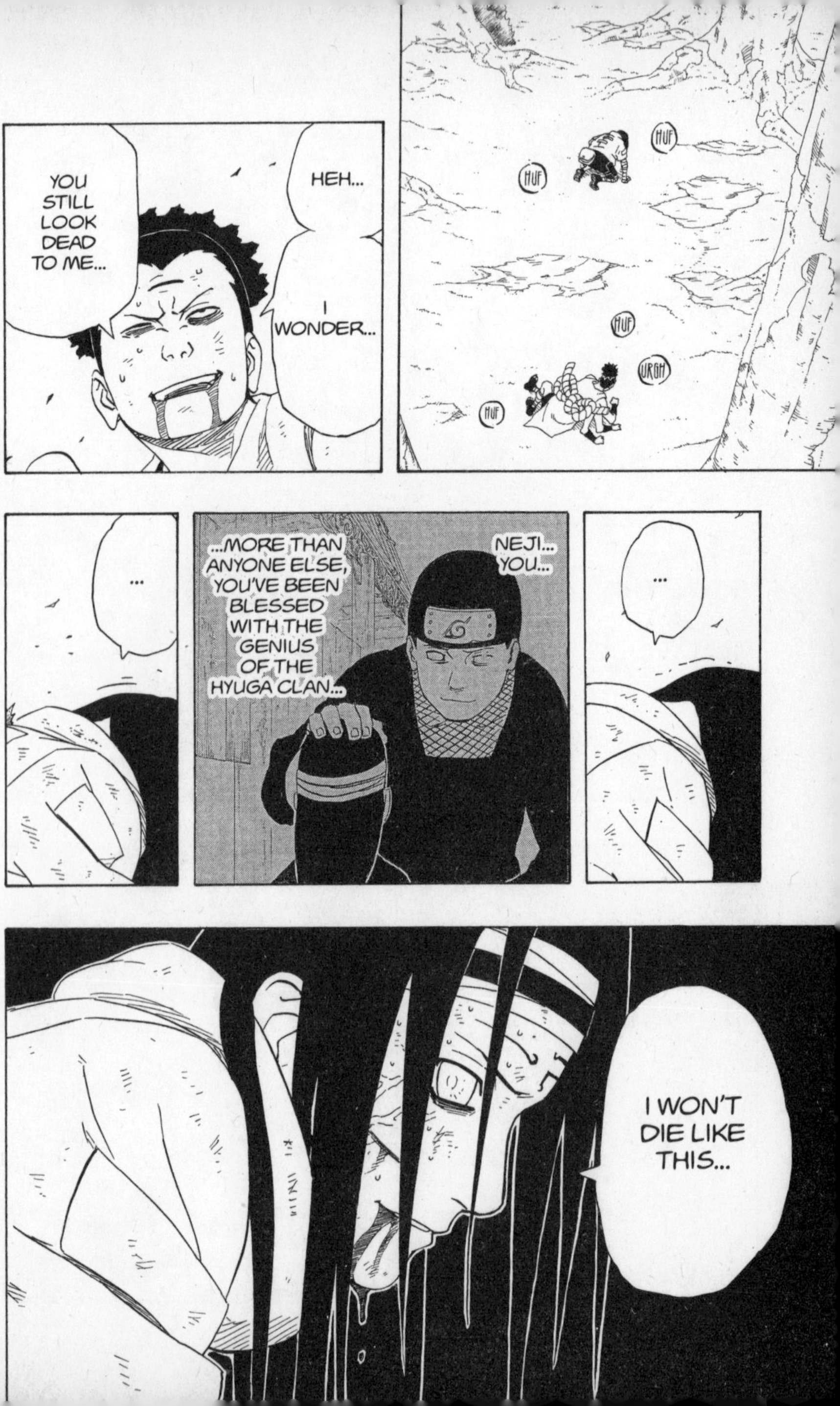
HUF
HUF
HUF
URGH
HUF
HEH...
I WONDER...
YOU STILL LOOK DEAD TO ME...
...
NEJI... YOU...
...MORE THAN ANYONE ELSE, YOU'VE BEEN BLESSED WITH THE GENIUS OF THE HYUGA CLAN...
...
I WON'T DIE LIKE THIS...

READ THIS WAY

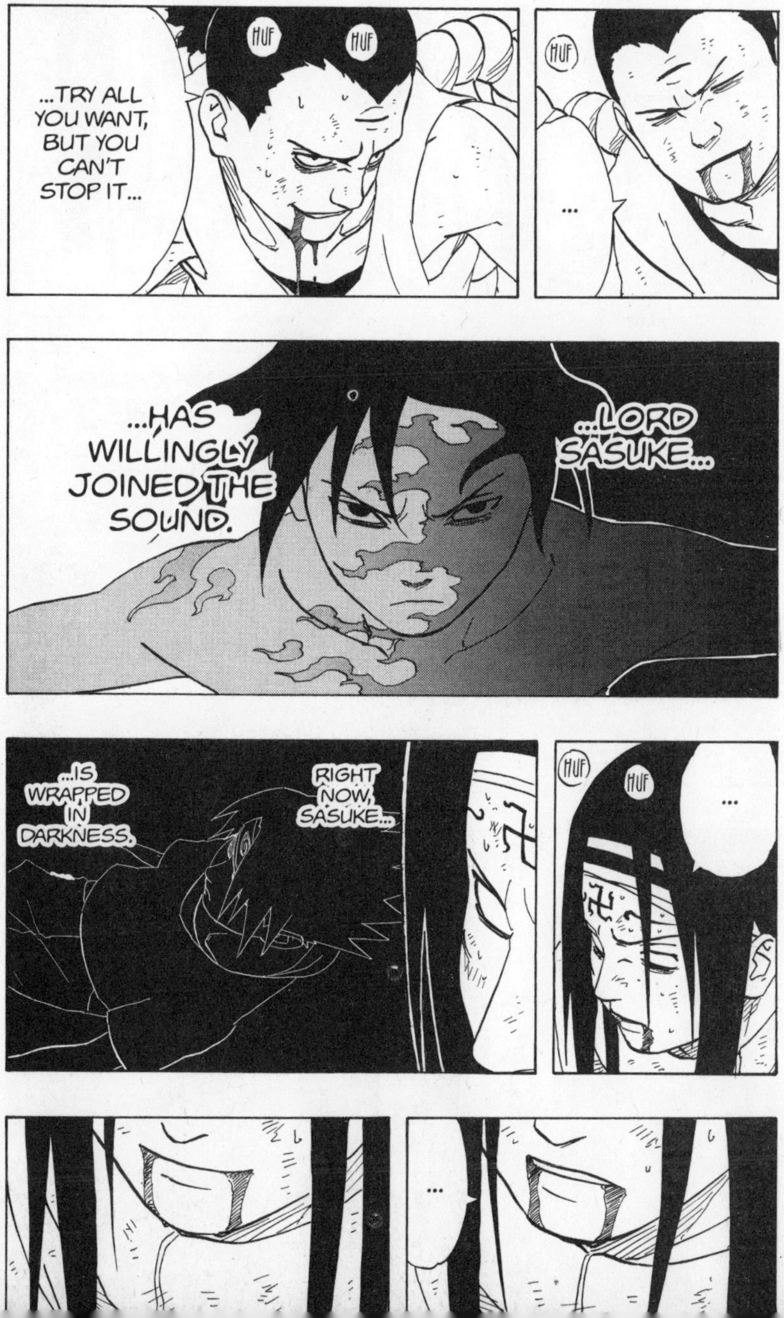

HUF
...
HUF
HUF
...TRY ALL YOU WANT, BUT YOU CAN'T STOP IT...
...LORD SASUKE...
...HAS WILLINGLY JOINED THE SOUND.
HUF
HUF
...
RIGHT NOW, SASUKE...
...IS WRAPPED IN DARKNESS.
...

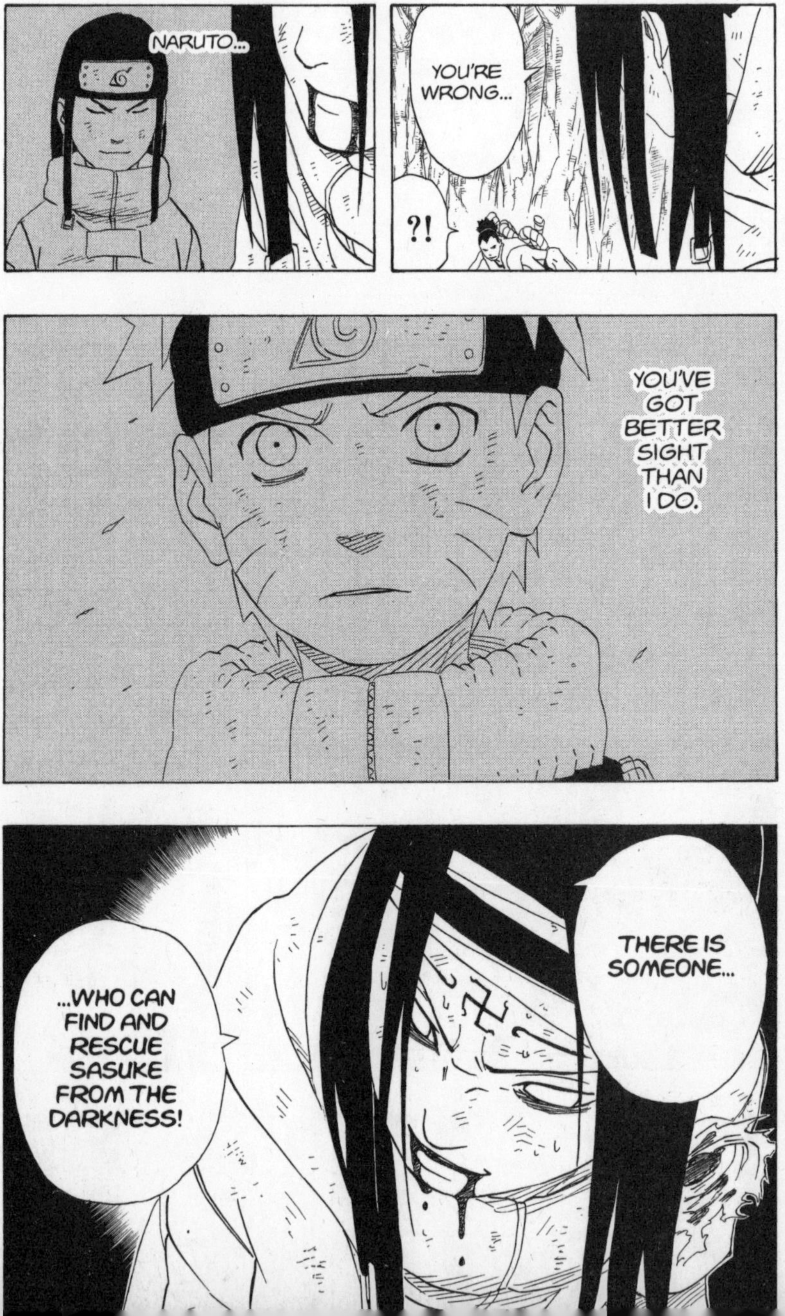
YOU'RE WRONG...
?!
NARUTO...
YOU'VE GOT BETTER SIGHT THAN I DO.
THERE IS SOMEONE...
...WHO CAN FIND AND RESCUE SASUKE FROM THE DARKNESS!

READ THIS WAY

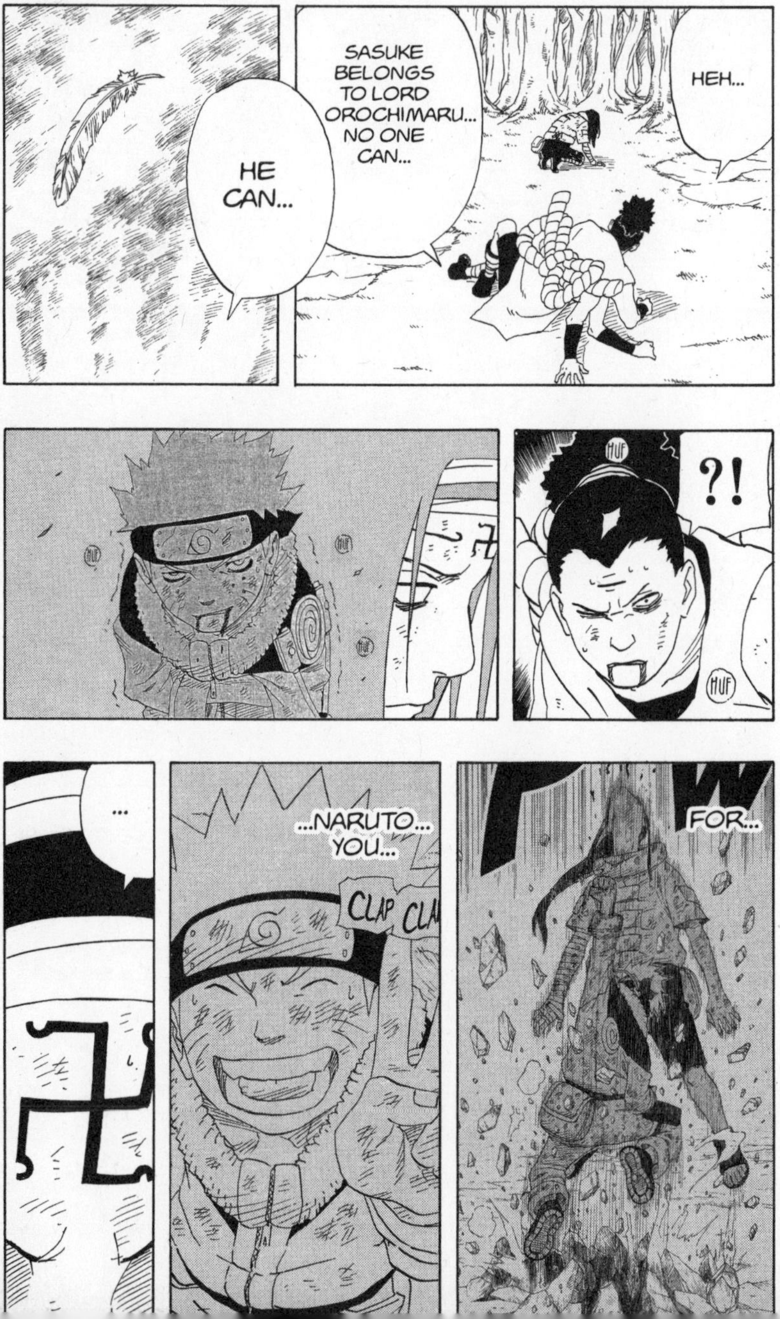

HEH...
SASUKE BELONGS TO LORD OROCHIMARU... NO ONE CAN...
HE CAN...
?!
HUF
HUF
HUF
HUF
HUF
FOR...
...NARUTO... YOU...
CLAP
...

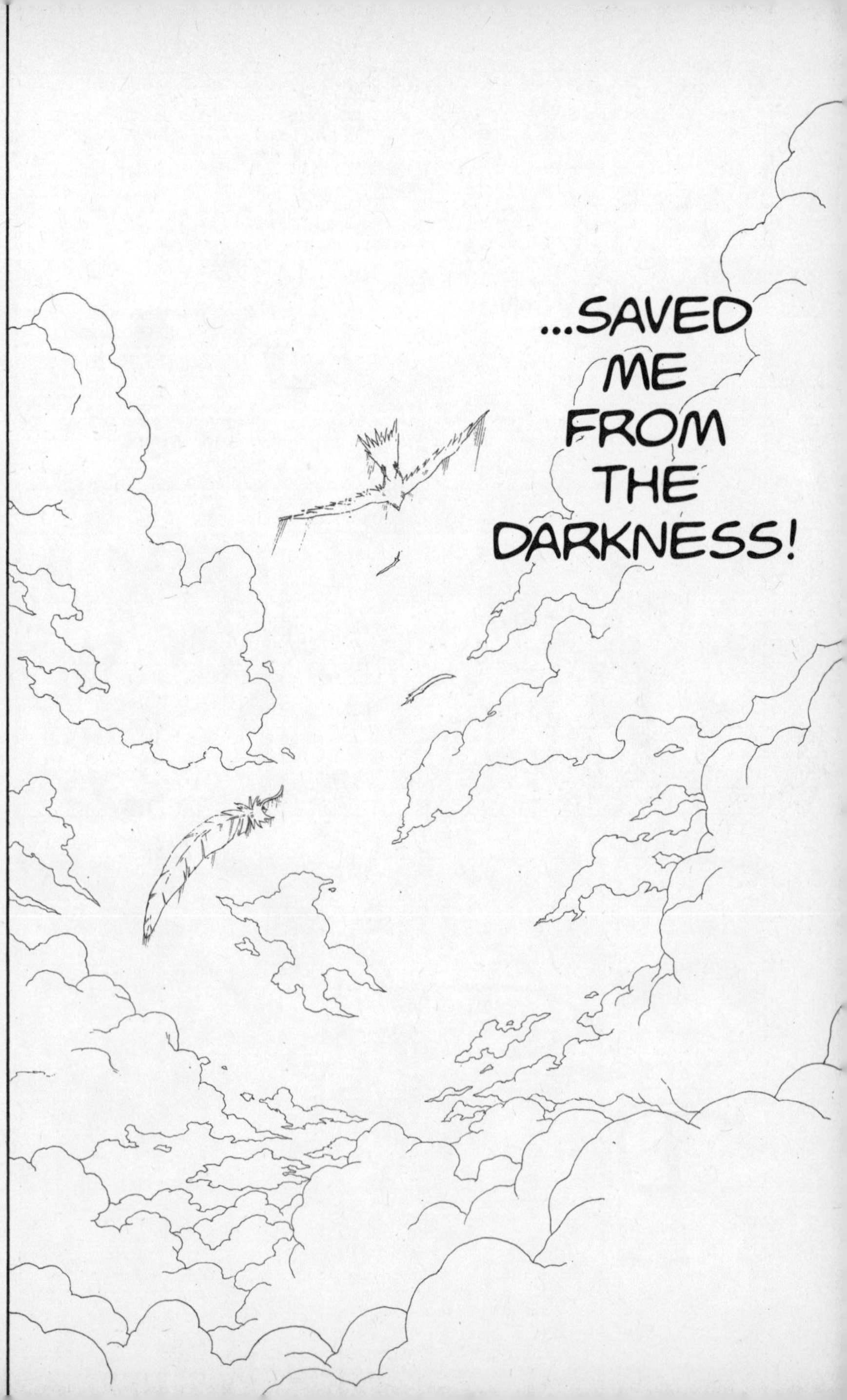
...SAVED ME FROM THE DARKNESS!

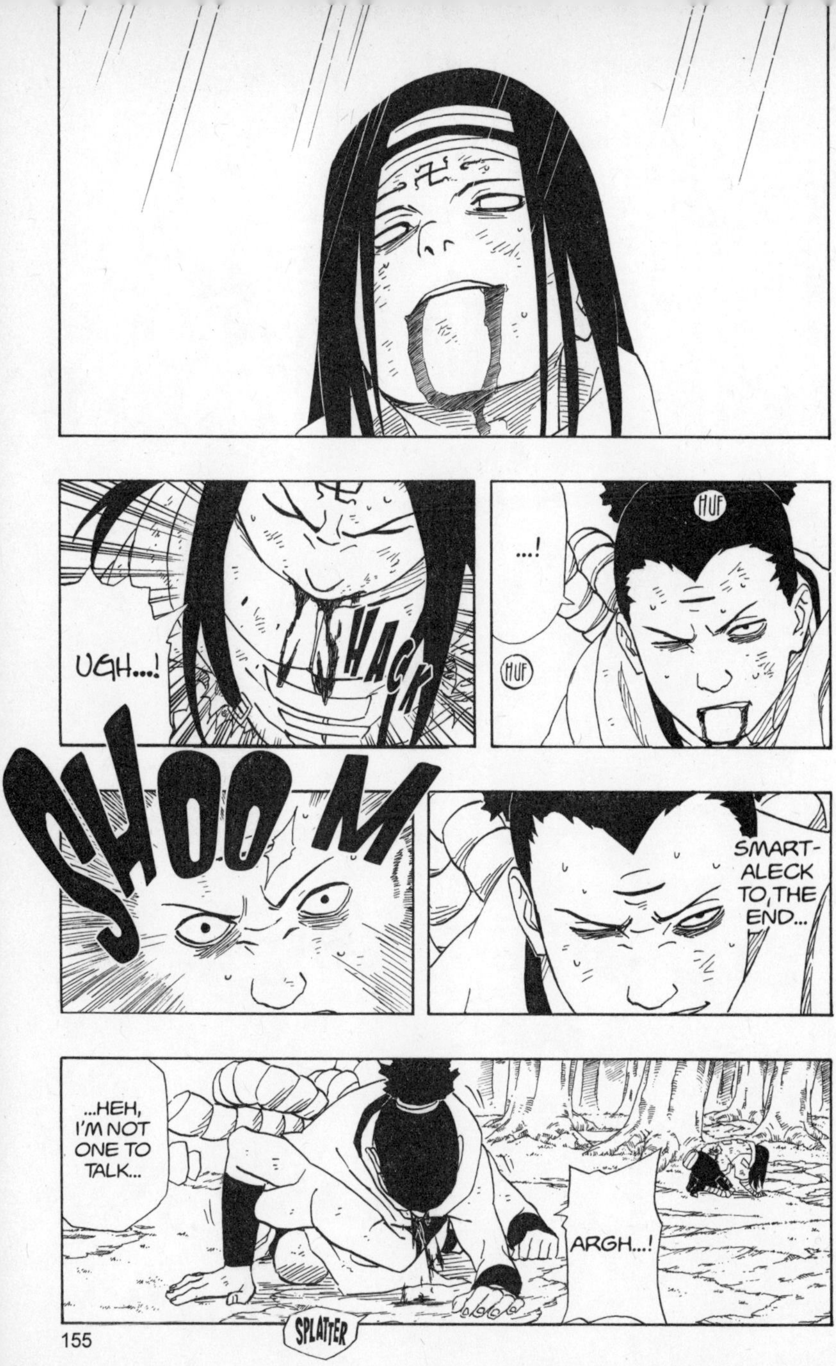
HUF
...!
HUF
UGH...!
HACK
SMART-ALECK TO THE END...
SHOOM
...HEH, I'M NOT ONE TO TALK...
ARGH...!
SPLATTER

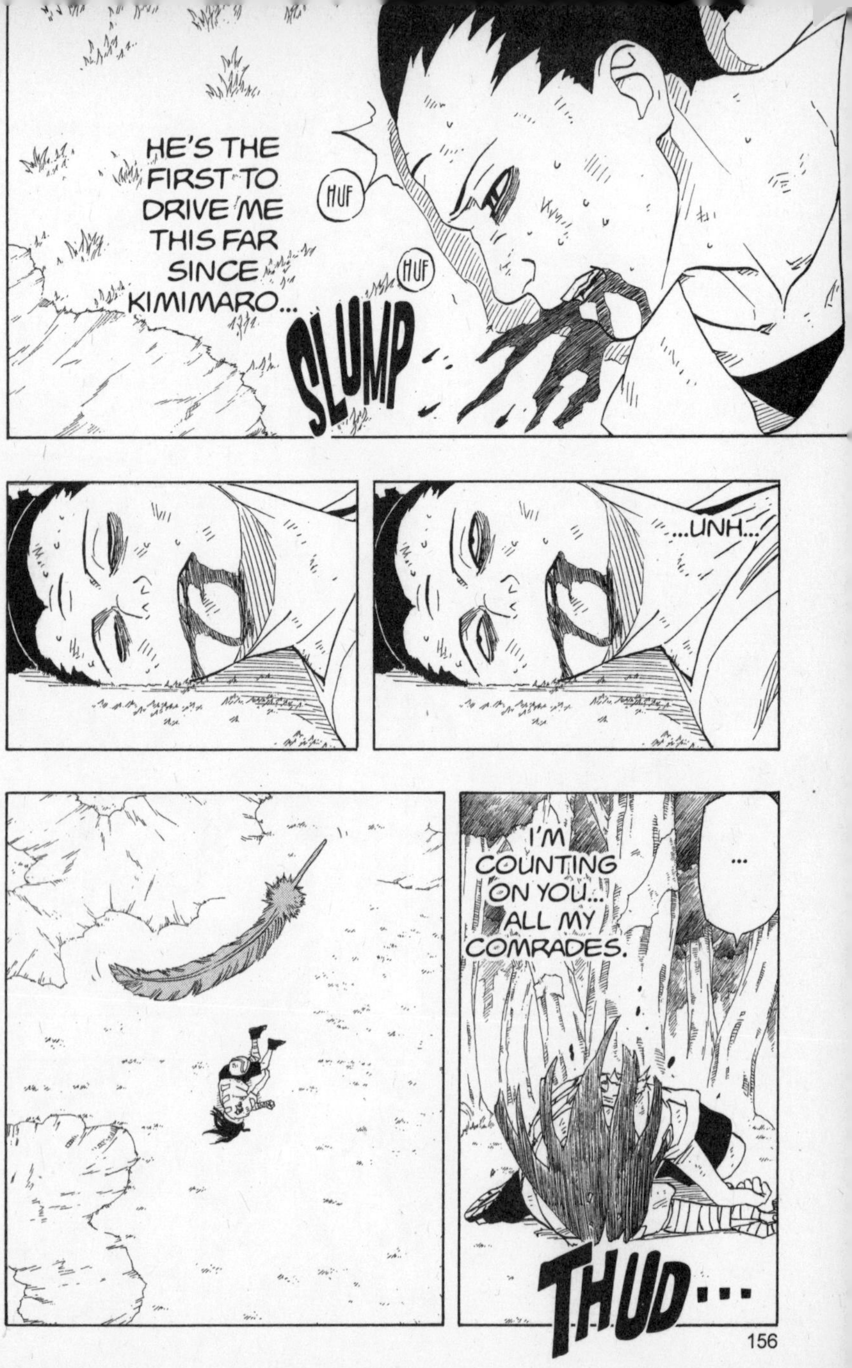
HUF
HUF
HE'S THE FIRST TO DRIVE ME THIS FAR SINCE KIMIMARO...
SLUMP
...UNH...
...
I'M COUNTING ON YOU... ALL MY COMRADES.
THUD...

READ THIS WAY

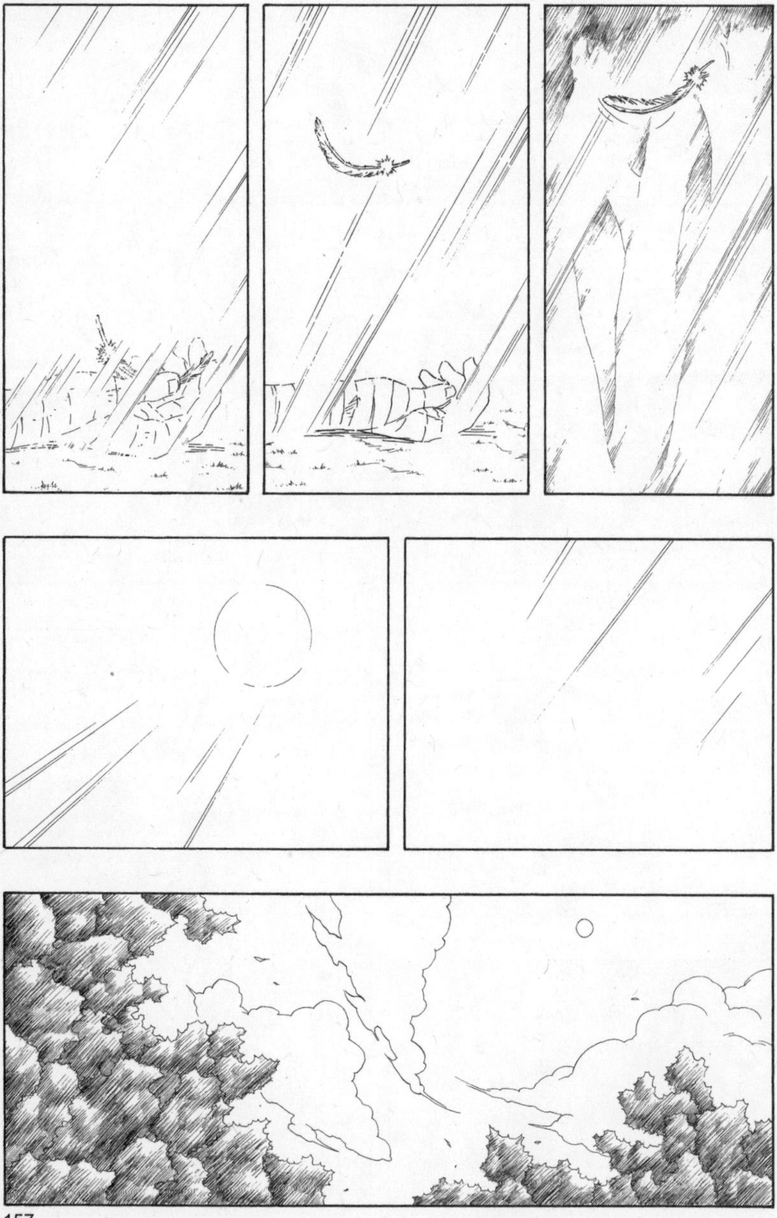

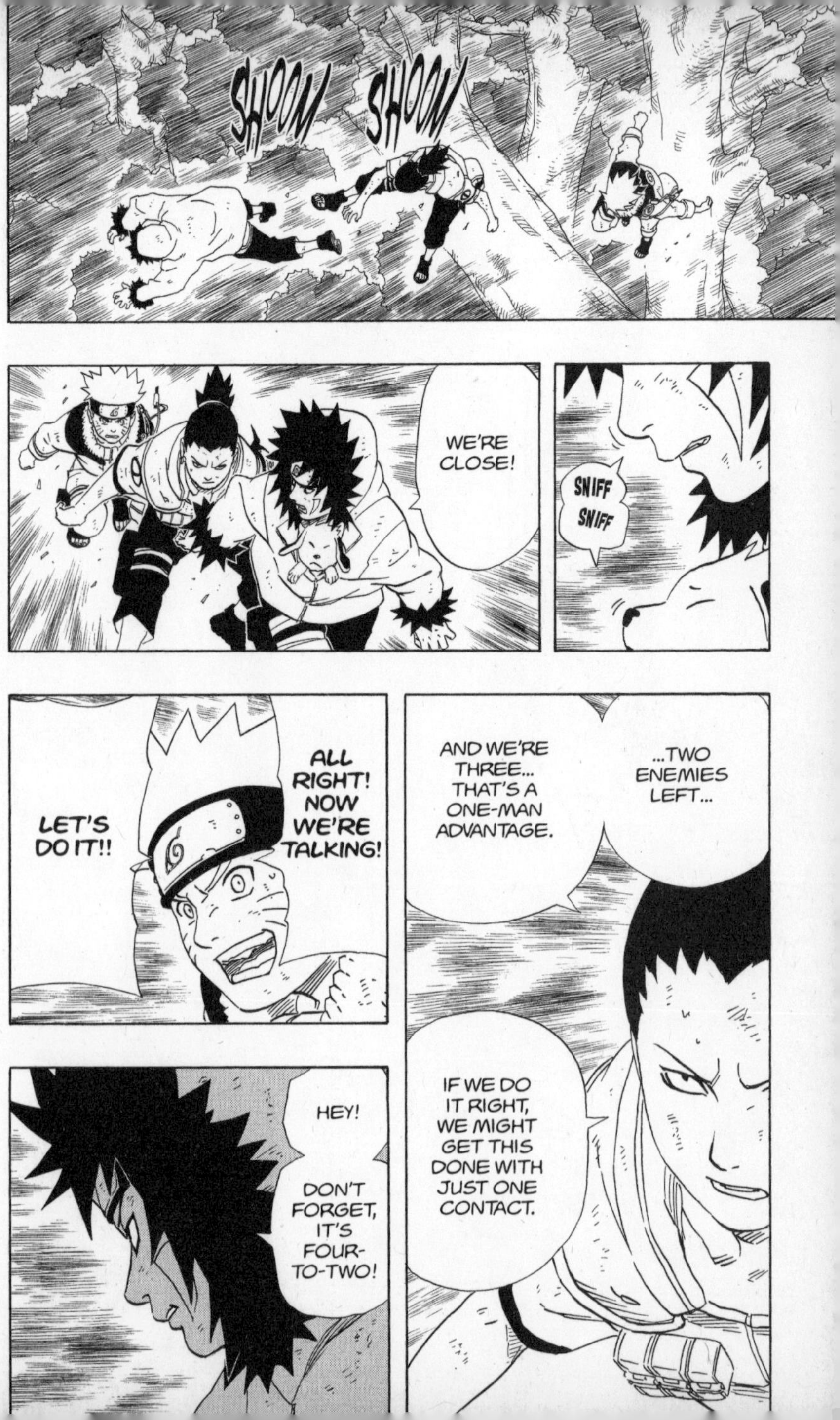
SHOOM
SHOOM
SNIFF
SNIFF
WE'RE CLOSE!
...TWO ENEMIES LEFT...
AND WE'RE THREE... THAT'S A ONE-MAN ADVANTAGE.
IF WE DO IT RIGHT, WE MIGHT GET THIS DONE WITH JUST ONE CONTACT.
ALL RIGHT! NOW WE'RE TALKING!
LET'S DO IT!!
HEY!
DON'T FORGET, IT'S FOUR-TO-TWO!

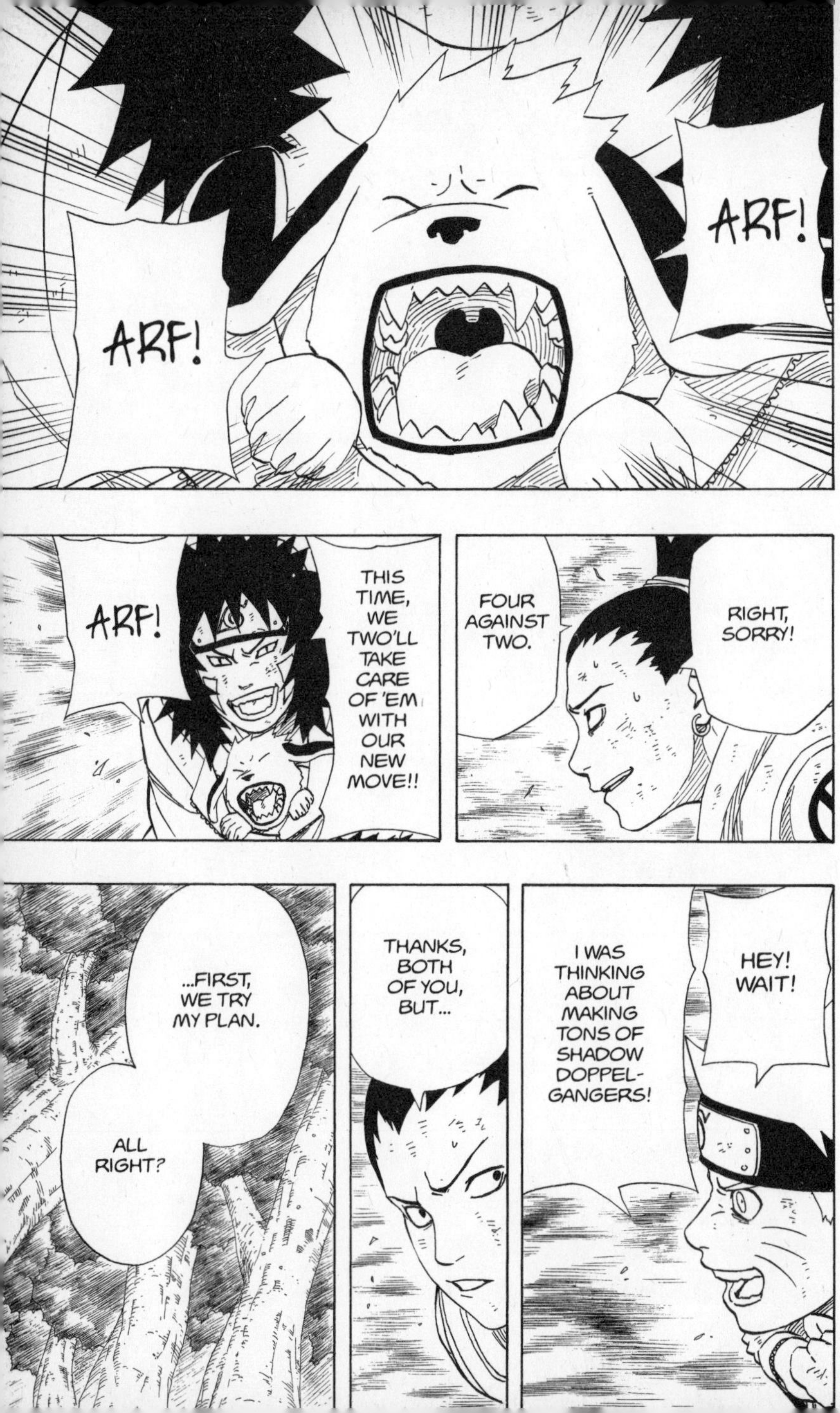
ARF!
ARF!
RIGHT, SORRY!
FOUR AGAINST TWO.
THIS TIME, WE TWO'LL TAKE CARE OF 'EM WITH OUR NEW MOVE!!
ARF!
HEY! WAIT!
I WAS THINKING ABOUT MAKING TONS OF SHADOW DOPPEL-GANGERS!
THANKS, BOTH OF YOU, BUT...
...FIRST, WE TRY MY PLAN.
ALL RIGHT?

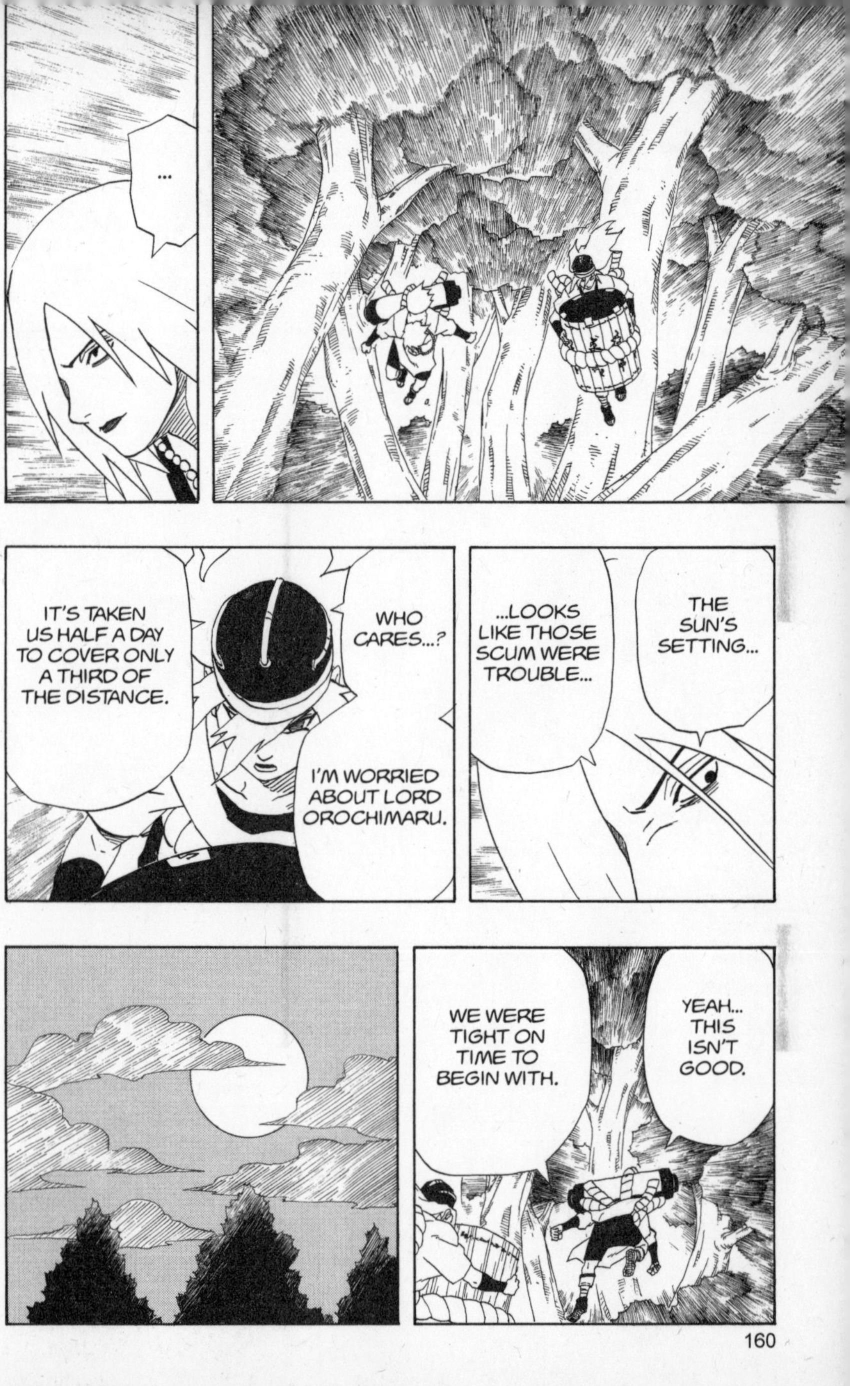
...
THE SUN'S SETTING...
...LOOKS LIKE THOSE SCUM WERE TROUBLE...
WHO CARES...?
I'M WORRIED ABOUT LORD OROCHIMARU.
IT'S TAKEN US HALF A DAY TO COVER ONLY A THIRD OF THE DISTANCE.
YEAH... THIS ISN'T GOOD.
WE WERE TIGHT ON TIME TO BEGIN WITH.

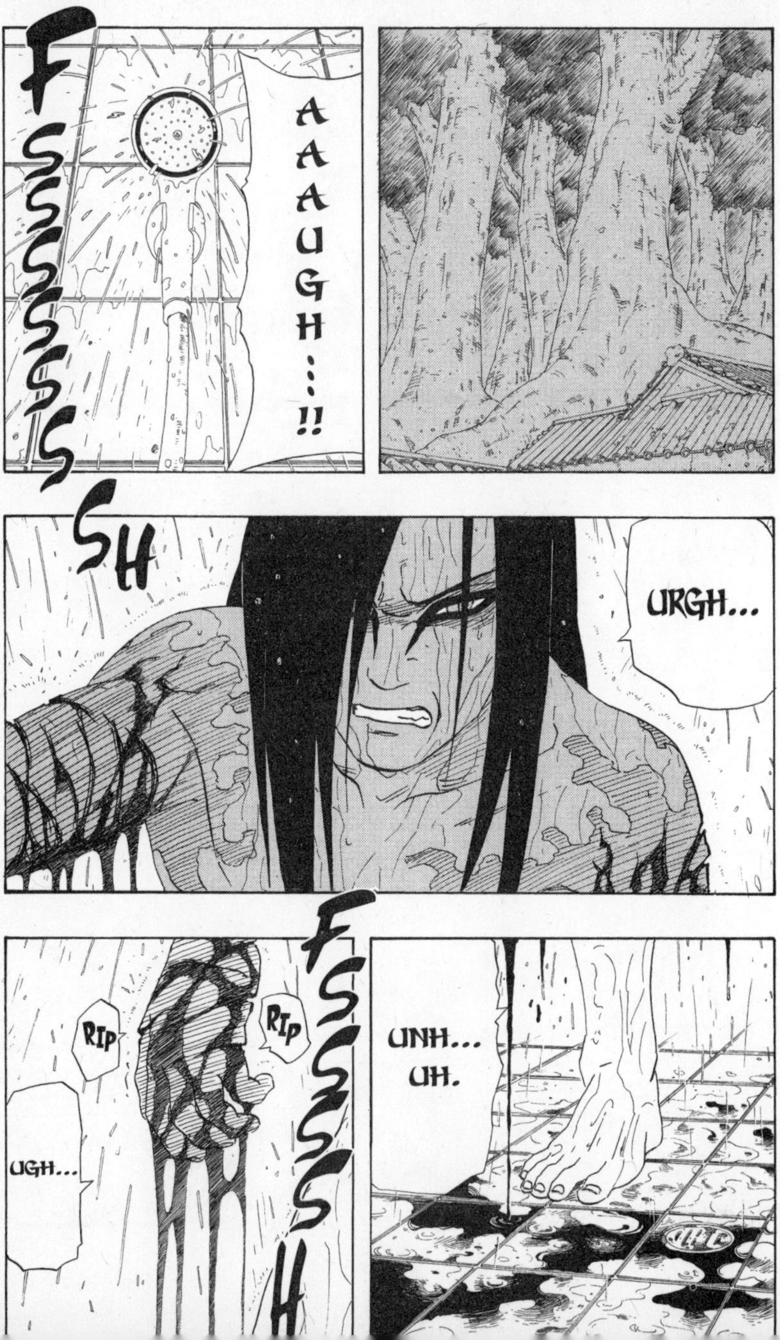

FSSSSSSSH
AAAUGH...!!
URGH...
UNH... UH.
RIP
RIP
UGH...
FSSSSH

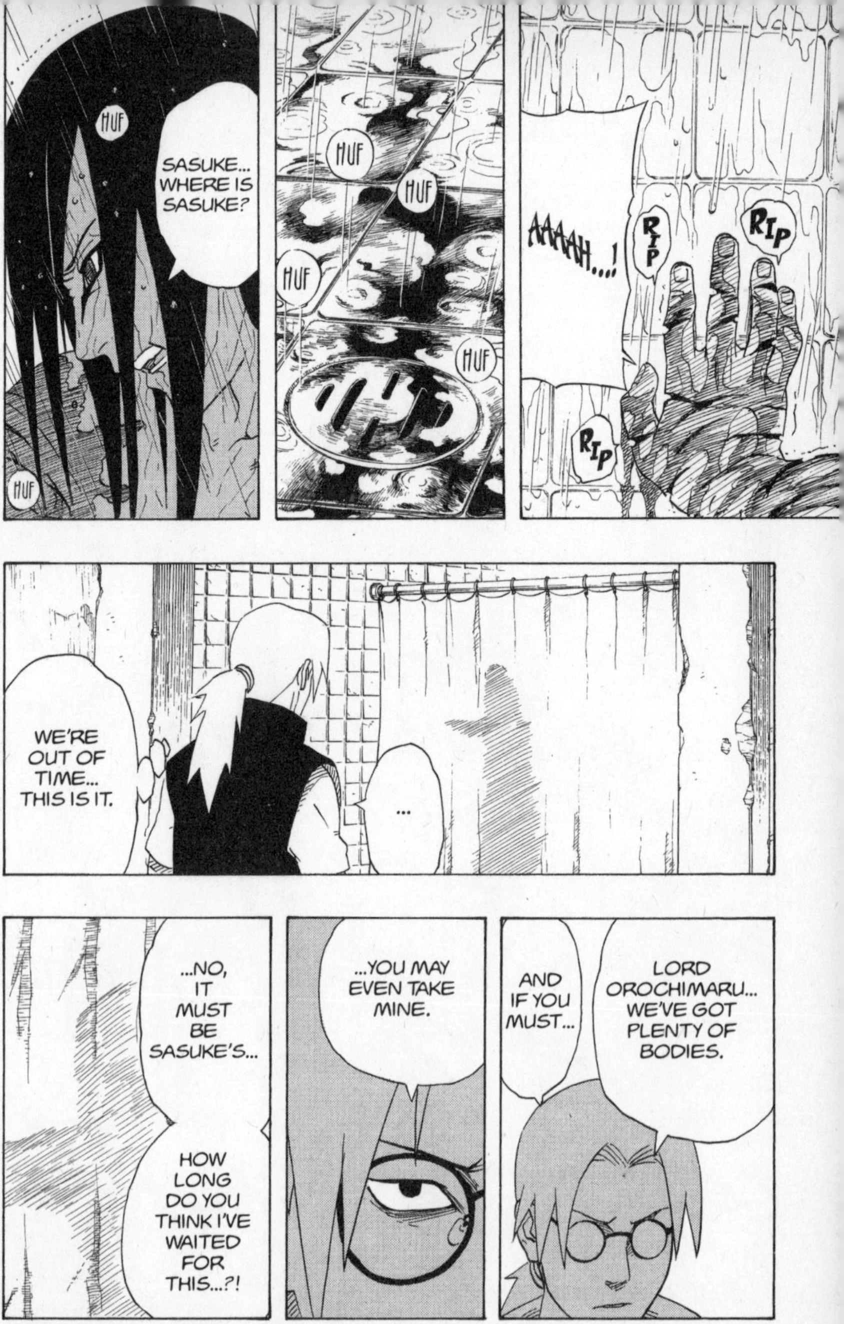
RIP
RIP
AAAAH...!
RIP
HUF
HUF
HUF
HUF
HUF
SASUKE... WHERE IS SASUKE?
HUF
...
WE'RE OUT OF TIME... THIS IS IT.
LORD OROCHIMARU... WE'VE GOT PLENTY OF BODIES.
AND IF YOU MUST...
...YOU MAY EVEN TAKE MINE.
...NO, IT MUST BE SASUKE'S...
HOW LONG DO YOU THINK I'VE WAITED FOR THIS...?!

READ THIS WAY

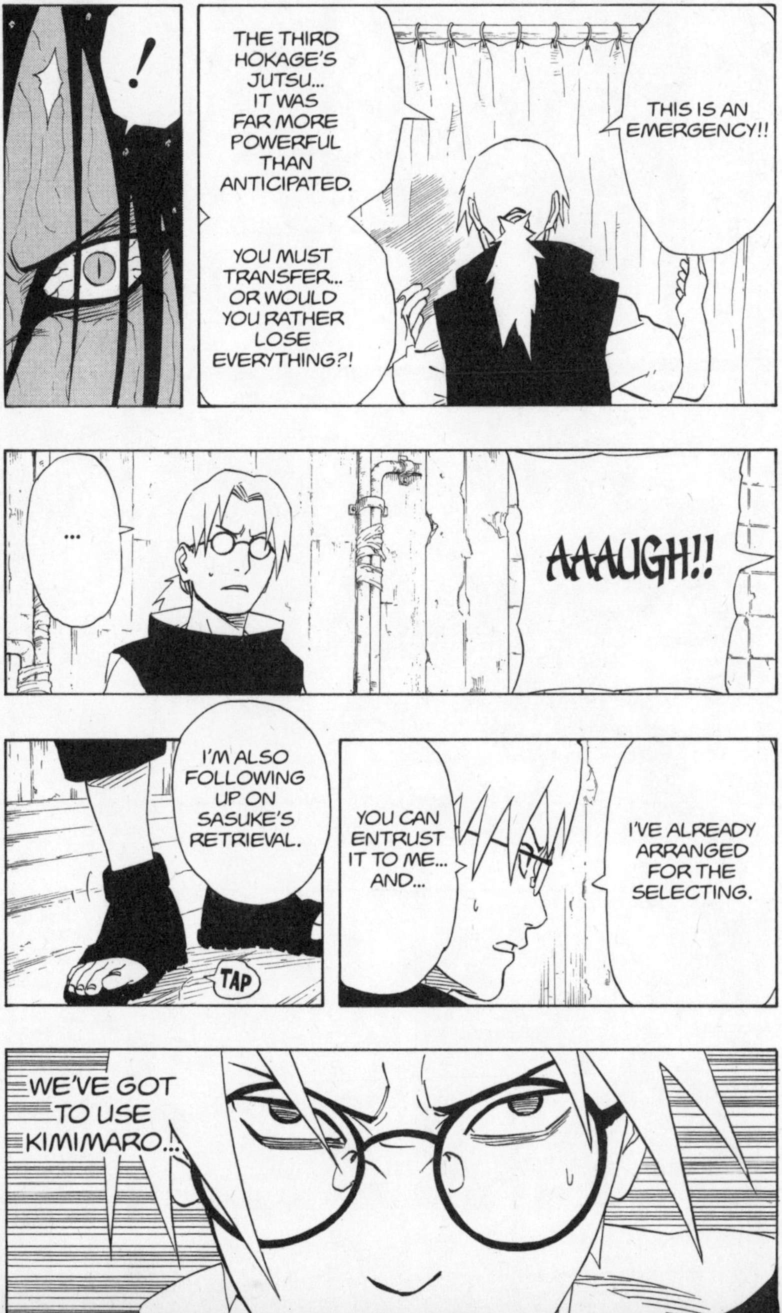
THIS IS AN EMERGENCY!!
THE THIRD HOKAGE'S JUTSU... IT WAS FAR MORE POWERFUL THAN ANTICIPATED.
YOU MUST TRANSFER... OR WOULD YOU RATHER LOSE EVERYTHING?!
!
AAAUGH!!
...
I'VE ALREADY ARRANGED FOR THE SELECTING.
YOU CAN ENTRUST IT TO ME... AND...
I'M ALSO FOLLOWING UP ON SASUKE'S RETRIEVAL.
TAP
WE'VE GOT TO USE KIMIMARO...!

CURSE
YOU,
THIRD
LORD...!

RIP

SSSS

SSSS

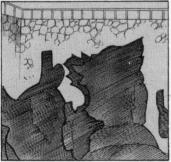

LISTEN
CLOSELY...

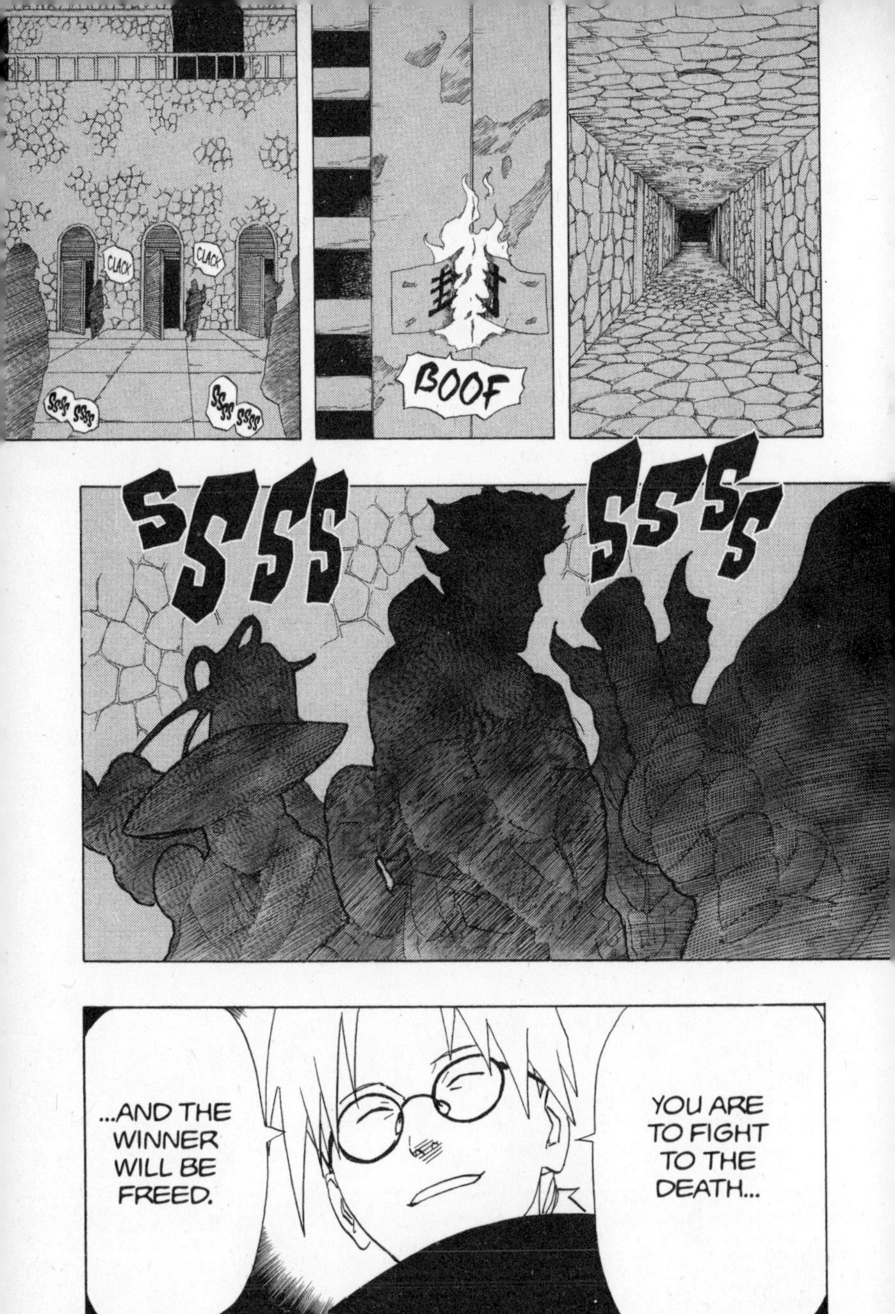
BOOF
CLACK
CLACK
SSSS SSSS
SSSS SSSS
SSSS
SSSS
YOU ARE TO FIGHT TO THE DEATH...
...AND THE WINNER WILL BE FREED.

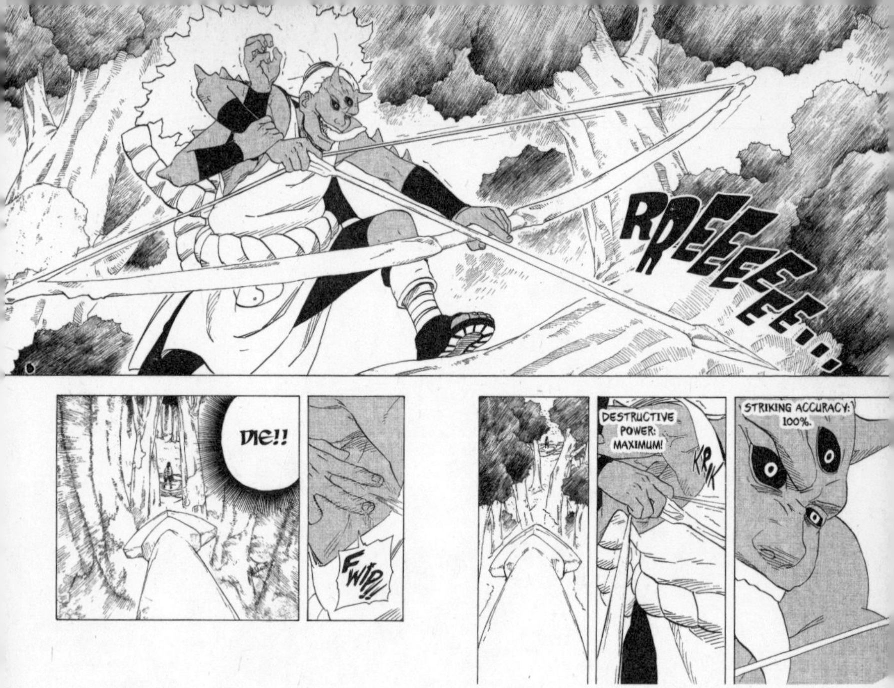
RREEEEEE...
STRIKING ACCURACY: 100%.
DESTRUCTIVE POWER: MAXIMUM!
KRIK
FWIP!!
DIE!!

KISHIMOTO MASASHI'S REJECT MANGA SPECIAL

THE TWO-PAGE SPREAD ABOVE WAS WHAT WAS ACTUALLY PRINTED IN WEEKLY SHONEN JUMP, BUT...

...WHEN MY TWIN BROTHER SAW IT, HE PESTERED ME SO MUCH WITH "IT'S SO UNCOOL," "BORING," "DO-OVER" THAT EVEN THOUGH THERE WASN'T MUCH TIME, I DID REVISE AND REDRAW THE TWO PAGES FOR THIS GRAPHIC NOVEL EDITION.

SO, DEAR READERS, CAN YOU GUESS WHICH PAGES WERE REPLACED...?

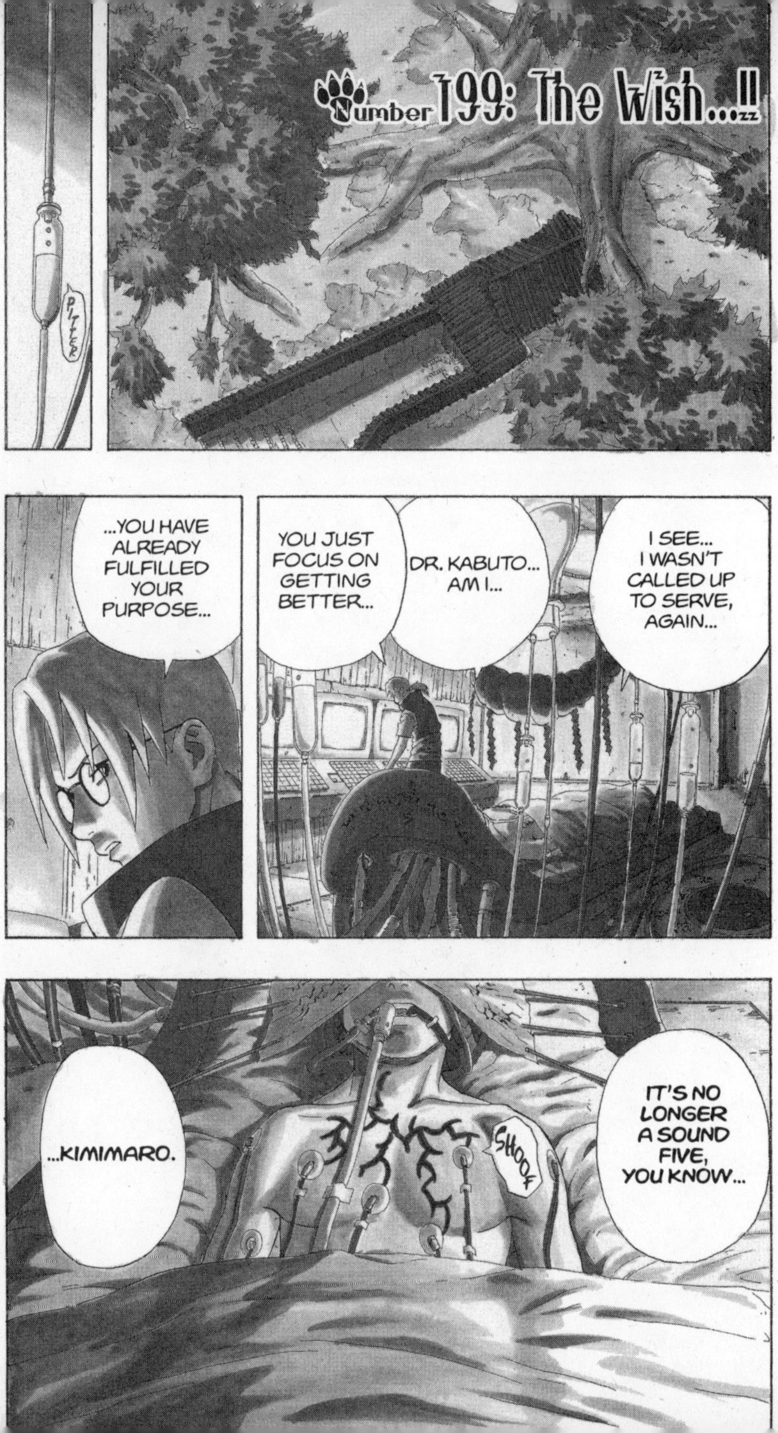
Number 199: The Wish...!!
PITTER
I SEE... I WASN'T CALLED UP TO SERVE, AGAIN...
DR. KABUTO... AM I...
YOU JUST FOCUS ON GETTING BETTER...
...YOU HAVE ALREADY FULFILLED YOUR PURPOSE...
IT'S NO LONGER A SOUND FIVE, YOU KNOW...
SHOOF
...KIMIMARO.

THE RESULTS OF THE FOURTH CHARACTER AND FIRST JUTSU POPULARITY SURVEY!!

CONDUCTED IN JAPAN.

SURVEY RESULTS ❸

11TH PLACE/NINJA CENTERFOLD	1,013 VOTES
12TH PLACE/1000 YEARS OF DEATH	909 VOTES
13TH PLACE/CRESCENT MOON DANCE	864 VOTES
14TH PLACE/BARRAGE OF LIONS	700 VOTES
15TH PLACE/UZUMAKI NARUTO BARRAGE	666 VOTES
16TH PLACE/THE COFFIN OF CRUSHING SAND	641 VOTES
17TH PLACE/LOTUS	610 VOTES
18TH PLACE/TSUKUYOMI	597 VOTES
19TH PLACE/IMPLODING SAND FUNERAL	566 VOTES
20TH PLACE/THE NINJA HAREM	493 VOTES

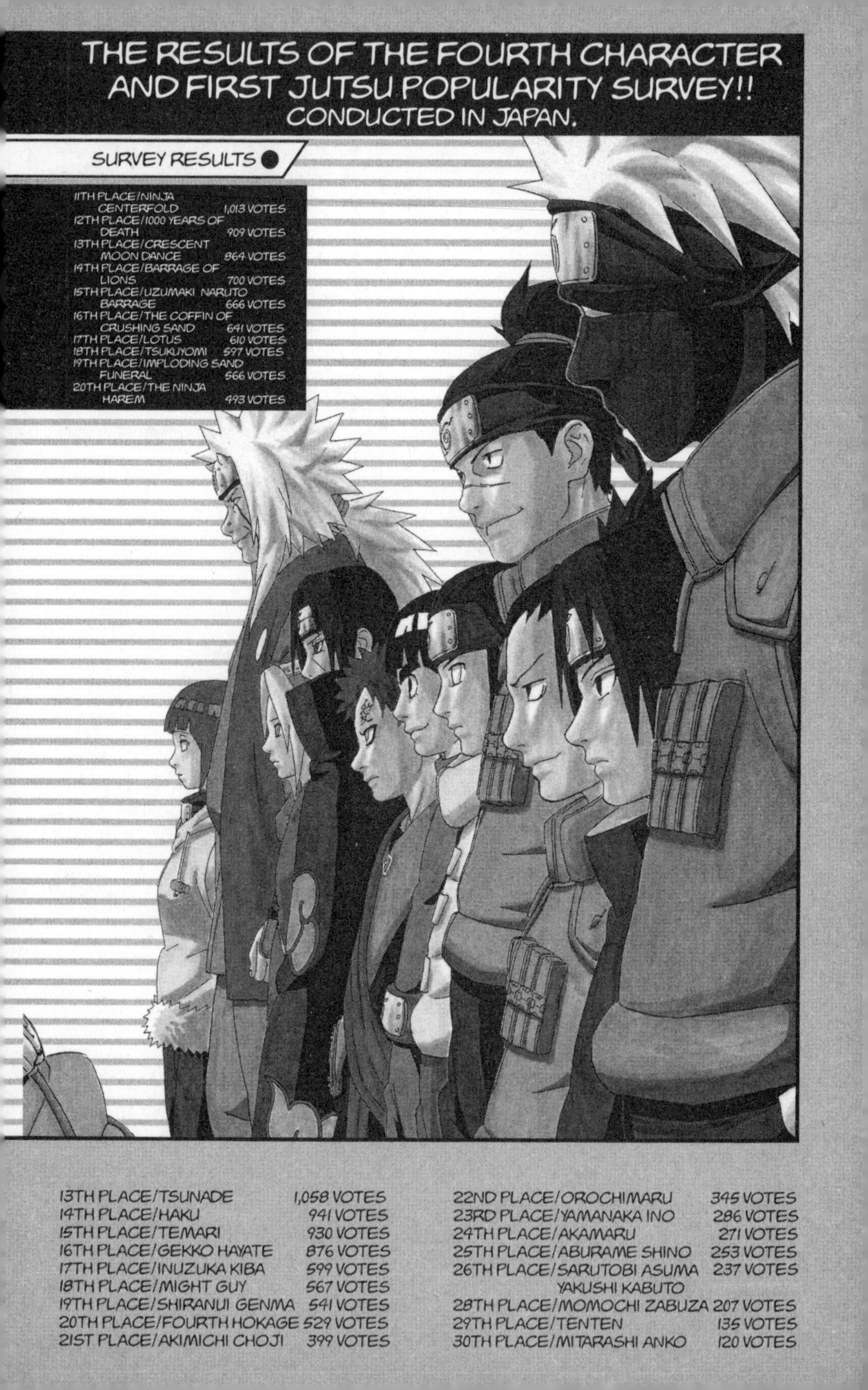

13TH PLACE/TSUNADE	1,058 VOTES
14TH PLACE/HAKU	941 VOTES
15TH PLACE/TEMARI	930 VOTES
16TH PLACE/GEKKO HAYATE	876 VOTES
17TH PLACE/INUZUKA KIBA	599 VOTES
18TH PLACE/MIGHT GUY	567 VOTES
19TH PLACE/SHIRANUI GENMA	541 VOTES
20TH PLACE/FOURTH HOKAGE	529 VOTES
21ST PLACE/AKIMICHI CHOJI	399 VOTES
22ND PLACE/OROCHIMARU	345 VOTES
23RD PLACE/YAMANAKA INO	286 VOTES
24TH PLACE/AKAMARU	271 VOTES
25TH PLACE/ABURAME SHINO	253 VOTES
26TH PLACE/SARUTOBI ASUMA	237 VOTES
YAKUSHI KABUTO	
28TH PLACE/MOMOCHI ZABUZA	207 VOTES
29TH PLACE/TENTEN	135 VOTES
30TH PLACE/MITARASHI ANKO	120 VOTES

Number 199: The Wish...!!

● THE JUTSU POPULARITY

1ST PLACE/RASENGAN	5,128 VOTES
2ND PLACE/LIGHTNING BLADE	4,395 VOTES
3RD PLACE/CHIDORI	3,216 VOTES
4TH PLACE/SHADOW POSSESSION	3,160 VOTES
5TH PLACE/SUMMONING	1,897 VOTES
6TH PLACE/BYAKUGAN	1,728 VOTES
7TH PLACE/SHARINGAN	1,639 VOTES
8TH PLACE/SHADOW DOPPELGANGER	1,415 VOTES
9TH PLACE/REVERSE LOTUS	1,400 VOTES
10TH PLACE/8 TRIGRAMS 64 PALMS	1,162 VOTES

1ST PLACE
UZUMAKI NARUTO
7,689 VOTES

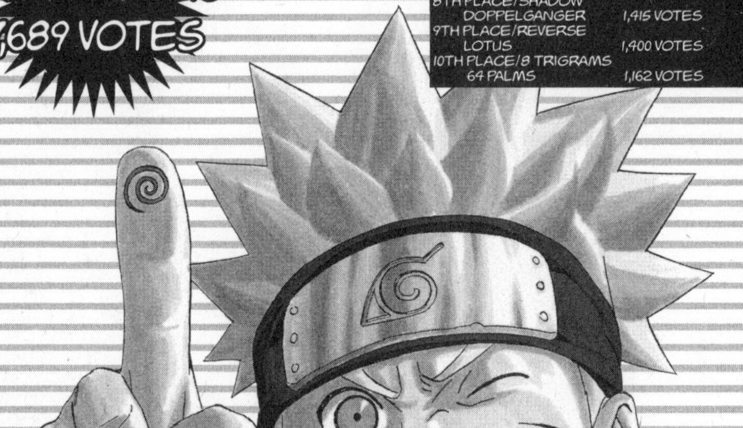

● THE REST OF THE CHARACTER POPULARITY SURVEY RESULTS ●

2ND PLACE/HATAKE KAKASHI	6,560 VOTES
3RD PLACE/UCHIHA SASUKE	4,843 VOTES
4TH PLACE/NARA SHIKAMARU	4,700 VOTES
5TH PLACE/UMINO IRUKA	3,855 VOTES
6TH PLACE/HYUGA NEJI	3,222 VOTES
7TH PLACE/ROCK LEE	2,522 VOTES
8TH PLACE/GAARA	1,868 VOTES
9TH PLACE/UCHIHA ITACHI	1,619 VOTES
10TH PLACE/HARUNO SAKURA	1,348 VOTES
11TH PLACE/JIRAIYA	1,235 VOTES
12TH PLACE/HYUGA HINATA	1,182 VOTES

NARUTO -ナルト-

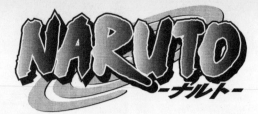

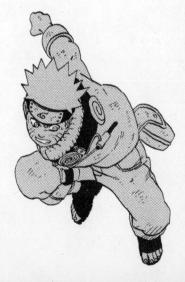

I...
CAN
STILL...

YOUR
SUCCESSOR
HAS BEEN
FOUND...

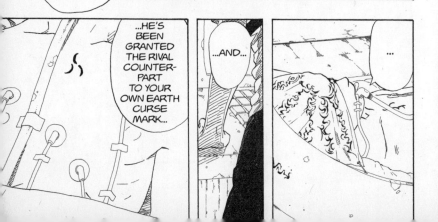

...HE'S
BEEN
GRANTED
THE RIVAL
COUNTER-
PART
TO YOUR
OWN EARTH
CURSE
MARK...

...AND...

...

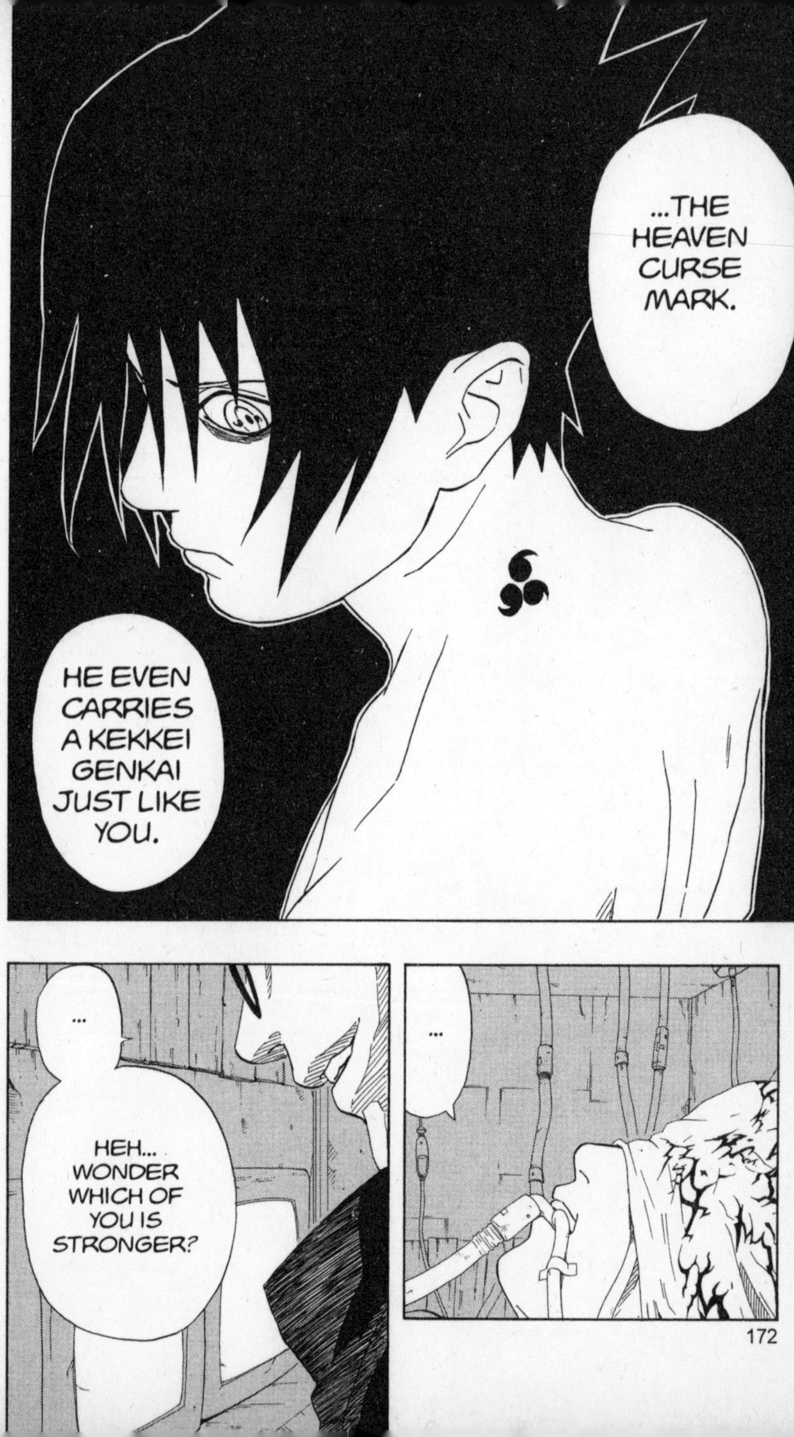
...THE HEAVEN CURSE MARK.
HE EVEN CARRIES A KEKKEI GENKAI JUST LIKE YOU.
...
...
HEH... WONDER WHICH OF YOU IS STRONGER?

READ THIS WAY

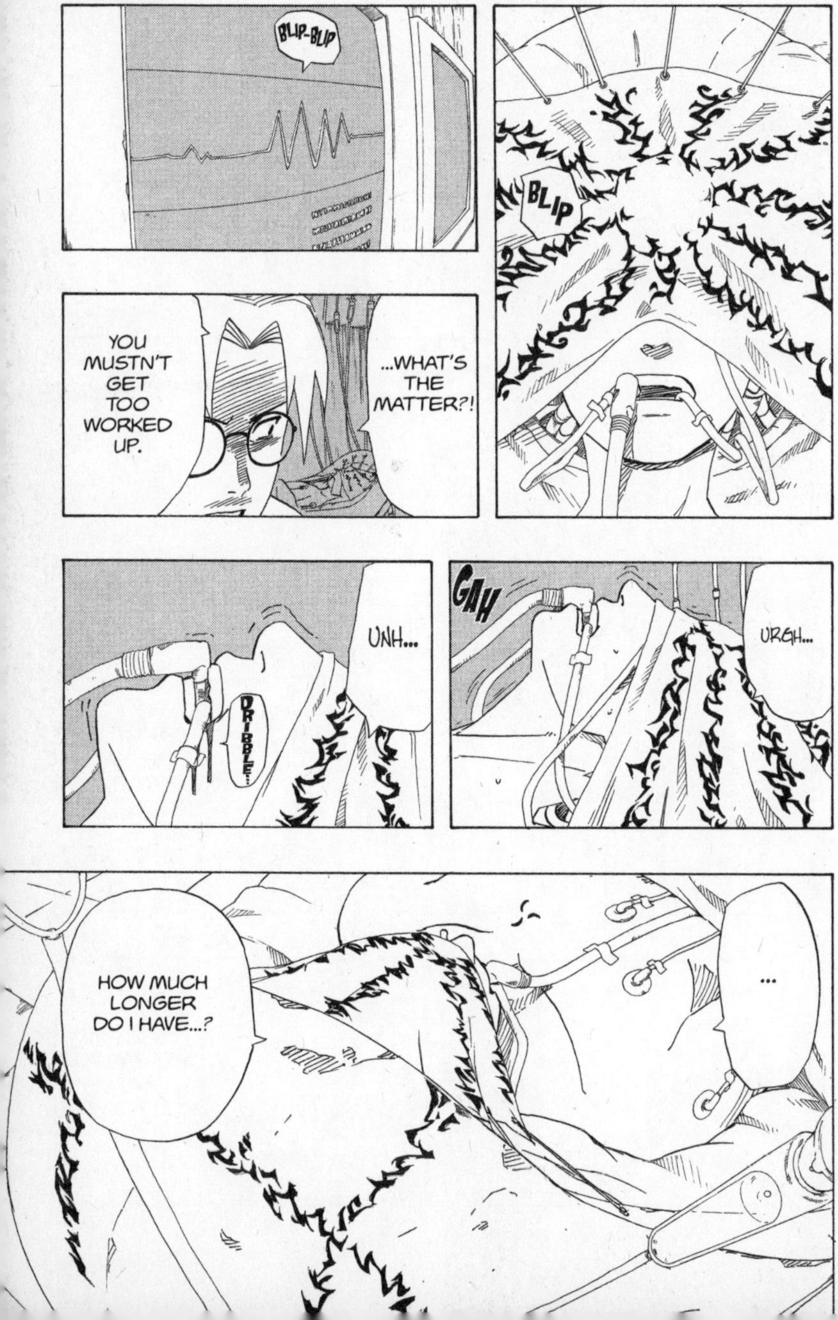
BLIP
BLIP-BLIP
...WHAT'S THE MATTER?!
YOU MUSTN'T GET TOO WORKED UP.
URGH...
GAH
UNH...
DRIBBLE...
...
HOW MUCH LONGER DO I HAVE...?

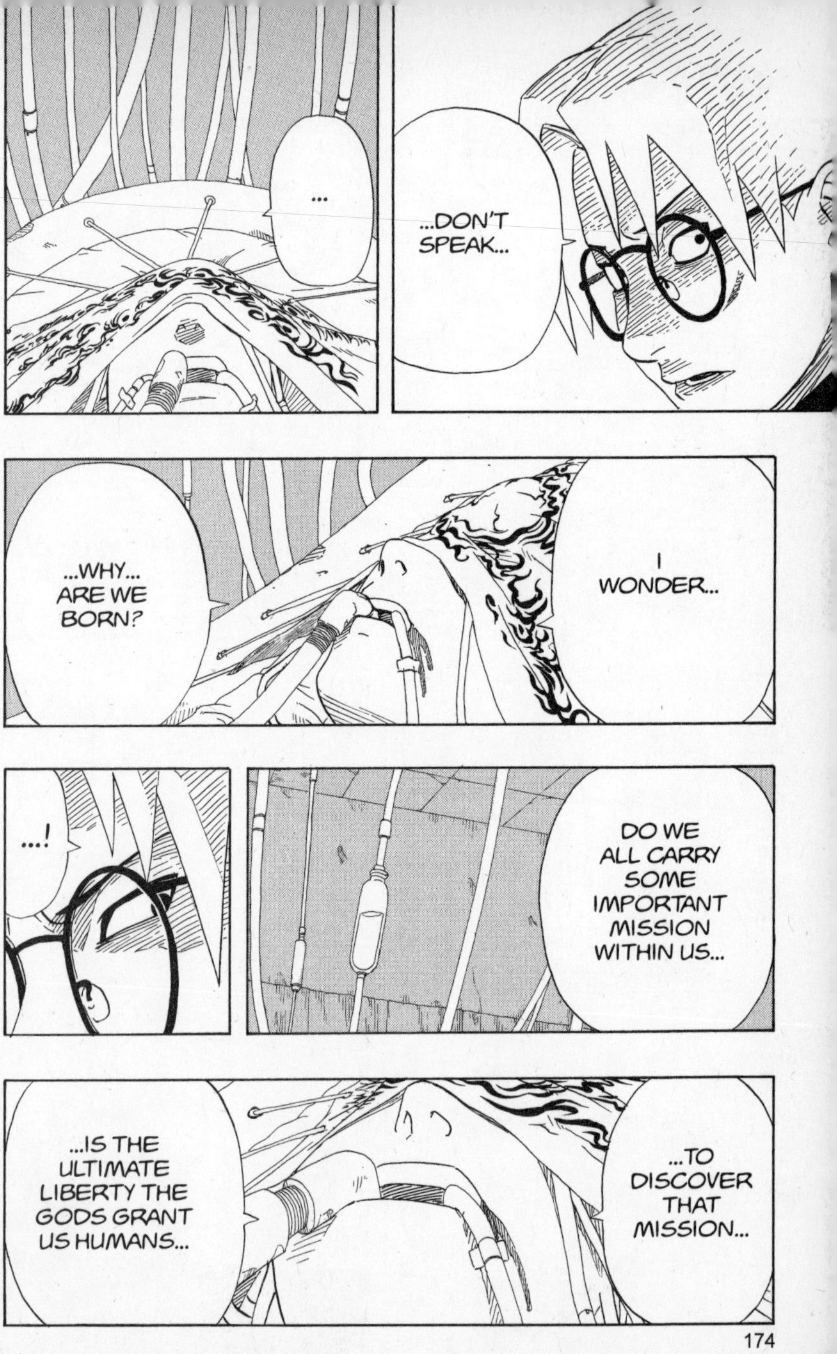
...DON'T SPEAK...
...
I WONDER...
...WHY... ARE WE BORN?
DO WE ALL CARRY SOME IMPORTANT MISSION WITHIN US...
...!
...TO DISCOVER THAT MISSION...
...IS THE ULTIMATE LIBERTY THE GODS GRANT US HUMANS...

READ THIS WAY

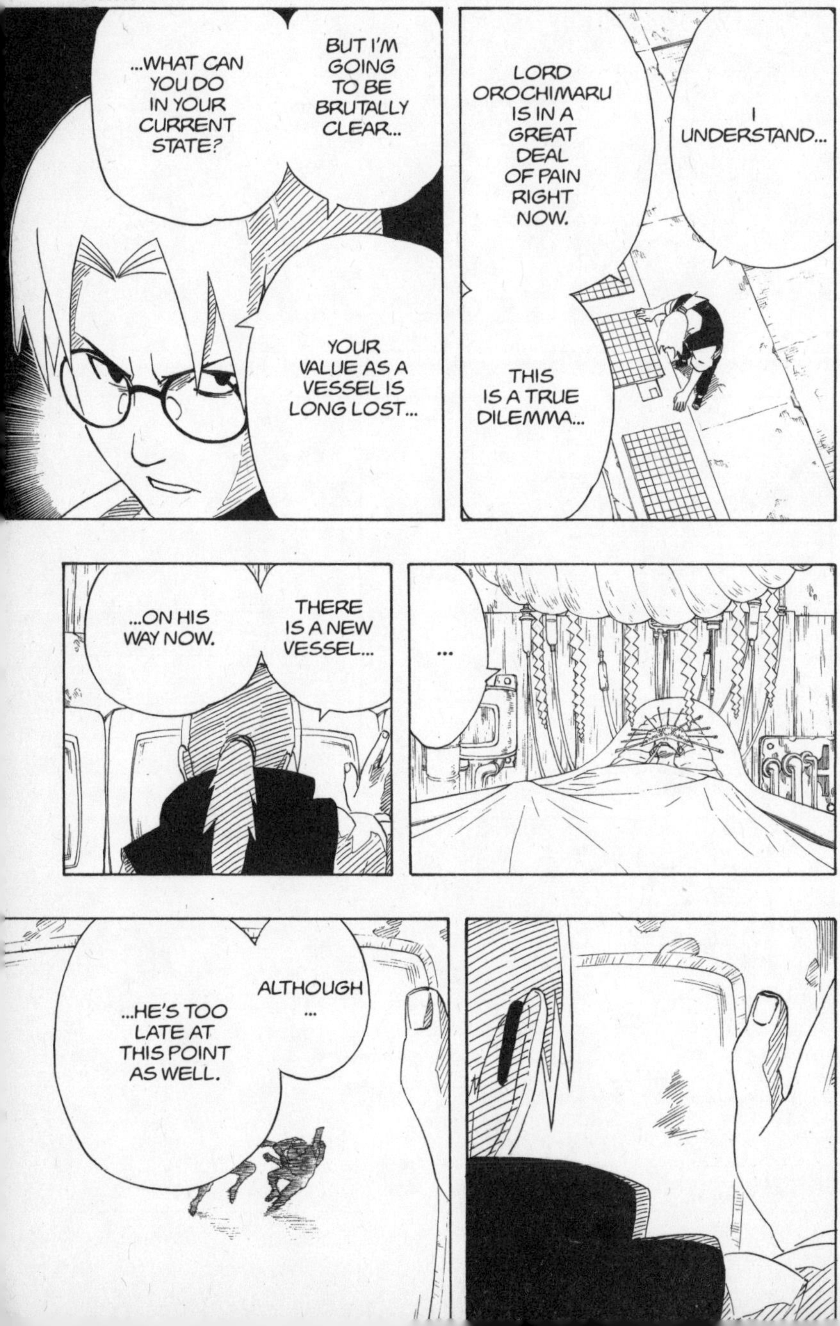
I UNDERSTAND...
LORD OROCHIMARU IS IN A GREAT DEAL OF PAIN RIGHT NOW.
THIS IS A TRUE DILEMMA...
BUT I'M GOING TO BE BRUTALLY CLEAR...
...WHAT CAN YOU DO IN YOUR CURRENT STATE?
YOUR VALUE AS A VESSEL IS LONG LOST...
...
THERE IS A NEW VESSEL...
...ON HIS WAY NOW.
ALTHOUGH ...
...HE'S TOO LATE AT THIS POINT AS WELL.

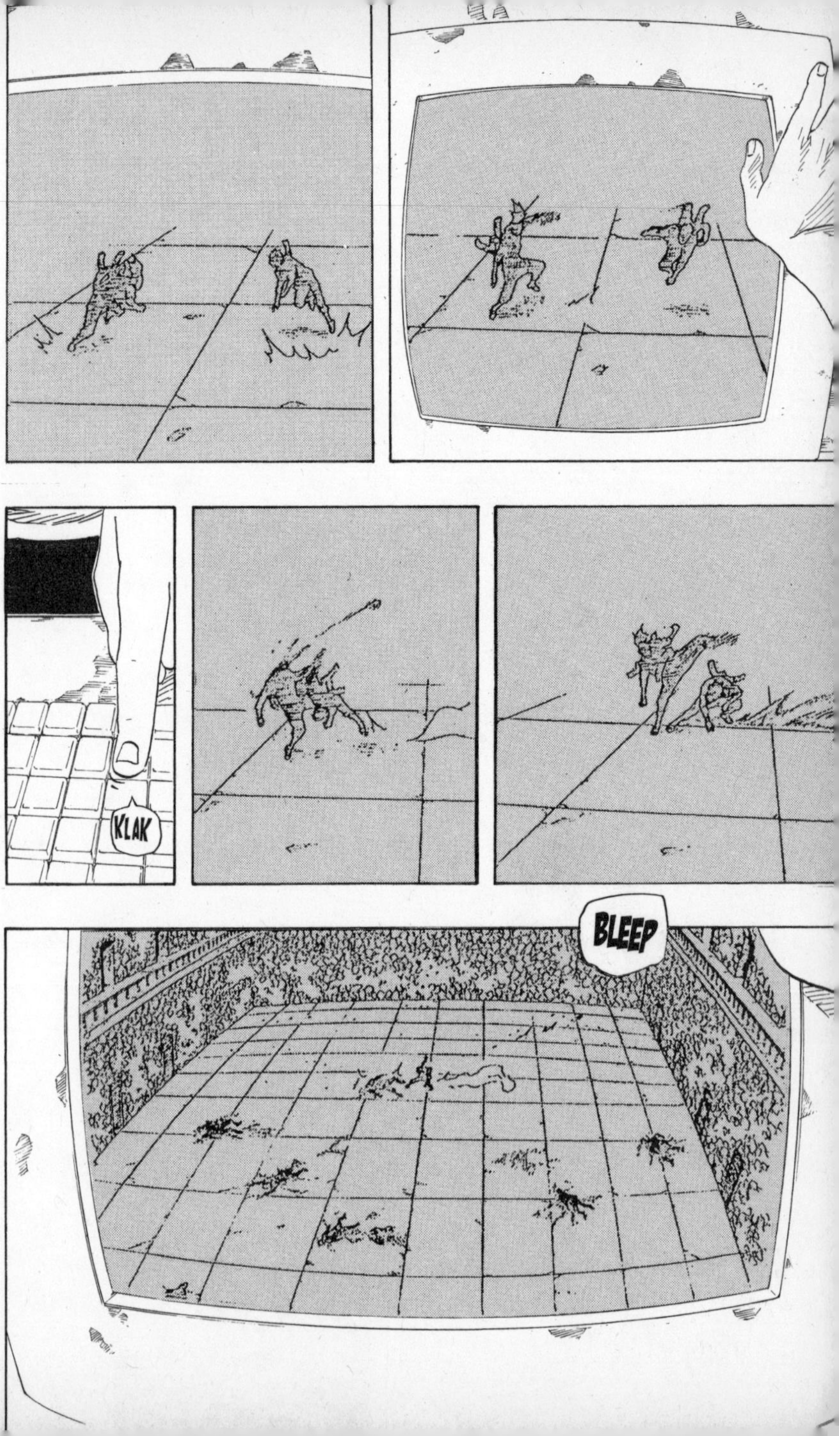
KLAK
BLEEP

READ THIS WAY

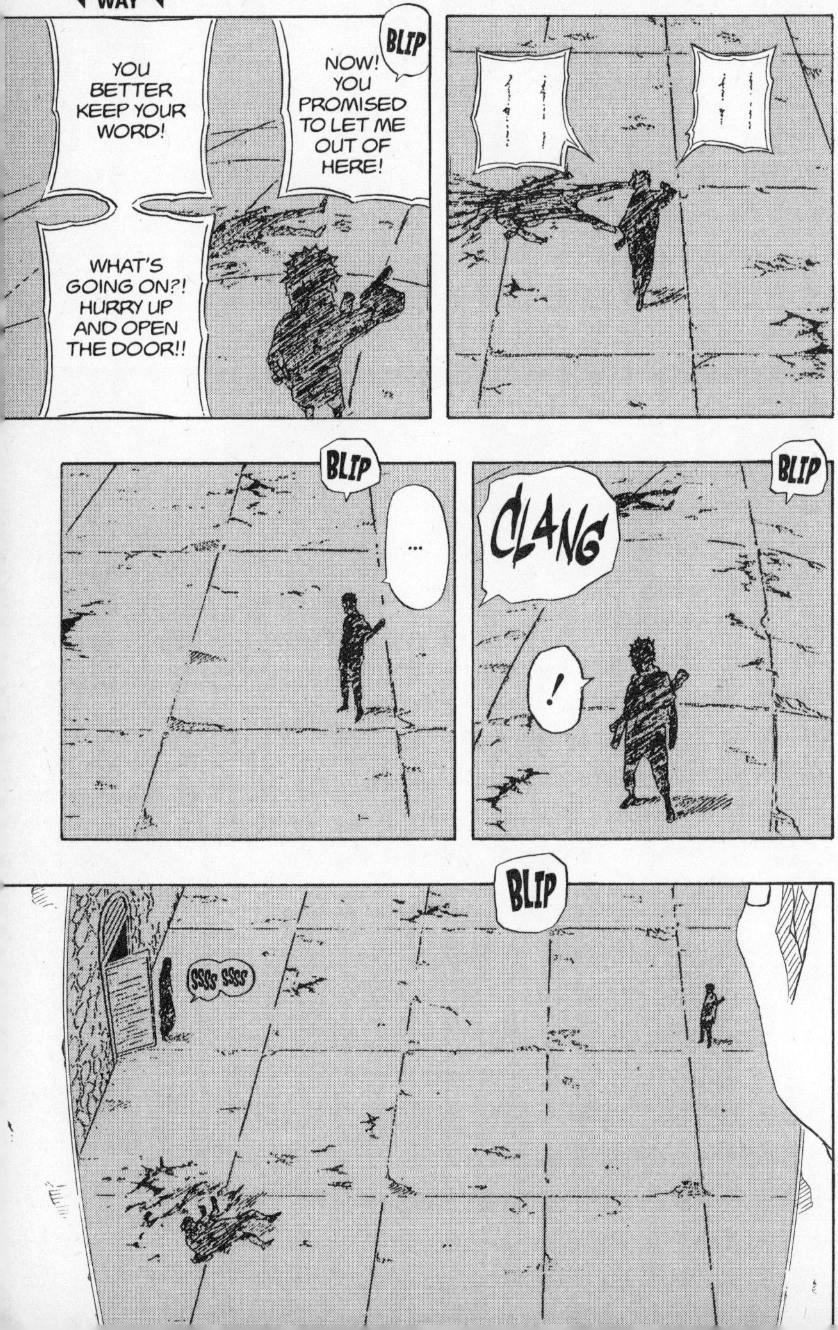
BLIP
NOW! YOU PROMISED TO LET ME OUT OF HERE!
YOU BETTER KEEP YOUR WORD!
WHAT'S GOING ON?! HURRY UP AND OPEN THE DOOR!!
BLIP
CLANG
!
BLIP
...
BLIP
SSSS SSSS

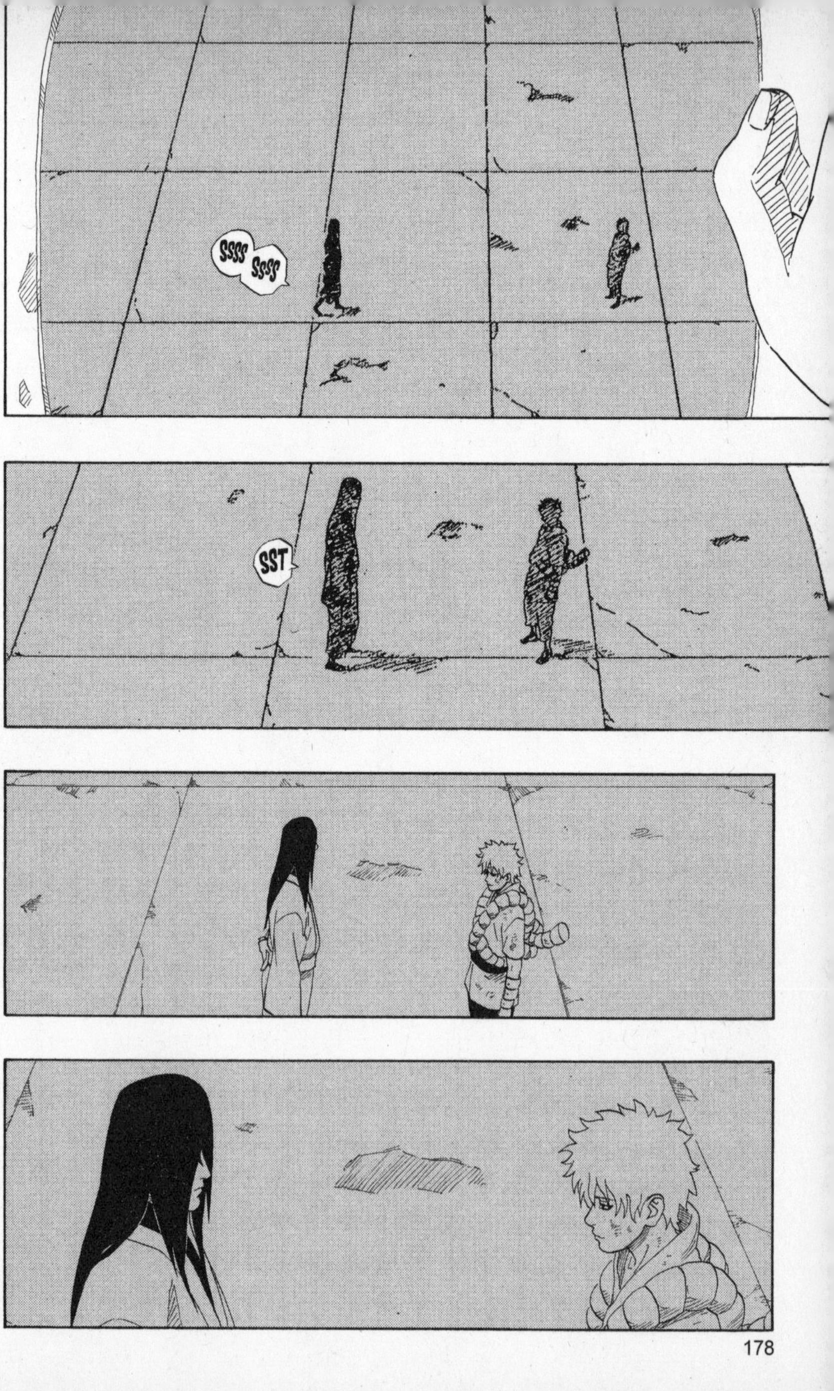
SSSS SSSS
SST

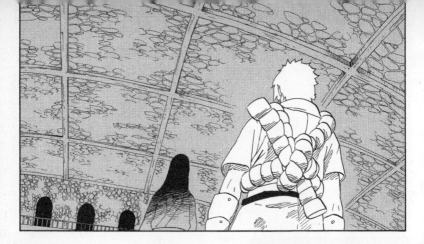

FINE, LET'S...

THERE WAS ONE MORE OF YOU...?

WHAT?!

...

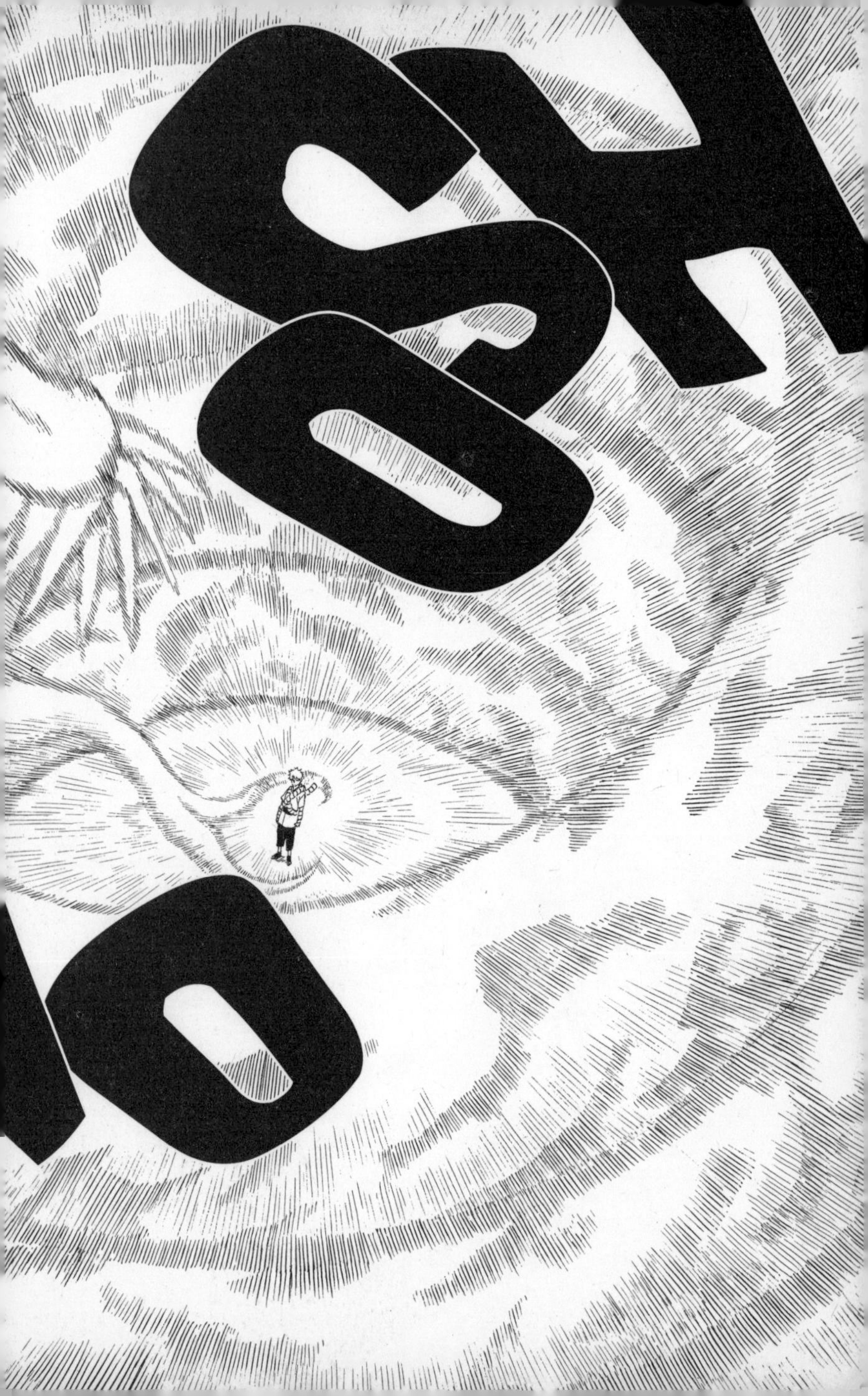
OOSH

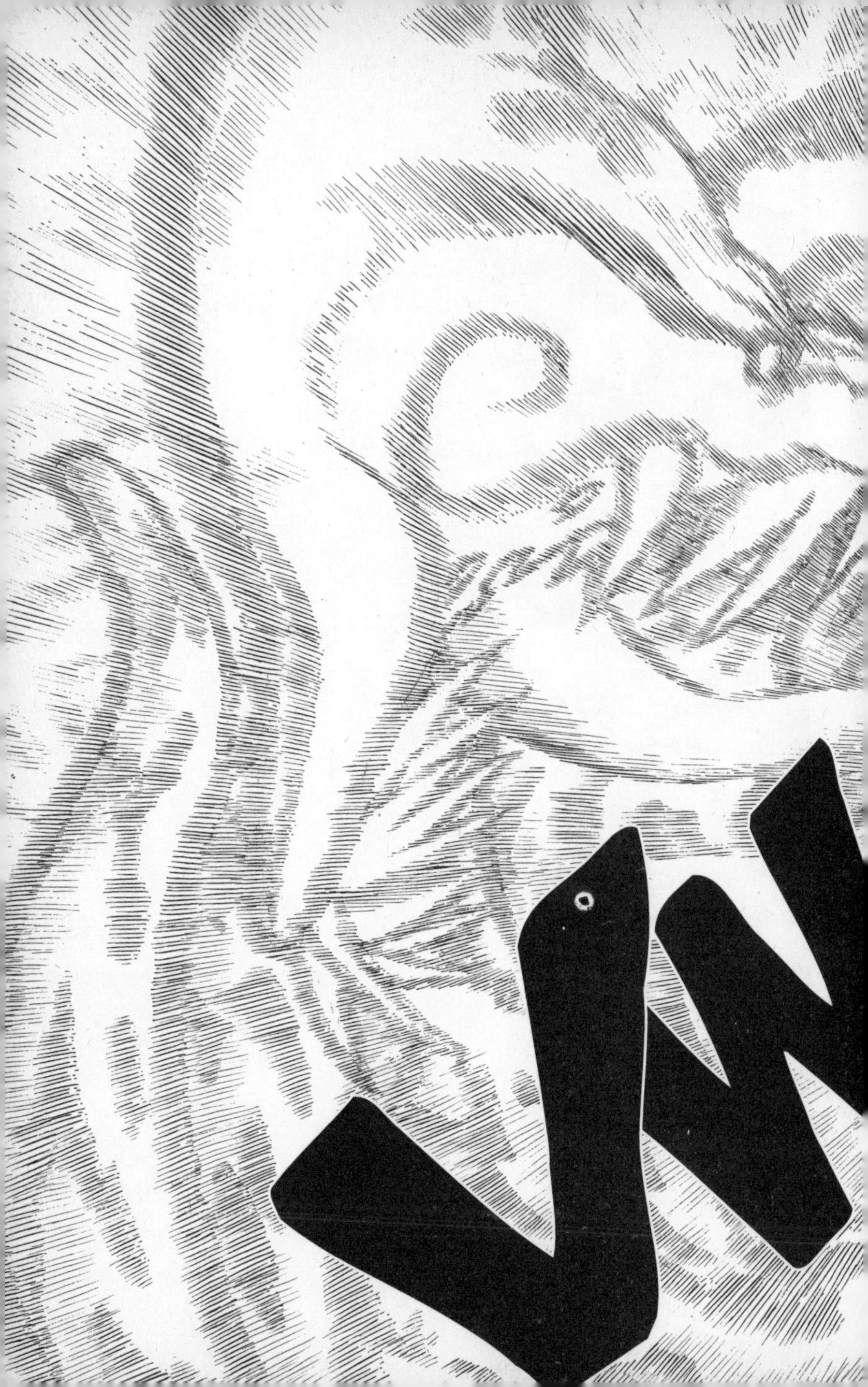

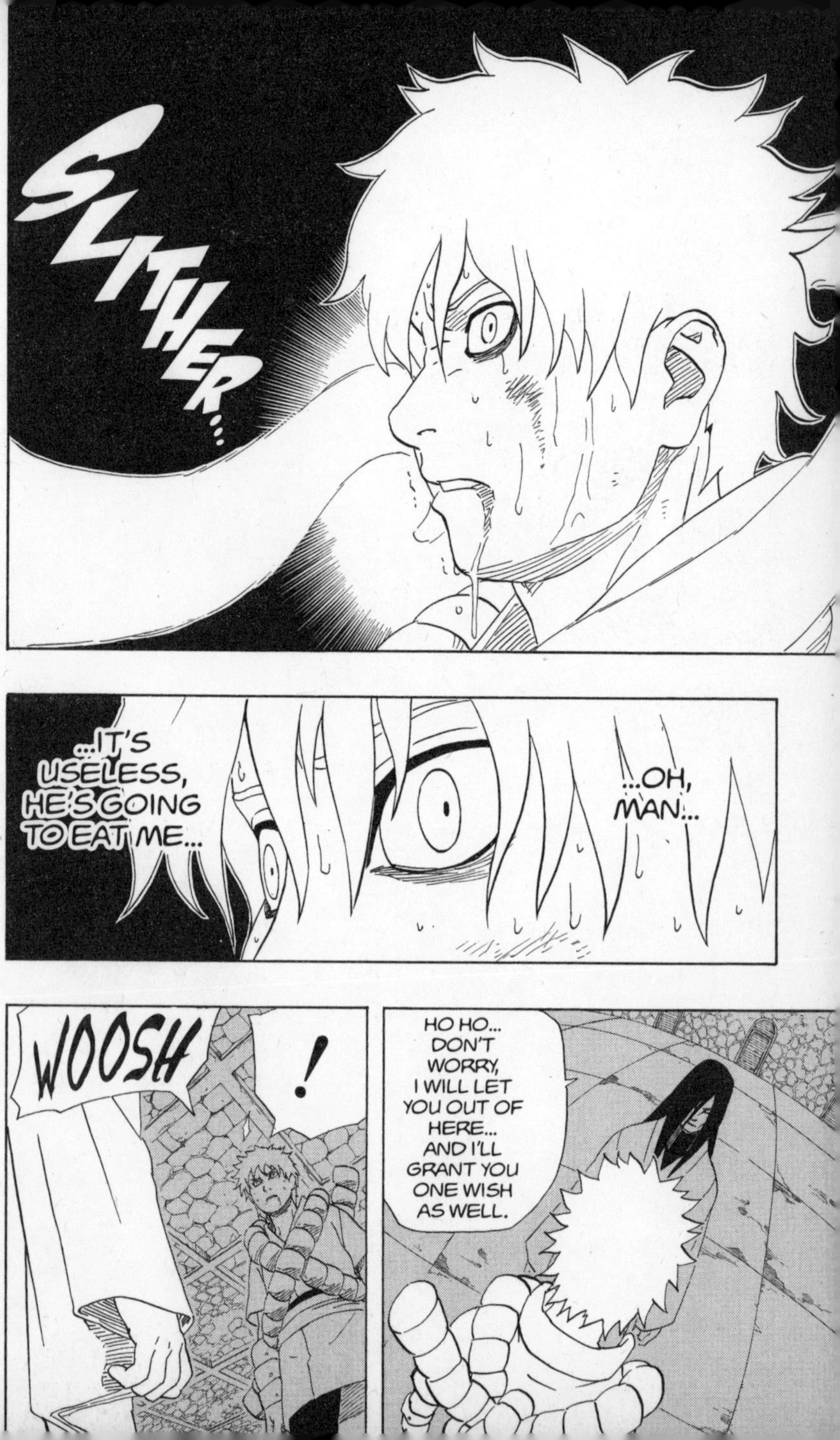
SLITHER...
...OH, MAN...
...IT'S USELESS, HE'S GOING TO EAT ME...
HO HO... DON'T WORRY, I WILL LET YOU OUT OF HERE... AND I'LL GRANT YOU ONE WISH AS WELL.
WOOSH
!

READ THIS WAY

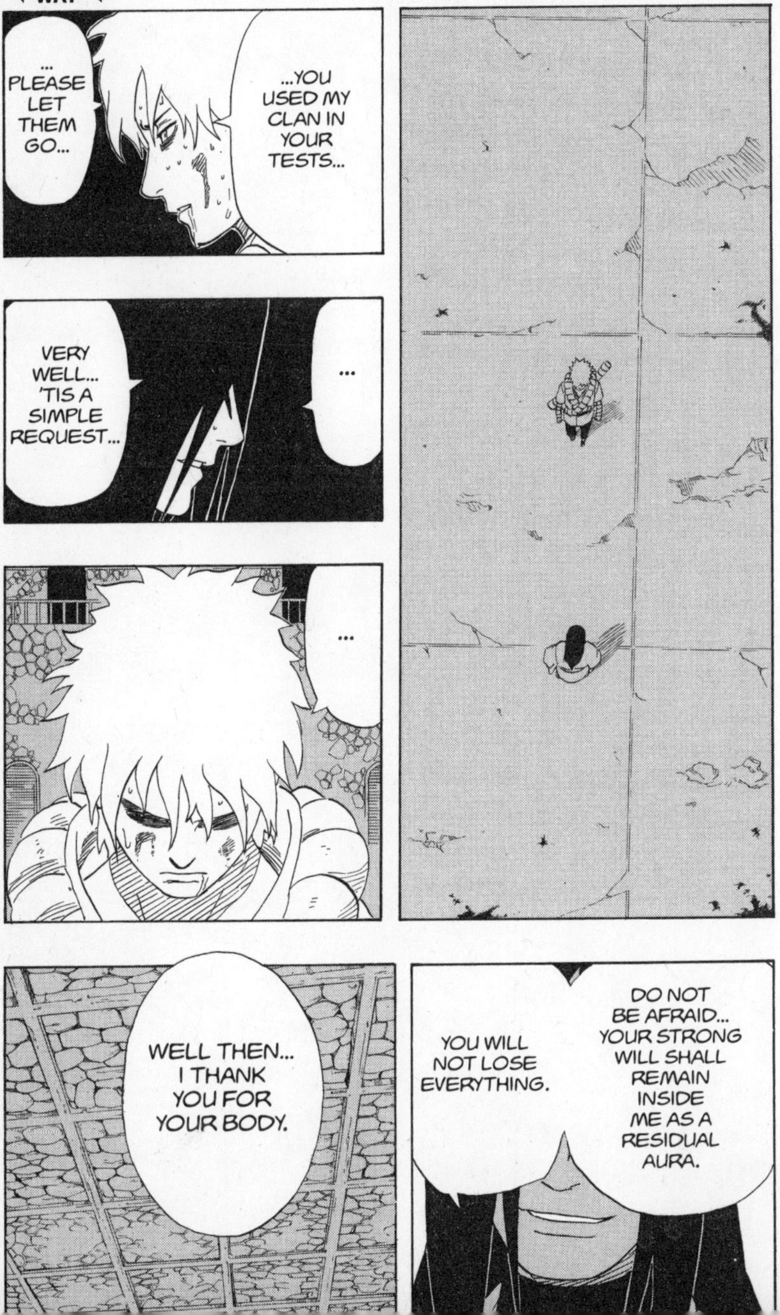
...YOU USED MY CLAN IN YOUR TESTS...
... PLEASE LET THEM GO...
...
VERY WELL... 'TIS A SIMPLE REQUEST...
...
DO NOT BE AFRAID... YOUR STRONG WILL SHALL REMAIN INSIDE ME AS A RESIDUAL AURA.
YOU WILL NOT LOSE EVERYTHING.
WELL THEN... I THANK YOU FOR YOUR BODY.

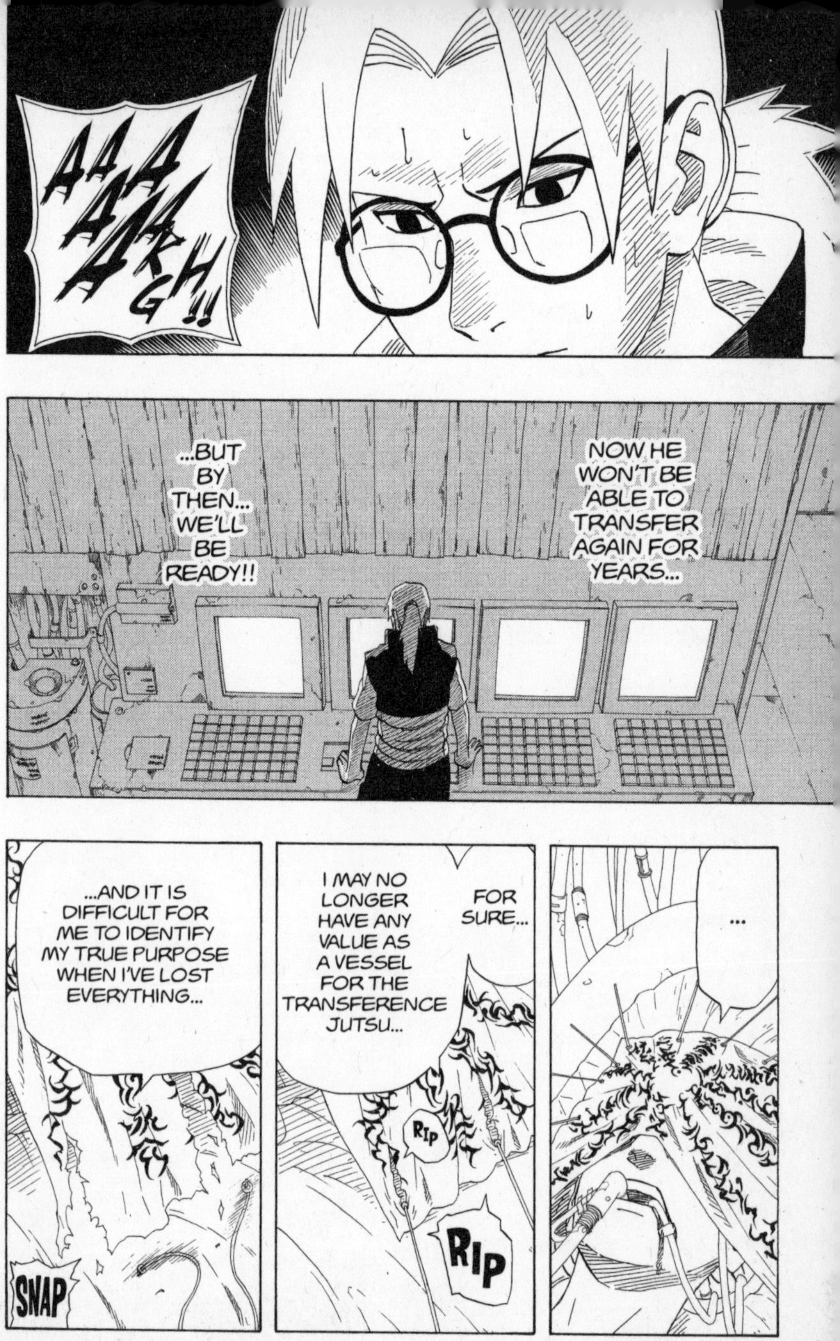
AAAAAAARRGH!!
NOW HE WON'T BE ABLE TO TRANSFER AGAIN FOR YEARS...
...BUT BY THEN... WE'LL BE READY!!
...
FOR SURE...
I MAY NO LONGER HAVE ANY VALUE AS A VESSEL FOR THE TRANSFERENCE JUTSU...
RIP
RIP
...AND IT IS DIFFICULT FOR ME TO IDENTIFY MY TRUE PURPOSE WHEN I'VE LOST EVERYTHING...
SNAP

READ THIS WAY

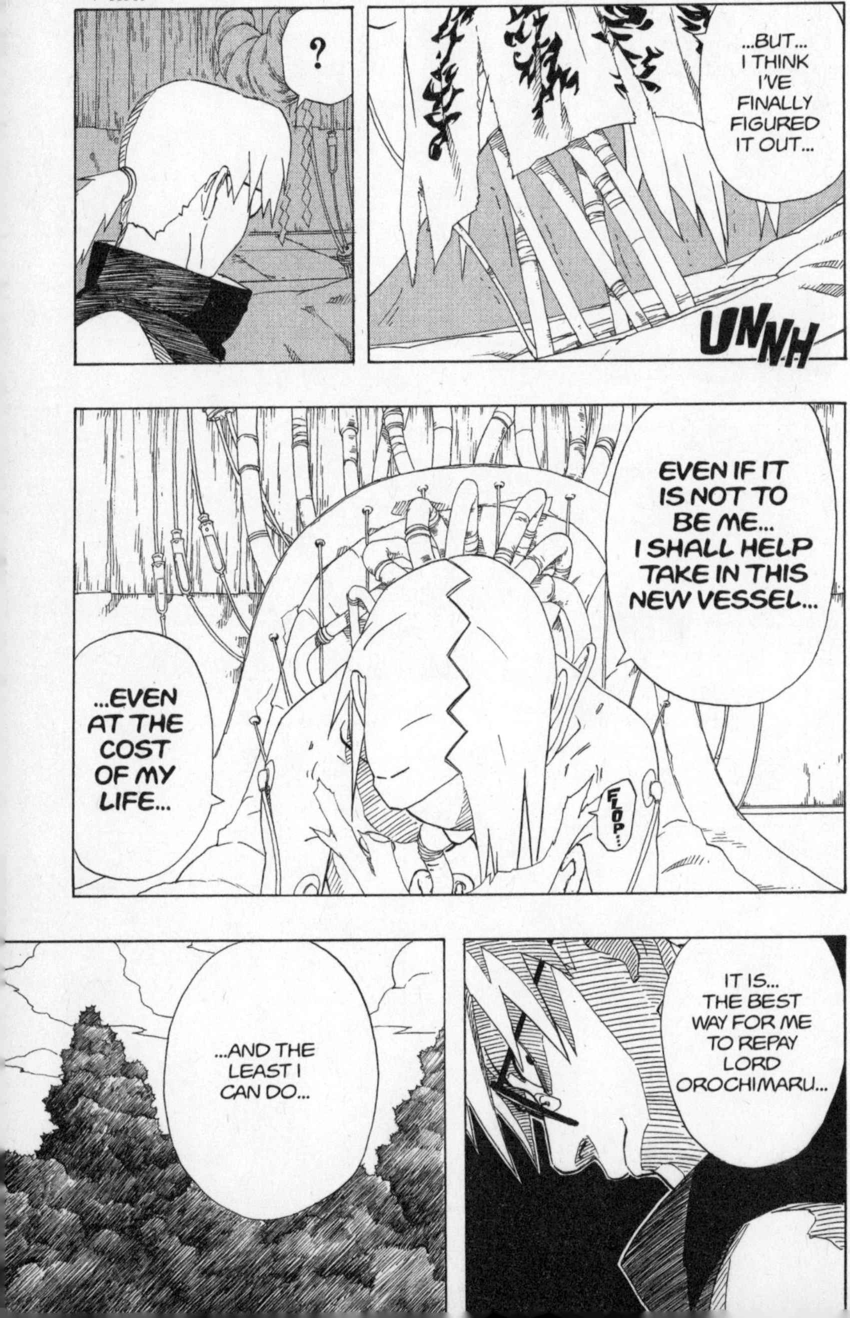
...BUT... I THINK I'VE FINALLY FIGURED IT OUT...
UNNH
?
EVEN IF IT IS NOT TO BE ME... I SHALL HELP TAKE IN THIS NEW VESSEL...
FLOP...
...EVEN AT THE COST OF MY LIFE...
IT IS... THE BEST WAY FOR ME TO REPAY LORD OROCHIMARU...
...AND THE LEAST I CAN DO...

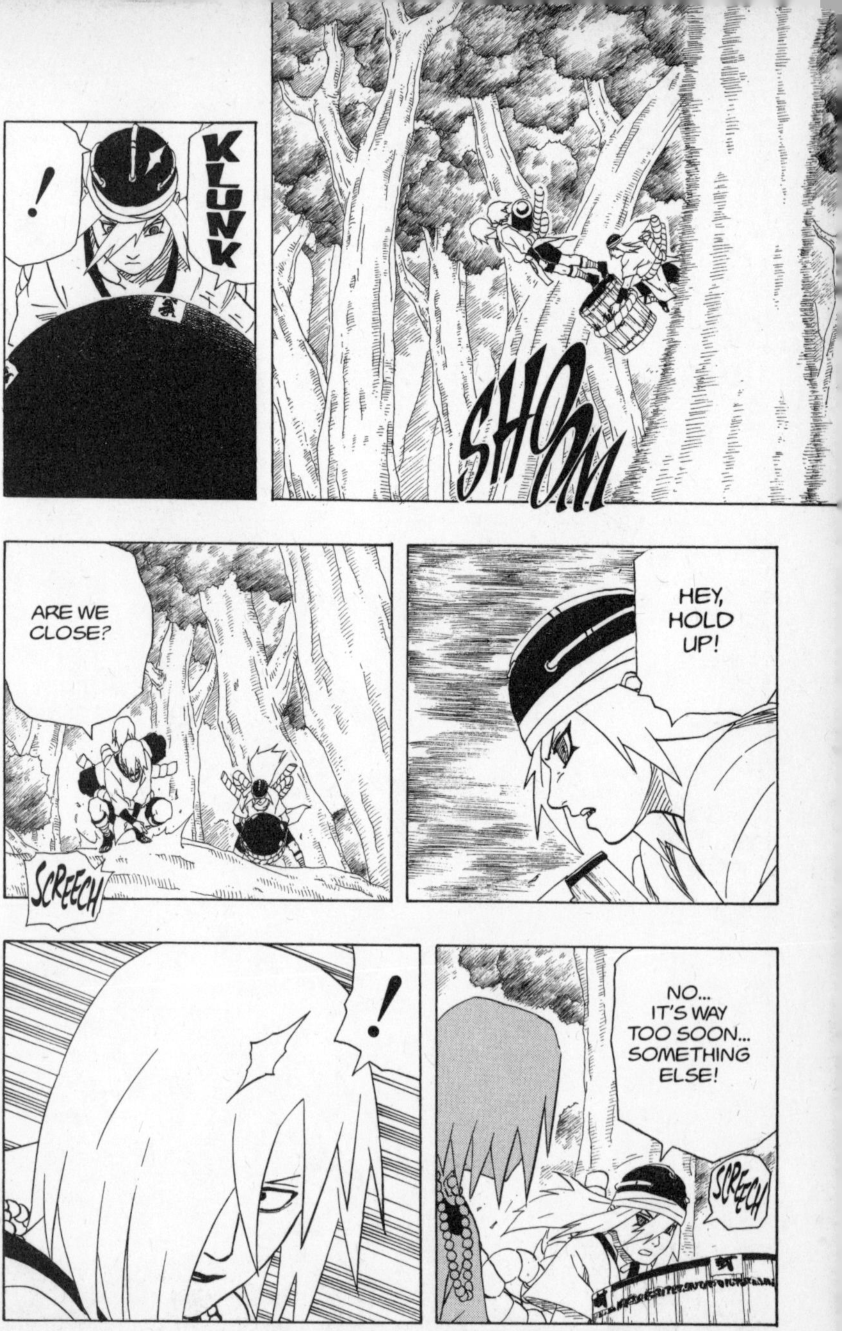
SHOOM
!
KLUNK
HEY, HOLD UP!
ARE WE CLOSE?
SCREECH
NO... IT'S WAY TOO SOON... SOMETHING ELSE!
SCREECH
!

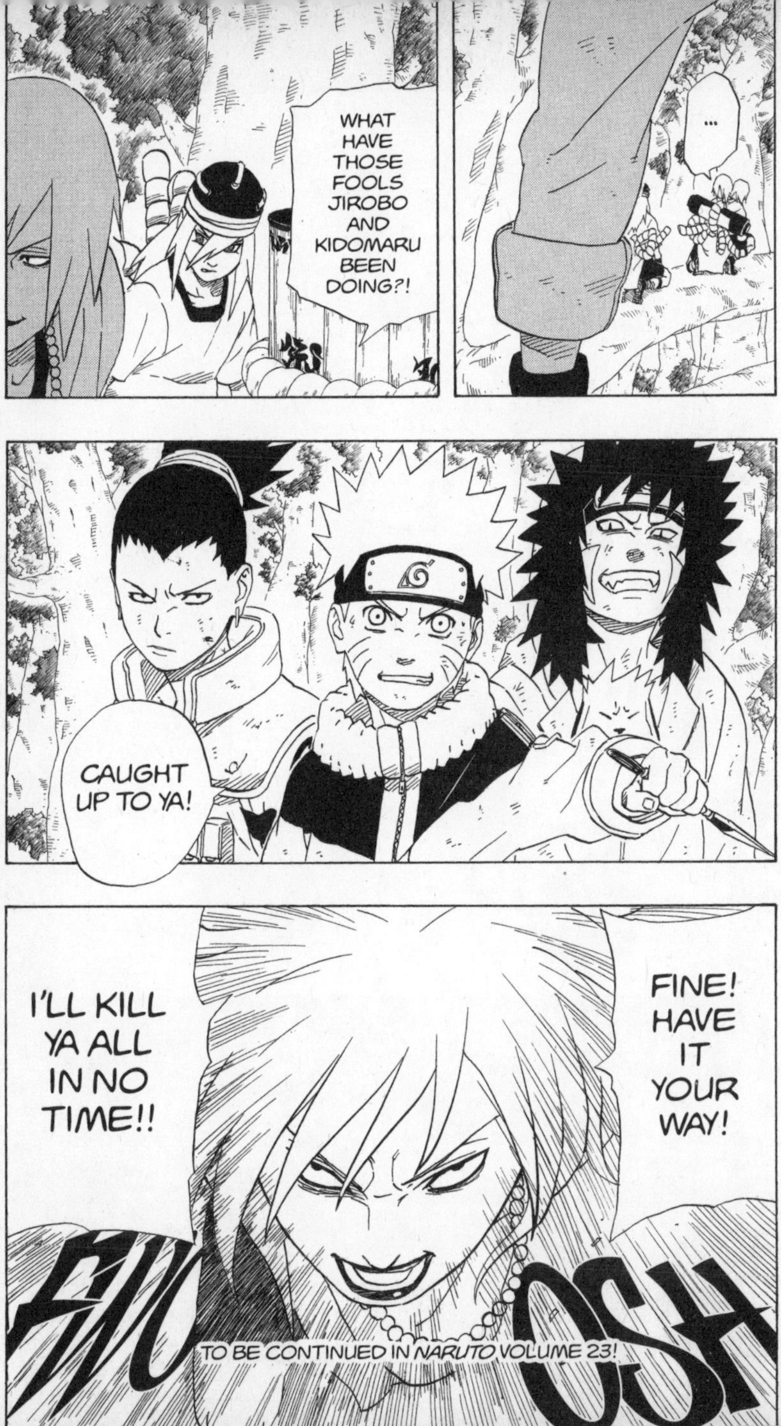
...
WHAT HAVE THOSE FOOLS JIROBO AND KIDOMARU BEEN DOING?!
CAUGHT UP TO YA!
FINE! HAVE IT YOUR WAY!
I'LL KILL YA ALL IN NO TIME!!
FWOOSH
TO BE CONTINUED IN NARUTO VOLUME 23!

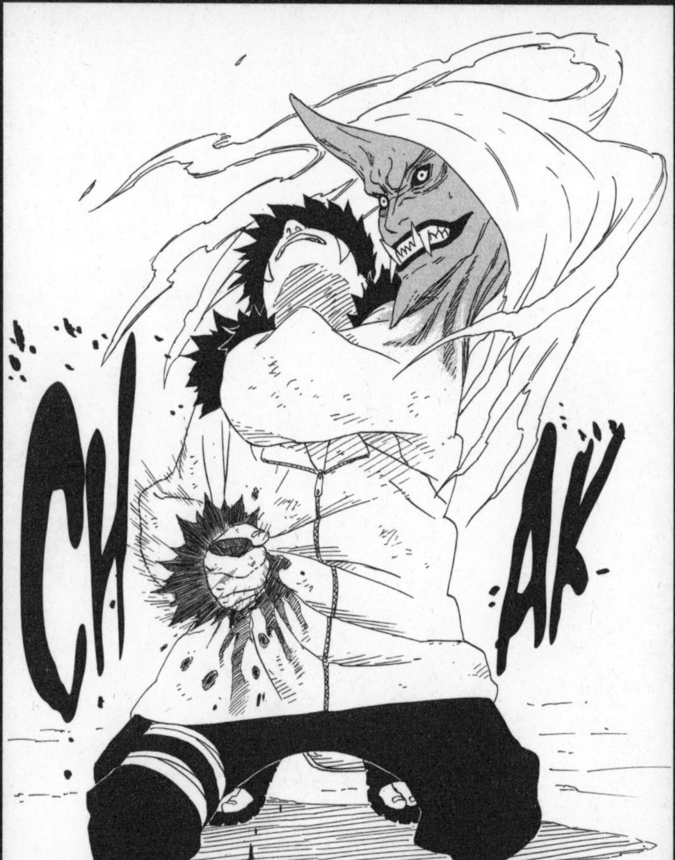
CHAK

IN THE NEXT VOLUME...

PREDICAMENT

Orochimaru's nefarious plans for Sasuke are revealed, and Naruto vows to save his friend. But first he must battle the mysterious Kimimaro, who has deadly past ties to the Sound Ninja Four!

AVAILABLE NOVEMBER 2007!

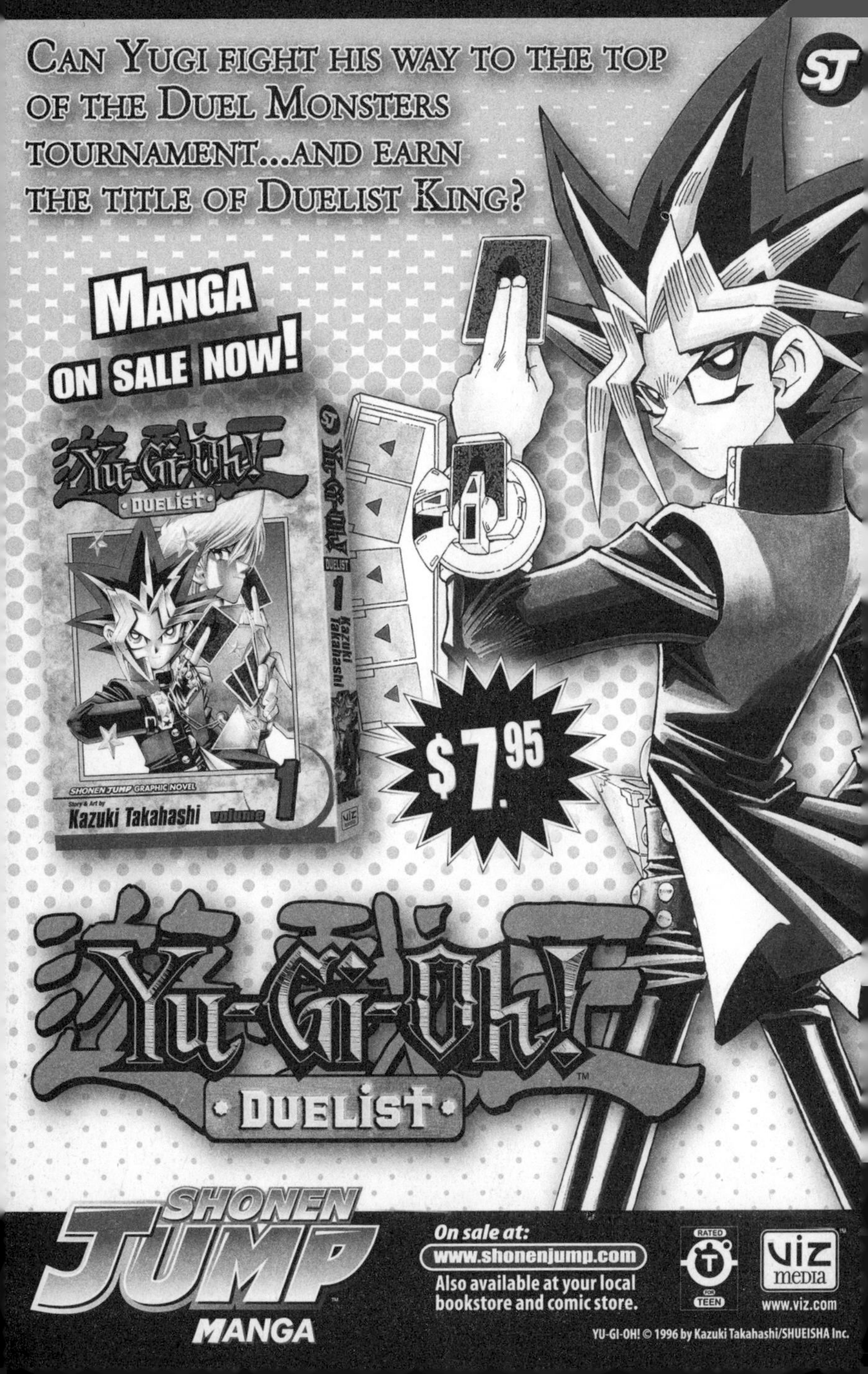
CAN YUGI FIGHT HIS WAY TO THE TOP OF THE DUEL MONSTERS TOURNAMENT...AND EARN THE TITLE OF DUELIST KING?
SJ
MANGA ON SALE NOW!
YU-GI-OH! DUELIST
SHONEN JUMP GRAPHIC NOVEL
Story & Art by
Kazuki Takahashi
volume 1
$7.95
YU-GI-OH! DUELIST™
SHONEN JUMP MANGA
On sale at:
www.shonenjump.com
Also available at your local bookstore and comic store.
RATED T FOR TEEN
VIZ media
www.viz.com
YU-GI-OH! © 1996 by Kazuki Takahashi/SHUEISHA Inc.

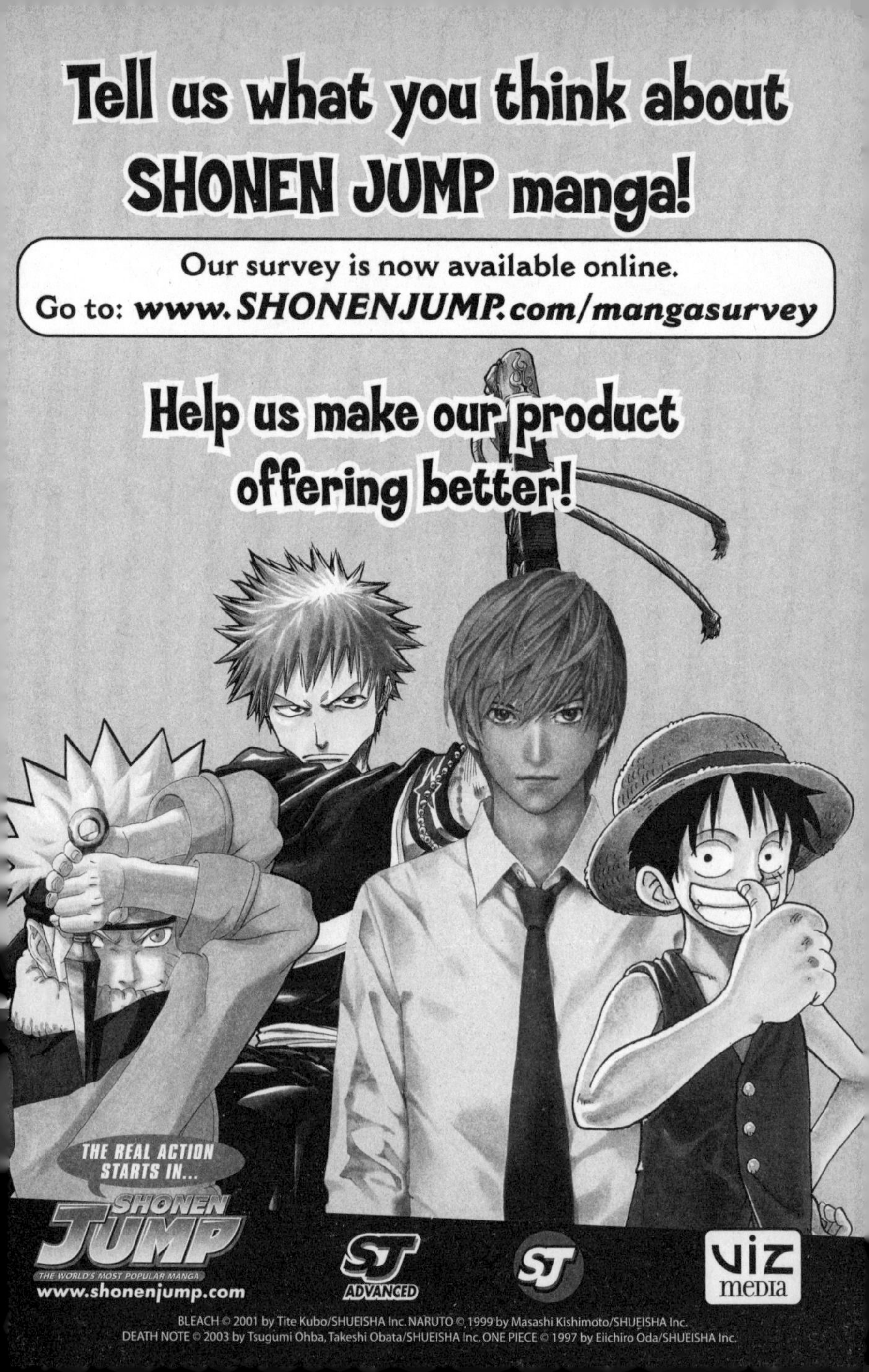